SUNLIGHT
ON
SHADOWS

Embracing Great Compassion

Lama Shenpen Drolma

 Iron Knot Press

INTRODUCTION

I met Tibetan meditation master Chagdud Tulku Rinpoche in the mid-1980s while searching for a spiritual practice to support and sustain my social activism. I was astounded to meet *bodhicitta*—the Sanskrit word for the awakened heart/mind of great compassion—for the first time in the example of Rinpoche's extraordinary wisdom and ceaseless, compassionate activity. Through him, I began to receive training in the path of the *bodhisattva*—a "spiritual warrior" who's committed to uprooting the suffering of every living being until all abide in the awakened state of utter peace.

This is a big undertaking! It isn't just a conceptual commitment but involves a profound transformation of mind and heart. In this training, I found everything I'd been searching for: how to access, enhance, and express our positive qualities so they serve as a steady source of strength, courage, and inspiration as we deal with the challenges in our lives and in the world. This step-by-step training can be practiced and accomplished by anyone, anywhere, who sincerely wants to change their minds and hearts, their own lives, and the world around them.

This training comes from the vast Buddhist tradition of the way of the bodhisattva. I was deeply moved to encounter such a rich and extensive training in the wisdom and compassion of the bodhisattva. I was also profoundly affected by Rinpoche's example. Rinpoche is an honorific Tibetan term that means "precious one." Having endured the loss of homeland and family during the upheavals of the late 1950s in Tibet, he held no bitterness, only compassion, for all involved. He'd been serving in various Tibetan communities in northern India and Nepal for 20 years when he met some Americans who invited him to the United States, where he moved in 1979.

The bodhisattva path was first taught by the Buddha 2,500 years ago and has been maintained over the centuries—

generation after generation—as a living tradition that's been profoundly transformative for anyone who practices it sincerely and diligently regardless of culture and background. As such, this training is extremely relevant and urgently needed during the challenging times in which we find ourselves.

For myself, it changed everything, inwardly and outwardly. I'd been searching for methods to address the limitations of my social activism, which I'd encountered most starkly in the context of my efforts in the 1970s to address the immense, 24/7 suffering of battered women. At the time, there were no services for abuse victims or training in domestic violence for police, social workers, or those working in criminal justice. We were trying to create shelters, hotlines and other services, change laws, and educate the public as well as those working in the criminal-justice system, because the predominant perspective at the time was that domestic violence was a personal issue and that women who were being beaten asked for it.

I realized I didn't know how to remain deeply engaged without my negative habits overwhelming my compassion and compromising my effectiveness. I finally recognized that my issue was a spiritual one, so I left the movement in search of a spiritual answer. In this quest to expand my ability to help others, I met Rinpoche.

From him, I began to learn about bodhicitta—the way of the bodhisattva. I also spoke with him about the many people I'd worked with over the years who I thought might also benefit from the training but, like many others with the same yearning to be of greater benefit in the world, were unlikely to ever go to any kind of spiritual or religious teaching.

He told me we could offer these teachings in a non-denominational context so they could be used by people of any or no faith who sincerely wanted to reduce their harmful impact on others and become better able to help. The format he developed, especially accessible for Western students, he called the Bodhisattva Peace Training (BPT). Drawn from the vast training of the bodhisattva, Rinpoche thought it was important to include the word "peace" in the name of this training, because it's the English word that comes closest to encapsulating both the inner process that we cultivate to be of greater benefit and the outer impact in creating a more harmonious world.

In 1996, Rinpoche ordained me as a lama ("teacher/minister") and later invested me with the responsibility to ensure the BPT would survive and flourish. I began by compiling and editing transcripts of some of his Bodhisattva Peace Trainings into a book called *Change of Heart: The Bodhisattva Peace Training of Chagdud Tulku.* After offering the BPT around the United States for a number of years, I spoke with Rinpoche about the need I saw for more extensive bodhicitta training to be made available in the form of an institute. In 2001, a year before his death, he gave me the broad outlines of what such an institute might entail.

Since then, and relying on the depth of wisdom, compassion, and blessing I've received from Rinpoche and many kind and extraordinary teachers I met through him, I've been offering week-long Immersion Retreats for the study and practice of bodhicitta. The teachings, accompanying questions and answers, and meditation instructions in this book come from edited transcripts of trainings that took place from 2013 to 2019 at Iron Knot Ranch in New Mexico. These aren't intended as a conceptual introduction or overview of teachings on bodhicitta but rather as an offering to anyone sincerely interested in exploring or undertaking the depth of experiential transformation embodied in the bodhisattva path.

I'm forever indebted to Rinpoche for teaching and exemplifying the spiritual principles and path of the bodhisattva. May the radiance of bodhicitta illuminate the minds and hearts of all who encounter these teachings and pervade their lives and communities until wisdom and compassion prevail throughout the world.

CHAPTER 1. ENTERING THE PATH OF THE BODHISATTVA

The spiritual principles and methods we'll be discussing in this book are at the heart of the path of the bodhisattva. The bodhisattva—the awakened warrior—is one who's committed to ending suffering and bringing about happiness for all beings throughout time and space.

This may sound like an impossible goal that has nothing to do with our daily lives. But the way of the bodhisattva can be practiced by anyone, anywhere, at any time. To the extent that we practice it, we can be certain we'll be of true and lasting benefit to ourselves and others. We'll learn how to do that in this book.

Bodhi (pronounced "bo-dee") is a word from the ancient Sanskrit language of India that means "awakened." It refers to the purity that is our true nature, imbued with limitless wisdom, loving kindness, compassion, and the ability to benefit others. *Sattva* can mean "hero" or "warrior."

Another Sanskrit word, bodhicitta (pronounced, "bo-dee-cheet-ah") means the heart of wisdom and compassion—great compassion for all living beings, equally, for all time. All living beings means everyone—from someone we might think of as the worst human being on earth to the smallest of creatures.

Everything the bodhisattva does comes from this heart of wisdom and compassion. To be able to do this, the bodhisattva trains their mind in bodhicitta for the purpose of increasing their positive qualities and decreasing whatever stands in the way of their being of the greatest benefit to others. This book is concerned with how we give rise to bodhicitta—how we practice, stabilize, deepen, and, ultimately, realize it.

To the extent we do that, we're able to make positive causes that produce positive results. Our good heart becomes more and more available—and not just to ourselves. As it expresses itself in the world at large, it increasingly becomes a cause of benefit for others. There's more kindheartedness in the world, more fortunate circumstances. On this path, we're training in methods that dispel our confusion and awaken our mind's natural beneficial qualities. Every one of the methods we'll be learning does both.

Medicinal and Toxic Seeds

In our current culture, success is often measured in a competitive framework that requires us to put our own needs first. We aren't encouraged to help others as much as we are to be better than others. We're taught that this is how we'll stand out, so we'll be recognized and rewarded. We often justify this by telling ourselves that our needs and goals are more important than those of others. But, if we understand that this kind of thinking only makes problems in our relationships over time, we see that we don't want to keep acting on habits that end up harming ourselves and others.

Avoiding such habits is a hard thing to do. Obviously, we all want what's beneficial, and we don't want misery and misfortune. Creating positive outcomes is like planting seeds. We start to learn which seeds we can plant in the ground of our mind and in our lives that will produce healthy and nourishing fruit. We also need to learn which seeds to avoid because their fruit is poisonous and harmful. Becoming more informed about what kinds of seeds will produce what kinds of fruit empowers us to make more skillful choices with each other in every arena of our lives.

Beneficial seeds, medicinal seeds, are those positive actions of body, speech, and mind that are genuinely concerned with the welfare of others, making the welfare of others at least as important—if not more important—to us as our own. Poisonous or toxic seeds are seeds of self-importance and self-centeredness, where we place our own needs ahead of the needs of others. When we do this, we're not being truly respectful of and responsive to the concerns of everybody around us.

One of the basic principles that we work with on the bodhisattva path and in the Buddhist tradition in general is that of cause and effect. This is the understanding that every action creates a reaction in the form of consequences or outcomes. As we begin to understand how this plays out in our workplaces, our homes, and our lives overall, we begin to see which kinds of actions of our mind and heart can produce the outcomes we want.

To benefit ourselves and others to the greatest extent possible, we need to plant a garden and eventually a forest filled with nothing but medicinal seeds. If we have the confidence that the seeds we're planting are purely medicinal, we know that, at some point, they'll bear healthy fruit. That understanding nourishes and supports us and gives us patience even though, outwardly, everything isn't necessarily going the way we want in the moment. Life's obstacles often confound our best intentions, and the path is not always straight or easy. No matter what difficulties we meet along the way, we have confidence in the benefit of doing everything we can with our body, speech, and mind for the sake of all beings. That vast intention is what we call "pure motivation." When we understand the importance of pure motivation, pure intention, each and every one of us has the power and opportunity in every day of our lives to grow to be of greater benefit to all beings.

Questions

Doug: I personally believe in this wholeheartedly, but how do we protect ourselves from others who don't believe this, who would never think about helping others, only themselves. Wouldn't practicing this all the time make us vulnerable?

Lama: Actually, it's the opposite. We're vulnerable and powerless when we're not connecting with and expressing our positive qualities. Our power lies in our wisdom and compassion— compassion for those who don't know anything other than harming others, who don't understand that the outcomes they're creating in the long run are the opposite of what they want. We're also empowered by the compassionate wisdom to know when and how to say to them that enough is enough—for their sake as well as for the sake of those they're harming. Cultivating such wisdom and compassion is part of the training of the bodhisattva that we'll be learning here.

1 Reflecting on Our Lives

Take a few moments to review your life choices and see if you find a connection between what was in your mind and heart at various times and the outcomes.

Think back through your life—the months, years, and decades—and recall how often you've ignored the needs of others when you've been gripped by negative emotions. Recall times when your mind was filled with toxic emotions—self-centeredness, self-protection, attachment to what you wanted, or anger and aversion—that clouded a genuine concern for others. Attachment includes a wide range of emotions ranging from the slightest fanciful inclination to full-blown obsession, all of which stem from wanting what we think will bring us happiness.

Aversion refers to the feeling of not wanting what we think will bring us suffering or prevent our happiness, and it ranges from the slightest irritation to full-blown rage. Maybe you stormed out of an argument and slammed the door, or you yelled insults that later you realized you didn't really mean. What were the immediate consequences of your actions in those relationships? What were the longer-term consequences? If you look back over the years, what happened to those relationships? Are you still in the same job or community? Do you have a good relationship with those people?

Next, think back on the times when your heart was open and filled with concern for others, when your motivation was truly pure, and you had no agenda other than to love someone and let them know they were loved. Maybe you were able to see things from an opposing point of view and recognize another person's fear, for example, and maybe you didn't condemn them. Maybe it was in a family or other challenging situation, but you were able to break through and put their needs before your own. Reflect on the outer and inner consequences of your actions over time.

Which choices gave you confidence, nourished you, and allowed you to keep trying to benefit others? Which choices caused you to feel resentful or shut down or disappointed? What was your motivation at the time? When your negative emotions took over, did you have some kind of attachment or ulterior or mixed motivation?

When you think about situations in which your motivation wasn't so positive, consider what might have happened in those circumstances if you'd focused instead on pure motivation. What would have happened if you'd checked your mind and heart and asked yourself how you could be of greater benefit to everyone equally? How could you have balanced not just the short-term but the long-term benefit of everyone involved? If you'd brought that kind of thought process to your planning or activity, how might the outcome have been different?

From I, Me, and Mine to We, Us, and Ours

One translation of the Tibetan word for meditation is "to repeat." Through the practice of meditation, we become more aware of and clear about what we're repeating and what we want to repeat in our mind. For our whole life, every single one of us has been meditating every minute of every day, though we're not aware of it. All the thoughts we focus on are a form of meditation. Every time we repeat something in our mind—such as, "I don't like that person"—we're making a meditation out of that thought. The more we repeat it, the harder it is to see that this person may not be at all like we think they are. Once we begin to gain insight into what may be causing them to behave the way they are—that they may be dealing with tragedy or loss, for example—our meditation about them changes. Through learning methods that empower our positive qualities, we become able to choose what to repeat in our mind that will produce better outcomes—in this case, bringing compassion and wisdom to our understanding of that person.

Throughout our lives, unless our meditation has been informed by wisdom and compassion, it has led to suffering rather than peace or happiness for ourselves and others. Now, instead, we want to become aware of the thoughts that repeat in our mind, stop our meditations that lead to suffering, and begin meditations that create benefit for ourselves and others. On the bodhisattva path, the purpose of meditation isn't to produce temporary blissful experiences or to escape from difficult feelings or circumstances but to uproot the suffering of all beings by awakening and actualizing our intrinsic wisdom and compassion.

What seeds are we planting in the ground of our mind? Medicinal seeds—thoughts that are virtuous and kind—will produce medicinal fruit that will benefit everyone who eats it. Toxic seeds—self-centered, non-virtuous thoughts—will produce the opposite. Because we've been unaware of this principle, out of our lack of understanding and confusion, we've been repeating self-centered thoughts and actions and believing they'll lead to happiness. We've been repeating "I, me, mine, I want, I need," every single day for decades, yet we haven't found stable happiness or contentment. These self-involved meditations neither lead to happiness nor do they benefit others. Instead, we end up in endless cycles of suffering that we, ourselves, perpetuate.

This is true no matter why we're repeating, "I want, I need, I have to have." We could be wanting something for ourselves—a new car or job, something for our community, for our team to win the Super Bowl, or even something with a seemingly selfless motivation like passing a new law to help end poverty. It doesn't matter what it is that we want. Repeating it again and again in our mind reinforces the idea that what we want is more important than what others want. So, once again, we're putting our own needs before those of others, which never ends well.

We've been using the wrong method to produce benefit and happiness. Our daily mantra of "I, me, mine" shapes who we are and produces a habit of planting poisonous seeds. These seeds ripen, we don't like what they produce, and then we react in the same way—over and over again. In this way, we continue in the same cycle in which we suffer the consequences—the fruit—of these toxic seeds.

Once we understand that the cause of our suffering is in the mind, we begin to realize that the solution can be found in the mind as well. Up to this point, we've been repeating, "I, me, mine." So now we need to begin repeating the remedy for that, which is, "we, us, everybody."

The only method we can trust to achieve stable happiness is one that focuses on, "we, us, ours," the wish for the benefit of others. When the intention of our actions of body, speech, and mind includes or makes most important the welfare of others, we change the habit of thinking of ourselves as most important. By making the welfare of others our motivation, we decrease our self-centeredness.

The mind is like a muscle. We're building strength, so we need to repeat certain motions again and again. To strengthen our spiritual muscles so they can carry us through everything we do, we have to repeat these principles in our mind. This is how meditation transforms our old habits that lead to negative outcomes into new habits that lead to positive outcomes. We're able to change our lives in a very real way—but, like trying to change the direction of an ocean liner as it heads toward an iceberg, we have to apply effort. That means we have to practice. As our practice grows stronger, we'll see the direction of our mind and heart turn, and our ability to benefit others will increase.

Breanna: I've noticed in my own life that I can't find true contentment if I focus on my own happiness alone—gathering food, friends, material possessions. I've tried this, and it ends up failing me. It's entirely different to focus on others—I feel more grounded and stable. Virtue opens my heart, and creating virtue is a better way to live, but I don't understand why or how.

Lama: As we avoid self-centered actions of body, speech, and mind; increasingly act in ways that are kind and caring; and are conscious of the needs, wishes, and welfare of others, we start creating virtue, which is the cause of happiness. As we avoid non-virtue—the cause of suffering—and engage in virtue, we experience the benefit of that arising as positive outcomes. Concern for others creates virtue, and self-centeredness creates non-virtue.

If what we're repeating in our mind is virtuous and positive, it will produce a positive result—happiness and contentment. If what we're repeating is non-virtuous and negative, it will produce a negative result—suffering. Virtuous actions won't produce lasting negative outcomes any more than non-virtue can produce lasting positive outcomes. Wheat and corn stalks might appear the same when they first poke out of the ground, but once they've matured, wheat can only produce wheat, and corn can only produce corn. Similarly, when the sprouts of medicinal or toxic seeds appear in our lives, they may both look nourishing, but, ultimately, can only produce opposite outcomes.

2 I, Me, and Mine

Start by examining, deeply, in your life and the lives of others:

—How has what you repeat in your mind created certain outcomes?

—Has acting in a self-centered way—putting your needs before the needs of others—caused harm?

—At times when you weren't conscious of the needs of others, were your actions toward others careless or harmful and, if so, how?

—If your motivation isn't truly pure, does this compromise your future ability to benefit others in some way and, if so, how?

—Have your actions created a forest that produces plenty of pure medicine that you've been able to share with and benefit those around you, and how has that happened? If that hasn't been your experience, do you feel it's important to increase your capacity to make that happen?

Contemplate each of the above questions repeatedly, from many different angles, examining the circumstances of your own and others' lives.

Closing the Gap

So how do we nurture the qualities within ourselves that could produce beneficial and harmonious outcomes? How do we make sure that our day-to-day actions are based in our values? We begin by developing awareness of our motivation in each situation and learning how to expand it to include others.

This is difficult. As we look at our mind and our lives, we see our values, and we also see whether we live those values. The values we hold in our heart aren't always the values reflected in our everyday actions. And there are all kinds of emotions in between—our feelings about ourselves and others, what we want, what we don't want.

If our motivation isn't completely pure, we may, for example, want to do something to benefit others, but there's self-centered attachment involved—perhaps to a certain outcome or to being praised for our work. Maybe we're helping others as a means to feel better about ourselves or to avoid something painful going on with us. If any of these things are present, even if we think we're doing what we're doing to benefit others, the seeds we're planting are a mixture of the pure wish to benefit others and self-centered motivation. What grows from these seeds will then also be a mixture of medicinal and toxic. That will be our future experience—a garden filled with both poison and medicine.

Sometimes, what's mixed with our wish to help is aversion, a whole range of emotions about the things we don't want—which we can experience as anything from mild irritation and impatience to outright rage. Anger, for example, can arise when we're attached to a particular outcome and things don't go the way we want.

Then there are times when we act truly selflessly, with no attachment or aversion. We might feel heartbreaking compassion—not just for the choices others are making or the pain they're feeling in the moment but for all the underlying conditions that are causing them to make those choices. Maybe they don't know other choices are possible.

Sometimes, there's nothing we can do but love them. For example, if we're with someone in our family or community who's dying, and we bring no agenda of our own about the right way to die or leave things with their family, we're able to simply let them know they're loved unconditionally, so they don't feel alone as they leave this life. We're just there, loving them, as they leave their body.

Some of what we'll be discovering in this training involves learning how to work with our emotions in a way that transforms self-centered and negative habits into genuinely compassionate, kind, and caring qualities and responsiveness to others. We'll learn how to close the gap between what we say we value and actually living that value.

Tonya: I've noticed that I spend a lot of time thinking about or concerned about others—what they do and say and think. But, I'm realizing there's often some background concern about myself. I realize I'm still motivated by concern for myself.

Lama: That's great that you're seeing the difference. If we look closer at our motivation, sometimes we can see where we did things that outwardly appeared to be for the benefit of others, but there was some twist to it. Maybe we tried to help a friend through a breakup or job change but harbored some more dubious intention to sway their decision in order to increase or decrease their dependency on us. Perhaps we wanted recognition or acceptance, to be loved, approved of, or thought well of, to feel less insecure or boost our ego. Maybe we were raised to believe that we weren't a good person, or our family couldn't survive if we didn't place others' needs before our own. So, we have a strong habit to please or to uphold others, but that's laced with lots of fear of the consequences if we don't. If we're honest with ourselves, we can see these layers of hope and fear that get mixed up with our motivation to help and, when that happens, we plant seeds that are a mix of poison and medicine. Therefore, the outcome will be mixed as well. It won't produce lasting benefit.

It's not that, every time we try to act with good heart, it immediately and magically produces all kinds of wonderful outcomes. Seeds take time to ripen, and the conditions have to be right. There's cause and effect in individual situations in which we have some control, and there's also cause and effect when the actions of others have an influence. We have to be particularly skillful in situations like that, and we may not see positive outcomes right away. It's important that our motivation be pure, so we can be as skillful and creative as possible in any situation—no matter what else is going on.

3 A Daily Practice of Pure Motivation

In each moment, ask yourself what your motivation is for everything you do.

Each morning, establish your motivation for the day as soon as you wake up. Make a commitment that everything you do today and every future day will be for the purpose of true and lasting benefit—not just to yourself but to those around you and, ultimately, to all living beings equally, in the short and long term.

Take a moment to set your motivation for working with this material: That whatever you learn, and whatever you practice may truly be of benefit—not just to a few but ultimately to every living being, now and in the long term. Make the wish to increase your pure motivation in your mind and heart, and bring that motivation into the thoughts and actions of your daily life, so it's not just an idea in your head, an empty value, but it becomes you and is expressed in everything you do.

CHAPTER 2. PURE MOTIVATION

Pure motivation—the heart of bodhicitta—involves making the welfare of others as important to us as—or more important than—our own. Pure motivation is like good heart steeped in wisdom—the wisdom of considering not just the short-term but the long-term welfare of all others. It becomes our fuel and our way of being in the world in a stable, powerful, and courageous way as we blend the contemplations and meditations on pure motivation with our mind and heart. Over time, through our practice, we develop trust that pure motivation is what will create the greatest benefit for ourselves and others in the long run. This allows us to walk through our lives with confidence, even if, in the short run, we encounter great hardship. Our certainty that pure motivation is the way to go nourishes, sustains, and holds us as we deal with any difficulties that arise. Therefore, we must genuinely and deeply explore why this intention is beneficial and how we can move it from a new and unfamiliar concept to a fully engaged experience.

At first, this process of generating bodhicitta involves contemplation, because we're learning a new habit. As we start on this path, most of us already have good heart and have spent a vast majority of our lives trying to help others in some way—family, children, parents, animals, the homeless, the abused, the ill, or others. Our willingness to be of benefit isn't the issue. We need to understand the difference between that impulse to be of benefit and bodhicitta, and why bodhicitta—the motivation to benefit all beings for all time—is so essential if we want to create the greatest benefit possible. We do this by contemplating the difference between bodhicitta and simple good heart, and by giving rise to bodhicitta as much as possible in everything we do throughout the day.

Two-Legged, Four-Legged, and No-Legged Alike

We begin by reminding ourselves that every single being, just like us, wants to be happy. There isn't a single being that wants to be miserable. This includes those we have a direct connection with, those we have a less direct connection with, those we've only heard or read about, and, ultimately, all beings—two-legged, four-legged, and no-legged alike.

Every being is just like us. Until we start to understand that the causes of our happiness are virtue and positive actions of body, speech, and mind, and that the causes of our suffering are negativity and negative habits of body, speech, and mind, none of us knows how to find our way toward the happiness we're looking for. We're all, always, trying to control, change, and manage everybody and everything, not understanding that the change we want has to begin in our own heart. Every living being that doesn't know how to move toward the causes of benefit and happiness and away from the causes of suffering and misery is actually creating—moment by moment—the opposite of what they want, working at cross-purposes to their own goals—just as we've done so often, again and again. We're all in the same pickle.

We've all gone through life thinking about who we are, what we want, and what we need, but rarely do we think about what others need. That's why there are so many problems in the world. Including others in our thoughts and wishes awakens our compassion, love, and responsiveness. This takes us out of negative feelings about ourselves and others into the sense of our common reality—the tragedy that all of us want to be happy but endlessly create the opposite. With that understanding, and through remembering everyone else, we bring our mind back to pure motivation. We aren't developing the motivation only to benefit those close to us. Instead, we realize that, as we help those around us, they're able to help those around them, and those help others around them, and so it goes out into the world.

Just as we know how much it benefited us any time somebody was kind and helped us when we were struggling, we can offer the same to those around us. So, we create an intention that's as vast as the countless beings throughout time and space and that benefits every single one, because we all share the same wishes, hopes, and fears.

We look at the difference in our mind and in the impact on those around us when bodhicitta is our foundation as compared to just thinking of one person or a few people experiencing one kind of suffering. We don't have to deny trying to help a particular person or that we love that person, but we can think of that person, in this moment, as the representative of all beings. We include all beings in the scope of our intention when we act and imagine that we're serving the needs of all beings through serving the needs of this one person. Perhaps this person is suffering from cancer. We don't just want that person to be free of the suffering of cancer but of all illness and, further, any kind of suffering. And not just this person but all beings.

In everything we do, we cultivate a sense of the ocean of suffering beings, the ocean of beings yearning for help who are all present in this person or situation to which we're responding. Each moment provides us the opportunity to bring the power of bodhicitta to every action, expressed through our love for whoever we're with and our wish for them to be benefited. Then, whatever we do is purely for their sake and that of all beings without a personal agenda.

Equally vast is the timeframe of our concern for others' welfare. We've seen, from our own experience, that any well-being we've found has often been unreliable. If the cause of our contentment is due to things coming together over which we have no control—a job, the economy, or a relationship, for example—and we're counting on others to fulfill our wishes, we may find ourselves trying to change other people and situations in the hope that this will bring us happiness. Most of us who've tried that learned pretty quickly that it doesn't work so well.

We need to understand that none of these things is permanent. The economy goes in a certain direction—up or down—and that's not going to last. Our workplace being a certain way won't last. There are always forces at play that cause change. We've all had the experience of relying on outer situations to try to ensure our happiness, and we've all seen such happiness evaporate. This is true for everyone.

That's why we don't wish for ourselves and others a happiness that's unstable, unreliable, and subject to a million causes of change. Instead, we wish for every living being a happiness that's stable—not just in the short run but in the long run and not just on the level of survival but on the level of complete opening and awakening to the limitless range of all of our own and others' positive qualities.

As we access, realize, and express those qualities in our lives, we'll experience their results—lasting benefit and happiness. This is sustainable, because it doesn't rely on anything outside of ourselves that we have no control over. Rather, it relies on the infinite positive qualities that are the radiance of our bodhicitta. That's what we mean when we talk about long-term benefit—that complete awakening—and this is what we wish for every living being. In so doing, we begin to embody the very qualities we're looking for and want to see in the world. Instead of looking to others to be the solution, we start to become the solution.

4 Reviewing Teachings on Pure Motivation

Review everything we've discussed above, paragraph by paragraph, reading and thinking about it but also examining and contemplating it as it applies to your own life and experience. Ask yourself if the framework and the principles make sense.

Have you seen, in your own life and the lives of those around you, that including the welfare of others in your intentions and actions creates more benefit than just thinking of your own, and, if so, how?

Have you seen that including the long-term as well as short-term welfare of others in your thinking brings more benefit, and, if so, in what ways? Has it brought more insight? More maturity and less reactivity?

Carolyn: You said we might eventually put other people's needs and benefits ahead of our own. How do we do that without feeling resentful?

Lama: First of all, we start out with the mind training of making the needs and benefit of others equal to our own. We aren't denying our own but including everybody within our wishes. As we go deeper in our training, our love and compassion increase and our bodhicitta naturally arises more strongly until love and compassion are all that's going on with us. All we want is the welfare of others. That's where we're at.

If you're feeling resentment when thinking of others' needs ahead of your own, start by including others in your own actions of body, speech, and mind. For example, if you're hungry and wanting a good meal, think to yourself, "May all beings have the nourishment they need." That way, you aren't denying your own needs. But you're including others within the scope of your wishes for your own welfare, so there's less self-centeredness and more virtue, and you're expanding your capacity for love and compassion at the same time.

It's not meant to be an insincere or phony practice in which we force ourselves or pretend to feel something we don't, and then feel resentful. It's a mind training. Through the training itself, our capacity for love and compassion increases. Therefore, our natural wish for the welfare of others increases. Over time, the welfare of others actually becomes more important to us than what we've perceived as our own welfare. Our need becomes whatever is best for everyone. That happens naturally, and it starts by including everyone in our thoughts as we move through our lives. When we start our day and think about whatever it is we want, we add the wish that, through our efforts, all beings may be fulfilled in the short and long run.

Carolyn: So, it's not that I'm denying my own needs, I'm just including others?

Lama: We start out including others and, over time, it's almost like the center of gravity in our heart shifts until it's all about everyone—and we're included. Our welfare is accomplished by caring for others, because every act of bodhicitta, every act of pure love and compassion, creates so much virtue that it naturally fulfills our own needs.

Wanting to benefit all beings doesn't mean all beings except us. It starts out as us and all beings and, slowly, over time, it becomes all beings including us. However, we aren't motivated by wanting to include ourselves. We have the confidence that everything we're doing is what's most beneficial not just for others but for us as well. We have the certainty that the virtue we create will bring benefit, and we aren't excluded from that benefit. We're fulfilled as our practice deepens, our capacity increases, and we're better able to help others. When we see that someone has genuinely benefited from our efforts, that fulfills us. There's no corner from which resentment would emerge. Don't worry that you're trying to force yourself to do something, and that's not where you're at. Your capacity will grow naturally.

Tonya: Meditation with the idea of producing change feels like something imposed. There's a subtle sense of there being something wrong with what I'm experiencing.

Lama: If we're bringing a value-based, moral judgment to our emotional experience—overlaying someone else's value system on our emotional experience and judging it according to that— we're going to rebel. That's why we spend so much time at the beginning analyzing the process and the path, so we don't feel we're doing it because it's the right thing to do according to somebody else. We *want* to examine what happens when we make certain choices to determine if they lead to benefit or harm. If we continue to examine our experience, it will lead us to trust that particular actions lead to particular results. That realization comes from the inside out. It's not an external form or belief system being imposed on us.

We listen to teachings, contemplate, and examine them according to our own experience. We each ask ourself if they ring true. Do they make sense? If they make sense, out of our own conviction and based on our own experience, we'll *want* to practice. As we do so, if we see benefit for ourselves and others, if our negativity decreases, our heart opens, and our positive qualities emerge, we'll naturally want to make different choices.

Ocean: Can you say something about the difference between practicing mindfulness versus pure motivation?

Lama: We want to ask ourselves what we're being mindful *of*. What are we remaining one-pointedly aware of and focused on? Is it about ourselves or about others? What are the habits we're reinforcing in the mind through repetition?

Pure motivation will always produce benefit however and wherever we express it. This is different than learning mindfulness in the context of our personal goals and not thinking about the needs of others—training to be a corporate raider, for example—because the motivation there is completely different. By practicing pure motivation, we can never go wrong. It can never create harm. It can only benefit.

Doug: How do we care equally about someone who's harming us or others?

Lama: We remind ourselves that we all want positive circumstances. We want what's beneficial to ourselves and others, and we don't want misery, suffering, and misfortune. That's pretty universal. But each of our ideas of what's beneficial is different, so there's conflict. Conflict arises because we're all equally committed to what we think are the causes of happiness, and each of us believes that what we think would produce the greatest benefit and happiness would really do that. We're completely sure, of course, that our way is the only way, and that people who disagree with us are wrong. We often have all kinds of righteous ideas about the choices we make and righteous judgment about choices other people make. That's a big problem if we want to benefit others.

As a student in school, a healthcare practitioner, a community organizer, or an environmentalist—in whatever way we're engaged in the world—we're pouring our heart and our effort into what we're doing because we believe it will be beneficial. Of course, we always encounter others who disagree with us and who are working for the opposite of what we believe in and with the same force that we bring to the work we do. If we engage in that activity and interact with others with the complete certainty that we're the only ones who are right and that others are wrong, we often judge them harshly. This compromises our capacity to bring benefit, because we're not coming from an equal commitment to and respect for everybody.

To truly bring equanimity—equal regard, equal respect, equal commitment, and equal responsiveness to all living beings—into our hearts and minds, it has to be more than an idea. It must be a lived experience. We must truly be committed to everyone we encounter and do everything we can to listen well, to hear them, and to be responsive to what they need. In everything we do, we try to find a way through that's equally respectful and beneficial to all.

When we're trying to be of benefit, often we think of the choices we make as either for or against this or that thing. The truth is, to find our way through, we need to come up with creative alternatives that aren't divisive but instead arise from a commitment to and respect for everyone equally. An appreciation of harmony, cooperation, community building, and problem solving requires skills we don't necessarily learn in our families, in our communities, or in our schools. Learning these skills requires putting time in, and practice.

Whenever we find ourselves strongly judging and disliking others' choices, we can do a meditation called, "Just Like Me." We walk ourselves through the process of remembering, that just like us, this person wants to be happy, doesn't want to suffer, has the potential to make different choices, and yet is bound to the outcomes of their previous actions. In this way, we're giving rise to a very humble point of view and recognizing our common frailties rather than our differences. We remind ourselves that everyone's true nature is a state of limitless purity, but, not knowing that, they work at cross purposes to their own wish for happiness, just as we've done countless times.

5 Just Like Me

Begin by establishing pure motivation for doing this meditation. Imagine someone you're biased against, and remind yourself, "This person—just like me—wants to be happy and doesn't want to suffer, yet, out of ignorance, they're working at cross-purposes to that very goal. The actions I've judged so harshly actually result from their efforts to be happy or stop suffering." Ask yourself how many times you've done the same thing. You may have acted to differing degrees than they have, with differing kinds of beings in differing arenas with differing values, but your thoughts, words, and actions have all stemmed from the same attachment to your own ideas of what's best, and you're both caught in the same counter-productive cycle. How tragic!

Expand the visualization to include others who behave similarly to this person. Remind yourself that they, like you, want to find happiness and avoid suffering. Unaware of the actual causes of happiness and suffering, they're sowing seeds of future misery, just as we've done and continue to do, in each moment, day after day, in the confused belief that pursuing our own needs and desires over those of others will produce stable well-being.

Continue to expand the content and scope of your meditation, in stages, to include more people with whom you disagree, those with whom you agree, and those toward whom your attitude is neutral until, eventually, you open to a pervasive awareness of everyone's shared human experience.

The Means and the End Are the Same

Bodhicitta includes both the process of awakening and the result. It's the foundation of the path, the process of change, and the final result.

We're relying on our positive qualities to increase our positivity—in the sense of virtue—and purify our negativity—non-virtue—so we can awaken the limitless positive qualities of our true nature. Every single tool we use both removes what's obscuring and supports us in recognizing, strengthening, and nurturing the positive qualities that are naturally present. As we go through our daily lives, we're able to practice the spiritual path by bringing pure motivation to everything we do. That way, every action of body, speech, and mind supports our ultimate awakening.

Rinpoche used to use the metaphor of the quartz crystal as it's formed in the ground as a symbol of our true nature. Our ordinary mind is like the ore covering the crystal. How we appear to ourselves and to each other is very ordinary, and this ordinary appearance obscures our natural purity and positive qualities. All the ideas we have—such as the shape and color of the ore that we do or don't like, everything we're relating to in ourselves and in each other, our emotions, and the habitual responses we've developed over time—are like layers of ore concealing the crystal.

The point of the path is to remove what's obscuring the crystal and reveal the essential purity of the crystal itself—and not only for our own sake. When the sun shines through the crystal, there's a rainbow radiance of tremendous beauty that brings joy. This is the case with our true nature as well. As we're able to reveal it, our pure qualities can be a cause of joy and benefit to those around us. In the Buddhist tradition, we call this "awakening" or "enlightenment."

Talking about enlightenment can sound like some ancient, foreign idea that's impossible for us to even begin to relate to. However, it simply means removing all the ore from the crystal. All we're doing is waking up to what's already there. We're empowering what's ultimately true instead of what's temporarily, superficially, apparently true. Simply through the process of recognizing and sustaining what's ultimately true— our natural positive qualities—and bringing that to everything we do, the ore sloughs off the crystal. Whether the methods we use are like water in a gently moving stream or like a rock tumbler or a vat of acid, we're removing the ore of our obscurations.

First, we recognize that these pure qualities are there within us, and then we cultivate a relationship with them and learn the methods by which we actualize them. That's the path. But it's also a principle and the goal. This is our true nature, so we want to assure that every action of body, speech, and mind will reveal those positive qualities instead of further obscuring them.

When we have a decision to make, for example, we do so from pure motivation. This means we ask ourselves what choice we think will produce the most benefit and least harm for the most beings, both in the long and short run. We do so with our outer choices and actions but also with the source of those actions in the mind. We look at which choice is most likely to uplift and empower our own and others' positive qualities. What's most inclined to increase positivity and decrease negativity?

We can learn how to refrain from harmful thoughts and choices and how to turn the mind in a positive direction by repeating in the mind, again and again, the cultivation and the expression of mind's positive qualities. The more we repeat those, the more we change the ratio of positivity to negativity in the mind. We're strengthening the presence of the positive, powerful qualities of mind.

As we do that, the negative habits that have arisen from our lack of recognition of our true nature are cleansed and purified. Just like when the sun comes out, shadows naturally dissipate, it's the radiance of our positive qualities that dispels the temporary, confused experience of mind's negativity. To the extent that we give rise to bodhicitta, all the shade, all the negativity that's arisen from not knowing our true nature naturally dissolves. Through that awakening, like the dawning of the sun, bodhicitta dawns in our heart and mind. Everything that isn't bodhicitta is naturally dispelled.

If we understand that process, the path becomes very simple. All we have to do in each moment is give rise to and maintain the practice of bodhicitta. Along the way, we may or may not have profound moments of insight or sublime visionary experiences, but those come and go. The only reliable sign that can give us confidence that our practice is working is if our negativity is decreasing and our positive qualities are increasing. That's the whole purpose of the spiritual path.

When this happens, we'll be of more benefit to ourselves and others. Wisdom, love, compassion, and virtuous skill are the expression of the inherent purity and goodness that's our true nature. As we recognize, stabilize, and grow our awareness of these qualities, our ignorance is dispelled. As our ignorance fades, our awareness of the presence of mind's inherent goodness becomes even more evident.

To the extent we do that, we're empowered to act in beneficial ways. The dynamic energy of mind expresses itself through kind, uplifting, and virtuous actions. This creates positive causes that produce positive results. The goodness of our heart becomes more and more clear and available—and not just to ourselves. As it expresses itself in the world at large, it becomes increasingly a cause of benefit for others. There's more virtue, honor, and inspiration in the world.

6 Cultivating Bodhicitta

Explore whether focusing on your self-centered needs and wants has been a cause of stable benefit for yourself or others. Then observe what the awareness of the needs of others does in your mind. Does it relax or transform your focus on yourself? Does it expand your love and compassion, and, if so, how?

Follow these three steps in your daily life and observe any changes that happen in your mind and outwardly in your life:
—Include the needs and wishes of all beings in any experience you're having.
—Join your thoughts and wishes with those of every being with the aspiration that we may all find the short- and long-term fulfillment we're looking for.
—Think of yourself as not separate from the needs, purposes, and wishes of all beings but as part of a whole. When you do so, are you more inclined to respond to others' needs without thinking, like the hand responding to the needs of the foot?

Breanna: I work as a nurse in the ICU, and one of the things people in my workplace talk about a lot is compassion fatigue—how we have to shield ourselves from burnout and be more self-protective. How can I increase my compassion without overdoing it and burning out?

Lama: This is such an important question about a very common misunderstanding. Using again the metaphor of the crystal covered by ore, we could say that the crystal obscured by ore represents a limited compassion. It's like a 9-to-5 or 6-to-6 compassion, depending on our work hours. It's limited, and it's also compromised by our own personal goals, whether to be recognized, to be right, to receive a promotion, or even to just look forward to the end of our shift when we're exhausted. Our compassion is limited, and our motivation is mixed, because we're trying to help people in the workplace, but we have our own things going on.

When we try to draw on that compassion, it *feels* limited because it *is* limited. This is why people encounter what's called compassion fatigue. We're not drawing on our deeper compassion, which is one of our inherent positive qualities. If, instead, we connect with our natural compassion, we're able to purify what's standing in the way of making it more sustainable.

That's the framework of these practices—learning how to draw on our inherent positive qualities, because they're the expression of our true nature and sustain us rather than drawing on what's temporary, which isn't sustainable. Whatever it is we're doing, if we use methods that increase and strengthen those positive qualities, we find our compassion, our caring, and our loving kindness increasing rather than diminishing. We begin to draw from the deep well of bodhicitta, which has no limitations.

Breanna: You used the metaphor of the crystal for our positive qualities such as love and compassion. Could you describe them in more detail?

Lama: Love, in the Buddhist context, means wanting happiness for others. When we talk about loving all beings, this means wishing for the welfare and benefit of all beings equally. Compassion means wanting others not to suffer. Using the example of your ICU, this love and compassion may begin with one person or a dozen people in that part of the hospital. Then we expand it to others in the hospital and continue expanding it until we're including every living being who doesn't understand that the cause of benefit and happiness is virtue and the cause of suffering is non-virtue—harming others instead of helping them. We realize that, in the very course of trying to create happiness, beings are creating the exact opposite. Thinking in this way is the basis for compassion for all living beings—wishing for the welfare of others and acting on that wish. We realize that the causes of suffering are being careless with, disregarding, or actively harming others. We create those causes instead of the causes of benefit and happiness as we try to find happiness for ourselves.

It's the same for us all: On the one hand, we want happiness, and, on the other hand, we don't understand the causes of that happiness, so we work at cross-purposes to that very goal. This is something we've all done, and it's something we all share. For that reason, it's the basis of compassion for all of us equally. That's another natural quality we all share—equanimity—recognizing the equalness of all of our circumstances and our true nature.

There's this underlying basis of compassion for every living being, within which there are the individuals we interact with. There are the patients in the ICU, the nurses and doctors and other healthcare professionals who are burned out, and there are the administrators who are trying to deal with a flood of data and information—including constantly shifting politics about how healthcare should be organized—and trying to manage healthcare services. There's a lot of stress and a lot of suffering in a profession that's focused on the welfare of others. That's the basis of compassion for everybody in the healthcare system.

For example, in your ICU, there isn't a single being who isn't worthy of compassion. There isn't a single being who isn't worthy of your love—which manifests as wanting them not to be stressed but also wanting them to find solutions and make things better. That's a huge arena, and there's nobody who isn't eligible for your care, your concern, and your kindness.

On the other hand, if we're working in the ICU, for example, we're attached to benefiting the patients and to positive outcomes. Part of why we're attached to positive outcomes is because we care about these people. Just like us, they want to be happy, and they don't want to suffer. Things are going wrong with their bodies that they don't understand. Maybe the doctors and nurses don't understand how scary that is. Just like us, these patients have lives and want to live them, but, because they have no control over what's happening to their bodies, they must depend on others to get that ability back.

So, you have attachment to helping them and aversion to not being able to help. What if you can't figure out what's wrong, or what if it's an inaccurate diagnosis, or what if the medicine isn't the right one? There are all kinds of fears about making mistakes. There are hopes about doing a good job. All of that comes from wanting to help the people under your care, but there's also wanting to do a good job, so you don't get fired. There's also not wanting to make mistakes, because you might be demoted or viewed poorly by your peers.

When we're in a lot of pain and suffering, many of us tend to lash out. Some people are kind when they're suffering, but others have a habit to blame. Therefore, no matter how hard you try, you'll probably get a fair share of blame and reactivity in the form of patients or their families thinking you're not working hard enough or responding quickly enough to their calls. In the middle of trying to help with all your best intentions, you may get a whole bunch of blame.

Of course, there's aversion to the blame, and there's attachment to praise, to being recognized when you do a good job, when you're responsive, and, in spite of all kinds of challenges, show up for a patient when they ask and provide all the things they need.

There are all these things at play in our mind when we're trying to help. So, when people talk about compassion fatigue, often the exhaustion is caused by all this stuff going on that's about us and not our efforts to benefit others.

Ocean: Regarding these self-centered habits, it's not like we shouldn't have them, especially wanting praise and feeling bad when we're blamed. Those feelings come out of insecurity, so, if we want to not have them, does that mean we have to cultivate a sense of security?

Lama: What we're learning how to do is develop security and confidence in our positive qualities instead of looking for feedback from others and other kinds of undependable support.

I don't want to use the word "should," because, as you said, we all have these wishes and feelings. It's not like we're bad because we react in this way, we're just human. At the same time, we need to recognize what the consequences are if we don't deal with our stuff. It leads to outcomes that aren't preferable for ourselves and others, including a lot of stress. It's not really compassion fatigue but a kind of "stuff fatigue." Actual compassion is tremendously energizing, because we're not drawing on a source within ourselves that's limited or compromised. It's limitless.

What limits us is our stuff—the things that get in our way. These include our attachments to getting what we want, whether it be praise, recognition, a raise, or time off; and our aversion to what we don't want when it happens, our harsh judgments, blaming ourselves and others, and so on—the poisons of our mind and the habits that arise from those poisons. As we transform our stuff, our compassion becomes increasingly unbounded. We need to remove the stuff to let our inherent limitless compassion express itself, which is a source of tremendous energy, inspiration, capacity, and potential.

7 Practicing Pure Motivation

Establish pure motivation throughout the day. When you see what's in the way of your being able to do this, think of others with the same kinds of challenges and wish that they may be able to overcome them. Make a commitment to apply the remedies for change on their behalf, beginning with pure motivation in everything you do.

Check your mind as you go through the day. Are you repeating the "I, me, mine" mantra all day, every day? Are you being a good listener, paying attention to and being responsive to the needs of others? When you've refreshed and acted from pure motivation, have you been happier and more content or more miserable? If you become lost in old, self-centered habits and apply the remedy to think about others, does that change your experience and, if so, how? Has developing pure motivation helped sustain your energy to benefit others? In trying to benefit others, have you experienced more compassion fatigue or stuff fatigue? Have you been more effective in bringing benefit when acting from your positive qualities? Do you see an increase in your positive qualities? If not, what needs adjustment in your practice?

As you go through your day, do you regularly generate and check your motivation, and is it producing change that's beneficial? What kinds of reminders could you structure into your day to bring your mind back to bodhicitta, such as setting an alarm to go off at regular intervals or remembering bodhicitta each time you open a door or answer your phone?

Anthony: I can't imagine being able to develop this kind of ability to practice.

Lama: Devoting time to practice is such an important part of developing confidence. Seeing the gap between our beliefs and what's really going on in the mind gives us a sense of urgency and determination to practice. We won't be motivated to do the hard work of practice unless we can't bear our old habits. And the results depend entirely on how much we apply the methods for change.

We all have habits to develop confidence based on aspects of our personalities that are impermanent. This means our confidence can be affected by things outside of ourselves or inside of ourselves when we're triggered. Confidence in our practice has to do with confidence in the qualities of limitless wisdom, loving kindness and compassion, and the capacity to benefit, all of which are natural aspects of our true nature. Developing confidence in those qualities, in those aspects of our experience, shifts us away from temporary, ego-based confidence.

Our self-concept—the way we think about and identify ourselves in the world as family members or co-workers, for example, and the sense we have of our capacities, strengths, weaknesses, and skills—has to do with personality traits that have been gathered in the course of a lifetime. However, none of those are stable. At any time, our identity, our sense of purpose, or our orientation to life can shift. For example, perhaps we've developed confidence in ourselves as a parent, but who are we when the kids leave?

Breanna: As you talk about confidence, the word faith keeps coming to mind.

Lama: Through our own experience, we've seen the power of our practice change us. As it changes us, it changes our relationship to outer and inner experiences. We develop confidence based on our practice, and you could say this confidence is similar to the idea of faith. We develop confidence not just in the practice but also in the presence of our positive qualities when we take the time to pay attention to, cultivate, and nurture them. When we do so, we draw on a source of strength, courage, inspiration, and possibility in our lives that isn't limited, impermanent, and bound by causes and conditions. Rather, it's a completely reliable source of everything we need to move in the world the way we want to move in the world and to create the benefit we want to create.

As we develop our practice, we cultivate a deeper connection with our positive qualities. As we do that, we bridge the gap between an identity that experiences itself as separate from our true nature and the true nature of all beings. If we rely on a sense of identity that's separate from our true nature to feel confident in whatever we do in the world, it's a false confidence. It won't support us.

Based on that relationship with our positive qualities, we're able to interact with others in a way that's more consistent with our values. This starts out as a relationship between an experience of ourselves and that of our positive qualities— which seem separate from each other. But, ultimately, the more we embody those positive qualities, it's no longer a relationship. There aren't two things that are relating anymore. We become aware that these positive qualities are the expression of our being-ness. This is the ultimate confidence, which will hold us through everything in our lives.

Riding the Wave to the Far Shore

If we develop the habit to make pure motivation the foundation for all our choices, no matter what situation we're in, we'll ask ourselves what our motivation truly is. We may have a genuine desire to benefit, but there may be layers of attachment to things going our way—because we think that would produce the most benefit—or aversion to things going in a way we don't agree with—because we think that's going to produce more harm.

So, in the case of the natural environment, for example, we may have a genuinely selfless intention to do something to stop climate change. Within that is our attachment to preservation of life on earth and aversion to its destruction. If we aren't checking our motivation, we may not notice our anger and judgment toward those we think are responsible for its destruction, making it very difficult for us to develop compassion for them.

It's not enough to act with just the idea of trying to stop or reverse climate change. To create the positive momentum needed to produce change of that magnitude, we must act with compassion and a commitment to the welfare of every living being equally. That includes the polluters, the people who are removing environmental protections, and those running the corporations that are spewing toxins into the atmosphere. They're operating according to a belief system that they think will produce happiness. And, of course, they're sure that having more wealth for themselves and their families is a way to find that happiness, and that they'll be able to buy their way out of whatever problems they're causing. They aren't thinking about the inconceivably toxic seeds they're planting that will create toxic results for their children and grandchildren and the whole world to deal with.

If we understand that they're making choices out of the same wish we have—to be happy and not suffer—we can stop dehumanizing them and start to think more clearly about possible solutions. If all we do is react with anger when we hear about harm to the environment, we're reinforcing the underlying belief that we're powerless. If we want to create sustainable change, we need to learn to be proactive, motivated to act *for* what we believe in, not just to react *against* what we don't.

If we want to come up with creative solutions for sustained benefit, we have to develop sustained positive motivation, sustained positive qualities, and a sustained, positive approach that's capable of drawing on our strengths and empowering ourselves, our positive qualities, and the positive qualities of those around us. When we do so, it's like we're riding a wave of virtue. That wave will carry us all the way to the far shore as long as we understand how to ride it, how to stand on top of it, and how to keep going.

When we did the contemplation in which we reviewed our past, we saw that acting based on our negative emotions didn't produce positive outcomes in the long run. That's true not just for ourselves individually—our individual outcomes—but also our collective outcomes. If most people are acting out of rage, bitterness, judgment, and righteousness, how can that produce a positive collective outcome? Rinpoche used to use the example of demonstrating for peace with a mind filled with hatred and anger. If our own mind isn't kind and caring, how are we going to create communities, workplaces, families, and a global community that are caring and harmonious?

It has to begin with us. As we empower our own positive qualities, we have the possibility of recognizing, encouraging, and empowering those qualities in others. If, instead, we view another's actions through the lens of our own negativity, we can't see each other's positive qualities. It's like we're wearing glasses colored by all our suspicions, judgments, righteousness, and pride. We're sure our way is right, and the ways of others are wrong. If we can't see each other's positive qualities, how can we encourage, inspire, and uplift them, and how can we go forward with any kind of certainty?

As we develop the confidence that those positive qualities are in our own hearts, we slowly cleanse the clouded lens of how we've viewed ourselves and the world in the past and begin to see the positive qualities in the hearts of others. With that certainty, we can begin to more clearly find creative solutions and ways forward that aren't stuck in the extremes of good and bad, us and them, but all of us together. We see how what we do with our body, speech, and mind can uplift everybody instead of only some at the expense of others.

We've seen this happen throughout history. When people try to uplift themselves at the expense of others, it's not sustainable. No one wants to see other people uplifted at their own expense, so there's a negative reaction. If we want to see sustained, positive outcomes in our family, in our relationships, in our workplace, in our communities, in our activism, or wherever it is, we have to create that cause in our own mind and heart. If we want to see outer positive outcomes, we have to create inner positive causes. This is true for ourselves personally, and it's true for ourselves collectively.

So, take a moment to set your motivation to think about and make this wish—that through whatever understanding and practice you develop, whatever actions you take, you may be the cause of awakening to the limitless positive qualities of yourself and every being throughout time and space.

8 Practicing Bodhicitta in Daily Life

Contemplate the difference between bodhicitta and simple good heart.

Give rise to bodhicitta as much as possible as the basis and reason for your meditation practice. Start by thinking of those you have connection with that you want to help, and then slowly expand that intention to include more and more beings you'd like to be able to help until it includes all beings. Reflect on how everyone's moments of happiness are impermanent, and wish for all beings that they find fulfillment that's not subject to change.

In your daily life, give rise to bodhicitta with everything you do.

Doug: Why would I want to love and make somebody happy who's doing everything they can to destroy the environment and make money off of it? What's the benefit created by loving that person? It would make me unmotivated to act.

Lama: It's a misunderstanding to believe loving someone means just sitting back and doing nothing while they destroy the environment, for example. If we really love someone, we want not just their temporary but their ultimate welfare. This means we want them to have the causes and conditions of benefit, happiness, and fulfillment that are lasting. Destroying anything or anyone for one's own selfish purpose creates outcomes that aren't going to benefit them. It won't create harmonious relationships in the short run, and, in the long run, the negative and destructive outcomes of their actions are inconceivable. If we're truly thinking about them—not only those currently impacted by their actions—our urge to intervene would only become stronger.

Tonya: Often, the things we want to manifest can begin with a pure motivation but, when they reach the world stage, ego and attachment crop up. In those moments, how can we return to that initial pure motivation for our actions?

Lama: Whether we're working in social-justice activism, counseling, teaching, or in whatever way trying to help others, if we're honest with ourselves, we'll see that, although what we're doing outwardly appears to be for the welfare of others, it's often about our own benefit. If we have attachment to achieving our goals, aversion to others' actions, attachment to people agreeing that our way is the best, and aversion to their disagreement, that means it's really about us. It's about *our* idea and how *we* think things should be. If we're sure our idea is the best, that's pride. If we feel it's necessary for us to convince everyone else, that's competition or attachment to our own way and aversion to others'. All of these poisons of the mind come out of a basic, self-referencing habit. Every meditation we talk about in this book and every meditation on this path is about eroding that self-centered fixation and undermining that as the basis for the choices we make in our lives.

To make these changes, we have to put time in on our practice of meditation. There's absolutely no replacement for that. We may like these ideas, go out into the world, and try to make sure our motivation is pure. But then we encounter our strong emotions and patterns, and the only way we can prevail is to make the force of our meditation stronger than our old habits. The only way to do that is time in with meditation—again and again and again. If we haven't put the time in on our meditation so that the force of our pure motivation is stronger than all our other habits, when we hit all of those circumstances, we lose it.

Rinpoche used to use the metaphor that intellectual understanding is like trying to repair a hole in our pants by simply placing a patch of the same fabric and shape on top of it. It might look really good and appear to be fixed—until we stand up and the patch falls off. We have to stitch the patch into the fabric of the pants so it will hold. Meditation is that process of stitching understanding into the fabric of our being.

Every time we relive a scene from our day, we think how it might have played out differently if we'd done this or that—if we'd done this with our meditation or we'd said or done that. Every time we do that, we're adding a stitch, so eventually the patch becomes part of the integrity of the fabric of our being.

There's no replacement for that stitching process. That's what changes us. Who we are changes. Our habits change. Our responses change. How we think about things changes. The amount of time we've put into our practice will affect the quality of our responsiveness when we're out in the world.

Ocean: I've recognized that one of my past survival strategies was to focus on the positive as a way to avoid feeling the negative. I see that's still about me and self-referencing, and I see how cultivating gratitude and noticing the positive are different from one another. I'm wondering what that looks like. Does it mean we no longer see the negative? I don't want to be trading one coping mechanism for another that ends up just reinforcing old, self-important habits.

Lama: No, it means we won't be seeing whatever's happening through the lens of denial, judgment, or other past survival strategies that are ultimately about us. Instead, we're simply witnessing suffering, and we respond with love and compassion instead of old behaviors that further obscure the crystal and inhibit our capacity to help others.

Ocean: I think I have a habit of eating the blame or eating the pain, so to speak, in relationships in an effort to maintain harmony. I struggle with wanting to come from a place of benefit for all beings in my relationships and, at the same time, not wanting to stuff a lot to be able to be in relationship. Maybe it's a boundary thing.

Lama: It's about motivation (surprise!). Outwardly, being co-dependent, as opposed to taking relationships onto the path, can look the same. We might still choose to say things or not say things or do things or not do things to try to maintain harmony. But why would we want harmony? Is it an old, neurotic pattern, part of past familial survival strategies, and we automatically go there, or is it really because our motivation is bodhicitta and we think our choices would not only produce harmony in the short run but also produce greater benefit in the long run? For example, do we believe our choices would create more virtue than non-virtue or model a different way of being for other people?

If we want to create harmony because that's how we learned to negotiate our family dynamics—by always being the peacemaker, for example—then it's about us and not about others. Refining our awareness of what's really going on in our mind is critical. Of course, it's easy to think that all we want is virtue for the sake of all beings, but, when we become more familiar with our mind, we see that this is a concept or value we've accepted, but it may not be what's really driving us in any given moment.

What we're trying to do is increase our understanding of the motivation for our choices, because that's what will determine the long-term outcome. Of course, we try to establish pure motivation to be sure we think carefully about whatever we can do to be helpful. At the same time, we have to watch our mind, using the interaction as a mirror to see what's actually going on with us.

Rinpoche used to say that when we engage the world in a material or worldly way, it's like we're looking through a window—we're looking outside of ourselves and seeing everything going on outside of us. We have opinions and judgments and likes and dislikes and, when we act on those, we plant seeds.

However, when we're doing our spiritual practice, it's like we're looking into a mirror. We allow whatever arises in our experience to reflect back to us. We're aware of the mind that's judging, that's attached or averse rather than being lost in the attachment, aversion, or judgment. We're learning to bring to our mind that quality of awareness that observes what's going on in the mind, because each of the meditations we're learning is meant to be applied to a different mental state to produce change.

If we have the illusion that our heart is always full of bodhicitta, we won't be inclined to examine our motivation and remedy anything that isn't bodhicitta. If we're really looking into the mirror of the mind and being honest with ourselves, we see that we often care about our job, our reputation, whether people like us, that we have a good meal at the end of our shift, or whatever our attachments are more than we care about the benefit of others. When we're aware of these, we can transform them. Whether it's emotional states, memories, ideas, a tendency to problem-solve, or whatever method each of us uses to organize our life and our experience, we need to develop the capacity to be aware of what's going on that's not steeped in bodhicitta, so we can apply tools for change. Most of us have a strong habit to look through the window.

Each of these teachings is meant to be used like a mirror, a means for us to look at, take responsibility for, and change our own mind and heart. They're not meant to be turned outward and used to judge other people. These are tools that empower our positive qualities insofar as we apply them. As our positive qualities increase, our capacity to benefit others increases.

What's important is that we're in it. We're not separate and having a concept about a process of change. We're actually engaging the change and, in doing so, we're immersed in a process that's impacting and changing our experience, not just our ideas.

When the mind isn't connected with the meditation or with what's going on in our heart, there's a separation, and the methods don't produce change. The whole point of meditation is to produce change for the better. If our negativity is increasing—we're becoming more attached, averse, proud, competitive, or whatever it is—there's something we need to adjust.

In everything that happens, in every interaction we have—even as we're doing what we can to create benefit—we're watching our mind and trying to be as honest as we can about our real motivation. For example, why are we saying this thing to this person or giving them a gift? Is it because we want something, like praise or recognition, or we're hoping to get something in return?

As we start looking into the mirror of the mind, we see more clearly the layers of our motivation. At first, it can be discouraging. We can think we're becoming a worse person than before we began practicing! But it's actually an indication our practice is working when we're no longer kidding ourselves. We might have thought we were doing everything for the sake of others and putting their needs before our own. But, in fact, we had all kinds of conflicting emotions, and that's why our speech sometimes came out a little unskillfully and our relationships got a little sticky. When we start to meditate, we begin to see all of that and can be more honest.

For our practice to be effective, we need to use the tools that are meant for where we are right now, based on our actual experience instead of our conceptual understanding. Otherwise, we can become less grounded and more proud, identifying with books and teachings we've been exposed to rather than being honest about where we really are.

With each step we take up the stairs, we gain a different perspective. We can't jump up to the rooftop at the beginning, as much as we might appreciate the idea of the perspective we'd have from up there. We have to create a way to get there, which begins with being honest with ourselves and practicing with what's actually going on with us.

9 Mirror of the Mind

Begin by establishing pure motivation. Watch your mind as you think of more and more beings and their long-term as well as short-term benefit. What's actually taking place in your mind? Are you remaining one-pointedly focused on their benefit, or do you get carried away by thoughts or stories about them? If and when you become aware of being lost in distraction, bring your awareness back to pure motivation.

Then, observe your mind while imagining or replaying an emotionally charged interaction. Notice the ways in which you judge the other person's speech or behavior. Do your thoughts and feelings stem from self-centeredness? Do you place your own opinions, needs, and desires first? If so, reestablish pure motivation. Reviewing recent events and anticipating future ones, continue to watch your mind as if looking into a mirror.

As you become more familiar with this meditation through your formal meditation practice, try it during actual conversations, beginning with situations that don't bring up strong emotions. As your ability to watch your own mind develops, you'll learn to create enough space in your mind to check your motivation before speaking. No matter what thoughts are arising, always bring the mind back to bodhicitta.

Carolyn: How do we care for and have compassion for ourselves on this path?

Lama: One way is to remember that we're included in the phrase "all beings" when we establish the intention to help everyone equally. However, it's most important to contemplate the true causes of happiness. Only our intention and actions to benefit others plant the seeds of happiness. The intention and actions to benefit ourselves plants seeds of suffering. The best way to care for ourselves is to care for all beings.

Tej: It's pretty amazing how much the culture has shifted in just the last few years to the point that, in students as young as 15, their victimization is the only currency they bring to the table—not their dreams, not their intellect, not their skills. It's like the marketing of suffering. In your example of the nurse in the ICU, I know kids that would ask, "Did she get the patient's consent to practice on them?" These tools you're describing work, because they've been around for 2500 years, but, given these times, the shift in the culture, and the increased prescribing of behavior-modifying medication for younger and younger kids, do you see a need for any change in the approach? A lot of principals in big city schools tell us to never, never say we love our students. I don't want to give in to that kind of fearful thinking.

Lama: Certainly, there's a big issue with language. In a Buddhist context, we can use words like love and compassion. However, I don't think I'd use those words with those big-city principals. You can talk to them about what's effective and empowering and will produce change. People want to be more effective, empowered, and capable of producing positive outcomes. In anything we do, we have to listen carefully to the people we're trying to help so we know what their goals and wishes are and the language they use to express them. Then we can better help them to understand how these tools can help to accomplish those goals.

Tej: What about when you've made large life choices not out of a desire to benefit all beings but on the basis of what you have an interest in or what's beautiful and inspiring to you? How do you then think about your life going forward? Do you have to change your entire life?

Lama: This is an important question, because most of us haven't made all the choices in our lives out of pure motivation. The first thing we can do is recognize that whatever we're doing now, based on choices we've already made, is because we wanted to be happy and we thought this was an avenue that would bring benefit for ourselves and perhaps for those around us.

So, the first thing we do is remind ourselves that everybody wants to be happy, and everybody is making all their choices based on what they think will bring them benefit and happiness. We open the frame of reference in our mind and our heart to include not just a few people around us but everybody. In this way, instead of experiencing ourselves as separate from the flow of humanity, we experience ourselves as one with the wishes, hopes, and dreams of everybody. This creates a huge shift in our awareness and, the more we do this, the more it informs all of our choices and how we see everything we do. Going forward, we find ourselves thinking more and more in terms of, "I could make this choice for myself, but what about others?" It will start to shift that way.

For example, you're doing a PhD in computer science. That's clearly in demand. You're going to be able to make a good living. So, then you think, "As I study and learn and continue to develop my capacity, how can I bring the most benefit with what I'm doing?" Your intention is that, as you work and learn, you do so through a different framework: How can I use what I'm learning to benefit more beings?

You can start to apply that in your workplace and in everything you do. Make that your motivation as you go into the workplace: "May everything I do here be of benefit, not just for myself, my family, the people I work with, or the company I work for, but truly of benefit to every living being." This will change your approach to what you're doing, and it may, over time, start to inform some of the choices you make at the workplace or in the course of your studies. When those choices are motivated by this idea of the greatest possible benefit for the most beings, that naturally includes how to avoid harming.

There are a lot of big problems in the world these days because of choices being made by those involved with technology. What an amazing opportunity for someone who has a PhD in computer science to come up with solutions that would be beneficial to all beings, that would limit the harm and increase the benefit. The world is waiting for your motivation and your skills and your insights to come up with better solutions for some of these huge problems. I've never encountered a situation or a workplace where there wasn't a great need—and, therefore, a great opportunity—to come up with solutions that are more beneficial to more beings.

CHAPTER 3. ADDING OIL TO THE LAMP

As our negativity decreases and our positivity increases, we'll be of ever-greater benefit to ourselves and others. More and more, we'll come to recognize our wholesome qualities and learn how to stabilize and grow that recognition. To the extent we do that, mind's energy expresses itself through goodness, positivity, and virtuous action —positive causes that produce positive results. The goodness of our heart becomes increasingly obvious—not just to ourselves but, as it expresses itself in the world at large, it becomes increasingly a cause of benefit for others. This results in more goodness in the world, more honor and inspiration.

There's a Sanskrit word (*puna*) that we translate as "merit." Merit refers to the power that virtuous actions have to create this kind of positive momentum. It also refers to the beneficial results of that momentum. Gathering merit benefits us as our practice blossoms, producing more and more positive circumstances. To be of greatest benefit to others, we need the resources such merit makes possible. For example, it's difficult to feed people who are hungry if we don't have food. More deeply, we can't help anyone if we don't have love and compassion in our hearts. Both are made possible through our accumulation of merit.

Turning up the Heat

The fastest and most powerful way to gather merit is to make bodhicitta our motivation for everything we do. With that motivation, everything we do accumulates merit, awakens awareness of mind's natural positive qualities, and purifies old habits, negativity, and ignorance of our true nature—all at the same time.

We need to accumulate enough merit to make it possible for our practice to take root in our mind and change us. When this becomes possible, we start practicing more and accumulating more merit. The practice of bodhicitta helps our practice to grow instead of our becoming more lost in old, negative habits.

The more merit we've accumulated, the more our positive qualities emerge. As long as our negativity overwhelms the positivity, we'll always see everything through that lens, and that makes it difficult to benefit others. The lens may be one of low self-image, feeling we don't have the capacity, fear of change, blaming others or the teachings, running away, closing the door, or whatever it is for each of us that isn't allowing the process to work.

However, if we gather enough merit, we can get things cooking. We have a pot—the container of our practice—into which we put a number of ingredients using a recipe that's been handed down for generations. We have to have the correct ingredients in the right amounts, and the heat has to be just right— determined by our accumulation of merit and the purification of all of our stuff. Using this awesome recipe, if we put in the right ingredients through our practice of bodhicitta and turn up the heat the right amount, what we create will be nourishing and of great benefit to ourselves and others. The more familiar we become with the recipe that allows us to recognize and express mind's positive qualities, the more our activity for the welfare of others can flourish.

The Pot that Overflows

We can see the presence and power of merit all around us, wherever people's actions are motivated by selfless wishes and intentions. For example, wealthy people who have the vast intention to end illness such as malaria throughout the world are riding a huge wave of merit that they've accumulated in the past and are further creating huge amounts of merit as they go. They take action and use their resources to wipe out malaria. They're making merit because they're joining the power of their positive actions with the motivation of not just trying to help a few people but to eradicate malaria everywhere.

When we develop bodhicitta, we expand our motivation from thinking about all human beings who have malaria, for example, to all beings throughout time and space, no matter what their illness or suffering is, and wanting their benefit not just in the short run but in the long run over time. As we take action to help those with malaria, cancer, COVID-19, or any other illness, for example, we do so for the temporary and ultimate health of all beings for all time.

By ultimate health, we mean complete awakening to our true nature. When all the ore is removed from the crystal and light is refracted through it, the rainbow display radiates beauty in all directions. In the same way, when we completely awaken, our positive qualities radiate to all beings, bringing limitless benefit. Temporary health means freedom from any sickness or disease along the way to that awakening. The merit that's created with that shift in motivation toward the ultimate health of all beings transports the actions of the mind beyond our ordinary, limited views of life and reality toward the possibility of awakening to the true nature of mind itself, which is limitless.

The more we understand the importance of gathering merit and how we can increase and direct the merit we create, the further empowered we are in our efforts to benefit others. It's like filling a pot of water until it overflows. We learn how to direct the water to bring the greatest benefit. When we have this vast motivation on the path, the force of our merit will propel us in the direction of the limitlessness of bodhicitta. Otherwise, the results of our gathering of merit will be more limited in scope.

Our compassion, by its nature, is limitless. Our love for beings, by its nature, is limitless. The wisdom mind that realizes and expresses that love and compassion is limitless. The method by which we can arrive at that limitlessness is bodhicitta, because the motivation is limitless. We do what we do not just on behalf of a few beings, not just those who are ill, not just human beings, but all beings—humans, animals, and those in unseen realms. It's not just for this lifetime, this year, or this season, but for all time, through the generations, and, if you believe in reincarnation, throughout limitless lifetimes. There's no limitation. This is the methodology that leads us to the limitlessness of mind itself and the limitless, positive qualities that lead to limitless benefit for all beings for all time.

Otherwise, to use a limited method to try to awaken to limitlessness has its limitations! If we want a limitless result, we need a limitless process. That limitless process is pure motivation, which makes possible a limitless gathering of positive qualities and merit that can produce limitless benefit for limitless beings.

Carolyn: Are you saying that the problem with good heart as our motivation is that it produces less merit?

Lama: There's no problem with good heart, ever! Good heart is so needed in this world. We're just learning how to expand it. Without a good heart of kindness and compassion, there's no possibility of genuine bodhicitta. But, if we develop bodhicitta atop the essential foundation of good heart, we can vastly increase the power of our practice, our merit, and our capacity to benefit others.

However, if we don't understand the difference, we can think we're giving rise to bodhicitta when we're being selfless and acting from good heart—for example, caring about and helping a particular person in trouble. We do what we can to help them, but, in the moment when we act, we're not thinking of all beings. Or, in that moment when we act, we may be thinking of all beings, but we aren't necessarily thinking of all time. As a result, our gathering of merit is more limited and ultimately of less benefit to all beings now and in the future.

For example, if we're a health worker or researcher, we might think that pure motivation means we make the wish that, through our efforts, cancer be eradicated, not just for those we're working with in the moment but for everyone. This is an amazing goal in itself. It's also a very important first step in establishing the motivation for our work. But, at the same time, it's a limited timeframe and a limited number of beings. We aren't thinking of all the other illnesses that may arise in the future or all the different kinds of suffering experienced by all beings throughout time and space.

Pure motivation involves a complete shift in our awareness and orientation to life itself. It means we expand our intention and actions from thinking only of those we're trying to help in the immediate moment—for example, someone with cancer—to thinking of how to create benefit and happiness for all beings for all time. Because beings are limitless and the goal is limitless, the motivation to benefit all beings for all time expands our gathering of merit beyond the realm of limitation.

Anthony: How can we know we're on the right track as far as bodhicitta? I think I know what good heart feels like when I'm cultivating it, but, when I try to bring in "for all beings and for all time," I try to picture what that means—all beings and what they're going through. Sometimes I get a vague sense of people on the other side of the globe and what they might be going through. Is there a way to know if I'm doing that successfully?

Lama: There's a quality of utter selflessness that arises when our motivation is bodhicitta. When there's a limited scope of entities we're trying to help and a limited timeframe, there's usually some attachment to helping, to things going a certain way, or to a certain outcome—we want to produce benefit, and we want a certain kind of suffering to end. Maybe we want to be recognized for how hard we're working. We may feel we want some help, or we want a break. When it's more limited in scope, it's easier for the presence of the self and all the self's agendas to manifest.

When our motivation is to act for all beings for all time, it's possible for the experience of the self to disappear. There isn't an identity. There isn't a person wanting. There isn't an agenda or a sense of us doing things separate from others. There's a sense of great commonality—not just of beings but the great pervasiveness of the positive qualities that are our true nature. We're accessing our immeasurable love and compassion, which is purifying everything that makes our ordinary love and compassion measurable. It's awakening the immeasurable qualities in our mind and heart, which are qualities of our true nature and aren't ego-based or separate from others. Bodhicitta isn't separate from our true nature or the true nature of every living being.

Anthony: For me, it's an amazing thing when I can truly think of someone other than myself. When I get to the point of feeling that open heart, I feel this process is working. I feel I maybe do care about other people. Are you saying we keep going with that method and eventually we get to the place where there's no longer a "me" feeling my heart space expanding?

Lama: When we're practicing well, our negative habits and psychology are purifying and diminishing, and our positive qualities are awakening and increasing. Some might call it grace. I experience it as blessing in the sense of transformation—the blessing of my lamas and that of their lineage lamas back through the centuries—in helping me to understand and to practice. It's an experience of transformation that isn't measurable, isn't conceptual, isn't ordinary, isn't describable, and isn't something we can grasp with the ordinary mind. Something else is going on that helps to awaken our practice and can awaken the practice of others. In their lives, their minds, and their hearts, something immeasurable is happening. That's the power of bodhicitta.

We look at what's happening in our mind and we ask ourselves, Is it measurable or immeasurable? We look at the impact of our actions on others. Is it measurable or immeasurable? Does it have a quality of benefit that's not ordinary? The rational mind can't grasp and understand what's beyond the rational mind—this process of transformation that arises in a way that isn't definable or isn't measurable. That's the power of a great gathering of merit. If we start with a measurable motivation, it's hard to arrive at a measureless result. We need to begin with a measureless method to produce a measureless result.

Inez: You've talked about how bodhicitta is limitless, but normally we think there should be a limit to things, even good things. We think, "If it's limitless, I can't do it. It's beyond me, I can't measure it." However, this idea is very freeing to me. All I have to do is to just keep putting it out there and being pure-hearted in my motivation, because that's what one does. The work of being human is to continually help end the suffering of others. I find it very freeing to think that, just as the suffering is unlimited, the antidote is unlimited, too.

Lama: Wonderful! What you're referring to when you say you just keep going with it is you keep generating bodhicitta. At some point, the merit you generate, the momentum you're building—which is also, ultimately, limitless—will produce a realization that goes beyond the concept of you as a limited being incapable of accomplishing this. How we get there is exactly what you're doing.

Breanna: When I get into an activity or even a practice, I feel I can only do one thing at a time. When I think of my true nature and compassion and put forth effort to connect to limitless beings, I don't always have an awareness of my motivation. I'm just doing it.

Lama: That's true for most of us as we start. Generating bodhicitta is more contrived, and it feels separate from our actual experience. How it changes our experience is through constant repetition. It starts out with the experience that what we're repeating in the mind is separate from the "me" that's repeating it. Through steady repetition, we're blending what's being repeated—in this case, bodhicitta—with our ordinary experience to transform it. Bodhicitta has the ability to transform that experience but only through diligent repetition.

At a certain point, something shifts in our awareness. By blending bodhicitta with the ordinary mind, a transformation happens. What creates the illusion of separation falls away and reveals there never was any separation. Bodhicitta is all there is. Bodhicitta isn't just the nature of our mind or of other's minds, it's the nature of everything, and nothing is separate from it.

As we purify our sense of identity, what's revealed is the essential purity of all that is. We realize that, ultimately, there's no such thing as Breanna separate from bodhicitta, although the current experience of Breanna may be separate. How we get there is through repeatedly giving rise to bodhicitta. That purifies what's standing in the way and, at the same time, helps us realize what is and always has been true.

Breanna: It's about remembering to bring it to mind, whatever it is you're doing in your life. It could be anything— even taking a shower. We bring that thought not just to ourself but consider other beings in the process, correct?

Lama: If we haven't created the habit to bodhicitta, it can fade. The more we remind ourselves that every aspect of our practice supports the development of bodhicitta and also expresses it, the more natural it becomes and the more confident we are in the process. It's the same, whether we're taking a shower, cooking dinner, or working directly for the benefit of others. Our shower, the dinner, our work becomes less and less about us and more and more of an offering to those around us, and, ultimately, to all beings. It happens through repetition—bringing it to mind, again and again, so there's never any aspect of our experience that's separate. That's what meditation is—to repeat again and again and again—and that's what produces transformation. The more steady the repetition, the faster the transformation.

Breanna: What about merit?

Lama: The more we practice bodhicitta, the more we're accumulating vast, inconceivable merit that supports the process of transformation. It's all part of the whole. Our confidence in both the power of merit and virtue and the harmful consequences of non-virtue will deepen. Increasingly, virtue and the gathering of merit will become the framework we use to inform our choices. Is there more virtue in this or that choice? Are we being more beneficial if we do this or that? That framework will become more and more blended with our lives.

10 Creating Merit

Contemplate the benefit of making your motivation limitless.

What's the benefit of thinking of all beings—not just human beings and not just beings we can see, but, if there are any other beings, for them too?

What's the benefit of thinking "for all time?"

Notice the difference in the impact in your mind and heart when you establish pure motivation with the understanding of the limitlessness of the scope.

What's the difference in the quality of the action, of your relationship to the action, and of your relationship to the results of the action when the scope is so vast?

A Butterlamp in a Dark Room

In speaking of merit, Rinpoche used the metaphor of a butterlamp in a dark room. The butter or oil in the lamp is like our merit. The more merit we've gathered, the more oil in the lamp, and the brighter and longer the wick will burn. No matter how many of us are in that room, we all benefit from that light. Anyone who adds oil to the lamp will ensure that there's more light, and everyone in the room will benefit. The process of adding oil to the lamp with the motivation to bring more light for the benefit of everyone in the room is called "dedication of merit." We're dedicating, or directing, the merit we're gathering to all beings for all time.

Although we can't always see it in each moment, every time we dedicate merit, we're contributing to the amount of light in the world. This helps us develop confidence so we don't become discouraged in the face of obstacles—when everything going on in the world seems so huge, and we feel there's no way that our tiny efforts, our tiny voice, or our tiny organization can make a difference. As long as our motivation is pure at the beginning of all our actions, and we dedicate the merit we've created at the end, we've added more oil to the lamp of awakening for all beings. That lamp will burn brighter and longer in proportion to how much each of us continues to add oil to it.

The power of dedication is profound, because it ensures that, in those moments when our mind is disturbed and we get angry, for example, that we won't tip over that lamp and cause all the oil to spill out. We don't want to do anything to destroy the merit we've created. Instead, we want to constantly dedicate it—at the end of every practice, activity, and day—to the short-

and long-term benefit of all beings. In this way, we can be certain that everything we do adds oil to the lamp and, no matter what happens outwardly, we're contributing to the illumination of the dark room.

This makes our lives meaningful, no matter what the temporary individual or collective circumstances of beings looks like. Maybe we're riding a wave of merit that joins with a wave of collective merit of beings and has a big impact. Maybe we're riding a wave of our own negative outcomes that intersects with a wave of the collective negative outcomes of the human population, and it looks like we can't help at all. But this is just a temporary condition, and we mustn't forget what's underlying it: wherever there's virtue, there will be benefit and happiness, and where there's non-virtue, there will be suffering. If all we ever do is make sure we add oil to the lamp, we can be confident in the underlying power of the merit we've created. Over time, as the oil is replenished and the lamp burns brighter and longer, there will be certain benefit for all beings.

Through dedication, we can protect and nurture the virtue we've created—not for our own sake but for the sake of others. That virtue is no longer living in the realm of ordinary mind and, therefore, is no longer subject to the actions of the ordinary mind. The drop of water has joined the ocean of bodhicitta and been given to limitless beings. This means that any later moments of anger or regret can't destroy it.

For example, in a moment of sincere generosity and love, we may give money to someone in need, but later, have regret when we realize our bank account is empty. That regret will spoil the virtue if we didn't dedicate the merit at the time of our offering. Our virtue can even be compromised through boastfulness. Any time we create virtue joined with self-important thought, we're overlaying self-centeredness on that virtue. Boasting is a powerful way to solidify self-importance. Any amount of virtue that's bound by limitations is, by its nature, limited. Like moisture on hot desert sand, it will swiftly evaporate.

Ida: You said we can create and dedicate merit even if we can't do anything outwardly to help someone. Maybe this is too blunt a question, but I still don't understand. How does that help?

Lama: To go back to an earlier metaphor, it's like each of us is sitting on mountains and mountains of seeds that we've planted. Some of them are purely medicinal, some of them are completely toxic, and most are a mixture. When the conditions are right, they'll all sprout. When somebody is suffering, the only difference between us and them is time. For them, right now, toxic seeds are ripening. For us, right now, maybe medicinal seeds are ripening. Before long, our toxic seeds will ripen, and their medicinal seeds will ripen. Until we understand the principles that allow us to choose to plant medicinal seeds, there will be a mixture.

We suffer when the toxic seeds we've planted ripen, but the conditions have to support that happening. No seed will ripen without the necessary warmth, moisture, and soil. Our dedications of merit change the conditions so that medicinal seeds can sprout, and toxic seeds will remain dormant. Ultimately, it's up to each of us to uproot the toxic seeds we've planted, but others' prayers and dedications can buy us the time to do that by changing the balance between our mind's positivity and negativity—creating the conditions for those seeds to sprout.

The process is intangible. We can't see it, and that's part of why the dedication of merit counteracts doubt. We can have doubt about the invisible spiritual principles underlying our lives until we practice and see their effects in our own experience.

Tej: To me, merit seems like believing in God. Merit doesn't seem scientific, and it's not something I can intellectually grasp. I can only have faith in it.

Lama: That's true, but it isn't a blind faith. You just need to have enough faith to check it out. Of the three kinds of faith, the first, the faith of awe, involves an initial connection with the path or the teachings on bodhicitta. Something happens in our mind when we hear about it, and we want to know more. It's enough faith to motivate us to learn more and contemplate it.

The next kind of faith, yearning faith, arises when we start exploring and practicing. As we see change, that increases our trust in the process. As our trust in the process increases, we do more practice. As we do more practice, we see more change, and our faith grows. Most of our practice life is based on that kind of faith. It deepens through practice.

Eventually, there's a point where the experience of our own and others' positive qualities become stable and unshakable. Rinpoche used to say that, even if a thousand buddhas appeared and told us our confidence in wisdom and compassion was wrong, we'd know we were right. That's how unwavering it can become. We don't have unshakable faith at the beginning, but practicing is how we get there. Through practice, it becomes true for us, because we've experienced it.

In the case of dedication of merit, it's one of those spiritual principles that isn't visible, but we don't have to accept it on blind faith. We check it out. We can dedicate merit to people we know who are suffering. We create merit and dedicate, create and dedicate, and we see what happens. Nothing will change overnight, but we watch what happens over the course of weeks and months, even years, to see if we notice a change for the better. It might take a lot longer than we want it to, but something may shift internally in their mind and heart or outwardly in their circumstances. Someone may hear about an apartment for rent that's affordable, an abusive ex-husband may get a transfer across the country, a child may have an experience that causes them to want to be more focused on their studies. If we weren't paying attention, we might just think these things were lucky happenstance.

Through this process, we start to realize there are principles at work that govern our lives and our experiences. If we understand them, we become empowered to create the kind of changes we want. If we don't understand them and work with them, we remain clueless about the whole process. We're trying to help others, but what we could be doing to produce benefit is so much deeper, richer, and vaster.

The same thing is true of seed planting. The seeds we plant don't sprout right away, but, if we look back over time, we see the general direction. We plant a seed in the ground and, usually, we forget about it. We don't remember we planted it and then, all of a sudden, there's the right temperature and moisture and there's this beautiful blossom! We didn't even notice or remember we planted the seed, because there's a gap between the time of the planting and the time of the ripening. That's what makes it invisible.

Some of the seeds we plant ripen in the course of this lifetime. Over years and decades, we can see this, so it's not quite as invisible as the effects of the dedication of merit. However, the effects of dedicating merit *are* visible when we start watching. If we're dedicating to all beings rather than somebody in particular, it's harder to see, because the effects of the collective seed planting are so huge and complex. But if there's someone we're concerned about, and we keep creating and dedicating merit to them and to all who are suffering with the wish that their suffering be completely uprooted—and we keep doing this again and again—we *will* see change in that person's experience. We may see this within a few weeks, but it more likely will take months or even years, depending on how disciplined we are and the amount of merit we create.

Doug: It seems to me that many of the people who have the most power are doing evil things. Have they accumulated a lot of merit to be in a position of having power over other people?

Lama: Can you imagine having accumulated enough merit to have billions of dollars and a whole bunch of power—for example, being the director of a huge corporation that affects the lives of millions of people around the world—and not using it for benefit? To have accumulated that much merit and, in the course of one lifetime, to destroy it all through creating harm? Talk about tragedies! Talk about objects of compassion! Think of that—someone has enough merit to have all that but not enough connection with a path of virtue to turn their heart toward others' benefit.

Rinpoche used to say it's like a hot-air balloon. It rises into the air and then, at a certain point, the air inside cools, and it starts to sink. However, if we're up there and keep generating heat, we remain aloft. If our actions of body, speech, and mind are based in self-referencing, and we're harmful toward others, we use up all that merit quickly, and then we fall. If that merit is joined with the yearning for virtue, the yearning to benefit beings, the yearning to use this opportunity to benefit as many as possible, we keep creating merit. We create a cycle of increasing merit instead of a cycle of destroying it.

Carolyn: I think I know what you mean by accumulating merit, because I have a great feeling when I'm doing it.

Lama: We aren't doing the practice to have a particular experience, sensation, or feeling. We're doing it to increase our capacity to be of benefit. It may or may not evoke a shift in our physical or subtle body experience, but, if we aren't experiencing that, it doesn't mean we aren't effectively accumulating and dedicating merit.

As our merit increases, our positive qualities such as love, compassion, and generosity arise more often and more spontaneously. Our negativity toward others in the form of anger or judgment decreases naturally as does our negativity toward ourselves—such as low self-image, depression, or despair. The presence of merit in the mind empowers our selfless confidence and commitment to the welfare of others. It's also reflected outwardly, so our opportunities and capacity to bring benefit increase. For example, we may find a job that pays us to help others, or our organization receives a grant that enables us to serve more people.

Remember that every time we dedicate, it's like adding water to the pot and directing where it goes when it overflows. We're joining the power of the positivity we've created to our intention. If we're not conscious of giving it for the benefit of others, that merit can even join with whatever passing thing is going through our mind, like, "I want a new red truck." We might even be able to get a new red truck! But, if our merit's been side-tracked to fulfill our short-term personal wishes only, when it's used up or destroyed by future actions, we could end up being distracted by the red truck and losing our bodhicitta, forgetting or abandoning the causes of reliable long-term benefit for ourselves and others.

Ida: I'm grappling with a lot of doubt about all of this. I feel I can't do it right or that there's one pure way the practice should be done that I don't believe in at the moment. What do I do with that?

Lama: We were talking earlier about the spiritual principles underlying our lives—how, if we want positive outcomes, we must create positive causes, and what those positive causes look like. These causes start in our mind, and they begin with pure motivation. When we feel we can't access our own positive qualities or believe in the positive qualities of others—such as the qualities of faith and trust in the spiritual path—sometimes what's going on is there's an imbalance in our own mind of positivity to negativity. The seeds that are sprouting in the garden of our mind and heart happen to be more negative than positive. The remedy is to create as much merit as we can. We don't do this for ourselves but because, even though right now we're not necessarily experiencing it in a genuine way, we know that, deeply, we do care about the needs of others and, deeply, we do want to be a force of benefit in the world. Even if it's just an idea, we connect with that motivation and, based on that motivation, we try to do whatever we can to accumulate virtue and positivity.

One of the swiftest ways to do that is to rejoice in all of the virtue that's being created all over the world. You can think about all the people working in ICUs and hospitals in every country around the world and all the people working in refugee camps and displaced-persons communities who uprooted their own lives to try to save the lives of others. We think of all of those people who've gone into war zones and put their own lives on the line to help others who are suffering from war as well as the uprooting and destruction of their communities and their homes.

Think also of all the people around the world in situations that aren't so dramatic—like schoolteachers who, in spite of great difficulties, are showing up every day, loving their kids, and doing everything they can to help them learn with a truly selfless motivation and intention. Think of the firefighters walking into the middle of huge fires. They put everything on the line to save the lives and homes of other people and animals. We think of the selflessness of their efforts. And we can walk through our own examples—whatever it is that moves us. In the same way, we can delight in all these activities of good heart and virtue. When we do this, we accumulate the same merit as those taking those actions.

Also, remember that, no matter how much merit we've accumulated, if we haven't given it away, dedicated it to the benefit of others, it's living in the domain of our own ordinary mind. This means it can be diminished or destroyed by our own future actions. For example, every time we feel resentful about something selfless we've done that wasn't recognized by others, it erodes some of that virtue.

As well, every moment of anger destroys our virtue. The great, eighth-century Indian Buddhist master, Shantideva, used the analogy that if the amount of virtue we've accumulated is like a mountain of dry grass, all it takes is one spark, one moment of anger, for that whole mountain to go up in flames. Of course, all of us get angry and give in to and express our anger until we've developed alternatives. This is just a human reaction. If we've had periods of anger since the last time we generated pure motivation, for example, we might have burned up some of the merit we created if we didn't dedicate it.

Every single moment that we act from self-centeredness—wanting what *we* want, not wanting what we don't want, not bringing awareness, pure motivation, or love and compassion to our actions—we plant toxic seeds. We may believe we have positive qualities in our minds, we may have good intention, we may be really trying and genuinely care about those we're interacting with, but, at the same time, for example, we're attached or averse or we want praise and don't want blame. When that's happening, we plant mixed seeds.

Using Shantideva's metaphor of the mountain of dry grass, we're all sitting on mountains of seeds we've planted—some positive, some negative, and most in between. When they ripen depends on various conditions—the weather, the temperature of the soil, the moisture, the fertilizer, whether the seeds fell on fertile ground or on rocky soil. When the conditions arise that allow them to ripen, they'll bear fruit.

So, there's no moral judgment that we're bad people if difficult circumstances are arising. Instead, we need to understand that each of us, equally, has planted mountains of seeds. The point of the path is for us to recognize this without blame, shame, embarrassment, or self-hatred. As those seeds bear fruit, we want to always bring good heart, love, and compassion to those situations, so our future experience only improves.

As Rinpoche said, just one moment of pure compassion can purify eons of toxicity. One big chunk of that mountain can get purified by one moment of sincere compassion, because compassion that's genuine is purely selfless. For example, when our heart is breaking for somebody, there's no self-referencing, no idea of what we do or don't want. Our wish is entirely for that being's suffering to end. That quality of compassion is so pure that it has the capacity to torch many of the toxic seeds we've planted. It's super-virtuous and creates inconceivable amounts of virtue.

Generating compassion is tremendously beneficial, because we're both accumulating merit and purifying past negative actions, doubt, and whatever else is obstructing our bodhicitta. This will help to shift the balance of what's ripening in our mind at the moment and in the future.

Of course, we want to do this with pure motivation—not just for our own benefit and happiness but for the sake of all beings. In doing so, we change the balance of positivity to negativity in our own mind, so it becomes easier to remember, develop, and act on our positive qualities.

This isn't easy in today's world. In the news and social media, there's a lot of negativity. There isn't much that's uplifting. This is one of the results of our collective seed planting. But, when we see degrading or snarky comments on social media, for example, instead of contributing to that negativity, we can generate compassion for that person who didn't know another way to deal with whatever's going on with them and respond with kindness. In this way, we can use whatever's arising as a basis for our spiritual practice.

Try all of these things. I'm not saying you'll all of a sudden have total faith in pure motivation and virtue, but if you feel a shift in your mind—a receptivity, or a little less distrust—that's already huge.

11 The Effects of Gathering or Depleting Merit

Think back through your life to periods when you were consumed by self-concern, whether it was in the form of ambition, great bliss or suffering, or anything in between. What were the short-term consequences in your outer circumstances such as jobs or relationships? What were the consequences in your mind—the presence of altruism, selfishness, or anything in between?

What were the longer-term outcomes in your outer and inner circumstances?

Think back to periods when you were guided by selfless concern for others, whether in your personal, work, or community relationships. What were the short-term outcomes, including confidence in your positive qualities or opportunities to benefit others?

What were the longer-term consequences in your outer circumstances as well as in the presence of positivity or negativity in your mind?

Tonya: Are there beings that are simply hopeless, even though we're sending out positive energy? I know people I consider to be beyond help. They're drowning in negativity, and they're a disaster for themselves and others.

Lama: This is due to the imbalance of positivity to negativity in their mind. Don't give up on them. Instead, pick one of those people you think is beyond help and accumulate and dedicate to them and all beings as much merit as you can for a year, two, or even more. Do this with the aspiration that no one ever be beyond help, that the power of love and compassion ignite their mind and heart so they awaken to their true nature. Then watch what happens.

We need to do this practice for our own sake as much as theirs. It diminishes us to give up on anyone. If, instead, we keep going, and keep trying, that helps us to remember the presence of our own positive qualities. We may need to accept that there's nothing we can do outwardly to help. But inwardly, we never want to abandon a single being.

Inez: How do we help someone who, because of trauma, has difficulty feeling self-worth, who has self-esteem issues and difficulty accepting, believing, and trusting the expressions of love shown to them?

Lama: Basically, there's not enough merit in their mind to hold the positive. There needs to be a container of positivity to hold the positivity. As we were just talking about, we do as much as we can to generate and dedicate merit for them. This will help them, over time.

Hillary: I've had a habit of not being so intentional about dedicating the merit. I thought it was included if we're doing something for the sake of others or we're working on refreshing our motivation. I don't usually stop what I'm doing to dedicate unless someone reminds me.

Lama: You don't have to go through a long dedication. You can just make the dedication that whatever virtue you've created benefit all beings for all time. It can be that simple. If you're busy or with people, you may not even have time to find the words, so be aware of that heart-space of giving it away. Just don't mindlessly dedicate without a sense of the longer-term purpose. Make sure to join the merit that you accumulate and dedicate with a very conscious and intentional dedication to their enlightenment. That way, you're producing an interdependence for that merit to contribute to that being's full awakening in some lifetime.

The idea is, we create pure motivation at the beginning, we continue to steep the entire action in that motivation, and, at the end, we dedicate it. From beginning to end, it's complete generosity and selflessness, and that's what makes it limitless and indestructible.

Tonya: I still don't understand how we work to end the suffering of all beings and to bring them happiness without attachment and aversion. Aren't we just continuing that habit?

Lama: When bodhicitta is the motivation, we have a commitment to the full awakening of all beings. That's our purpose. That's the ultimate goal of everything we do. With that view and motivation, we keep practicing and doing all we can to help. At the same time, we aren't attached to certain results short of that ultimate goal. So, if things are moving slower than we want, or not working out at all, we aren't completely devastated. Bodhicitta gives us the strength, the courage, the power to act in whatever way is of greatest benefit that we're capable of at any given moment, without attachment.

We let go of the ordinary, short-term, goal orientation as our purpose for the activity. Instead, we let bodhicitta inform everything we do. Never losing our bodhicitta—because this is what makes that long-term benefit possible—becomes our continuous focus and goal, always. We have the confidence that the merit we've accumulated and dedicated will produce benefit in the long run. No matter how things are going in the short run, we're on track for long-term benefit.

Tej: Do you think that dedicating merit to my neighbor who's always yelling at his kids could help change that situation?

Lama: The great master, Shantideva, said, "Wherever there's happiness, there has been the practice of virtue. Wherever there's suffering, there has been non-virtue." When we see such suffering, we need to know we can accumulate and dedicate merit to help change the balance of positivity to negativity. That's not nothing. Everyone in that situation is drowning for lack of merit. Whatever we can do to accumulate and dedicate merit will benefit them over time.

But we won't always see the change. Sometimes the pile of poisonous seeds that are ripening is much larger than what we're able to see transform in the relatively short span of time during which we're close to them.

It's important to know that there's always something we can do and why it works, especially when we feel out of options to help someone or a group of people. It's important to know it can make a difference. This is an essential part of our practice. Otherwise, why would we be inspired to accumulate as much merit as we can? We won't know unless we try it. We have to do our own kind of science experiment.

For example, say you're trying to help a group of addicts in recovery. You continue to do everything you can to help outwardly and, at the same time, you accumulate and dedicate merit to them. It's not as if everyone is suddenly addiction-free, but there may be just a little more clarity, a little more space within which change can happen, and the whole situation gets a little lighter. There's more room for love, more room for compassion, more room for the participants to reach out and help each other. You'll be able to witness the little wonderments that no one else would recognize. But you know they're miracles for the people who are suffering so greatly. There will be more and more of those moments.

At the very least, we need to suspend our disbelief, suspend our certainty that things that can't be seen and aren't provable to the five senses aren't true. If we suspend our disbelief, that's its own miracle. Then there's room for the power of transformation, the power of blessing to occur. However, if we're so sure we're right and that principles that can't be proven are wrong, there's not much room for wonder.

Hillary: If we recognize our own good fortune and make a wish that all beings have that same good fortune, is that another way of generating merit?

Lama: Yes, definitely. Any time we think of others, any time we wish for their welfare, generates merit. The practice of love and compassion always creates virtue. If we do that practice with bodhicitta as our motivation—which is vast and limitless—by thinking of others, wishing for their welfare, and dedicating the merit to the uprooting of suffering for all living beings, this creates a limitless, inexhaustible form of virtue.

Exhaustible virtue is created in all those moments of good heart we have every day, when we aren't acting for the sake of all beings and dedicating the merit. It's like an annual plant—there's a virtuous seed that's planted in the ground that will produce a beautiful blossom. If the right conditions—water, moisture, sunshine, fertilizer—are present, the seedlings will come up and they'll be beautiful, but, at the end of the season, the plants will die, the roots will die, and that'll be that.

We plant a medicinal seed when we help someone who's hungry or homeless. This is, without question, virtue. If, on top of that, we add the motivation that, by serving this person, the needs of all beings will be fulfilled, temporarily and ultimately, and dedicate in that way, it's transformed from an ordinary, exhaustible virtue to an extraordinary, inexhaustible accumulation of merit.

If we take that same action—helping that same friend with the medicine or the food they need—but with the motivation to do so for the welfare of every living being in the short term and long term, our mind becomes as vast as space. We've used concepts to stretch the ordinary mind beyond its conceptual framework to include countless beings for endless time. By serving the needs of this one person, we aspire that the needs of countless beings for infinite time be fulfilled. That transforms the same action from what we call ordinary virtue into extraordinary virtue. We make the same effort, and add the same moisture, water, fertilizer and so forth, but it's like planting the seed of a perennial. With the right conditions, it will grow beautiful blossoms, beautiful medicine, season after season, and produce more and more fruit that will in turn produce more seeds, more plants, and more blossoms.

At the end of the season, the flowers will die, but the roots will remain intact and the plant will sprout again in the next season to create more flowers and more seeds. The principle of multiplication is always there, whether the virtue is ordinary or extraordinary. But, if we want ultimate welfare for ourselves and all beings, we have to create the causes—and one cause is a mind that can embrace all beings for all time.

This usually starts out abstractly. We can't even conceive what countless beings or infinite time means. But, if we keep doing this, again and again, we're creating momentum that's beyond concept. We're planting seeds of virtue that can't and won't be destroyed, and that has its own momentum that continues day and night as long as we don't uproot or interrupt it. That carries us. It carries our minds and hearts into the future.

Hillary: I assume the other side of that coin is when we experience suffering ourselves, we can hold others who may be experiencing the same kind of suffering in our thoughts and, as we're wishing for our own freedom from suffering, we wish that they, too, be free of misery?

Lama: Yes. We make the aspiration that, through our suffering, no one may ever have to suffer again, that, through our pain, no other being will ever again have pain. We always include everybody else in the scope of our experience. If we're having enjoyment, we wish that all beings may have enjoyment. If we're suffering, we wish that it purify the suffering of all beings.

In this way, we're never separate from the sense of all of us in this vast ocean of suffering, and everything we're doing is for the sake of all of us, together. Any time we do that, even if it's not bodhicitta, even if it's not vast and limitless, we're thinking of others. We're wishing their suffering would end. We're wanting them to be as happy as or happier than we are. That's pure love, pure compassion, and that will create pure virtue.

If, on the other hand, we're involved in activity for the benefit of others, but we're attached to certain outcomes, and we get proud about it or competitive about which organization gets the grant to do their compassionate activity, for example, that compromises the merit we generate. If we're working 24/7 doing everything we can and are completely exhausted, but all we get in return is resistance, we may feel aversion, which also compromises the merit we're generating. Our mixed motivation produces a mixed result. It's a little bit of medicine, a little bit of poison, and whatever grows from that will be a mixture of medicine and poison.

This is why we emphasize taking the time to, first of all, purify our motivation before we act, so it isn't mixed with poison. We then expand our motivation from one of short-term benefit for a few beings to one of ultimate benefit for all beings. We create a limitless accumulation of merit when we do that.

If, on top of that, we dedicate merit with the wish to unite our intention with that of all awakened beings' dedication of merit, even though we may not have great wisdom and compassion present in our mind, our dedication is transformed from one that's more ordinary to one that's extraordinary by joining our mind and wishes with their vast merit and wisdom.

If we really understand this principle, it makes sense why we might take extra time in the morning to walk through the steps to give rise to pure motivation before we go running out into the world to create benefit. If we haven't done the mind training, if our motivation is mixed, then, even though we're out there doing everything we can to help, that merit won't be nearly as huge as if we take the time to give rise to bodhicitta first. Even if the time we take to give rise to bodhicitta means a little less time to do the activity in the world, the accumulation of merit will be vastly greater. And then, if we dedicate at the end of the day just as all awakened beings and bodhisattvas have done, the accumulation of merit and wisdom will be infinitely more beneficial.

We can learn about all these different ways to accumulate merit, but are we doing it only for our own personal happiness, with the understanding that we can't move along the path without it? Or are we doing it because we're attached to helping a certain person or certain organization? We know they need merit, so we're out there scrambling to accumulate it. If bodhicitta isn't our motivation, we aren't going to be nearly as effective as if we took the time to establish bodhicitta and then engage in whatever activity we do. When we bring bodhicitta to beneficial activity, that's the best of everything. To the extent that this is difficult, to the extent that we're exhausted by it, to that extent we purify negativity and obscurations. If we keep bodhicitta as our motivation, we're purifying attachment and aversion and creating limitless virtue. It's a huge, vast benefit.

Inez: Sometimes, I set a stopwatch that reminds me to reset my motivation every 20 minutes. Are there other things we can do to help us when we're going into activity, so we don't get so lost?

Lama: Everything you learn on this path will contribute to that. In some ways, the most important practice is to accumulate and dedicate merit. Bodhicitta is the natural expression of the merit present in our mind. Of course, it's a cart-and-horse situation, because you need to give rise to bodhicitta to make the most merit.

Remember all the skillful ways you're learning to accumulate and dedicate merit. Just keep doing it. Every moment in which the mind slides back into self-centeredness—especially when there's irritation and strong aversion to circumstances or people or events—we exhaust the merit we've accumulated. Accumulate and dedicate frequently throughout the day, so you can't burn it up the next time you're disturbed or impatient. Otherwise, our habit is to become involved with our attachment and aversion and constantly diminish instead of increase our merit.

12 Dedication of Merit

Contemplate everything we've addressed here, paragraph by paragraph, and see if it makes sense in your experience.

Check out the power of dedicating merit in your own life. Choose a person you have enough contact with that you can observe them over months or maybe even years. Start each day by giving rise to bodhicitta and, as you go through the day, create and dedicate as much virtue as you can and avoid non-virtue. At the end of the day, dedicate the merit you've created through all your efforts to that person's and all beings' temporary and ultimate happiness.

Do that every day, and observe what happens to that person and to your own mind over time. Do you have glimpses of principles at work that are invisible to the ordinary mind and senses?

CHAPTER 4. HOW THE SPIRITUAL PATH CHANGES US

Of course, we want to be happy, and we want others to be happy. If we start to develop a relationship to and appreciation of the deeper causes of happiness, we'll most likely practice them—not because somebody told us to, but because we have first-hand evidence that virtue creates happiness and benefit. The more we experience this, the more eager we become to create virtue—as much virtue as we can—for the sake of all beings. The merit produced by that virtue makes our practice joyous and more diligent, because we've laid that foundation. If we don't lay that foundation, the path becomes a bunch of *should*s that we rebel against.

If we don't trust in the power of virtue based on our own experience, this path will seem to be simply a curious belief system that came from halfway around the world and has no relevance for us. We'll be trying to overlay a foreign belief system onto our ordinary mind and our cultural habits. It's only through practice that we learn for ourselves, from the inside out, what works and what doesn't.

We Can't Just Leave It on the Shelf

This is why, first, we need to examine carefully the principles we're learning to see if we believe they're true in our own experience. We then have to understand how to integrate them and, finally, we have to practice them and learn how to deal with all the stuff that comes up when we do. If we don't take the time to internalize our understanding when we first begin to learn from spiritual teachings, we might feel charged up at the beginning and believe we're going to completely change our approach to life. But, when the rubber meets the road, that change doesn't stick. The principles stick to the degree that we practice them.

We have to make the path our path. It becomes our path when we're exposed to teachings, contemplate, meditate, and join our new understanding with our mind so our awareness grows to encompass that understanding. Then, it's truly ours.

If we only listen to or read teachings, it's like going shopping at a market with an amazing variety of foods. We might buy our favorite foods, get all the best ingredients, and put it in our pantry. But if we never take it off the shelf—never cook or eat it—we could have the best foods in the world and still starve to death. We can read hundreds of books and attend hundreds of workshops and lectures, but, if we don't nourish ourselves through contemplation, meditation and applying what we've learned, we aren't partaking of the nourishment that gives us the life-force energy we need to carry those spiritual principles into our lives. We may have a million great ideas stored in our mind, but, spiritually, we'll starve. If we're spiritually malnourished, we won't be able to keep up our efforts to bring benefit and we'll burn out.

We have to have enough exposure through reading or listening to the teachings to understand the goal and methods of the path. Then we have to contemplate them enough to know how to meditate. The process of contemplation is like looking at the list of ingredients on a box of food, studying and researching them, and learning how they nourish us. We research, prepare and cook, because we're convinced the meal we've created will be healthy.

Eating and digesting is meditation. If we don't meditate, our spiritual values and beliefs don't become part of us, and we can find ourselves in the middle of all this plenty and still be starving. We can read and listen non-stop to spiritual teachings, but if we never blend them with our mind, our negative habits won't decrease and our positive qualities won't become more available. We need to examine our experience when we practice to see if it's good for us. Do we get indigestion when we try to integrate what we're learning? Does it give us energy to be more helpful to others? We have to go through that process and, when we do, we find what's nourishing. That makes us eager to partake of it. Then, when we ingest the food, it's no longer separate from us. It becomes us, sustains us, fuels us, and gives us the strength we need to keep going. We have to contemplate *and* meditate.

The Three Kinds of Wisdom

To fully integrate the teachings, we must cultivate three kinds of wisdom: listening or reading, contemplation, and meditation.

Listening or Reading

The first kind of wisdom arises from listening or reading, during which the rational, cognitive mind is exposed to ideas. We need to listen or read carefully to understand what's being presented. In the case of these teachings, we need to deeply understand the goal, the methods, how they work, and how they're applied, so we'll be able to use the tools well.

Giving rise to this wisdom is largely a conceptual process, though we can have spontaneous, non-conceptual moments of insight if we have a strong, heart-opening experience at the same time. Depending on our openness to these ideas, we may be changed by them, but it's not a change that lasts. We can be inspired by a book or lecture, because it speaks to everything we want to be or believe in, but, as soon as we meet situations that bring about a strong emotional response, the change we felt vanishes, because it hasn't been blended with our mind.

Contemplation

The second wisdom comes through contemplation, which means working with the material and examining it in light of our own experience. We need to think about it, but not just abstractly like in school—where we may have learned ideas and facts and were able to repeat them—but really examine it. Does it ring true for us? Can we think of any experience that we or others have had that contradicts it? Do we have doubts about the basic beliefs behind the principles? Do we have hesitations about how to apply it? When we identify our misgivings, questions, or resistance, that's when we need to ask questions. This is important, because, otherwise, there will be a part of us that likes the ideas but also a part of us that always has doubt.

This isn't a path of blind faith. There are traditions where establishing faith is the basis for one's spiritual practice. On this path, faith is developed through a process of examination, exploration, and application. We could say it's a 50-50 process. We rely on the blessings and the teachings that have been practiced successfully for generations, but we also have to do the work. We have to receive the teachings, understand them, contemplate them, and apply them through our practice.

If the process of contemplation brings us to a confidence about the need for the practice, we'll be inspired to try it through meditation. If we don't have that confidence, our meditation isn't going to be very effective, because we won't go into it with a full heart. If there's always a part of us holding back because we're not sure it works or if we really believe in it, we won't apply it as it's meant to be applied, and we won't experience the results.

Meditation

Rinpoche sometimes used the metaphor of a two-pointed needle when speaking about how we approach meditation. If we try to sew with a two-pointed needle, we aren't going to get very far. We have to join our mind with the material being presented using a process of inquiry and self-reflection. We resolve our doubts, resistance, and confusion through contemplation, and we become one with the meaning of the teachings through meditation. Then we can stitch what we're learning into the fabric of our being in the certain direction of benefit for beings.

Meditation carries us in our lives and gives us genuine enthusiasm for our spiritual practice. We have the tools that support the development of wisdom and compassion. If the mind is like a roller coaster of thoughts and emotions and we never meditate, we're not going to gain deeper insight. We might have ideas about deeper insight, but those ideas can become part of the barrier to our genuine experience, because they're concepts *about* insight, not insight itself.

Rather than reading and listening to more and more ideas about wisdom and compassion, we need to work with the practices that will awaken wisdom and compassion in our mind. Then, through our own experience, we start to develop insight. We need to build the foundation, step by step, to create change in our mind and heart so we become more deeply receptive to what we're reading or hearing.

It's important that we understand why and how to do each meditation so we're comfortable with the meditation itself and feel confident it's a tool we can put into our toolbox to carry with us and use throughout our lives. We have to go through this threefold process to take our conceptual understanding from the surface of our minds and hearts and make it one with us.

There are both effortful and effortless meditations, and alternating between the two is an extremely powerful method for change. Otherwise, trying to simply rest the mind can be a contradiction in itself. We all have a strong habit to use effort to create change. So, when we first start to meditate, as soon as we let the mind rest, we can get involved with thoughts like, "Is this it? Am I resting in the right place? Is this what rest looks like? Should I be doing something else?" We have the habit to try to get to a place that's different from where we are. Or, if we have the idea that it's not someplace else but "here," we wonder what "here" looks like. There's a tendency to orient to a certain mental state or object or things to be done, all of which require effort.

Instead, when the mind starts stirring from a state of rest, rather than attempting to make it stop, we use that energy of mind and direct it to the next stage of the meditation. We might think about others who are suffering in similar ways or others who are suffering in other ways. We then let go of the effort, and let the mind rest. We alternate in that way—effortful meditation and then rest—for example, thinking of one person we want to help, then resting the mind, then thinking of others we'd like to help, then resting, and so forth.

We're all very familiar with mind in motion, and yet, through alternating that movement with rest, we make space to become more familiar, in a nonconceptual way, with the essential nature of all that motion. We're introducing the mind to a different habit. Instead of holding on, we're learning to let go. That way, we can have glimpses of the possibility of genuine rest. As we continue to alternate, we refine away mind's extremes so that, within the motion, we can begin to experience rest, and within the rest, we experience the ceaseless play of movement. The ordinary mind, like a perpetual-motion machine of endless, self-referencing thoughts and feelings, can begin to calm down. In moments of stillness, we recognize the presence of awareness and, within that undistracted awareness, we begin to know choice: what to abandon and what to engage.

Rinpoche used to say that, at first, we're usually only able to genuinely rest the mind less than 1% of the time. But that 1% is truly at rest, open and aware. So, it's most useful to spend the remainder of our meditation time using effort to transform what's preventing our ability to rest. We purify whatever's blocking our awareness of and ability to access our positive qualities. We then rest in that recognition—as long as our mind is genuinely restful. We then go back to the effort and, slowly, over time, the ratio of effort to rest will change. At some point, we'll be doing effortful meditation 98% of the time, and 2% of the time we'll be resting, then 97% of the time using effort, and so forth.

Through that process of alternating, we're practicing both. We're creating transformation in the effortful process, so we're not using effort in a way that's counterproductive by *trying* to rest, which is impossible. We don't use the motion of the mind, which is accustomed to effort, in a direction that's only going to cause frustration and impatience. Instead, we take that motion and use it to create change by directing it toward something transformative like pure motivation.

When we give rise to bodhicitta, for example, the motion itself and the habit to be effortful start to relax a little. When there's genuine relaxation, we rest there, and let the blessing of bodhicitta sink in. When our mind is no longer restful, we direct it toward the next effort that will produce change—for example, expanding our awareness of beings who are suffering. By doing this, every minute is truly transformative. There's not a moment in our meditation that's wasted in frustration. Every moment of the meditation is designed to produce benefit for all beings, more virtue, less non-virtue, more positive qualities, less obstruction of our positive qualities, greater capacity to benefit, less interference to our capacity to benefit, and more confidence in the process, the methods, and the presence of our positive qualities. Change is happening all the time, and it's change that will always be beneficial to others.

Ocean: I've received these teachings before, but, this time, I feel like I'm hearing it all differently. Why's that?

Lama: When we're first exposed to teachings such as these, we can only experience them through the lenses and filters of our mind as it is at the time. There are layers of psychology and habit through which we interpret what we're hearing.

The more we practice, the more those lenses clarify and those filters dissolve, so we hear more each time we listen. The more we're able to hear, the more we understand where we've previously gotten confused or fallen short. We apply that understanding to our practice and gain more clarity. With that clarity, we do more practice. Our practice has more clarity and more intention, and the process deepens.

Using the metaphor of a crystal embedded in ore, the teachings are ultimately pointing out the nature of the crystal. When the crystal is obscured, we can only hear the teachings through the ore—however thin or thick it is, which has to do with our obscurations. Through our practice, we're continually in the process of removing the ore and increasingly recognizing the qualities of the crystal.

Ocean: I know that my practice is working on one level because my understanding is increasing. But my mind's poisons still keep coming up, and sometimes I feel as if there's been no change at all.

Lama: As we purify, over time, mind's poisons erupt less often and last less long when they do because we see through them and can transform them more quickly. When they're up and we're gripped by them, it can seem like they're all we've ever known. But, each time, they're a bit thinner, like the blemish on an onion that becomes smaller and more transparent as we peel away the thicker outer layers until, finally, there's no more blemish, no more layers.

Ocean: I've kept a personal journal for years. Is it helpful for me to journal about the insights that come up as I practice?

Lama: As we practice, different emotions and insights can arise. The point of our practice isn't to increase our fascination with the story of our lives but to transform and free old habits so we're capable of benefitting others to the greatest extent possible.

Journaling can have the unintended consequence of reinforcing self-important thought, even as we write about bodhicitta! It can still end up being all about us, how we're practicing, if it's going well, how much we are or aren't changing.

So, instead, it's best to use the time we might have spent journaling doing practice. Whatever arises in the mind that isn't bodhicitta, we bring bodhicitta to that. The next thing arises, and again, we don't want to get lost in our fascination with observations about the story of ourselves or others. Instead, we purify and transform these through bodhicitta. The more we practice, the more we strengthen our facility with the tools of meditation, so we always have tools available to help ourselves and others in each and every situation.

Carolyn: Doing this practice takes a lot of faith—the faith that it's true, because the mind is so conditioned to experience reality in a certain way. I'd like to learn how to quickly rest the mind in our positive qualities because, when we're in the world, all this stuff is coming at us so fast.

Lama: There's no reason that any of us would have instant and unquestioned faith in any of these principles as we begin. First, we're exposed to the general overview, like we've been talking about, and then we start to learn methods for cultivating those positive qualities. Next, we start applying those methods when we experience old negative habits arising and, through the application of the meditations and seeing them transform the negative habits and give rise to positive qualities, we develop what you could call faith. You might prefer to call it trust or confidence that the methods work—and, not only that the methods work but, as we apply them, we see change, and we see our positive qualities increasing and our negativity decreasing.

Becoming aware of that gives us more confidence, more trust, more faith.

It's a process, and it's based on our own experience. It's not based on hearing what someone else says and automatically agreeing with it. As you pointed out, our experience of reality is informed by our projections, so how we see the world based on those projections of our ordinary mind creates our experience now. If somebody says to us, "Well, that's not ultimately true," why would we believe that? We aren't going to believe it until we see change in our own minds. Through that process of change, we start to see that something else is possible and something else is true.

On the bodhisattva path, we talk about the different kinds of faith, all of which have to do with developing a relationship to the practice—the methods that produce change and are beneficial to ourselves and others. First, we need to have enough faith to want to read a book or receive teachings and do practice. Then, if we understand the benefit of applying the methods and we practice them, we see an impact in our mind that produces a deeper kind of faith based on our experience. This isn't stable, because our experience is still shifting and can change over time. We don't develop an unshakable faith until our relationship to and confidence in the presence of positive qualities in the minds of all beings is completely unwavering in every situation.

13 Alternating Contemplation with Rest

Use the method of alternating between contemplation and resting the mind to reflect on what we've covered so far. For example, you might begin by reflecting on the consequences of your past choices and their outcomes. Think about the short-term outcomes when your actions of body, speech, and mind arose from toxic emotions. Then, rest the mind. Next, think about the long-term consequences of those actions, and rest the mind. Think about the short-term outcomes when you acted from love and compassion, and then rest the mind. Reflect on the long-term outcomes of those same actions, and then rest the mind.

Always begin with pure motivation, and end with dedication of merit. You can use this alternating method to contemplate each of the subjects we'll be covering going forward to reflect, examine, and blend your mind with the meditation itself.

Winning Our Personal Tug of War

We need to take the time to pull away from our daily lives and do what we call "formal meditation practice." This is when we focus our body, speech, and mind one-pointedly on the meditation instructions. Change doesn't just happen through changing our ideas. If we have ideas that we think we believe in, and then our life experience seems to challenge them, we can lose faith in those ideas. If we don't think deeply about new ideas and blend those contemplations with our mind and heart, our understanding can fall away in stressful situations, and we'll go back to our old habits.

In our formal meditation practice, we pull away from other people, so we're not distracted or interacting with others. However, outside of our formal meditation time, when we *are* interacting with others, we don't want to waste or lose any opportunity for practice. We apply the tools we've developed familiarity with in our formal practice as we go about our lives. Whether we're talking, washing dishes, or whatever it is that involves our body and speech being engaged in another activity, we can still focus our mind on meditation. "Informal practice" is what we do with our mind as we go through the activities of daily life. An example is doing everything we can to bring pure motivation to all our interactions with others.

Rinpoche used to use the metaphor of a tug of war: If you have 23 people on one end of the rope and one on the other, who's going to win? If we spend an hour every day in our formal practice and 23 hours reinforcing our old habits, which is going to win? We need to learn how to bring our practice into every aspect of our lives. This informal practice is essential, so we don't lose the opportunities found in those 23 hours. The 24th hour allows us to dive deep and make a concentrated effort toward transformation. In this way, we become clear about the practice and develop our meditation muscles, so we have the strength during the other 23 hours to lift the load of our daily lives.

In one way, formal meditation is preparation for the other 23 hours. In another way, when we have that undistracted time where we don't have to think about the consequences of what we're doing in a worldly sense, this imprints the mind in a way that creates powerful change.

For example, if we're trying to practice good heart with our boss as she's telling us to be more cutthroat in the work we do or that competition is a good thing, it can be hard to bring to mind a meditation method if we haven't developed that muscle. If we practice compassion toward our boss during our formal meditation when we're alert and undistracted, who we are at the end of our practice time will be a little bit different that who we were at the beginning, and that's who we bring to our boss the next time we encounter her. It may not be anything we say outwardly to her that's different, but, when we interact, our heart is a little bit different, so our response has a different tone. This is why we need to do both formal and informal practice. Both are essential.

Through this process, we acquire confidence as we increasingly understand how and why the meditation methods work so they become tools we can use. For example, if we're learning carpentry, we can't simply listen to someone tell us how to hold a hammer. We have to hold the hammer. We have to hit the nail on the head. We have to try it and see if it works, and then we'll have that tool for our toolbox.

Closing the Gap

In proportion to how much we do the meditation, that's how quickly we'll see change happen—or not. That's the difference between liking the sound of the teachings and actually practicing. It's the practice that changes us. It's the practice that allows us to walk the talk to the extent we're able to. The more we walk the talk the more we can help others.

The world is full of words and information—more so today than ever before—and we're exposed to all this information every day. It's everywhere we turn, and it's hard to get away from it. But, among all those who are talking—ourselves included—how many are living what we talk about? Meditation supports us learning how to live our values.

The gap, for all of us, between our values and our lived experience can produce cynicism and despair. What opens our heart and inspires us is encountering those who walk the talk, who are living their values. When we encounter these people, we know it's possible for us, too. When we meet people who are living in the midst of great difficulties, aggression, hostility, and hatred and still remain kind and loving, it changes us, because we know another way is possible. But, until we see someone demonstrating it, it's hard to believe it and easy to be suspicious.

To the extent that we practice, we can live it, and, to the extent we live it, we can help inspire others to want to live it. It's a process. We can have a beneficial kind of impatience that inspires pure motivation: we can't bear the suffering of beings and so we know we *must* accomplish enlightenment *in this very lifetime* for the sake of all beings. It's important to have that sense of urgency about our practice, because that's the only power that can cut through the inertia of our old habits and the influence of the larger culture that's so strongly reinforcing the concept of self, self, self. To cut through all that, we must have that sense of urgency, of feeling that we have to do this *now*.

Of course, it doesn't happen that quickly, but we have to remember that there's no replacement for the time we put into meditation, both formal and informal. That's what will cause the change that allows us to model a different way of being.

Through our formal practice, things will come up, and we might gain insight into why, for example, it's so much easier to stay busy or be engaged in the welfare of others outwardly instead of looking at and being honest about what's actually going on in our minds.

Hillary: I have so much going on in my life that I really don't have time for formal practice. Is it enough to just practice informally?

Lama: Devoting the time to really immersing in formal practice is such an important part of our path because, in our daily life, it's so easy for our ordinary mind to consume us. Psychologically and culturally, we have a habit for developing confidence based on components of our personality that can be affected by things outside of ourselves or even inside ourselves when we're triggered. What we're talking about here in terms of confidence in our practice has to do with confidence in qualities that are characteristics of our true nature, such as limitless wisdom, loving kindness, and compassion. To develop confidence in those aspects of our experience, we have to put in the time to recognize and stabilize them.

Through practice, we shift away from self-concept—how we conceive of and identify ourselves in the world as a family member, or a co-worker, for example. We all have a sense of identity, of our capacities, and of our strengths and weaknesses. All of those have to do with features such as skills and identity that have been gathered in the course of a lifetime. None of those are stable. Our identity, our sense of purpose, or our orientation can change. For example, we develop an identity and confidence around being a parent, and then our kids leave. Who are we then?

To develop the confidence necessary to stay steady in the face of the shifting circumstances of our lives, we have to identify with what's a reliable source of benefit for ourselves and others—our positive qualities. That's a very difficult transition to make if we don't put in the necessary time into formal practice.

Look at your daily life and see if you can find even just short periods of time here and there to do formal practice. Rinpoche used to say that the ordinary mind is like a paper bag—every time we bring the mind back to practice, it's like we're poking a hole in the bag with a needle. At first it doesn't seem like much, but, eventually, if we keep going, the bag will shred. It's often far more effective—especially as we're starting out on the path—to bring the mind back to bodhicitta for short periods frequently than to try to stay focused and do our practice all at once for a longer period, especially if we're really busy.

Anthony: I have a fear of the idea of sitting down to practice, and maybe this is what's kept me from doing it. I picture myself isolated like a yogi in a cave and, instead of dealing with the fear, I bounce around and stay busy with other things.

Lama: The cave can be a metaphor for pulling away from the busyness of our lives and doing formal practice—whether that be for some time each day or some days each month or some weeks or months each year. As we begin on the path, it's hard to rely only on formal practice without the presence of teachings and other practitioners and activities that create merit. The habit to self-involvement is so strong that it's easy to get lost at first. We may start out genuinely practicing for the sake of all beings, but then the habit to self-centeredness can seep into everything. Initially, it's hard to sustain bodhicitta when we aren't interacting with others who are suffering or with those who are trying to help those who are suffering or when we aren't receiving teachings or creating merit through activities to benefit others.

It's helpful, at first, to alternate being alone with our minds and then interacting with people and activities that confront the ego, our self-involvement, and pride. If we're alone and not dealing with stress and suffering, it's easy to get self-contented and think we've got it all together and are close to enlightenment. It's a huge tragedy to have enough merit to go into a solitary retreat, for example, do practice, and get lost in pride. It's the worst kind of obstacle, because, if we're proud, we think we don't have anything more to learn or any reason to. We just sit there using up our merit.

We have to be skillful with the back and forth of being alone with our practice and being active in the world, especially at the beginning. We need to put all the right ingredients in the pot, have it set at the right temperature, and keep the lid on! Once it's cooked, we can serve it, and share with others.

Anthony: I think that's what was happening for me—a lack of good formal practice for who knows how long.

Lama: It sounds as if you're noticing the difference in your mind when you do formal practice and when you don't. You're learning about your mind, your practice, what's supportive, and what isn't. I wouldn't draw a grand conclusion and scare yourself with judgments about choices you're making. Right now, you're learning. Sometimes we learn by contrast. Do what you find to be the most supportive, and then observe the impact on your mind. It takes time for the teachings to sink in, to cook. Just accept the process of integration, work it, and let it work you—and it *is* working you, in case you haven't noticed!

Hillary: I want to share proof of what you just said, Lama. I left the retreat center where I was living 15 years ago, and it seems I let everything steep for all of that time. Even though I didn't do very much formal practice during those 15 years, my mind is significantly different now than it was then.

Lama: That's an example of informal practice, taking your life as practice.

14 The Benefits of
Formal and Informal Practice

Do a session of formal practice with any of the topics we've discussed so far such as establishing pure motivation. Notice the change in your mind from before you start the practice to after the practice.

Next, observe any change in your mind that takes place between the time you start and end a period of informal practice. For example, you might establish pure motivation on your way into work, bringing the mind back again and again to that motivation throughout your shift, and dedicating the merit at the end.

Notice any differences between the quality and power of your practice in the formal and informal practice sessions. Do they support each other?

Reflect on the changes in your mind at times when you only did one or two sessions of formal practice each day. Then reflect on the changes that took place when you didn't do formal practice but tried to practice throughout your daily life. Think about times when you did both.

When did you see the most genuine change?

Working with the Wild Horse of the Mind

If we find ourselves frequently distracted as we meditate, we can try moving to another meditation we've learned. Rinpoche used to say this process is like we're taming the wild horse of the mind. If we try to put it on a short tether—working hard to keep our mind focused and not allowing any movement—the horse will rear up and fight us, maybe even break its neck. Instead, we want to give it a big corral and let it run and run so it has the experience of freedom. That corral is a corral of virtue, wisdom, and compassion. If our mind is stirred up and there's a lot of emotion, we make sure to direct the emotion always in a virtuous way and bring our mind back to one or another meditation.

If we can't calm down, we might listen to or read another teaching, but we don't just leave it at that. We then contemplate that teaching or pause and practice what's been taught, and then continue reading. We do whatever works for us as long as it's always a process of change that's beneficial for ourself and all beings. We always allow the mind to run within that virtuous corral. Eventually, the horse gets tired and comes right up to us. We can even give it an apple or a carrot. At that point, when the mind finally relaxes a bit, we can nourish it with deeper insight.

Distraction can also be related to certain aspects of our lifestyles. We can pay attention to see if our distraction is greater if we try to practice at a particular time of day, or we try to practice right after or in the midst of emotional upheaval or a particular kind of activity, or if our practice seems to be affected by certain dietary choices. When we eat more sugar or drink caffeine, are we more distracted, and, when we eat more fat or oil, do we calm down more? Are we less distracted after a good night's sleep?

Some of the recommendations in Tibetan Medicine for doing this are to make sure we have enough sleep, minimize stress, eat small portions more frequently, and/or create a diet that has more cooked than raw foods, more oil in it, and, if we're not vegan, more dairy or meat. All of these calm us down. Baths with oil in them are better than showers. Warm, non-caffeinated tea is calming. We notice these lifestyle factors and change them as needed.

All these things are helpful for calming down the body's subtle energies when they're disturbed. As the subtle energies calm down, the mind calms down. It's said that the ordinary mind is like a legless rider on a blind wild horse, which represents the subtle energies. We're trying to calm down the mind, but the rider is legless and the horse is wild and blind and scared. That's why it's so supportive to our meditation practice to calm down the subtle energies.

Ideally, when we meditate, we sit upright with our back straight. When our spine is straight, our subtle channels are as well, and the subtle energies can move smoothly. If we can't sit cross-legged, as long as the spine is straight—whether we're sitting in a chair or on the floor—it's helpful.

Doug: In the process of doing my practice, there are times where I drift away or get disturbed by my thoughts, or the stream of thought takes me for a ride. How can I work with that?

Lama: In general, as we're doing the various meditations, we're also cultivating an ability to be aware of what's going on in our mind. To do any of the meditations, we need to bring the methodology directly to our mind. We can't do this in a way that's relevant and impactful if we aren't aware of what's going on inwardly. When we bring that quality of awareness to our meditation, we'll notice when we're distracted. This allows us to bring the mind back to the exercise we're working with.

The process of transformation happens through that blending of the ordinary mind and its habits with a methodology that's designed to produce change. To do that requires concentration, so we have to be aware when we've spaced out, or else we aren't going to realize we need to bring the mind back. It's rich territory as we learn what's going on in our mind—and take responsibility for and change it—as we engage with others. It's not that we're denying what's going on for them, but we're simultaneously taking responsibility for what's going on in our own mind and committing to a process of transformation so we can be more effective, more responsive, and more beneficial to others and to the conditions of our lives.

Meanwhile, in our daily lives or formal meditation practice, whenever our minds start to run wild, we remind ourselves not to get lost in these emotions that rob us of the opportunity for transformation. Through our practice, we undermine and purify these habits and mental poisons and awaken our positive qualities. We establish the foundation of bodhicitta, create virtue through that awakening, and dedicate the merit in order that this may be of benefit not just to a few but to all beings and not just for now but for all time.

Each of the moments in which we do that nurtures our entire path. It supports us creating less harm and so not using up, but instead, adding oil to the lamp. It benefits those we're connecting with. It supports our own awakening, and, eventually, the awakening of all beings.

Ocean: What do we do with all the stuff that arises during our meditation—not just negative thoughts but insights and experiences?

Lama: In looking at our ordinary mind, we could use the metaphor of viewing a mountain shrouded in fog. The power of our awareness can be like a ray of sunlight that causes some of the fog to disperse. We might see a waterfall, and then the fog covers that over. The fog thins again, and we see an amazingly beautiful cliff face. We might have all kinds of ideas about the cliff face—how steep it is, what kind of rock it's made of, and so on—and then the fog covers it again. This process of temporary glimpses of the mountain keeps happening—we see a forest and then a snow-capped peak and so on. Not one of those images is the whole mountain.

Similarly, if we grasp at our meditation experiences, we might start analyzing the cliff faces of our mind and thinking of all the cliff faces we've ever noticed. We start journaling about them, "This cliff reminds me of this and that." The more we get into that process, the farther away we move from awareness of mind itself, because we're attached to one or another aspect of our experience. In addition, we create ideas about the mind instead of letting the sun shine, the fog disperse, and the mountain emerge, which is the practice.

A traditional metaphor for meditation is that of building a fire. The purpose of the fire is to produce heat and light. Although it produces smoke and sparks, they aren't the purpose of the fire. If we become fascinated with the smoke and sparks, we stop feeding the fire, and it goes out. Smoke and sparks represent temporary meditation experiences—psychic experiences and moments of bliss, clarity, or stability. To the extent to which we become fascinated with them, we don't rely on the methods that are designed to produce transformation and the profound change we're seeking.

Ocean: Are you saying that some of that stuff may be useful in the short term but not in the limitless way we're seeking?

Lama: Sort of. It's a different frame of reference. The frame of reference we're developing is one of wanting all beings to be free of suffering and to awaken. We use methods that will produce that awakening in ourselves and increase our capacity to inspire others to awaken rather than simply to negotiate, gain insight into and make decisions about our daily lives. Those are short-term survival methods as opposed to waking up.

Carolyn: Each of us has different experiences. If someone has the inclination to sing, for example, are they using that as a method, or is that just their inclination?

Lama: It depends on their mind and their motivation. Those experiences, how we understand them, and what we do with them come from the ordinary mind, the mind that doesn't know its own nature. Out of the not-knowing of our own nature, each of us has been trying to figure it all out by ourself.

Obviously, you're a seeker, and you've been yearning for wisdom and compassion and whatever will help you find that. We can only try to pull it together for ourselves until we encounter a tradition that provides this guidance. Then all that's required of us is to practice it! Once we encounter methods given to us by enlightened beings that are designed to transform ourselves from the root—and we see how effective they are—what we rely on shifts, if we want it to. This doesn't mean whatever method we've been using is bad, but we need to be sure the tradition is authentic and guaranteed to produce the outcome we want.

The only way we can know if these methods will work for us is by trying them. If the change that we experience is of a different quality, caliber, and potency than the change we've experienced before, we're inspired to continue to rely on these methods. It becomes our experience, and it creates a shift in orientation.

This isn't to say we can't have insights from dreams and various kinds of experiences, but we have to remember that, no matter how old we are, we don't have much time in this life. It's easier when we're younger to have the illusion we have a lot of time. When loved ones or friends our age or younger die, it's an important wake-up call.

The time and circumstances of our death are completely uncertain, but the fact of it is certain. None of us knows how much time we have. We could keep trying to come up with our own methods to achieve wisdom and compassion based on our limited life experiences—or we could try these methods from enlightened beings and see what happens in our mind and heart. Do our positive qualities increase? Do our negative habits decrease? Does our capacity to benefit others increase? If so, we'll be more inclined to practice these methods with whatever time we have left. It's up to each of us, and we have to explore, examine, and do exactly what you're doing. We ask questions and examine what truly produces benefit.

Carolyn: I've definitely seen positive outcomes from doing the practice. That's why I'm here, and that's why I want to keep going. However, other methods I've used in the past and my temporary meditation experiences haven't gone away, and I find they're still useful sometimes.

Lama: As long as you keep practicing these methods, the process of transformation you're going through will, over time, help to put all your experiences in perspective. Your confidence in the power of virtue and the harmful consequences of non-virtue will deepen. More and more, this will become the frame of reference you use in your life to inform your choices: Is there more virtue or more non-virtue? Am I being more beneficial or more harmful? That framework will become increasingly integrated into your way of being and will help you to better understand your relationship to these other experiences, methods, and habits. You don't have to reject them. Just keep practicing bodhicitta, and it will become clear over time.

CHAPTER 5. THE PLAY OF KARMA IN OUR MOVIE

Each of us experiences life through the lens of what's familiar to us—the habits we have and the way we view reality. We're totally certain that how we perceive things is the way they truly are. It's like we're watching a movie while sitting in the theatre of this human realm. In the back of the theatre is an old-fashioned projector. The light it projects doesn't contain color or movement or drama or characters. It's simply pure radiance, a metaphor for the limitless potential of our true nature—the sacred essence of our being.

Our mind is that projector. Dimming the light of mind's awareness are the imprints that each of us—as the writer and director of our life—has made on the film that contains all the drama of our lives. As the film continues to roll and each new frame appears, we don't realize that we, ourselves, are acting as the producer, director, heroes, and villains who've created and star in our movie. We grasp at the events and people on the screen that we like and reject those we don't, composing future scenes with each motion of our mind.

It's easy to blame the characters appearing on the screen for the things we don't like. But, if we understand we're watching a movie that we've created, not only will we not experience ourselves as victims in relationship to those images, but we'll become empowered to transform them—because we understand their source. When all the imprints and filters—with their various degrees of density or murkiness—have been removed from our mind, what's left is the direct experience of the brilliance that's the pure expression of mind's essence.

Most of our lives are lived without that awareness. We're unconscious of the impact of our choices of body, speech, and mind on the film strip of our lives. Every single action imprints the film with the next scene, and that frame of the film passes over the light of the mind and projects an IMAX appearance we call reality, which we believe has nothing to do with us. We think of ourselves as innocent victims when bad things happen to us. We think we've always done everything right, and it's the rest of the world that's confused. We don't experience our lives as the unfolding projection of our ignorance, attachment, aversion, pride, or jealousy.

So, all we can do is react out of that misunderstanding, further etching the next frame of our life's film with negative emotions and habitual reactions arising from our lack of awareness. When these images are displayed, we once again react to them, creating further imprints to which we'll react in the future— entrapping us in a seemingly endless cycle of powerlessness and reactivity.

If we understand this basic principle, we understand that our future experience is up to us. Will we respond to what's unfolding in our lives as victims of all these events? Or will we understand that we're creators of our individual experience, co-creators of our collective experience, and that we have an opportunity to intervene in and change the ordinary unfolding of all these appearances? We can intervene by writing a different script, so different scenes unfold on the big screen of our life. It won't work for us to try to wipe away the imagery we don't like on our personal movie screen. If we want to change our experience, we have to change the film.

We're the Producer of Our Movie

Our individual experience of reality is the natural outcome of the imprints we've created in our mind—what we could call, in the most general sense, our personal karma. The understanding of karma as expressed in the Sanskrit language and the Buddhist tradition has a sense of causality, that actions have results. We do what we do with body, speech, and mind because of our past habits and actions, and those actions in turn will have certain results in the future. What we call "virtuous" actions have the sense of being healthy, beneficial, and wholesome—like nutritious food that's been prepared skillfully and is nourishing and supportive of positive outcomes. That which we call "non-virtuous" lacks skill and wholesomeness.

Each of us perceives the appearances on the screen according to our individual karma. This is why no single object is experienced the same way by everyone. Two people can be talking about a third person, and they can have completely opposite experiences of that person according to their karma, which influences how they see them.

Some of our experience is also shared by others, and that's what we call collective karma. All of us sitting in this same human theatre have differing experiences of the movie we're watching. We share the karma of sitting together in this theatre, but we simultaneously have our own individual experiences of the storyline being projected. Some people are sitting up close to the drama playing out at the moment. Others are sitting farther away. Some love the hero, while others love the villain. No matter where we're sitting, our personal karma outweighs the collective karma in determining how we experience the movie.

Through spiritual practice, we become increasingly aware that our entire reality is informed by the push-pull of our attachment and aversion in relationship to our experience. Appearances arise due to past imprints, yet our experience of them is colored by our current mental and emotional environment.

How we experience the display of our previous actions is affected by our current habits of mind. We might experience the same thing differently depending on whether we're in a good or a bad mood. If our hearts are wide open and full of compassion, we experience a scene or react to a person through the lens of compassion. Later, if we're disturbed or angry, we'll experience the same scene or the same person through the lens of disturbance or annoyance.

Seeing this, we'll be motivated to refrain from acting on negative habits and impulses that are harmful to ourselves and others. We understand that if we don't want to see that negativity playing out on the big screen of our life, we have to commit to changing our own mind and refraining from causes of harm.

As we refrain from non-virtue—the cause of suffering—and engage in virtue, the projections of our mind will change over time. There will be fewer frightening and painful experiences and more loving, kind, and harmonious ones. Slowly, the scenery starts to change in the inner landscape of our mind, and this affects its projection in our outer experience.

Each of the meditations we'll be working with accomplishes this by deepening our relationship to the principle and practice of virtue. We need to constantly ask ourselves if what we're repeating in our mind is positive. No matter what the imagery on the big screen of our lives, we respond with good heart, because we understand that, if we don't, the future scenes of our film will be filled with difficulty and misery.

Each of us, as the producer, director, screenwriter, and hero in our movie, has the ability to make a better future for ourselves and others, but we need to understand what will bring that about—virtue, compassion, good heart, and selflessness in relationship to others.

Depending on our religious background, our philosophical beliefs and so forth, we can have a different analysis and understanding of what created our experience. But no matter what our spiritual or religious understanding, there's a shared assumption that how we respond to our life's circumstances will determine future experiences for ourselves and others. For this reason, we're not focusing here on the causes of our experience, but rather we'll be learning how we can transform our responses and create the causes for a different experience in the future.

Carolyn: What about the idea that setting your goals and wishes, in and of itself, changes your experience?

Lama: If we could all influence what happens to us spontaneously by sheer will, this world would be a very different place! Some of us may be riding a wave of merit in this moment that's based on the effects of previous virtuous actions coming to fruition. It may seem like everything is aligning perfectly to make our life go well. It's expansive and exploding, so it's possible to think, "All I have to do is believe in what I want, and it happens," because that's how it appears in that moment. But, in that worldview, there's no understanding that everything appearing in that moment is the result of eons of past actions and habits. If it was universally true that all we have to do is set an intention and it will manifest, that would happen for everybody, but it doesn't.

The other thing that's often present in that worldview is it's all about one's self. We create a visualization of what *we* want, but there's no love and compassion inherent within it. It doesn't embrace the welfare of all others, so it doesn't create the virtue that would allow whatever the goals are to be sustainable in the long run. If we're riding a wave of positive outcomes due to previous past actions, but we aren't creating the basis for that to continue, at some point, the underlying causes will be exhausted.

Ocean: Hearing about karma has always made me feel powerless, because it seems like something I can't influence much less change. It's happening because of all these things I did before.

Lama: We *can* change it. That's the whole purpose of the path. Not only can we rewrite the script going forward, but, as we access and empower our positive qualities, they overpower and purify past negativity, like the power of the rising sun dissipates darkness. But we can't be naïve about the necessity for creating positive causes. We have to make sure, first, that every action we take with body, speech, and mind nurtures our capacity to continue creating more positive causes and, secondly, as we interact with others, that our impact on them inspires their virtue so that they, in turn, inspire virtue in others. In this way, we build a momentum that can impact the collective karma. Helping others long-term means modeling and supporting actions that are uplifting and compassionate rather than actions that tear down, so others are able to accumulate more merit, not just use up what they have.

Ocean: Would it be possible to reach a spiritual critical mass and change the world?

Lama: In theory, it is. It requires a lot of authentic spiritual practice on the part of a lot of people, and it can't be superficial. It can't just be intellectual or wishful thinking. We have to go through the hard places to get there. We can't bypass all the bumps we encounter along the way. We can't pretend those aren't there and suppress them. It's through the very process of being honest about, working directly with, and transforming what's in our hearts that we inspire others. Through us, they see it's possible. If we talk about it but haven't gone through it and lived it, others can feel it. If we really live it, that gives others the hope they can too. They can come to believe they can make it through the dark night of the soul, and have faith there's something beneficial on the other side. So, it's worth doing the hard work. Inspiring others to engage in authentic spiritual practice begins with doing it ourselves.

As we refrain from self-centered consciousness and actions and engage virtuous actions of body, speech, and mind, there's a thinning of the tumultuous phenomena we see on the big screen of our life. There's less upheaval, because we aren't so captivated by the objects of our attachment and aversion. As we experience less upheaval, we create less upheaval around us, less chaos and confusion resulting from wanting and not wanting, misunderstanding, grasping, and rejecting. As we pacify our negative emotions and habits and engage positive habits and qualities of mind that are a source of benefit for others, we become increasingly aware of the power of virtue and commit to practicing virtue as a method of change for ourselves and others. We begin to experience moments of lucidity in which we're aware that all our experience is ultimately none other than light through film, and that the true nature of our mind is radiant and pure. We start to have more glimmers of that, because there's less obstruction and overlay of confusion and delusion.

Tossing Pebbles

Karma is hugely misunderstood in Western culture as payback or punishment from an all-powerful outer force or being. Whether we've accepted and lived by this definition or rebelled against it, it's seeped into our consciousness, and our understanding of karma is often interpreted through the lens of that belief.

Karma perceived through the lens of punishment is based on the belief that people who are suffering deserve it. Implicit in that worldview is the assumption that, because those experiencing positive karma didn't make bad choices, they're in a self-righteous position to judge the choices others have made. This is looking at karma through the lens of reward and punishment. But if we see suffering and don't try to help, we're the ones making bad karma.

If this is our understanding, when we have periods of negativity, depression, sorrow, or challenging circumstances, we might ask ourselves what we did wrong to cause these things to arise and feel even worse about ourselves. We might view the misfortune of someone we don't like as them finally getting what they deserve. Yet, if this happens to someone we do like, we ask ourselves why bad things happen to good people.

But karma is simply the process of cause and effect—like the ripples that result when a pebble is tossed into water. If we've been continuously tossing pebbles, ripples have reached the shore and are coming back toward us. If we've been tossing boulders, it can feel as if a *tsunami* of karma is hitting us, and it's all we can do to catch a breath. But if we find ourselves in the middle of that tsunami and still breathing—and, we don't toss any more pebbles—we won't make more waves.

With karma, there's a principle of multiplication. If we plant an apple seed, we don't just get one apple—we get an apple tree that produces many apples that fall to the ground, create more trees, more apples, and so on. So, cause and effect is a big part of karma, but there's an additional, important consideration: we're all sitting on mountains of karma. Some of us may be experiencing positive karma at the moment, some of us negative karma, and many of us are experiencing a huge range in between. In the future, that will all change according to the causes each of us has set in motion in the past and continue in how we respond to our current circumstances.

If we happen not to be suffering right now, it's because we're experiencing a wave of positive karma rather than because an external source is rewarding us for our actions. The actions themselves create the outcome. What's ripening at any given moment is dependent on the karmic causes and conditions that make possible its fruition. The only difference between what's going on with any of us is where we are in time. It doesn't have anything to do with one person making better or worse choices. We've all created inconceivable amounts of good choices, bad choices, and everything in between. None of us is a better or worse person because of what happens to be occurring at the moment. We're all lost, we're all confused, and we all want to be happy, but we've often created the causes of suffering instead of happiness due to our ignorance.

Karma is entirely active. It's not a justification to sit back and not act. For example, if we have compassion for a victim of violence, aversion to the perpetrator, and we're motivated to act to protect the victim, it's virtuous to want to try to save or help somebody. But if we do it with aversion to the perpetrator, our motivation is mixed, and we're abandoning the perpetrator—the future sufferer. They're making karma, and they'll experience the results of their behavior in the future scenes of their movie. If, instead, we act to help the victim in the moment and protect the perpetrator from making that karma, we'll feel a much greater urgency to respond, because it's for the sake of both. If we understand karma through the lens of compassion, we'll see things very differently.

When waves of difficult karma hit, depending on whether those around us can catch a breath or if they're drowning, they may or may not have the space in their mind to notice if we're going through the world in a different way—with compassion. However, if we're always reaching out a hand to help pull them up, they'll notice it. To the extent that we're stable in our good heart, exemplifying a different way of being, and holding out a hand they can grab on to, they'll notice it and over time, be inspired to do the same for others.

Tonya: I'm realizing that I have this subtle punishment-and-reward understanding of karma that I didn't think I had. I'm worried that I'm actually reinforcing that habit by believing I have this deeper layer in which there's something wrong with me, or that I chose all of this suffering. What do I need to do?

Lama: You're already doing it, because you're practicing and seeing these aspects of mind that you didn't realize you had.

That awareness is the most important thing, because now it will be hard to indulge it. You'll be seeing your habit all over the place. Every time you see it, you can correct it and dedicate the merit of your practice to everyone with misunderstandings about the nature of reality, karma, and cause and effect.

Tonya: I think I don't feel deserving of whatever good fortune I have. It's almost like a consolation for how bad I am.

Lama: This means your bodhicitta is growing. The more you experience the presence of your positive qualities, the harder it is to refute that your nature is pure. You're seeing, by contrast, your old habit of putting yourself down, and it's not standing up to the power of your positive qualities.

Doug: You talked about having equal compassion for the victim and perpetrator. How do we actually do that?

Lama: When we understand that the only difference between a victim and a perpetrator is time, that's when we truly understand karma—cause and effect. Take the example of an abusive spouse whose behavior over time so alienates their partner that eventually the victim of abuse leaves. The abusive spouse may then find a new partner that they also abuse and who also leaves. Over time, the abuser accumulates ex-spouses and children who fear and hate them. When the abuser later becomes ill or is dying, they find themselves all alone with no one to help or comfort them. Their film has become a horror show. If we saw that old person all alone, we might think of them as an innocent victim and wonder why their family has abandoned them. This current victim is the previous perpetrator, and the victims that they abused might now be healthy and flourishing someplace else. The same characters play different roles in later scenes.

Can you imagine the awful karma of a heartless politician or corporate CEO with the power to make choices that affect the lives of people in this and future generations all over the world? What a terrible karma, because it's such a huge responsibility to hold the lives of so many beings in your hands and to not have what it takes to do that in a kind and compassionate way instead of constantly harming others.

We may believe we understand this conceptually and have an idea of compassion for these people who are doing these things to other beings and to the earth, but when we actually try to generate compassion for them, we can't get past our righteousness and our judgment. We think this an evil, terrible person and, even though the teachings say that everyone has inherent positivity, we feel this person is an exception. When we believe someone is an exception to the rule that all beings have pure nature, that's a big judgment! It's also an obstacle to us being able to genuinely give rise to loving kindness toward that person.

For example, if we're involved in social-change activity, this kind of judgment is an obstacle to being able to come up with creative, harmonious solutions to conflict. If we have this judgment about a person we interact with in the workplace or in the family, it's an obstacle to harmony within the workplace or family system. If it's somebody we have a close personal relationship with, we're in the position to be able to possibly impact their mind. We interact with them every day, so what we do makes a difference. If we're full of judgment and aversion toward what they're doing and hold the righteous belief that our way is the only way, we're not building bridges or creating a basis for harmonious solutions. Then it's hard to be proactive, and hard to help. Our own stuff is getting in the way, so we need to be able to work with our own judgment.

We can start working with this by thinking about situations where we may have been disrespectful or disregarded the needs of others—our coworkers or students in our classroom or neighbors making different choices than we're making, who are just as disrespectful of our needs or choices or wishes. Maybe we see somebody who's killing others, and we have a tremendous aversion and judgment about their act of killing. We have to own the times that we've been so careless or unconcerned that we've killed living beings—maybe not human beings, but four-legged, two-legged, and no-legged beings. If there were ants invading our house and crawling all over our counters, how many times did we carefully pick up every ant and carry it outside so that none were harmed? When termites invaded the foundation of our home, did we try to find ways to relocate them that wouldn't harm them?

Why is it that we thought what we wanted was more important than their lives? Why is it that we felt it was okay to kill them? They're living beings that, just like us, want to be happy and don't want to suffer. They're just trying to live their lives in the only way they know how, and yet we kill them to get what we want. We need to own that—not in a "I'm so terrible, this is another reason to hate myself" kind of way but on the level of humility. We recognize that we're not perfect, and we're not in a position to judge or find fault with another being that's behaving in a way that we find so objectionable. Every single one of us, at one time or another, has behaved in ways that were harmful. We need to own that.

In doing the Just Like Me meditation we learned earlier, we think about another person's choices from the point of view of our common experience. They're just like us in wanting to be happy, just like us in not wanting to suffer, and just like us in not knowing another way, so they produce the very thing they don't want—just as we've done so many times. Thinking it through that way helps to purify our judgment and pride and helps us generate equanimity and equal regard. We're no longer so inclined to demonize them and think of them as just this "other" who's so worthy of our hatred. If they knew how to create the happiness they want and avoid suffering without harming others, they'd likely do it. So, who are we to judge them, looking at our behavior during the many times when we didn't know another way?

Doug: If you've identified yourself in a particular way and are fixated on that label, how do you remedy that?

Lama: The fixation results from habit—reminding yourself again and again of that label, which reinforces it. To change it, you need to create a new habit. Our experience is formed by karmic causes—the seeds we plant—and the conditions that occur at any given point to allow those karmic seeds to ripen. We want to plant different seeds and gather different conditions. As we do this over time, we introduce a different ingredient into the recipe of our self-image. Every time we introduce a new point of view, contemplate it, integrate it, and let it blend with our experience, we're composing the future scenes of our movie. Slowly, over time, the outer and inner imagery will change.

Doug: We're planting new seeds with our positive actions, right?

Lama: Yes, but also, say you have a negative self-image oriented toward some particular label. You can make the aspiration that, by this past history, you may be able to uproot the suffering of everyone who has given themselves this label. You're not denying the old identification or the old label. You're wishing that it may serve as a cause of benefit and happiness for everyone who identifies with that label. By doing that, you're including others in the scope of your heart space. That shifts your identity a little bit. You aren't just that original label. You're also a helper of people with that label. Even though you aren't walking around with an, "I'm a helper" label, your heart space is oriented toward others with that old label. Just including others within that starts to change the label.

Breanna: I'd appreciate your thoughts about the fact that my shoes disappeared this past weekend. That's okay with me, but I hope whoever took them really needs shoes. As I sat with this, I felt something almost like grief that these shoes were taken. I've been watching my mind and working with this, because it's not really about the shoes. It's about sadness or feeling hurt.

Lama: Your instinct to make an offering to whoever took your shoes, so they don't have the karma of stealing, is wonderful. Who knows what really happened? Maybe they had the intention to take something beautiful that wasn't theirs, or maybe they need cataract surgery and couldn't tell which shoes were theirs. We can't know.

Whatever it was, you still offered to them, which is great. Your generosity of spirit changes the karma, which both protects them from the strong non-virtue of stealing and creates the virtue of offering.

At the same time, there was a boundary crossed, so there's a feeling of violation. But if you make the shoes an offering to them, they're no longer violating the boundary without your permission. It's no longer an intrusion or violation.

However, you might have the concern that your boundaries could be breached again and wonder if they'll continue to be. We can never be certain what our karma holds for us, so all we can do is change our mind about the broken pieces. We can make the aspiration that what appears as a breach fulfill those who are violating and be what they need. We have the understandable feeling of not wanting to be violated, of wanting to feel safe and stable and in control of our environment, and then we realize we're not any of these things nor can we be. But we can learn to gain control over our mind and, for example, make everything an offering.

Wherever we see a lack of control over our own environment, we think of everyone else's environment—entire countries being invaded by armies on the ground and bombs from above or submerged under water or ravaged by fire or wind. We think of all the women being beaten and raped and all those whose bodies are being invaded by disease. There's so much boundary-crossing going on in which there's much more suffering than what we experience. We make the aspiration that, by our experience of violation, no one else's boundaries ever be breached, that all of that boundary-crossing be subsumed within our own, so no one else ever has this experience of violation.

Working with it that way helps us to develop a greater capacity, because all kinds of boundary-crossing can happen at any time. There are so many things we take for granted—the ground not moving under our feet, our home not lost to fire or tornado. It's a good meditation for all of us to remember, wherever we have an assumption of safety or a fear of losing it, to think of everyone who's experiencing loss of safety in this moment with nowhere to go. We then dedicate the merit of our practice to them.

Breanna: Thank you. It was such a small thing, but it brought up so much.

Lama: Yeah, your instincts were great.

Purifying Karma

In looking back through our lives and remembering our thoughts and actions before we knew how to work with our mind, we might develop immense regret. We might find ourselves reflecting on what we wish we'd done better, the opportunities we missed, the ways in which we followed the poisons of the mind instead of being guided by pure motivation. If we don't have a method to take responsibility and own what we've done in an honest way so we can let it go, we might start thinking of ourselves as a bad person, holding onto self-hatred or low self-image or a sense that we're hopeless and can never change. Shame, embarrassment, and guilt can develop over time if we don't have a different way to deal with regret for mistakes we've made. If we identify with the regret, we might make up stories about how hopeless we are and become depressed and anxious. Instead of condemning, judging, and spinning old storylines about ourselves, we need to remind ourselves that, at the time, we didn't know better. We didn't have tools to do it differently.

There's a practice we can do to purify specific actions we regret as well as to purify our general karma and habits: the Four Powers of Purification.

The first step of this practice is to imagine, in front of and above us, whosoever or whatsoever embodies for us limitless wisdom, loving kindness, compassion, and the capacity to benefit others. We bring this to mind as the support or witness for our purification—a frame of reference for a sense of accountability to the values we hold and the positive qualities we're committed to awakening through our practice.

In the second step, we review our mistakes—the ways we've harmed others, either intentionally or unconsciously when old habits took over. We regret those things deeply, not superficially. Rinpoche used to say the regret we feel should be the same as what we'd feel if we saw a beautiful bottle of delicious-looking liquid, uncorked it, drank the whole thing, and, only afterwards, noticed that the label said, "poison."

This regret leads naturally to the third step in which we make a commitment not to repeat these mistakes. No matter what the circumstances, we understand that when we follow toxic emotions and act in ways that are harmful to others, it creates suffering for them and will cause all kinds of suffering for ourselves in the long run. If we acted out of a long-standing habit to anger, for example, we make a commitment to change that habit, so we don't repeat it. In this way, we aren't vulnerable to the power of our old toxic emotions but instead are committed to a process of change.

It's in this third step that change happens. If we don't take this step, we can confess again and again but not necessarily change. However, if our deepest commitment to others is not to harm and to do what we can to help, our regret will be heartfelt. So, we make a commitment to not repeat harmful habits, and change happens when we honor that commitment.

The fourth step is the power of the antidote, purification, and blessing. We imagine that, due to the sincerity of our regret and our commitment to change, a purifying light radiates from the representation of mind's limitless positive qualities that serves as the support for our purification. In this way, their limitless wisdom, loving kindness, compassion, and capacity to benefit washes through us. We imagine it washing away negative habits and imprints and uprooting all the toxic seeds we've planted.

If we do this each evening as part of a review of our actions of body, speech, and mind during that day, we go into the next day free of the imprints we made that day in the film of our lives. If we do this practice often, it can purify imprints from days, weeks, months, and years previous. It's very helpful to uproot daily the seeds we've planted before they can take root, grow a big tree filled with pinecones that fall to the ground, multiply, and eventually become a great forest that's far more difficult to uproot.

We dedicate the merit of this practice to all the beings that we've harmed—those we remember as well as those we don't— and all those we've helped or who have helped us and ultimately all beings. We pray that, through the merit of our practice, they may all awaken to the inherent purity of their true nature.

15 The Four Powers of Purification

Begin by establishing your motivation to do this meditation for the purpose of purifying whatever obstructs your ability to be of limitless benefit to all beings.

Imagine in the space above and in front of you the embodiment of the inherent purity of your own and all beings' true nature—limitless wisdom, loving kindness, compassion, and the capacity to benefit—as the witness or support for your purification.

Bring to mind and sincerely regret anything you've ever done that caused you to fall away from your inherent purity. Think about times you've overtly harmed others, and imagine the consequences in their lives and in the lives of those around them. As well, regret any habits such as anger, guilt, or low self-image that have added ore to the crystal instead of removing it.

Make a commitment not to repeat those actions and to a process of change to ensure you don't perpetuate them. Instead of repeating, "I, me, and mine," refresh your motivation and your practice for the sake of others who may or may not have the tools they need to find the happiness they seek. Commit to continuing to purify your old habits and to reinforcing new ones for the sake of all beings.

Due to the sincerity of your regret, of taking responsibility for your actions and habits, and of your commitment to change, imagine the radiance of limitless wisdom, loving kindness, compassion, and the capacity to benefit radiating from the representation of mind's purity in the space in front of you and washing through you, completely purifying whatever it is that's in the way—the ore, the mud, or the dust of obscuration—leaving nothing but the pure, crystalline nature of your being.

Then dedicate the merit of your meditation to those you're aware of having harmed, those you're not aware of harming, and, ultimately, all beings.

Tonya: I'm really hard on myself when I see I missed an opportunity to make merit or I said something stupid because I didn't have pure motivation. I can't feel pure regret, because I'm so busy kicking myself. Whether or not I said something that upset someone, it's not about them anymore. It's about me. I can go through my day and see every tiny thing—like, why did I say that, or where did that come from?

Lama: It sounds like you're lingering on the second step of your purification, lingering on regret.

Tonya: I feel it's because I somehow mutilate the process. Instead of having this pure, beautiful regret that you describe, I just see my foot as I look down. I look at it, and I'm not regretting non-virtue. I'm just regretting this despicable creature that should know better.

Lama: Do you get to the third and fourth steps?

Tonya: That's my problem, too. I make a commitment that every conversation going forward, everything I do, will have pure motivation. And then, the next day or whenever I catch myself doing the same thing, this anger at myself arises, because I can make these commitments, but I don't carry through.

Lama: Do you go to the fourth step of letting it go?

Tonya: How do I do that if I'm making it about me?

Lama: You're not the only one who has this issue. In those moments, generate compassion for everybody else who's trying to live up to their values but may not have the tools to help them do so. The genuine spiritual path isn't easy. It's not blissful all the time. It's hard work. Remind yourself that you aren't the only one who's getting down on yourself. It's not about you, it's about others, so redouble your efforts on behalf of everyone else. Then, on behalf of everybody else and in the context of the Four Powers, let it go. Dedicate the merit of your practice to anyone you may have harmed, including yourself.

Keep in mind that before we knew a different way to do it, we all made up stories about ourselves and others in an effort to make sense of what was going on. So, generate compassion for all beings who do that and are lost in their own stories. When you experience regret, you aren't just regretting whatever you did in the moment. You're also regretting the storylines and the habits to believe the storylines. Make a commitment not to repeat those habits, and then let it go. Let yourself receive the blessings of purification, and imagine letting it all go and it being washed away.

Whatever it is that we're struggling with, we bring it to this process and let it go. It's really important to go through the fourth step. Otherwise, the regret mutates and takes on another form—self-hatred, shame, or guilt—and it doesn't benefit anyone.

Hillary: How important are reparations in this process?

Lama: That depends on several things. If we've harmed someone, and we're purifying through the Four Powers, the idea of reparation may come up as one framework for working with what we've done. But we need to always check our motivation. For example, is our impulse to make reparations coming from a sincere desire to benefit them or as a way of dealing with our own guilt?

You can't know what they've done in their mind with whatever happened between you. If it was a long time ago, maybe they've truly moved on, and reaching out to them would only stir things up again. This doesn't mean that you abandon your commitment to benefit them. You always carry that in your heart, look for opportunities and interdependence (interconnected causes and conditions) in which you can help them, and you include them in your prayers and dedications of merit. Each of us has strong karma with someone we've harmed, so our commitment to them must be strong as well. We do whatever we can to help them going forward. If we remain aware, there may be some kind of opportunity.

In our practice, we always want to reinforce virtue and bodhicitta, not old habits and psychology. Through the practice of the Four Powers, we take responsibility for what we've done. With the fourth power, we receive the blessing by accepting the antidote—the purification—and then we let it go.

So how do we know when to do or say something to someone we've harmed? As with any action we take, it depends on our motivation. If we bring the incident to that person so we're less overcome with guilt, that's not taking responsibility for changing our own mind.

Once you've done enough purification practice to no longer feel possessed by your negative emotions about your previous actions, refresh your bodhicitta and pray that what's truly best for the other person becomes clear. Perhaps that person comes to you and wants to talk about the distance they feel has grown between you and figure out what the problem is. Of course, the door is then wide open for you to talk about it with them. If they haven't asked you, and there's no interdependence arising for you to bring it up, it's probably better to just take it into your own practice and have confidence in the purification and dedication you're doing.

Hillary: I've been wanting to end a friendship with someone who doesn't want that. How can I approach this?

Lama: You may or may not feel you have to withdraw from the friendship, but make sure you don't withdraw from your practice. Make sure you bring everything that's coming up in the friendship to your practice. In some ways, you'll become even more committed to the friendship, because it's such a cause of purification and transformation. Maybe, over time, you'll be more able to be engaged with that friendship without getting triggered and able to think more about their benefit.

Hillary: I pull back and feel bad, because I haven't been able to show up with bodhicitta.

Lama: You're sustaining and deepening your bodhicitta through your commitment to your practice. Perhaps, as a skillful interim strategy while you're cultivating bodhicitta, it seems like you're withdrawing from the friendship, but you're actually putting even more energy into it by working with it in your formal practice. From the point of view of your mind, there's no withdrawal, because there's an equal or stronger commitment.

Tonya: How do I not freak out when I work with the Four Powers and see how many actions of body, speech, and mind I've generated because of my self-loathing?

Lama: To begin with, think of everyone else who's struggling with self-loathing—all the different causes and conditions that lead to self-hatred in individuals or whole categories or cultures of people—and the amount of sorrow arising from what's basically a shared confusion of identifying with what's obscuring instead of with what's underneath. Think about how much suffering is in the world because of this confusion and all the ways that people behave in response to it that create more karma and suffering for themselves and others as well as reinforcing those habits.

Remind yourself that you can benefit them by purifying your own self-loathing, and dedicate the merit of your practice to them. Imagine the display of your innate purity—which you haven't yet fully recognized—as the witness or support to your practice. Regret whatever actions, karma, confusion, and habits have led to this misperception. Regret them deeply, even though you can't identify them, because you know that, insofar as you're captured by them, not only are you perpetuating causes of suffering for yourself but you're less available to all of those other beings who hate themselves and need you to be fully available to them. Commit to purify and not repeat this confusion. As your psychology bubbles to the surface and this misunderstanding becomes more obvious, don't engage, indulge, entertain, analyze, or resist it. Just keep bringing your mind back to its positive qualities for the sake of all those who don't know how to do that.

As you experience the sincerity of your regret and commitment, imagine the radiance of your essential purity flowing down from the top of your head and washing away all this self-hatred, all the causes and conditions of it, all the misperceptions that have arisen, and all the mental habits and poisons of the mind that you've developed in response to it. Then let that all go, and imagine yourself bathed in this great outpouring of purity, a purity that's flowing out to all the beings that you've ever harmed, all the beings you've ever judged, all the beings who hate themselves, all beings who yearn for happiness but don't know how to find it, and, ultimately, all beings. Then dedicate the merit of your practice to all those who are now completely awash in this radiant purity that's awakening in them, so they recognize and acknowledge their essential purity.

Remember not to approach this practice from the point of view of self-condemnation and purifying all the things you hate about yourself and all the mistakes that you've made. Rather, you're purifying the mistake of straying from bodhicitta by believing these misconceptions about yourself.

Ida: I had a terrible car accident recently, and I find that I've lost confidence in my ability to do my job well. I'm always second guessing myself and my karma.

Lama: As you do your purification practice, keep bringing the mind back to bodhicitta. Don't let yourself get distracted by the consequences of the accident and questioning yourself. That doesn't benefit anybody. As much as you can, try not to follow those lines of thinking or those fears and emotions. Remind yourself that you know what you're doing, you've worked successfully for decades, and you've helped so many people over the years.

Remember what the Buddha said to the man discouraged by how much farther he had to walk over the mountain to reach the Buddha and receive his teachings. Don't just look forward to where you're going. Every once in a while, stop and look back to see how far you've come. Remind yourself of how many worldly and spiritual resources you bring to your work. You have skills, aptitude, intelligence, and mental acuity. Keep bringing the mind back to bodhicitta and pray that every action of your body, speech, and mind be of infallible benefit to everyone you work with and, ultimately, all beings.

Don't scare yourself by second guessing what you might have done to avoid the accident. Until the seed we've planted has fully ripened and the fruit is ready to fall from the tree, there are still things we can do to purify and protect ourselves from the consequences of our previous actions. But once the conditions have all come together for the fruit to fully ripen and fall from the tree, there's nothing we can do except accept it and pray that, through our suffering, no one else ever has to suffer. Don't turn it into a *thing* that causes you to lose confidence. Have confidence in the power of bodhicitta to purify past actions and create the basis for beneficial outcomes going forward.

Breanna: How do we bring the understanding of karma regarding victims and perpetrators into our practice?

Lama: First of all, none of us could be experiencing the perpetrator's harmful actions if we hadn't sometime in the past created the causes for our suffering. We planted seeds, and those seeds are ripening. We need to have a huge perspective and accept responsibility for our part in what's happening to us. We're talking about countless, inconceivable numbers of lifetimes over which, out of ignorance, attachment, and aversion, we've planted seeds. We didn't know any better, and some of our actions ended up harming others, knowingly or unknowingly. We're all sitting on mountains and mountains of seeds of that kind of karma.

In this particular moment, if we or someone we love is suffering, it doesn't mean they're a bad person or somehow deserve that. It's not the victim's fault. Maybe 10,000 or 10,000,000 lifetimes ago, somebody could have been walking down a path and stepped on an ant, and now that person experiences injury or dies suddenly. This isn't punishment; it's just cause and effect. All of us, out of ignorance, have planted seeds and will have to deal with the consequences—not just once but hundreds of times as a result of the power of multiplication.

We can purify all the seeds we've planted through bringing bodhicitta to the Four Powers of Purification, but we can only do that if we never forget that this is our common experience and generate equal compassion for all beings—victims and perpetrators alike. We all need merit, so, on behalf of all beings, we do everything we can, always, to create rather than destroy merit, and dedicate again and again to the complete freedom from suffering and full awakening of all beings.

Ocean: If I'm driving and a butterfly hits my windshield and dies, do I need to bring that into my purification practice?

Lama: For a karmic act to be complete, it must have four factors. The first is the identification of the object. So, for example, you're driving home, doing everything you can to not harm any living being, and you don't see that butterfly. This means, there's no identification of the object. The second factor is your motivation. In this case, your intention is to never harm any living being and do everything you can to save the lives of all living beings. You had no motivation to kill the butterfly and you didn't even see it. The third factor is the action itself. The butterfly hits the windshield. The fourth factor is the consequence of your action. Maybe the butterfly dies or loses one of its wings. Maybe you didn't even see that the butterfly hit the corner of your windshield, so certainly there's no satisfaction or rejoicing in the outcome, which is a part of that karmic fruit. For a karmic act to be fully complete, it must have all four components. When all four factors are there, it's the strongest karmic imprint, but, even if they aren't all present, there's still karma that needs to be purified.

If we're bringing awareness of something like this to our purification practice, the Third Power, commitment to not repeat the action, is important to think about carefully. If we regret the past but keep doing things that hurt other beings— and we don't make a commitment to change—it's like confessing on Sundays but continuing to be non-virtuous all week. It doesn't change our behavior.

We could make the commitment to never kill a butterfly unwittingly again but, obviously, that's really hard to uphold. What's important is to bring our awareness to a process of change. We could make the commitment to bring to mind all beings we can't remember or didn't notice we'd harmed in all our prayers and dedications of merit. We could do the same for all the beings that died so we could eat. Maybe our commitment is to be more conscious and intentional. This means different things to different people, but, what's important is that we're being deliberate about taking the principle of not harming into our lives and integrating it as much as possible.

We all have different ideas about how to do that and what that commitment looks like for us. It's possible that butterfly lost its life but created the interdependence for us to make a huge commitment—such as never again taking a meal for granted or that we'll always remember all the butterflies, all the ants, and all the beings that died in the transportation or the packaging or the cultivation, harvesting, and preparation of the food we eat. For example, we might commit to offering every meal to whoever or whatever for us embodies limitless purity, loving kindness, and compassion, and dedicate the merit of that offering to all the beings that died or were harmed so we could eat that meal as well as all the meals we have eaten or will ever eat, all the clothes we wear, all the driving we do, and so forth.

We never want to be mindless about a connection we make that causes harm to another being. It has arisen karmically as a negative connection, but, through our practice and the power of our intention, we can transform what has arisen as a negative connection into a positive one. We pray that connection be the cause of freedom from suffering in all future lives for that being and all beings. By upholding whatever commitment we make, we change, and there's less harm in the world and more benefit.

CHAPTER 6. A SAFE HARBOR

When the play of our virtuous actions arises as fortunate circumstances—in our environment, our resources, our relationships—we experience happiness. However, every single moment of happiness is ultimately impermanent, because everything in our experience—any of the components of our body, speech, mind, and environment that create our experience—can change in an instant. These may be inner elements such as our health or frame of mind or outer elements such as our job, home, or community. All of these things can and do change quickly, as we're all currently experiencing. The rate of change in the world right now is breathtaking.

When we examine the different components of our experience, we realize that everything in the world as we see it is made up of multiple elements. The outer universe, earth, mountains, lakes, and forests are all composed of molecules, atoms, and sub-atomic particles. Our bodies are composed of flesh, blood, and bones, which in turn arise from countless specialized cells. If any one of these components is affected or changed by something else, we may experience injury or ill health.

Our ordinary mind isn't stable, either. We feel happy when things go well and sad or mad when things go poorly. Our mind is filled with all kinds of emotions, habits, and delusions. We may believe we've always been essentially ourselves, but, when we look back, we see that what was important to us when we were five years old was very different from what was important to us when we were 10, 15, 25, 30, or older. Our perspective on life, our goals, and our hopes and fears have been affected by outer and inner circumstances and have undergone constant change. There's no stable self that's survived through the decades. We can see that not only our experience but who we think we are is made up of countless components.

When we examine these aspects of our experience more deeply, we realize they are all, in and of themselves, impermanent. They can be affected by all kinds of things within and outside themselves. Right now, for example, we're seeing how imbalances in the outer elements accelerate with climate change, affecting every aspect of our lives. Causes and conditions arising in relation to each other—interdependently—are creating ever-greater and cascading imbalances in the fire, water, wind, and earth elements. After severe storms, tornadoes, floods, and fires, increasing numbers of people have nowhere to live, and others can't afford to rebuild. There's nothing in our experience that's free in the sense of not being affected by something outside of itself.

Yet, not having explored this truth deeply, we usually try to find happiness by grasping at and attempting to stabilize impermanent aspects of our lives, and we may even find a certain cluster of things that make us happy. The more these make us happy, the more we try to hold onto them and the more we suffer when the components of that cluster fall apart.

Whatever Makes Us Happy Is Already Falling Apart

As long as our happiness is based on outer material things and people behaving the way we want them to, we're destined to suffer. They either won't do what we want, or, if circumstances come together in a way we like, we'll suffer when they later change. And they *will* change, inevitably.

Suffering is built into our attachment, because whatever is making us happy is already falling apart. The seeds of separation are present in every single thing from the moment it first comes together, whether it be material substance, a relationship, an organization, our health, or a state of mind. Because everything in our world is composite—made up of multiple parts—it is, by nature, impermanent. If we try to stabilize these elements as the basis of our happiness, we're destined to suffer.

We grasp because we have the illusion that we can hold on to things even though, by their very nature, they're in a constant state of flux. Looking back, we can't remember the many things that were once important to us or what brought us together with certain people or informed the choices and decisions we made. All those people, dramas, and circumstances now seem to be no more than mirage-like appearances, wisps of long-forgotten, illusory dreamscapes.

Consider a house, which seems solid and real. If we look closely at the materials used to make a house, we find the brick, wood, and cement are made up of molecules, atoms, subatomic particles, quirks, quarks, and, finally, empty space. Ultimately, there's no *thing* we can call a house, though you wouldn't know it by our relentless efforts to stave off impermanence through maintenance and repairs!

For those of us who grew up studying science, the composite nature of a house seems obvious. But, to understand this truth intellectually through physics or chemistry is very different from meditating on it. Integrating into our being and our lives the knowledge that all appearances—everything we experience as reality—are composite, impermanent, unfree, and unreliable is quite another thing indeed.

Unfree phenomena constantly affect each other, and the outcome of those interactions is almost always beyond our control. None of these are free or independent. All are interdependent and influenced by each other. Sometimes, our hard work produces what we want or what we think is most beneficial and, sometimes, it doesn't. If we become attached to those outcomes, we're likely to be disappointed.

The effects of our actions are dependent not only on the virtuous roots of benefit in our own minds but also on the ripening conditions of our personal and shared karma—which are in constant flux and therefore unreliable and incapable of creating stable happiness. The outcome of our interactions with others may be very different than what we imagine or hope them to be. They're the result of the interplay among the effects of actions each of us has set in motion personally as well as the larger constellation of causes and conditions set in motion by societal or group actions.

16 The Causes of Happiness and Sorrow

Reflect on the things that you've looked to for happiness throughout your life. Are they composite? Impermanent? Are they free, or can they be affected by things outside themselves?

Have you been able to control whether you're able to find or hold on to those things?

Has your attachment to them produced happiness or sorrow?

What happened when you managed to find but then lost them?

Does the extent of your sorrow and disappointment when you can't find them, or find and lose them, correspond to the amount of your attachment?

Our True North

Exploring these ideas, we might despair that we could ever find stable happiness. We may think, "I'm reading all this to try to find a remedy for my depression, and now I'm even more depressed!" How do we engage with all the elements of our lives that are impermanent and not become discouraged? How do we go forward to create benefit for others and not be discouraged when that benefit doesn't happen?

We need to explore—deeply and relentlessly—until we discover what's truly reliable. Is there any cause of stable happiness within this world of composite phenomena?

All that we experience as reality, all the images at play in the movie of our lives, are so intensely captivating because we look to them for our happiness and to dispel our suffering. But, as we've seen, we can't change or erase them from the big screen of our lives without removing them from their source—the film itself.

As we begin to understand this, we're inspired to edit and rewrite our film to produce increasingly fortunate scenes. We engage in virtue and abandon negative, self-centered actions that are disturbing, chaotic, and produce harm. As we do this, our experience starts to settle down. Whether there's less drama on the big screen of our life, or our inner relationship to it calms down, or both, we begin to have a sense of the deeper presence of awareness that informs our experience of reality: each of the images in our movie is arising and not separate from the projector's light. What is that light if not the basis of all the appearances in our movie?

Thinking about this, we might find we believe there's some essence—something sacred, profound, and reliable—underlying our entire experience of reality. However, we don't have any idea if this essence is something we can relate to and rely on if we've only paid attention to the scenes unfolding before us rather than their luminous basis.

So, how do we explore that essence? Since it's not a *thing,* it can't be seen, heard, smelled, touched, or tasted. Yet because it isn't a *thing,* it's not composite and, therefore, it's not impermanent. It pervades the minds and hearts of all beings and all appearances throughout time and space. It isn't composite and therefore not impermanent, because it can't be affected by changes within and outside itself. That means it's free. If we want freedom from the endless ups and downs of hope and fear based on our clinging to illusion, we need to rely on something that is, itself, free.

This entire spiritual path is leading us away from the causes of suffering, toward the causes of happiness, and, ultimately, toward the freedom of the realization of our true nature. To awaken to this essence, we have to remove what's clouding that recognition—ultimately, the delusion of believing the movie is real. With every contemplation and meditation we do, we're removing what's concealing and coming closer to revealing that essence. The more we practice, the more we develop an increasing intimacy with our positive qualities, our true nature as the sacred essence of being. This is a deeper and far more stable experience than happiness based on composite and impermanent phenomena.

Instead of relying on material things and people, trying to control things outside our control, and hoping circumstances will go the way we want as our source of happiness and stability, we can rely on the spiritual principles and practices that lead us away from suffering, toward benefit for ourselves and others, and make possible the realization of our true nature.

We've been exploring the play of cause and effect in our lives and observing what happens when we create new imprints and habits in our mind. Through this process, we've begun to observe whether our relationships, over time, have become more harmonious; whether we're kinder, more helpful, more authentic; and whether we have a greater capacity to benefit others. To the extent that we've found this to be true, our confidence has been reinforced by our life experiences. This is how we come to depend less and less on composite, impermanent, and unfree outer conditions for our happiness. Increasingly, we find our fulfillment in what's absolutely free and reliable—the essence of mind and its positive qualities and the practice that leads us to that awareness. This is one way of understanding the meaning of virtue—that which leads to wisdom, an awareness of mind's true nature.

Through this practice, whether things go well or poorly, we bring everything in our lives onto the path of virtue, which sustains us and keeps us going. If we have confidence that it's working, we keep practicing and bring pure motivation to everything we do. Inwardly, we'll transform our minds and hearts and, outwardly, we'll express this by benefiting others and making the world a better place. No matter what happens outwardly, we're at peace inwardly, knowing that we're aligned with our values, our true north—always subduing our negativity, increasing our wisdom and compassion, and becoming more effective and beneficial. We develop a deep confidence and contentment that we're on track. Regardless of the external outcomes, our personal experience continues to improve, because we have less negativity and self-centeredness; more selflessness, kindness, and compassion; and a greater capacity to benefit others.

Over time, we gain greater insight and wisdom. As those develop, we'll have a presence of mind and stability of practice that we can bring to every situation, no matter how chaotic. When composite phenomena fall apart, we can offer a stable presence of calm. As we continue to cultivate these qualities in our formal and informal practice and express them in the world around us, we'll be a steady force for benefit wherever we go and whatever we do. We'll be able to look back at the end of our lives and recognize that, because of what we've done with our body, speech, and mind, the world is better for us having come through it. Even if we didn't intend to become enlightened or have no concept of what that means, we're on a path that will lead inevitably to that result.

Hillary: You talked about the luminous essence or basis of our experience. What do you mean by that?

Lama: The example of our dreams may help to explain. In last night's dream, you had an experience of a drama unfolding, but, when you woke up, you realized the drama never occurred. Maybe you dreamt that you won the lottery, but, when you woke up, your bills still weren't paid. You can't deny the unfolding of the dream appearances, but, in essence, they weren't real.

Luminosity refers to the quality of mind that knows and has clarity. It's not the mind of confusion. So, when you remember a dream, there's some clarity, some awareness, and yet, the content of the dream didn't ultimately happen. We could say that a dream is the display or the projection of mind's luminosity, like the scenes unfolding in our movie. Lucid dreaming occurs when we know we're dreaming, the mind is awake within the dream. When that luminous awareness is clouded by ignorance of the true nature of the dream, we're bound by confusion.

If we realize that our daytime experience is like a dream or a movie of our own creation, we're empowered to change the appearances on the big screen of life. When the power of our awareness is greater than the power of the appearances, change is possible. It's like lucid dreaming, in which we realize we're dreaming, so we can change what's happening in the dream. This is illustrated in a poster of a man being choked by a monster in his dream. He's terrified and cries out, "Oh no, what's going to happen to me?" The monster replies, "I don't know. It's *your* dream!"

Anthony: What more can we do to develop that wisdom perspective?

Lama: We can begin with the alternating meditation, alternating one of the Four Immeasurable Qualities or prayer with resting the mind. Impermanence meditation is also an extremely powerful method to loosen the ordinary mind's fixation on the seeming solidity of appearances. If we allow that meditation to become more subtle, we aren't just using the conceptual mind to think about outer phenomena as if they're self-existing. Instead, we allow ourselves to be open to and aware of the illusory nature of things by letting the mind rest within the rate of change of all outer and inner appearances. Being aware of the rate of change, everything seems more dreamlike. We then let go of that effort and rest the mind.

Rinpoche taught us to alternate in this way, because we start with an effortful meditation that, by its nature, is designed to relax effort, relax contrivance, relax fixation. We then rest the mind in the warmth of the effortless essence of the effortful practice of giving rise to our pure qualities. We use a method that leads to wisdom, but isn't, itself, the direct experience of pure wisdom. Rather, it's one of the methods the Buddha offered to point toward suchness, toward mind's nature. Depending on what's going on—our current fixation, poison, or experience—there's a way to transform it, using bodhicitta, that leads toward wisdom.

Thinking about our death is also a very helpful way of contemplating impermanence, because we're directly contemplating our own impermanence. Why would we think we have another day? Why do we believe, when we wake up, that we're going to have a whole day of life? We can't know that. What we can know is that having been born, we'll die. We just don't know when. Acting as if today is our last day will help us avoid doing things we'll regret later. We'll see that we can't assume we'll have time to purify or rectify harmful actions at some time in the future. Thinking this way can support a healthy framework for our choices, because we can't cheat karma. At the time of our death, karma will determine our future. Peaceful life, peaceful death.

There's a well-known Buddhist story that Rinpoche used to tell about a farmer who, one evening, discovered one of his mares was missing. His neighbors shared their dismay at what had to be his substantial loss, to which he replied, "Maybe."

The next evening when he brought his herd in from the pasture, he found a wild stallion accompanying the missing mare. His neighbors exclaimed how fortunate he was, to which the farmer replied, "Maybe."

The next day, trying to tame the horse, the farmer's son broke his leg. His neighbors all expressed their condolences at his misfortune, to which the farmer replied, "Maybe."

Soon, the army came through their village to draft young men for war, but, because the farmer's son had a broken leg, he couldn't go. Again, the neighbors rejoiced in the farmer's good fortune, and, again, he replied, "Maybe."

The story continues in the same vein, demonstrating the farmer's wisdom. Through his understanding of impermanence, he was neither attached to seemingly fortunate events nor averse to seeming misfortune. He displayed the wisdom of impermanence. His understanding of the truth of impermanence offered a stable way through the ups and downs of life, beyond hope and fear, excitement and disappointment.

17 Impermanence

Can you think of anything you've ever known in your outer environment that hasn't changed?

Observe how frequently you assume that things will remain the same. Are you surprised when they don't? Is that surprise a cause of sorrow, disappointment, or happiness in the short or long term?

Is there any aspect of your experience of yourself that hasn't ever changed? Do you assume it won't? Do you indulge hope and fear in relation to assumptions about your personal experience remaining the same?

Do you have relationships of any kind that haven't changed in some way? Do you have hope and/or fear that they will or won't change, and do you suffer as a result?

Inez: In my work with battered women, I feel like I've become a sponge for trauma. I've absorbed so much of it, because it's just in the air. Sometimes, specific things happen—a suicide attempt or a death—but mostly it's just the human tragedy I witness unfolding day after day. I don't know how to absorb all that without it taking a heavy toll on my heart or causing me to shut down emotionally.

Lama: Aversion to being the sponge for trauma or suffering is sticky. It acts like a magnet and causes all of that energetic contamination to wear us down.

Instead, we can purify our motivation enough so we're able to wish we could absorb all of the trauma so no one else ever has to experience trauma again. The power of that compassionate wish, in itself, can transform your experience so it won't weigh you down.

Over time, as your practice deepens, you'll develop more of a sense of the ephemeral and impermanent nature of all that's arising. It's a constant flow of wounded women and tragedy and sorrow, loss and trauma, grief and rage and violence—waves and waves and waves of it.

Through compassion, we can be aware of every single wave, every single woman, and be fully present for her and everything she brings to it. What we're doing in the face of it all is generating compassion and being as present as we can be.

At the same time, we can cultivate wisdom, recognizing the larger picture of all women, all beings, so much tragedy. Yet, even as it all arises, it's like a dream, a mirage, a movie, a phantom hallucination that arises as the play of impermanence—a constant, unceasing expression of the suffering of beings. To see it in this way doesn't deny the experience from the point of view of everyone in it. However, from the point of view of our mind, we have more breadth of perspective to draw on, which helps us to contextualize and bear it with compassion. We experience, deeply, that when we and all beings don't know our nature, don't have the tools to produce the happiness we want and avoid the suffering we don't want, this is what happens.

Our life is all about helping those very beings—helping them to survive, helping them to find a way through. You're demonstrating your presence to their pain in the context of compassion and love that's nonjudgmental and unconditional. You're simply receiving them and their suffering and offering a safe harbor. Right now, that's what your life is—and how extraordinary is that! To have a life dedicated to beings in that way. How fortunate you are to be living this life.

As you keep in mind that larger picture, your motivation remains steady: that, through your efforts with all these women or this effort with this woman on this day or as a result of this suicide, may no one want to take their lives ever again; may every being find their way through; may every being find safe harbor. By maintaining your unrelenting compassion within this larger perspective, you'll develop, over time, more and more confidence in the power of your wisdom and compassion, and that will sustain you. It's not magic. It doesn't happen overnight, but it *will* happen over time.

For those women, those beings, in this time, in this place, there's something for them, thanks to what you're doing. And always remember to dedicate to all those who don't have a refuge. You're not doing any of this out of pride or attachment but from a sense of gratitude and rejoicing that you have this opportunity to offer something in the midst of the ocean of suffering—a safe place, some solid ground. Constantly dedicate that all beings may have safety, comfort, shelter, nourishment, and rest when they're weary. Formal practice will really help, so do that as much as you can.

18 The Rate of Change

In this meditation, instead of using your conceptual mind to think *about* impermanence, simply pay attention and be open, through all your senses, to the rate and process of change taking place in every moment around you.

If you find yourself lost in thoughts or emotions related to the past or future, remind yourself that those thoughts themselves are examples of impermanence. You were aware of changes taking place within and around you, and then you lost that awareness. You reestablished it by bringing yourself back to the present moment.

Continue to observe directly that whatever happens doesn't last long—each and every moment is fleeting and can't be grasped. Repeat this meditation as often as possible and in different settings throughout the day.

CHAPTER 7. CREATING A
NEW SCREENPLAY

When we're captured by the images in the movie of our life—when we have hope for what we want and fear of what we don't want, mind's poisons—our negative emotions—seem very real. We experience ourselves watching the movie as separate from what's being watched. This duality—our basic ignorance—is the source of all the drama that is our lives.

Mind's poisons come from the tension between the mind that's watching and what's being watched. We like, want, and try to grasp at and hold on to what we're seeing, or try to reject what we don't like and don't want. But, ultimately, our negative emotions are nothing other than mind's radiance passing through film. Our actions based in attachment and aversion arise from this fundamental ignorance and create consequences—karma. We then develop habitual responses to the things we like and the things we don't.

Self-centered emotions, karma, and habits (both coarse and subtle) all arise from the mind that doesn't know its nature. Our coarse habits are like the ruts we dig when our vehicle is stuck in the mud or snow and we hit the accelerator, digging ourselves in deeper the harder and faster we try to escape. Our subtle habits are related to our belief that the movie is real. These are the four obscurations that prevent us from waking up to our true nature.

Any methods that purify karma and habits and transform negative emotions bring us closer to recognizing reality as it is—a pervasive state of limitless purity. If we were to examine what appears as white light emanating from the projector, we'd find all the colors of the rainbow—the radiance of infinite positive qualities arising as the display of our true nature. None of it can be captured, yet all is appearing as the moving pictures of our life.

Those four layers of obscuration create the filter through which we experience reality. We're bound by that misunderstanding and so relate to appearances as if they're real and even permanent. If what we perceive is something we don't want, we fear it will happen or will never subside. If it's something we're attached to, we hope it will never go away. We develop a huge emotional response to the projections of our habits and karma.

Because we're unaware of our true nature, we identify ourselves and each other with what's obscuring that luminous essence of being instead of the essence itself. We have attitudes about ourselves or others and, based on those judgments, we develop attachment or aversion to everything and everyone we encounter. We want the things we want because we believe, deeply, that if we can attain and hold on to those things, we'll have permanent, unceasing happiness.

This is something all living beings share. If we all had the same values, we'd all agree about what the source of happiness is, and we'd all want the same thing. Everyone would be harmonious and collaborative. Instead, we all have different ideas of what will produce the greatest happiness. Conflict arises because we want different things, but, ultimately, we're all bound by the confusion of believing our movies are real.

All the images in our film are composite, impermanent, unfree, and completely unreliable. It's confusion to let our projections convince us there's some kind of essential truth to these appearances. We're just watching our own movie. In the context of the movie, by generating and practicing "relative bodhicitta"—our commitment to the awakening of all beings from the cycles of suffering—our projections become increasingly positive.

As we develop ultimate or "absolute bodhicitta"—the wisdom that recognizes reality is ultimately like light through film—we'll no longer be bound by our projections. We gain confidence in the capacity for transformation, because we know, from our own experience, that the power of wisdom—inseparable from love and compassion—is greater than the power of our projections. Like the radiance of the sun, which shines everywhere equally, ceaseless benefit for all beings arises naturally from ultimate bodhicitta, the effortless expression of our natural state.

We Created Our Movie, So We Can Change It

If we want to change the images in our movie, we must start with our screenplay. To do that, we need to transform harmful emotional reactions to ones that are virtuous, kind, and will produce more beneficial outcomes. What will create the greatest benefit is to realize that our story is not ultimately true—nothing more than light through film. To the extent that we purify our misperception of reality, we recognize our illusory poisons for what they are and are empowered to more swiftly and deeply transform and uproot them.

This starts out as a conceptual process, but, as we practice more, our fixation begins to relax. Our practice of bodhicitta helps us to loosen that grasping so that, even as appearances unfold, our responses become more spacious. We can recognize them as reflections of our past actions and take responsibility instead of wanting everybody and everything else to change. We realize our past responses have been like trying to run up to the screen in the movie theater, wipe away the scenes we don't like, and paste new images on top. Through our practice, we realize we need to change the basis of our projections—our own mind.

Without the light of the projector, there would be no movie. So, to think those projections are more powerful than the light that's sustaining them is confusion. Every moment we give power to our projections rather than immersing in one or more of our positive qualities, we undermine our ability to benefit others. We can't ever forget that.

As we practice, we become more aware, even as the projections unfold, that they're none other than images resulting from causes set in motion through our past actions. Here they are, all coming to fruition. Realizing this, we can take responsibility instead of blaming others. We're the filmmaker, the producer, the director, and, of course, always the hero. But we're the villain as well, because it's our movie. We created the film, and we wrote the screenplay, so we can change it.

We change the script through formal and informal meditation practice. Slowly, over time, the power of our awareness of the deeper nature of our experience begins to penetrate our belief in the projections so we can make different choices. We're more informed, and, therefore, more empowered.

We start out by reminding ourself that these are our projections, our karma playing out, and that we need to apply the methods we're learning to produce change. Over time, this process becomes less conceptual. Instead of getting lost in our attachments and aversions and then reminding ourselves to antidote those negative emotions, our practice becomes more intuitive, spontaneous, and natural. We come to recognize our projections for what they are as they arise, take responsibility for them, and spontaneously apply whichever practice we've learned is most effective for creating transformation in any given moment.

"Bypassing" Doesn't Create Change

As we practice, we also realize that we have emotional reactions to our own mind. Whether we're the hero, the villain, both, or we're wearing multiple outfits as we watch the habits of our mind unfold, we may become depressed, discouraged, fearful, angry or even proud. Although this usually doesn't feel good in the moment, it means we're starting to take responsibility for what's there. Not only do we start to recognize the presence of these emotions, we also start to see whatever conscious or unconscious strategies we've developed to try to avoid difficult emotions or to numb our pain. Once we're no longer involved in all the ways we've been bypassing our emotions, we start to see what's really there.

Whether it's our own story or that of others that we're working with, we can learn how to apply spiritual tools rather than worldly ones to uproot the causes of suffering for ourselves and others, rather than perpetuating more of the same. With bodhicitta as our motivation, we can produce limitless benefit for ourselves and others rather than limitless suffering. Understanding the problem means we can address and transform these habits rather than using our spiritual practice like we've used worldly means—such as addiction to substances, relationships, work, busyness, or entertainment, for example—to try to bypass, avoid, or "process" difficult feelings. In doing so, we've been suppressing what was happening in our mind instead of penetrating and transforming it. We might have become frozen and numb or developed addictive habits to chase after things we hoped would make us feel better. Of course, whatever made us feel better didn't last, so we wanted more.

If we're seeing fear, for example, this insight, in itself, empowers us to transform it. If we're not aware the fear is there, we'll continue plunging forward with our lives and reacting to all our experiences without even touching on what's driving those responses. By looking at our mind, we realize we can change our behavior, because we're starting to understand what's going on under the surface, and we can apply the appropriate methods to produce the change we want. If we don't realize what's underneath, our practice remains conceptual—we're not connecting with what's actually going on in our heart and mind. That connection is necessary to create a new imprint on the film. If we want to change that imprint, we must join our practice with our current experience of reality.

It's by joining the two that transformation happens deeply, immediately, and powerfully.

Whatever is arising in the mind, we bring practice to that. If we don't, we continue to believe our projections and emotional states are permanent, solid, and real. Every time we respond to them as if that's the case, we, as the screenwriter, write the next scene based on that belief. There's no change, there's just reaction. That reaction might seem rebellious or outside our normal behavior, but we're still operating within the thread of the storyline as it's projecting. We believe it's true, and we write the next scene based on that same storyline. We're not addressing the underlying ignorance at all.

The whole point of our meditation practice is to awaken from that ignorance and change the script so that what arises isn't just the next predictable frame of the film but an entirely different movie, and, ultimately, the unfiltered radiance of pure being. The beliefs we've formed based on our projections are strongly imprinted by our psychology, our politics, our intellect, or any number of other influences. Of course, this has been all we knew, so how could we have done anything differently? Over time, and with practice, we become less and less gripped by our projections and the way the ordinary mind has tried to process, manage, and control our experience.

However, our habits are so strong that even when we start to practice and stuff comes up, our tendency is to use those habits to interpret it. If we indulge old psychological reactions to what's arising in our mind, we just perpetuate more proud, competitive, obsessive, self-hating, reactive, or other patterns that have dictated our past experience, as well as our past methods for trying to avoid those difficult feelings such as bypassing, armoring, freezing, fleeing, or resisting. We're experiencing our mind and process through our self-referencing lens rather than through bodhicitta.

To ensure profound transformation, we have to let go of those old modalities and turn our mind, steadily and repeatedly, toward reliance on bodhicitta.

Doug: I can see the presence of anger in my mind, and there are degrees of it—from subtle to not so subtle. The same happens with attachment. How can we recognize ignorance when it's the prevalent thing going on in our own mind? What are the characteristics of ignorance?

Lama: We can think of ignorance as confusion, a lack of awareness, no sense of orientation to what makes sense. In some ways, it's easier to identify in relation to moments of clarity, wisdom, or insight. Then we see, "I was so confused. I didn't get it." Because it's a kind of mental dullness, it's hard to realize that there's no recognition.

Doug: How can we transform the mental dullness we experience as confusion and distraction? The only thing I know to do is to pray, because, if the confusion and distraction are intense enough, I can't make my mind do anything.

Lama: Wisdom is the antidote to ignorance. We can use a method that leads to wisdom, such as impermanence meditation or prayer, and then rest the mind in its empty resonance. If our impermanence meditation becomes more subtle, we can allow ourselves to be open and aware of the rate of change and then let go, relax contrivance and fixation, and alternate between the two. In doing so, we loosen our fixation on the things we're attached and averse to, so the future scenes in our screenplay are less troubled, and the light of wisdom can further penetrate our experience.

Anthony: I'm wondering if anger can be figured out by working backward from the other poisons of the mind. If we get angry, can we look back on how we were feeling before we got angry? Were we in a state of ignorance and absence of bodhicitta?

Lama: That could be one way. Ultimately, the poisons of the mind come from basic ignorance of our true nature—duality—out of which arises the tension between the experience of self and other. You could think of it that way, and examine it that way.

Hillary: I've been stuffing my emotions since a recent accident. I had a lot of terrible grief the first few days afterwards, and then I got into managing my life alternating with bouts of sobbing. I don't know what to do when that grief comes up. I don't want to indulge it, but I don't want to stuff it.

Lama: It's important to have the grief. Whatever the emotion is, feel it. Don't try to stuff or bypass it. Just try, as much as you can, to include the grief of all beings within your own, so your heartache becomes part of this ocean of sorrow. Your grief becomes inseparable from your compassion and love. When something is uncorked in you, always bring others' pain to it. If you're feeling anger, bring others' anger to it, so you have the sense of all of us together in this ocean of suffering.

That will purify the causes and results of how you've dealt with your emotions in the past. Let yourself genuinely have the feeling, and bring to mind the experience of others having the same emotion. Wish that, through your grief, the grief of all beings be purified and no one else ever has to experience it. Don't abandon your heartbreak, and don't abandon others. They're joined in your mind and heart through your compassion.

Hillary: I'm not sure I understand how to avoid bypassing our emotions and what to do instead. It's about allowing the feelings to arise, and then what?

Lama: Basically, when an emotion arises, we don't ignore it and do something outwardly to compensate or avoid it as if it's not really there. If we do, the actual poison of the mind hasn't been penetrated and transformed. Once we let ourselves experience the emotion, we use practice to transform it.

Hillary: I think I do that—ignore what I'm feeling. Sometimes, I don't let myself go there, while at other times, I almost think I'm recognizing it's actually light through film—but I might be bypassing. How do I know?

Lama: If you're not admitting to yourself that you're having that emotion and/or you're bringing the *idea* of light through film to it, you're bypassing it. Instead of letting yourself have the emotion, you're bypassing it using a spiritual idea. That spiritual idea isn't a spiritual practice that can penetrate, transform, and purify the emotion. Instead, it avoids it, the emotion doesn't change, and your practice doesn't deepen. On the surface, you seem okay, and can keep going, which is better than making non-virtue. But we want to uproot, purify, and transform all those poisons so we can realize mind's nature and actualize our intrinsic positive qualities.

Hillary: Sometimes, I want to push away what I'm experiencing, and that can also make it easier to think of others.

Lama: The purpose is to bring others into it—not try to avoid our current experience. We're not rejecting our experience, and we aren't attached to changing it but, out of love and compassion, we want to include everybody else.

Ideally, we don't just flip through our meditations so quickly that they remain superficial or conceptual and don't produce change. At the same time, we're not so fixated on creating change that our attachment gets in the way. We take enough time with our meditation to create a different imprint. The next scene is a little different than it would have been without that new imprint. We don't want to skim through the meditations so fast that there's no imprinting.

19 Transforming Fear

Start with pure motivation and then look at the presence of fear in your mind. Does fear underlie whatever other emotion you may be aware of? Whether you're feeling upset, angry, prideful, or any other strong emotion, ask yourself if fear is present as well. Is there fear in your response to an onslaught of things to deal with? Is there fear under pride or other compensating emotions?

If you're able to see fear, examine its presence in your mind. If you're not feeling fear right now, evoke a time when you were. Before exposure to bodhicitta practice, how did you respond to your fear? What were the mechanisms you used to deal with it? Did you become aggressive, withdrawn, shut down, or try to avoid it through busyness?

Then ask yourself if whatever you did in response to your fear was effective in overcoming it. Did it purify or transform it? Did it allow you to create benefit? Did it give you more confidence? Has it worked for you as an ongoing strategy?

Next, as you let yourself be aware of the presence of terror or dread in your own mind, become equally aware of its presence in the minds of others. Think of others you know who share your fears, and make the wish that their fear be evaporated by your own, so they never again have to experience it. Wish, as well, that their suffering be contained within your own, so they never again have to experience it themselves. Then let your mind rest.

Next, think of others who share similar anxieties— those you know as well as those you've only heard of or can imagine. Again, make the wish that their anxiety be contained within your own, so they never again have to experience it, and then let your mind rest.

Allow yourself to be aware of the presence of fear in your personal life, in your community, and in the world. With the intention to free all beings from fear, make the aspiration that the suffering of all beings be contained within your own, and that, by your own experience of fear, no one else ever need experience it. Then rest the mind.

Keep expanding the scope of your meditation— including more and more beings who are afraid due to different and varying circumstances—until eventually you're including all beings, because no one has ever known a life without fear. Then rest the mind for as long as it's genuinely restful. When thoughts or emotions stir once again, think of everyone else dealing with similar habits, and then again rest the mind. At the end of your practice session, dedicate the merit.

This meditation can be repeated with whatever other emotion is present in your mind.

Creating a Channel for Our Emotions

Whichever meditation method we use changes our screenplay and our projections. We're no longer creating an endless, rollercoaster, Hollywood film-type drama. There's a qualitative difference in our movie that's the reflection of what's ultimately true instead of the reflection of our not knowing what's ultimately true. That difference in quality is like night and day.

As we start looking at our mind during practice, we can become distraught when we see the contrast between our values and what's actually happening in the moment—the tumult of our emotions, ideas, and old behavioral patterns that have served as our coping mechanisms for so long and which we feel we have no control over. But that's actually a good sign and considered to be the first stage of meditation.

There's a metaphor that's used to describe how our mind appears when we first look at it—like water cascading over a steep cliff. Our thoughts and emotions are non-stop. There's no rest, and no basis for rest. There's no awareness. Of course, this has always been the case, but we didn't realize it until now. When we meditate, we begin to see the extent to which we've been lost in and reacting to our projections.

Realizing this is a big step forward. It means our practice is working. It means we're starting to meditate and, slowly, the methods we're using are capturing and redirecting the current through a canyon. The walls of that canyon are the container of our practice. The water is still flowing rapidly, but it's no longer a chaotic tumult. It's contained within our commitment to bodhicitta: not to harm, to create as much benefit as possible, and to transform our minds to make that possible.

This is the second stage of meditation, and it becomes our lived experience as we learn to bring that practice to our daily life. That's what the methods we're working with are intended for— to harness and subdue that tumult and direct it in a virtuous way. We're constructing a framework that can support the redirection of mind's energy, a vast river of our everythingness flowing in a virtuous direction that eventually leads to a depth of still water.

Creating this framework starts with the intellectual understanding that our true nature is pure. We realize the way to reveal that is to practice what we believe to be true even though, at the beginning, it may not be our direct experience. We're drawn to practice because we value mind's positive qualities. We start to practice with equanimity, for example, even though, at first, it may seem contrived and not at all like our present state of mind, because our current experience is this cascade of thoughts and emotions.

At the same time, we're creating a container to hold and direct the energy of that tumult away from non-virtue and toward virtue through effortful practice. And it *is* effortful. It's like we're *trying* to be compassionate equally to all beings, and we're *trying* to be loving equally to all beings, so it may feel insincere. But we make this effort because we have confidence that the container we're constructing will channel the tumult in a direction that will be of greater benefit to ourselves and others. So, we're motivated to use effort to construct that container for our mind's activity.

Slowly, we start to realize that, even though the flow of our mind's habits is so powerful, our awareness of what's going on is increasingly in charge and able to create change—a different direction of the flow, a different imprint on the film. We're starting to gain control—not total control yet, but the idea that we can choose what to do with our minds instead of remaining powerless in an endless cycle of reactivity.

Just having that idea means we realize there's something else that's true besides our present emotions. We know there's a larger context we can bring to our experience, and that larger context is our practice. It's the power of awareness—the awareness of the screenwriter to rewrite the script. This is evidence of a huge change. Instead of feeling lost in the display of our inner and outer phenomena—even though we may not like what we see—we understand that these emotions are the basis for change. If we aren't seeing what's there, we can't apply methods to redirect it.

When we first attempt this, we might feel like we're being carried away by the current, and we identify with that current. We feel out of control and helpless against the power of our emotions, as if possessed by them, turned upside down and inside out by the rapids. Our emotions appear so true, so valid, and so righteous that we act on them. And, of course, we feel justified to harm or impose our way on others according to the dictates of our emotions.

As we start to create this container of practice, we're reminded there's something else that's true about us, there's another possibility other than identifying with the eddies and undercurrents that capture us and make us feel we can't catch a breath. We start to realize the picture is larger within the container of our awareness. That, in itself, is a different experience. Our honesty with ourselves about what's there and our growing confidence in the power of practice to transform our experience gives us the strength to keep going. We realize we have the power of pure motivation, awareness, will, and diligence that we can bring to bear to redirect and transform the tumult in our mind. Eventually, the channel begins to expand, and the flow of water slows and starts to calm down.

Tonya: With what's going on in my life right now, I don't have the ability to practice anything that resembles bodhicitta, because my emotions are so intense. So, I tell myself to be patient and gentle and do what I can to make merit. Is that a good starting place? Can I trust that the process will keep unfolding?

Lama: It's a great place to begin. In general, as we learn different practices for giving rise to bodhicitta, we notice that different methods are more or less effective in different situations. Have you tried different methods that you've learned?

Tonya: I've tried various contemplations, but the result, so far, is that I shut down. It's too much thinking.

Lama: Your instincts are right on target. You're remembering that, in a situation where there's so much suffering, there's an absence of merit. Therefore, one thing you can always do is create merit. Even if it feels contrived, you have that basic understanding. If that's all you can do, that's already so much. It's okay that you aren't able to be more present with your emotions. That will change over time with practice.

Tonya: I hope that, as I accumulate more merit, the next steps will become obvious. I also wonder if I could be doing more to help those I'm worried about that are struggling.

Lama: Sometimes, the situation is so intense, so entrenched, that there's not a lot you can do until you've gathered and dedicated more merit. What you're doing now is confounding your old habits of how to help. You're recognizing the longer-term causes and conditions of benefit and not just the immediate ones, so you're also purifying your old habit of always trying to fix things, accepting that there are some situations that, outwardly, in the moment, you can't fix, even though you can always create and dedicate merit.

Don't scare yourself because your feel your mind is blown, and you can't use any of the methods that involve more awareness. Sometimes, it's just like that. You now have a new habit to make merit and know what to do even when your mind is blown—and you're doing it.

Reining in Our Emotions
through Alternating Meditation

Our present experience is of being habituated to the screenplay, to mind in motion. It's what we've believed to be reality and of greatest importance. The deeper nature of mind in motion—the basis of all the causes and conditions that have come together to create our drama—is mind at rest—vast, spacious, and luminous like the radiance of light from the projector.

We've started with effortful practices that work with mind in motion to harness and transform the direction of that motion into something that's increasingly beneficial for ourselves and others. At the same time, if we neglect to pay attention to mind at rest, it will be harder to recognize the deeper nature of that motion—a profound state of peace. So, we also need to develop a relationship with mind at rest and notice the presence of the restful mind, even if, at first, it's just a millisecond of restfulness.

A powerful way to examine and transform our relationship to our emotions is to alternate between transforming our experience of the emotion itself and resting the mind in the ultimate nature of that emotion. We apply an effortful meditation to transform the emotional experience and then let go of the effort and insight, and simply let the mind rest.

Rinpoche used to explain that because our minds are so busy, when we start trying to rest the mind, it keeps on being busy. Instead of trying to squelch the busyness, we transform negative, non-virtuous busyness into positive, virtuous busyness. Ultimately, we need to purify the habit to busyness itself, and we can establish the basis for that through this alternating meditation.

In the moment when we first let go, the mind has the possibility to be fresh and open. By alternating back and forth between effort and rest, we can begin to lessen the attachment to our experience being "a thing," meditation a thing, light through film a thing. We're slowly building the basis for non-dual awareness that's not stained or compromised by attachment.

20 Alternating the Investigation of Emotions with Rest

When your mind is filled with constant, self-perpetuated thought and emotion, examine your current emotional experience and ask yourself:

Am I angry and trying to find ways to justify my anger? Explore, then let the mind rest.

Am I scared of something, trying to create protection and figure out how to be free of suffering in the future? Examine, and then rest the mind.

Am I attached to an object of desire and trying to figure out how to get it and hold on to it? Investigate, then rest.

Alternate exploring your emotional state and then letting go of the effort to understand, and let the mind rest.

To do this meditation effectively, we must be honest with ourselves about our emotional experience and then apply a method, a container, within which it can be transformed. We alternate that effortful practice with resting in a space that allows us, over time, to experience the ultimate nature of that emotion. When the mind gets too busy to remain restful, we move back to the effort of transforming that imagery through another method and then, again, alternate that with the state of rest.

For example, if we're struggling with physical or emotional pain, we begin by letting ourselves be aware of our aversion to the pain, and then let the mind rest. Then we think of all others experiencing similar or greater pain, generate the wish that, through our pain, they no longer have to experience such misery and that they find not just relief from suffering but happiness and contentment. Then we let the mind rest.

As we go back and forth between examination and rest, we realize that, even within all that motion, there's a luminosity that lacks substantiality—what we might describe as empty luminosity, a pervasive state of utter peace. Within emotion itself, there's mind at rest. That mind at rest isn't ultimately separate from mind in motion, because the restful, peaceful aspect of mind isn't separate from mind's expression. Within that state of peace, there's constant display, and the density of the film being projected over it determines the quality of that experience. We use meditation to change the projection and alternate that with rest.

We need to work skillfully with mind's habit to motion—for example, when we ask ourselves, "Is this rest? Is there an image in this rest? What do I do if there's no image? Where do I put my mind?"—because, if we ask the mind to rest when it's so habituated to motion, the result will only be contrivance, suppression, and disturbance—in which case, we aren't receiving the benefits of a restful mind. Instead, we want to develop a relationship with mind at rest that's ever-present in the motion yet normally not experienced as such because of our orientation to the motion itself. By its nature, mind is awakened and luminous, like the light arising from a projector without the projection of storyline and drama.

The more we practice this alternating meditation, the more the state of rest remains genuinely restful for longer periods. We aren't trying to suppress thoughts or mind's motion. Mind, by its nature, is dynamic. If we suppress all of mind's dynamic qualities, there would be no basis for the arising of compassion or loving kindness or any of mind's positive qualities. All of that is the display of mind at rest. We're not trying to squelch it; we're trying to realize it. Within all the motion, mind's radiance is constantly giving rise to the ceaseless display of appearances that we call life.

Through our practice, we start to develop a capacity to recognize that, even as we watch the movie, it's light through film. No matter how dramatic or sorrowful or joyful, it's just light through film. We can then bring this insight to everything that happens, so we're less torn and tormented by the ups and downs of life. We start to develop some stability, a presence of wisdom awareness in the midst of all that's going on, which can then penetrate our experience so we can be more beneficial.

In doing so, our capacity to sustain meditative awareness grows. It's like exercising any muscle. Many of us have never gained any control over or insight about our minds, because we haven't tried. This is why we begin by meditating for only short periods of time—without any expectation we should be able to sustain it for longer. Alternating meditation works well for this.

As we practice this way, our meditative experience unfolds within a container of awareness and vigilance about what's happening in our mind. This is a new muscle we're developing, so we can't expect a depth of intimacy with it right away. But, as we become more adept at meditation and join our ordinary mind with these various meditations, the mind's motion slows. Over time, that rushing water emerging from the cascade of emotion and mental activity moves through a canyon of awareness to become the undisturbed, calm surface of a lake.

This process doesn't mean indulging or suppressing mind's energy and the habit of thinking. That's the expression of the motion of the ordinary mind—the constant, self-perpetuated thought process arising from self. Our involvement with the scenes unfolding in our life gives rise to emotions, and our habit is to try to make sense of our experience so we can negotiate it, navigate through it, try to control it, or not feel so terrified by it. Maybe we create barriers to protect us from the pain, fear, suffering, or the idea that more suffering will come, because that's what's happened in the past. Whatever the reason, if we can recognize our habit to do that, we won't feed it.

We realize we've been watching our own movie unfold and have developed a fascination—or even an obsession—with it. If, instead, we can remember it's light through film, we can ask ourselves, "What can I do to make the movie better, create scenes that are more beneficial for myself and others?" In that way, we're reining in that wild horse of the mind. We're not just letting it run wild and giving it total power over our life. Instead, we're determined to bring our mind back to bodhicitta.

Until we've subdued, purified, and transformed enough of our obscurations, we're not able to genuinely rest in the recognition of the empty luminosity of mind itself, in which thought and emotion could simply unwind and be free. So, we rely on bodhicitta, which, by its nature, will transform and purify those self-centered, negative emotions that temporarily overshadow our mind.

Carolyn: When I rest my mind, I arrive at a point that's similar to calm-abiding meditation. Is that okay, or am I doing something wrong?

Lama: It depends on what your experience of calm-abiding practice is. In recent years, many Westerners have been exposed to "calm-abiding" or "mindfulness" meditation to still or calm the mind, which is introduced many different ways, often outside the context of Buddhist or bodhicitta practice.

As we cultivate bodhicitta, we try to be careful not to accumulate even the most subtle habits of attachment. If there's some aspect, however faint, of trying to arrive at or maintain an experience, it's better to alternate, to redirect effort to the next contemplation, and then let it go. We use meditation to purify our attachment, aversion, and ignorance. To bring attachment, aversion, and ignorance into the meditation itself defeats the purpose.

Be as aware as you can be of what's going on in your mind. When the subtle energies start to calm down, everything can feel blissful or serene. It can feel so good that we slip into a subtle attachment to that state. If that happens, be sure to cut that attachment by bringing your mind back to the next contemplation. If and when your mind again becomes lost or out of control, let go of the effort, and rest the mind.

Carolyn: But we can enjoy the bliss while it's happening, right?

Lama: Yes, but share it and radiate it out to all beings, so it's not just your bliss but everyone's bliss. Doing this will help you not get attached to it, and your love and compassion will help to purify any attachment that might arise.

21 Alternating Exploring the Nature of Emotions with Rest

Identify the emotion uppermost in your mind without getting lost in the story in which it appears. Ask yourself questions such as, "What's the emotion? Is it real? Is it a thing I can find somewhere?"

If you can't find it, let go of the effort, and rest the mind. The intellectual effort to find becomes an experience of not finding, and, in that not finding, something begins to clarify: ultimately, there's nothing there, despite the vividness and intensity with which it appears.

Your mind may then become stirred up. "Am 'I' in the not finding? Am I finding something—a vibration, energy, or color—and is that the emotion? Is it inside the mind or outside?"

In this process, examine and analyze the emotion. Use effort to see if it has a color, a shape, or a size—because we're habituated to *things* having features. After spending some time trying to find it, let go of the effort, and let it sink in that you can't find this thing that's causing such pain and disturbance in your mind, your life, and, on a larger scale, all the disharmony in the world.

Each time you search for the emotion and don't find it, your heart can open a little more to an experience of more space, more compassion. Rest in that openness—love, compassion, the genuine wish for the welfare of others. Let that sink in without effort or thought, and rest in that awareness. When the mind starts churning again, think of everyone else struggling with similar emotions who don't know what to do with them. Again, rest the mind, and then use effort to change the emotion. Keep going back and forth between effort and rest for the duration of the meditation session.

Hillary: I had the experience of not being able to find where the negative emotion is, but suddenly I thought, "Wait a minute, I can't find where the compassion resides, either; and I can't find where the generosity, resides; and I can't find where the love resides." Aren't all of those things also dependent upon composite causes and conditions coming together? I'm confused.

Lama: Yes. Our *experience* of the positive emotions is subject to causes and conditions. But, ultimately, there's no such thing as positive qualities of mind or wisdom. Ultimately, there's no such thing as poisons of the mind. Yet, within relative appearances, there's this display. Insofar as we're able to recognize the deeper nature of our experience, the display becomes increasingly pure and positive, imbued with positive qualities and of benefit to beings.

That doesn't happen if we empower our negativity. All that happens is more negativity. The objects of our anger and aversion, of our desire and attachment, all become more real, and we become more oppressed by the weight of this seeming solidity instead of becoming free. The process is one of opening and increasingly realizing the nature of our experience, which empowers us in relation to the needs of others.

Hillary: Often during guided meditations, when we move the mind through several steps, I don't find a commitment arising from my compassion. I start worrying about whether I can uphold the commitment and censor it before I even make it.

Lama: In guiding us through those steps, Rinpoche created a structure within which we can cultivate what happens naturally in moments of compassion. If it's an obstacle for you to make a commitment, don't worry about it. As you develop more love and compassion, a sense of commitment will arise naturally as the expression of your care for beings.

Hillary: I'm asking the question because, when my practice is strong, I naturally feel a commitment. That's why I'm upset when it doesn't happen.

Lama: When you sincerely generate a deep love and compassion, there's less and less of a sense of a "you" doing it. There's just love and compassion. Don't worry and be so self-conscious about it, because that just pulls you out of the meditation. You're not holding yourself back by staying with love and compassion. They're the essence of the practice. Be love, be compassion, and let that be your practice on that day. Then dedicate hugely.

22 Alternating Meditation with Prayer to Transform Our Emotions

We can also use a more extensive alternating meditation to work with our emotions. To do that, we begin with contemplation. For example, we might begin by reflecting on our aversion to and judgment of the actions of someone who's harming the environment. We might remind ourselves of the teachings and meditations we've learned about karma. We could reflect on the fact that they're only going to suffer in the long run from what they're doing, and so we might choose to intervene in order to protect them from the consequences of their actions. We might consider how we could balance the short- and long-term benefit of that person with the short- and long-term benefit of all those they're harming.

Having reviewed or contemplated the teachings we've been exposed to in relation to this person and why we want their welfare, we let go of the effort to contemplate. Without effort, we let our conceptual understanding sink in for as long as it feels like it's making an impact on our mind.

Then, we go to the next effortful practice. We generate compassion for everyone who finds it difficult, in the midst of adversity, to genuinely want the welfare of others—those we perceive as enemies as well as those we perceive as compatible wayfarers on our life's path. We generate compassion, and then we let that effort go, allowing the compassion sink in.

We make a commitment to whatever arises from our compassion—for example, to strengthen our love and compassion, to grow and stabilize our capacity so that, no matter what we encounter, we're able to continue to be a force for benefit. Whatever that commitment looks like for us—to our formal practice, to our informal practice, to a certain kind of activity—we make that commitment and let it sink in as we let go of the effort.

Then, we pray. Through prayer, we open the door to the infinite positive qualities that are facets of our true nature. Perhaps we can't conceive of such positive qualities in ourselves, but we can conceive of them, or we've experienced them, as embodied outside of ourselves in a particular object of faith or refuge. We may experience ourselves as separate from the pure embodiment of positive qualities, but, through the process of prayer, that apparent separation relaxes, creating the possibility of a recognition less bound by duality. Our mind and heart open, and we rest in that openness. We access deeper wisdom, opening our awareness to those qualities, so they can be awakened and actualized for the sake of all beings.

In between each of these effortful practices, we rest the mind, letting go of fixation on whatever we do or don't want to happen. When we let go of the effort, we also let go of the habit to that fixation, the habit to solidify attachment and aversion to a particular outcome. We let what is, be.

Depending on our experience of our objects of faith, prayer can start out dualistically but lead to non-dual wisdom. If we experience ourselves as confused, powerless and incapable, not knowing what to do or where to turn, we pray to limitless wisdom, loving kindness, compassion, and capacity to benefit—however we may or may not conceive of them—that such capacity can be awakened in ourselves and all beings. Prayer can open the door to that capacity. Our mind's poisons dissolve within the warmth of the positive qualities embodied in our objects of faith.

As we begin to actualize that wisdom, mind's poisons can be seen through, and, ultimately, released without making new imprints. When we recognize that all thought, emotion, and mental events are none other than light through film, we don't become lost in the dramatic scenes of our movie. We can begin to exercise free, beneficial choices that aren't bound by old patterns.

We always want to pray for what's best for all beings, not just for ourselves and those close to us. To illustrate this point, Rinpoche used to tell the story of a Tibetan woman who was flying overseas and had a layover someplace where she didn't speak the language. She didn't understand the announcement that her flight was boarding, and she missed it. We might think this was unfortunate news, but the flight she missed later crashed. Her life was saved because she missed her flight.

We aren't omniscient. We can't see what's best in every situation—although we often think we can! However, we can always do our best to keep a pure heart, so we pray for whatever is best for whoever we're praying for. We pray that whatever is best for all beings comes to pass with the understanding that we don't have the wisdom to know what that is. In this way, we cultivate a depth of humility. When we pray, we pray not just for this being or this situation but for all beings and not just for their temporary happiness but for their ultimate happiness.

Returning to the example of the person harming the environment, we're praying for what's best for them, and all beings, in the short and long term, and dedicating merit that the causes and conditions of that benefit may ripen swiftly. We can't see, we can't know, what that would look like, so we pray with tremendous humility. Suspending our certainty that we know what's best antidotes our pride and attachment.

Breanna: As I pray, I find myself uncomfortably close to a situation in which I'm praying for a specific outcome. This is a habit of many years. How can I reframe that so it's genuinely purely motivated and not the old, grasping, self-centered sense of prayer—I want something, I'm asking for help to get it, I'm going to be good so I get it, and so forth?

Lama: When you come from a strong tradition of prayer within a dualistic framework, it's unrealistic to expect yourself not to continue in that framework initially. However, if we're praying from a framework of bodhicitta, we're joining our faith with our bodhicitta. We can think of our faith as a gold ring that joins the hook of the compassion of the enlightened beings we're praying to and who we're still conceiving of as separate and outside ourselves. That duality resolves within bodhicitta as the ring of our faith meets the hook of their compassion. In that transmission, the duality can dissolve, eroding the basis for mind's poisons to arise.

Our motivation determines much of the interdependence of the prayer. If our motivation is for what's truly best—without a concept of what that is and not just for one but for all living beings—that makes a huge difference in the outcome. The virtue that's created is limitless, and the amount of purification that happens is beyond concept, because we're bringing to it the limitless blessings of our objects of faith and the limitless expanse of our heart. The scope of our intention is limitless beings. We're bringing all these immeasurable components to it that have the power to interdependently create an immeasurable outcome.

Of course, there's still the force of old habit, emotions, and karma. If we're skillful about understanding what changes when we introduce spiritual practice into our circumstances, we can write a different screenplay. At first, the new scenes are mixed with the old storyline and the old characters, but we continue to introduce scenes into the screenplay that reflect the causes we've been creating on the path instead of old patterns from our past.

Our habit to duality is strong, so we begin by using that in our practice. Then, we rest the mind. We could pray that, by the blessings of our objects of faith, our compassion become non-dual, that we may realize the true nature of everything as pure, and recognize the sacred within apparent duality, thereby eradicating the source of mind's poisons. Even though our heart is reaching out from this initially dualistic framework, it's become wide open through our bodhicitta. Our heart has been opened through our effort. We then relax that effort, and what remains is vast spaciousness in which the resolution of duality can occur.

One of the things we always bump up against when we try to bring benefit is our lack of wisdom. We don't know what's best—what's best to do, what's best to pray for. Simply acknowledging we don't know what's best is a critical first step. When we have that humility, the power of our prayers, dedications, and actions isn't tainted as much by attachment, aversion, and pride. We're creating and dedicating virtue in a completely non-fixated way, with a receptive heart of wishing for true, unceasing benefit, whatever that may be. It's a heart of humility.

To rely on prayer to access a deeper wisdom, we can use a two-step process. We start with pure motivation—looking in the mirror of the mind, recognizing where our intention to benefit is being compromised by our stuff, and bringing practice to it to transform it. When our heart is more genuinely purely motivated, we take the second step, which is to pray for clarity and interdependence to make evident what's truly best. After taking these steps, the power of prayer is less compromised by our attachments and aversions. We're no longer interpreting the unfolding of interdependence through the lens of obscuration.

Anthony: It seems to me the process you're talking about when praying for interdependence and clarity requires a tremendous amount of faith to believe it can happen.

Lama*:* That faith grows like everything else—through experience. We can start with small things and, as we continue to see how our actions affect interdependence and produce different results, this gives us more confidence.

As we begin exploring our relationship with the sacred through prayer and open the door to our limitless positive qualities, our trust and faith in the process grows through practice. And, as with other aspects of our practice, this takes time. Our faith emerges through investigation, analysis, and our own experience. We check it out for ourselves. Does it work for us? In this way, our faith deepens over time, and this is why there's no replacement for practice and time in.

It doesn't mean there's something wrong with our prayer if lightning bolts don't fall from the sky, suddenly changing everything. Over time, through the power of our practice, our bodhicitta, and our prayer, the imagery in our movie will change. It's possible that the change we experience through prayer may be swift, especially on an inner level. Even if it isn't an outer change, if we pray in a sincere way, with bodhicitta as the basis, we can sometimes feel a shift in our heart.

For example, say we're so acutely aware of the limitations of our capacity to help another that it feels like our heart is shattering. We pray from that broken-hearted place that our ability to benefit increases. Even in the moment of our prayer, we may feel the most subtle shift in our heart. We go from feeling we can't bear our limitations to feeling we can, because we know what to do about it—practice. It's subtle, and it doesn't mean we're not praying well if we don't experience change in the moment. Over time, we can see the reflection of those inner shifts in our outer experience.

Doug: Honestly, I wouldn't even know how to begin to imagine putting that time into trying to develop faith in prayer. Throughout my life, I've heard people talk about prayer in a way that allows them to justify inaction and allows injustice to continue by saying, "I'll pray for them." I don't have faith in the existence of an almighty being or beings worthy of or responsive to my prayers.

Lama: Everything in our experience—everything we can see, hear, touch, or remember—arises due to interdependence. All phenomena that can be known through the five physical senses and the sixth sense of consciousness arise due to causes and conditions.

What we're doing through our practice—of which prayer is a component—is changing the causes and conditions. Instead of just relying on a material, dualistic perspective and material phenomena for making change, we're introducing causes that will produce different results.

Giving rise to bodhicitta and opening our hearts through faith creates an interdependence for us to be able to experience the sacred non-dualistically by praying and then resting the mind. Our prayers are informed by bodhicitta, which we join with the power of faith. Those together create an interdependence for an outcome that might not have happened if we didn't introduce bodhicitta and prayer.

Through prayer, we're cultivating a receptivity to the existence of limitless positive qualities that are embodied outwardly in great beings who, over lifetimes or even eons, have purified obscurations and gathered merit joined with dedication and aspiration prayers to be of benefit to limitless beings. Through prayer, we blend our intention and aspirations with theirs. It's as if the stream of our bodhicitta joins the great river of the enlightened intention, merit, and aspirations of all great beings throughout time and space.

CHAPTER 8. SUNLIGHT ON SHADOWS

The Dalai Lama said that the purpose of the spiritual path is to benefit others and to do the inner work that makes that possible. Even if we truly value the idea of working for the welfare of others as the purpose of our lives, we often worry that if we start to think of others as much as ourself, something bad will happen to us or, at the very least, we won't get what we want.

It takes a lot of courage to keep going while not having confidence in how to be of greatest benefit to others. It can be scary, because not only have we not yet realized our true nature, we have no idea how to make the needs of others equally important to us as our own. Had we known how to do this, we would have been doing it. We'd have known all along that this was how to create happiness for ourselves and others.

Although we can encounter that fear in the course of giving rise to bodhicitta, actually, the only thing more powerful than fear is bodhicitta itself and the positive qualities that are its foundation. For example, when we give rise to a depth of compassion, we have the experience of coming home to ourselves. This grounds us and gives us more confidence, because we know, especially in difficult situations, that it brings us closer to our true nature. So, we know it's reliable.

It's like the chicken and the egg. We want to make our practice of bodhicitta authentic, and we want to give rise to genuine good heart. For these reasons, we start practicing, which can expose hidden fears. We can get so scared that it's hard to recognize that the solution to that fear is bodhicitta itself.

When we rely on bodhicitta, we're relying on a deeper truth rather than the superficial habits and self-image we've developed over the years. All that psychology, all that behavior, those identities, defenses, and reactions were developed in the course of responding to things that arose due to causes and conditions, things that themselves weren't free. Good happened, and we were happy. We identified with it, and maybe we became proud. Bad happened, and we got scared or angry and developed the habit to shut down, put up a wall, or rebel.

Our identities were formed over time through our repeated responses to things that are composite, impermanent, and unfree, and we developed a sense of self that's also composite, impermanent, and unfree. Every single habit and emotion is composite and created by causes and conditions that produced that experience of reality and our reaction to it. None of it is solid. It's impermanent and can be changed by things outside of itself. It's not stable, free, or independent, and it's not our true nature. That's why what's obscuring our true nature is ultimately less powerful than our positive qualities.

To identify with and act from that identity places us in a position of weakness. We're always on shifting sand. If we try to act from that place to benefit others, we'll be operating out of what's undependable and unstable, because we haven't developed confidence in what's not composite or impermanent and is absolutely free—the pure essence of being, which is utterly reliable because it's utterly free. It can't be affected by anything. As we keep practicing and going deeper to try to find our true nature, we discover that, ultimately, there's no *thing* we can point to that's our true nature, even though the closer we get to its realization, the more we discover the limitlessness of our positive qualities.

When we alternate between immersion in methods that give rise to those qualities and letting go into a state of rest, we find there's nothing there. That not finding *is* finding. When we get to that place, we rest there. This helps us develop confidence in the meditative awareness that gives rise to the courage of the bodhisattva. Until we've stabilized awareness of our true nature, confidence is built whenever we're immersed in our positive qualities. Although our experience of those qualities is impermanent as we start out on the path, and the methods we rely on to give rise to them are composite, their practice leads to an awakening that's beyond what's composite and impermanent—a state of freedom found in the aftertaste of their expression, like the glow of alpine light on the mountainside after the sun has set.

When we have a profound experience of one of these qualities— like feeling compassion for a particular person or situation—it can feel like it cracks our heart open. In an experience like that, we recognize something profound about ourselves, which gives rise to confidence and trust. The more we have those experiences, the more we trust in the power of our positive qualities. Confidence from the experience of those positive qualities gives us courage and overrides our fear.

Working with Fear

Fear is one of the most pervasive obstacles to practice as well as an obstacle in our attempts to benefit others. We can learn to work with fear so it nourishes and empowers our practice instead of stopping us or slowing us down. Bodhicitta gives us the courage to do that. What makes us courageous isn't the absence of fear. It's what we do with it when it arises.

Sometimes fear comes up when we're practicing, because we feel naked and exposed. It may be that our ego is so mortified by what we find in our mind that we're simply horrified and can't bear to do it anymore. Other times, it's just plain embarrassing, and we can't believe we've been repeating these old patterns for decades!

For whatever reason, be it mortification, bodhicitta, or genuine renunciation—a sincere commitment to turning away from the causes of harm and suffering for ourselves and others—we aren't engaging those methods of suppression anymore, so we feel naked and wonder who we are without all those protective layers. These can be extremely fertile moments for practice, like planting new seeds in a field that's been carefully tilled and prepared for cultivation.

Anthony: Sometimes, when I listen to teachings, I find myself shutting down, because I'm scared of how vulnerable you're asking us to be. It doesn't seem like it could work in the face of what's happening in the world. How can we withstand that if we're so vulnerable?

Lama: That's a great observation. You've captured the sense of fear that many people have about cultivating a depth of practice.

Ask yourself this: do you experience yourself as being more capable of being effective or being a steady force for benefit when you shut down or when you open up? Think about that in terms of your life over time, in terms of each day and each interaction. Where are you most effective, and where can you be of greatest benefit?

When we're not shut down, when we let down our defenses and all of those habits and behaviors we've developed over time to protect ourselves, our initial experience can be one of great vulnerability. However, as we keep going with the practice, we realize our most vulnerable place is to be disconnected from our love, disconnected from compassion, disconnected from our positive qualities. This makes us truly vulnerable, because we don't have access to the source of strength that comes from everything that's beneficial for ourselves or others. So much of what's happening in the world is because so many of us are disconnected from our love, compassion, and spiritual practice. Many of our negative behaviors are an attempt to compensate for that lack of connection.

Our positive qualities give us courage and power in every single situation. It's when we aren't aware of them, when we don't have faith and confidence in them, and when we wall ourselves off from them that we lose our power. That's when outer circumstances can overwhelm us. Disconnected from our true nature, we don't have the strength derived from drawing on our positive qualities to bring to each situation. Being connected to our true nature and expressing it in every moment empowers everything we do to be of benefit.

The Dalai Lama, Chagdud Tulku Rinpoche, and all the great masters have practiced extensively, given rise to, and actualized their positive qualities, and that's what they express in the world. The force of that is immensely powerful. Most of us on the path haven't fully accessed all our positive qualities, but that doesn't mean we can't experience the power and confidence that comes from living those positive qualities when we do. What appears at first to be a vulnerability ends up being our greatest strength and source of courage.

Anthony: I'd be hesitant to try to communicate with people who are harming others if my defenses weren't up. It would take some preparation to feel love as a kind of armor. Maybe armor isn't the right way to think about it.

Lama: If you're dealing with someone who has armoring of all kinds—including weapons—remind yourself that this is someone who's doing what they're doing because they think it's the best way to get what they want—or at least to avoid more suffering. Our role is to simply love them. Genuine love has the capacity to overpower extreme negativity.

Congressman John Lewis, who worked with Dr. Martin Luther King, spoke of how those involved in the civil rights movement in the 1950s and 1960s often found themselves in intense confrontations, encountering tremendous hatred and violence.

On one occasion, when asked how to respond to certain kinds of provocations, Dr. King said, "Just love the heck out of them!"

What does it mean for us to love the heck out of someone? It means, in that moment, we're believing in and doing what we can to inspire the very best in them and to protect them from harming themselves and others. What can we give them in that moment that will uplift them?

Tej: Where I used to live, I had to walk by a church that has a big gas meter. I'd sometimes think this meter was a dog, and I have a strong fear of dogs. After a while, I was able to see it was a gas meter, and the fear went away, but what do I do with situations like that?

Lama: First, there's the fundamental misperception of believing that appearances are something other than our own projection, our own movie. On top of that, we overlay the habit of our fear—which, in your case, is a fear of dogs. We're immediately captured by the drama in our movie, unaware that it's just light through film and, within that, is a perception of "dog," which brings up fear.

Use one of the methods that we've been cultivating. For example, "By my fear, may no one else have fear. May the fear of all living beings be dispelled by my own." Always remember others. Think of all others who are fearful—no matter the outer or inner objects of fear—and then offer, "By my fear, may no one else ever have fear."

Repeat those meditations until the experience of the fear begins to relax, and you begin to realize it's just your movie. First address your fear of dogs and then keep going. Your fixation on appearance as self-existing will loosen as well. Over time, you'll purify the deeper habit, too.

23 Examining the Nature of Fear

After establishing pure motivation, try to find this fear that's so fully gripped you. This big, powerful fear—where is it? What does it look like? What's its size and shape?

Relax the effort to find it, and rest your mind.

Then, try to describe it—for example, its color—and again rest the mind.

If you think the fear's in your heart, try to determine if it's in the left or the right ventricle. Is it in the muscle tissue or in the blood? Could a heart surgeon find it? Could it be found with a microscope in the cells, molecules, or subatomic particles?

If you find there's *no thing* there called fear, then relax the effort to find it and rest in the not finding.

Hillary: What does it mean to experience the emotion of fear? If we see it, notice it, and feel it, is that the same as experiencing it? If we analyze fear, and it falls away as we look at it, did we actually experience it? In our efforts to not indulge or avoid it, how do we know we truly experienced it?

Lama: Since you're asking this question, it's possible you're not fully experiencing it, because when we do, it's palpable. If we have a habit to watch or analyze it, in the watching and analyzing there can be a stepping back from and not fully experiencing it.

Having fear means we're living it in that moment. It means all our perceptions in that moment are colored by or informed by that emotion. Even if we develop an ability to be aware of it as the play of our film, and we bring therapeutic or spiritual methods to it, there's still the experience of the emotion itself.

There's not just the intellectual understanding of what's going on. If there's an imbalance on the side of analysis and examination as opposed to experience, there's a distancing from it, and we prevent ourselves from having it.

In some cultures, there's a predisposition to suppressing or bypassing emotions. Depending on the family, emotions could be considered misdemeanors or even felonies, or, on the other hand, that having and expressing emotions is a civil right!

When we allow ourselves to have the emotion and bring practice to it, we have the experience of the emotion *and* the experience of the emotion changing as we bring practice to it. This isn't a sense of separation from it through watching it. It's having it and experiencing it as it transforms into loving kindness or compassion, for example. We're not separate from the experience of the emotion. We're in it. We're in that experience of reality and, through practice, we're transforming it. To the degree that we're distanced from the emotion itself, it's difficult to truly transform it, because then we're only imprinting and changing our ideas about—not our actual experience of—that emotion.

It's the same with any emotion that arises, and that's why it's so important to let ourselves be fully in it and, within the context of being in it, transform it. This will ensure it's purified and that there are no remnants remaining or any suppressing taking place. That's what's going to produce change.

Otherwise, the emotion remains, however buried, and we continue to project and experience appearances through that lens. This creates consequences in our mind, our relationships, our health, and every area of our lives. We might then perceive all beings and situations as objects of fear or anger, for example, to which we respond with more fear and anger. This only deepens our habits, further obscuring our perceptions and impeding our ability to see clearly and respond to people and circumstances in truly beneficial ways.

Tonya: What might it look like to purify fear? What must one regret or confess?

Lama: When we act out of fear, at the very least, we lose opportunities to benefit. When we're possessed by our fear, our own suffering is so predominant that we can't see the suffering of others. Or we feel so entitled to address the causes of our own fear that we don't think of how we could be harming others.

Our fear may be deep and pervasive, or maybe certain situations trigger memories of violent or traumatic experiences. When those are triggered or we feel possessed by them, we act out of that space of mind with no concern for others. Because it arises from the nonrecognition of our nature, it's self-centered. Until we've trained our mind with bodhicitta, all we want is to end our own suffering.

Ocean: When I think about the suffering of beings and how it seems there's so little I can do about it, I feel afraid for us all— for every being and the planet in general.

Lama: Pain and sorrow will come up as we contemplate suffering. Fear will come up. Anger. Waves of emotion can come up—emotions that we've suppressed or bypassed. They're just lying there, unresolved, and can come up in specific circumstances or in relation to beings in general when we give rise to bodhicitta. When we realize that so many of us don't know the power of our positive qualities—only the power of our emotions—deep sorrow can arise. Everyone works so hard to find happiness and yet frequently produces the opposite.

But if we bring our heartbreak into our practice, this only strengthens our compassion and our commitment—as long as we keep it about others and not ourselves. Stronger than the sorrow is our commitment to others. The sorrow doesn't eclipse our commitment to them or to our practice. Instead, we'll give rise to an even greater capacity to respond.

Taking Out the Garbage

As we deepen our practice, suppressed emotions can bubble to the surface. When we start purifying all the ways we've tried to hide, suppress, deny or avoid our emotions, we're left with what's underneath—uncomfortable and often painful feelings. There's no way to remove these without experiencing and dealing with them.

Rinpoche used the metaphor that when we're purifying, it's like taking out the garbage—some of it slops over the side on the way. However, compared to the years, decades, lifetimes, and even eons of karma, habit, and toxic emotions that we're purifying through our practice, there's very little spilling over into our current turbulence. Even so, as we experience it, it can feel huge, permanent, solid, and powerful—because it's our habit to see it that way. This is the reason we suppressed these emotions in the first place. They felt so overwhelming, and we didn't know how to deal with them. We masked them with layers of behaviors or beliefs about ourselves or others so we wouldn't have to feel what was really going on with us.

As Rinpoche said, one moment of pure, intense compassion can purify eons of karma. Due to the power of compassion, the purification we go through can be very profound and feel scary, as so much of what we'd suppressed comes up.

When we're really practicing, all of what we assembled to protect ourselves gets disassembled, and it can feel as if we're unraveling. In one retreat, someone observed, "It's all blowing apart. I don't know what just happened, and I don't know what I believe. All I know is my world just blew up." This person had the courage to let themselves unravel as they practiced bodhicitta.

Breanna: When I start to see all my habits, I feel ashamed. What do I do with that?

Lama: Even as we give rise to our positive qualities, our old habits feel threatened. As our crusty armor cracks open, all those broken bits of our heart and personality get scared and reactive. We experience the way our particular constellation of poisons of the mind, habits, and karma are configured as "who we are." The ego may react by grasping even more strongly at what it's known and say, "No way! You're not going to work on me."

Understanding this process helps us to not interpret it through the lens of our old patterns, such as condemning ourselves and others or feeling ashamed. The ego has a strong survival instinct, and that's how we got this far in our life. Remembering that, we're able to stop scaring ourselves and solidifying our old survival patterns. Instead, we can remind ourselves that we survived well enough to be able to ask ourselves the deeper question of, "Why is this going on?"

Like the power of the rising sun on shadows, the power of bodhicitta has started to dissipate these old habits. If we understand that's what's going on, instead of empowering old methods for dealing with what feels broken and scared and chaotic, we can bring the mind back to bodhicitta. The more we do that, the more we have confidence in the practice and the process, the presence of positive qualities in our own mind and in the minds of others. That confidence comes through repetition.

If we don't understand that, we'll be constantly reacting to our practice in the context of our old patterns, just as we've reacted to the outer appearances of our lives and continue to undermine ourselves. From the point of view of the ego, all this change is just more suffering. Of course, the ego does what it's always done in relationship to suffering and reverts to what's familiar as our way of coping. If we engage our old habits in relation to our purification, we might believe that everything we're going through is the fault of the practice, other practitioners, or the teacher. That's our ordinary mind kicking and screaming in its effort to retain and recapture some kind of control.

If we have moments of clarity in which we recognize we're undermining ourselves, and we experience shame or grief, the old pattern is to go more into our psychology to try to understand why this is happening. For example, we might be convinced that we're hopeless, the path is hopeless, everything is hopeless, and there's nothing worthy of our trust. But that's just a story we've told ourselves in the past. It's not ultimately true. By repeating it to ourselves, we scare ourselves and shut down more, using all the methods we've always used to shut down in response to pain.

Our ordinary mind is like an elastic band. We stretch it through our practice, but it can snap back strongly. Each time we bring the mind back to love, compassion, and bodhicitta, the rubber band loses more of its elasticity. We still have reactions, but, over time, the power of our practice stretches our love and compassion and weakens the integrity of the rubber band. Understanding this makes it easier for us to not indulge our old habits.

You're experiencing shame, but that's probably the reaction you've had in relation to worldly phenomena your whole life. Now you're having it with your practice. Understand that, and keep repeating the practice.

Remember that we're least effective when we identify with what's obscuring our true nature instead of with our positive qualities—the source of our strength, power, courage, and everything we need to benefit ourselves and others.

Breanna: What do I do when I'm so into the shame that I can't even remember the practice?

Lama: First, recognize the process, own it, and remind yourself that the rubber band snaps back because it's been stretched. If there were no stretching, there would be no snapping—or there would be snapping in relation to outer phenomena but not in relation to your practice. Change is happening. Then, decide you aren't going to indulge the old habits. Instead, you're going to strengthen your practice.

Sometimes, we might have a question about which practice to do when there's a huge reaction happening in our mind and heart accompanied by seemingly overpowering emotions. First, think of everybody else. As much as we can expand our practice to include infinite beings throughout time and space, the power of that expansive intention is greater than the power of whatever our own neurotic mind is doing in the moment.

Think of others who are experiencing similar emotions and feelings of powerlessness but don't have tools to transform them. Through compassion, our hearts naturally move, and we let our compassion express itself by thinking of others who are suffering in different ways, overpowered by negative habits and emotions, wanting so badly to find happiness but not knowing how. Even if they have a conceptual understanding of cause and effect, they may not know what to do in the moment when they're triggered, being reactive, or shutting down. You can equalize yourself with others, being aware of their needs and aspirations and wishing for them that they have everything they need. This could lead to a compassionate commitment to help them find what they need.

The point is, to the extent that we include others in the scope of our intention and motivation, to that same extent we put in perspective the drama of our own mind. When we think of the suffering of others who don't have tools and a way through, compassion arises. That compassion will naturally help to pacify the drama in our own mind and heart.

Working with Trauma

Tonya: Fear is my overwhelming, predominant habit. Ninety percent of whatever negative thing is happening in my mind is always fear.

Lama: When we're doing formal practice, we can't use any of our compensating behaviors—to be busy, to be productive, or to run away. We have to just be with the fear. But this emotional honesty is the basis for transformation when we bring practice to it.

Tonya: There have been times when it's been easy for me to cultivate love, so I know fear isn't all there is. However, it's very convincing, in the moment, to believe I'm only afraid, and I've never purely loved.

Lama: When stuff gets stirred up in our minds, as we practice or in daily life, especially when we're triggered, it can seem as though what we're feeling in that moment is what's always been true. We can't remember any other experience. We're completely convinced that this projection—this feeling and experience—is all there is.

It's as if our brain is composed of different files that store different kinds of information. When we're triggered, our awareness is transported to the "trauma" file, and we feel like we're back in the original traumatic experience that's stored there. Suddenly, we're five years old, experiencing violence or fear of violence, for example, and it's like we're there again and can't access anything else.

Through our practice, we're learning to be there *and* access the tools to transform those feelings at the same time. That's what you're doing now. I know it feels as though it's always been that way, but it hasn't.

Tonya: I know that, conceptually. It's partly that I'm also frustrated. There's nothing, in particular, that I'm aware of that makes me afraid, but there's this overwhelming physical experience.

Lama: Once we're triggered, we project onto everybody and everything around us. It's hugely painful to be so vulnerable and to confront the fear of letting down our defenses and opening up in the face of those big, gnarly guys or situations. We're learning to let go of all the adaptive behaviors we've built up that prevent us from being present, so that we can give rise to bodhicitta in every situation.

Tonya: What do we do in the actual moment when the triggering happens? If I had the presence of mind, I could practice, but I freeze. It doesn't have anything to do with what's happening outwardly or the person I'm interacting with. I'm just stunned, like I've received a punch in the stomach.

Lama: In those moments, we can disassociate, as if we're no longer present in our body. Rinpoche described this kind of shock using the metaphor of a jar of canned food that's been vacuum-sealed. If we open it, even for a millisecond, the seal has been broken. Outwardly, it looks the same, but what's inside has changed and continues to change. He used that example to describe what happens to the subtle life-force energy that connects the mind and body. When we're triggered, it's often reflexive, and we feel just like we did when the original shock happened.

Rinpoche was a doctor of Tibetan medicine, which has a profound and nuanced understanding of what happens to the subtle body when we're shocked. There are a number of things that are part of the prescription that a Tibetan doctor would give to a patient suffering from trauma and shock. To the extent that we do these things ongoingly in our lives, we heal the breach, the disconnect. When we're triggered emotionally in the future, there's less of a neurological, physiological, subtle-energy impact.

Trauma stirs the subtle energies, so the essence of the treatment is to rest and create as much of a stress-free environment and lifestyle as possible. That means, to the extent that you're able, going to sleep at the same time every night and as early as possible, and letting go of all the effort and striving. Turn off all your digital devices at least an hour or two before going to bed. Warm, soothing beverages or even warm milk helps us to calm down before bed. It's a good idea to eat before going to sleep and have a snack available containing oil and protein in case of insomnia. All these things contribute to the process of restoration that happens overnight. Then, upon waking, there's more of a sense of wholeness that we take into our environment.

Other advice from Tibetan medicine for recovery from subtle energy imbalances is to eat the same amount of food we'd normally eat during the day but in smaller quantities and more often, to help stabilize blood sugar. When the subtle energies are disturbed, the blood sugar can become unbalanced. This also means not eating a lot of empty carbohydrates or sugar. Instead, we eat foods with more protein and oil that break down more slowly, so the energy is released steadily into the blood. As much as possible, we want to eat warm, cooked foods. Taking baths with oil in the water instead of showers is also more calming.

To further help calm the subtle energies, we can take long, slow walks under a big sky or in gardens. We don't focus our mind outwardly or inwardly but simply rest the mind in that space between outer and inner. We don't race. The purpose isn't physical exercise. It's harder to fixate when we walk slowly and easier for the subtle energies to calm down.

In general, to the degree we're able to heal that breach ahead of time, we won't have as much of a physical or subtle-energy response when we're triggered. Otherwise, in the moment of shock, it's hard to remember what meditations to do or how they work.

Tonya: So, in the moment, if we have the presence of mind, we do one of these practices?

Lama: Yes. Do whatever practices you find most helpful for calming down. Think of everyone else who's facing trauma or in shock. All these methods connect you with your current adult mind, heart, and experience, so you don't fall into old habits. Whatever you can do to open to your environment and connect with other people helps to ground you in the present moment— where the trauma isn't happening—instead of being in the memory of what it felt like or looked like back when. If you have any kind of prayer practice, you can make a prayerful plea for help in finding a way through with bodhicitta that's beneficial for all concerned.

The more you prepare ahead of time, the more accessible those meditations will be in the moments when you need them the most. It's understandable to want a quick, easy fix that always works, no matter what, but they all work in proportion to how much we prepare.

Tonya: Sometimes there's just a certain tone when I'm around people, and that's a trigger for me. My method has been to disassociate. I could be in a social or work situation, and when I detect that tone or inflection, I immediately dissociate. What practice can I do in those moments?

Lama: The more practice you've done before these triggers arise, the more facility you'll have to deal with them as they happen. Start with the Just Like Me meditation, because then you won't see the person you're feeling triggered by as the enemy. Remind yourself that, just like you, they want to be happy and don't want to suffer, and it's because of that they're behaving this way. Your love and compassion will be generated so you have a sense of commonality.

Anthony: When I focus on this idea of looking back through the day and intentionally reliving and transforming my responses to traumas, I feel scared. I realize I could tap into something that would be a profound practice, but I don't feel super comfortable opening myself up.

Lama: That's not necessarily a bad thing. The ore isn't looking forward to entering the rock tumbler. You might consider when and where you could feel safe enough to do this meditation. If we don't have the tools to work with our emotions and our traumas differently, we put up all kinds of barriers and defenses to protect ourselves from those hard feelings. So, for example, we might not want to go there right before we leave for work when we know it will be a hard day and we must be super-present. At the same time, it's never going to be comfortable to take down our defenses, so you have to figure out where, when, and how to do this.

It seems you're aware of what's going on with you and being courageous about it. I think your fear is out of proportion to the experience, because it's not nearly as traumatic as the original situation, and you're bringing tools to it that you didn't have in the original situation. You're more empowered and, when you've done the practice once or twice, you'll have more confidence.

It isn't like therapy, where you're reliving the drama. We aren't getting into the storyline. We're remembering when we were triggered and applying a different method for dealing with it, and the method itself is transforming. It produces change.

That's what you'll be experiencing—the change, a new tool, and an increased capacity as opposed to all the feelings you felt before when you didn't have these resources.

Anthony: I think the way I'm approaching it is more therapeutic—reliving, retelling, and going back to those experiences. I think it's important for me to see the difference between what we're doing here and just feeling triggered.

Lama: It's a different method. Some of the more recently developed therapeutic models for working with trauma don't deal with the content. But with others, there's some measure of revisiting the old situation and unpacking it, so the feelings become more evident. This allows us to analyze them, but the analysis is from the point of view of the ordinary mind and from the point of view of the options that were or weren't available at the time and our feelings about that.

Here, we're not doing that. We're not analyzing the emotions or trying to determine why they occurred. Instead, we're learning to recognize what they are so we can consider the appropriate meditation to transform them. We have to know what's going on with us so we can change it.

Those of us who have a habit of not wanting to look at, admit, or deal with what's going on with us usually have developed all kinds of behaviors that allow us to avoid going there. It can feel scary, but it's nothing like the original situation, because we have more resources and, in the case of trauma, we're working with a meditation that will give us a different experience of the emotion. We must feel the emotion in order to transform it, but we aren't giving in to it, indulging or analyzing it, and trying to create change based on changing the storyline. We're creating change by applying different meditation methods to an emotional experience to bring our mind back to bodhicitta.

If we try to do meditation practice disconnected from our emotional experience, we aren't going to see much change. Instead, it's like the example Rinpoche used of pushing the pause button on a music device, which appears to create peace, but the same noise resumes when the pause button is released. We may be able to calm our emotions and feel better for a period of time, but all of those old habits and emotions are still bubbling under the surface.

The purpose of meditation is to bring our practice directly to our experience and transform it, so we're able to purify our negative emotions and create a stable presence of love and compassion.

Working with Anger

Anger abides along with fear on the spectrum of aversion. We're afraid of bad things happening and often angry when they do. When anger possesses our heart, it can cause us to harm others and compromise our ability to be of benefit. It's such a powerful force in our lives and in the world that we need to examine more closely its presence in our mind in order to harness and redirect its energy in the most beneficial direction possible.

When anger possesses our mind and heart, it causes such a great turbulence that we're unable to find the presence and stability of compassion and wisdom needed to see things clearly and to problem-solve effectively. Our anger arises in proportion to our attachment, which always leads to disappointment when things don't go the way we want. Caught in the great tumult of hope for what we want or fear of what we don't want, we're unable to stop the roller coaster of emotions that exhaust us spiritually, energetically, and even physically. As our anger consumes our merit, we're unable to find or create the inner and outer resourcefulness needed to uplift and inspire ourselves or others toward avenues of benefit rather than harm.

To avoid energizing and following our anger when it comes up, we can begin working with it in the same way that we worked with our fear—thinking about how many beings are trapped in endless cycles of angry reactivity and creating further suffering rather than the benefit they long for.

Then we remind ourselves of what we've seen happen in the past when we've indulged our anger. We can ask ourselves why we think things should go the way we want them to. We need to reflect on how much we suffer as a result of believing that things should go a certain way, and that they rarely do. If we can accept that things won't always go how we'd like them to, we would have less hope and attachment and then less anger and disappointment when they don't. We begin this process by examining the evidence of our lives.

For the same reason, we can't assume that bad things will happen, because they might not, any more than we can assume good things will. It doesn't help us to create big ideas about what will happen in the future, as this just increases our hope and fear about fictions of our imagination.

It's more helpful to recognize that sometimes things are good and sometimes they're bad, but, no matter whether they're good or bad, we just keep going and try to be kind, compassionate, and help others as much as we can. If we have an expectation that life should be a certain way (hope), that's going to automatically produce disappointment and anger (fear) when it doesn't go that way.

We need to accept that things won't always be or go the way we want, so we're not in a constant state of reactivity. This isn't the same thing as accepting that beings are suffering and doing nothing about it. This isn't acceptance in the sense of apathy. We accept that we don't have control over everybody and everything. That's the truth of it. Then, within the spaciousness of that acceptance, we have room to transform our hope and fear and give rise to bodhicitta, so we can remain steady with our practice and see more clearly how we can be a stable source of truly creative and proactive benefit for others.

24 The Consequences of Anger

Think through the times in your life when you acted from anger. What were the consequences of those actions in those relationships or situations in the short term? How did those circumstances play out in the long run?

Then rest the mind. Generate compassion for everyone who follows their anger without considering the outcomes, then rest the mind. Make whatever commitment may arise from your compassion, then rest the mind. Then pray for the wisdom, compassion and capacity to transform your relationship to anger so you can have more presence of mind and practice and ability to benefit others. Then rest the mind.

Ask yourself why you thought that this thing you're angry about should have gone differently.

Generate compassion, commitment, and prayer for all the beings who are angry when their expectations—however unrealistic—aren't met, alternated with resting the mind.

Think about the possible short-term consequences if you follow and act on your anger.

Think about the possible long-term consequences as well.

Then, rest the mind, alternated with compassion, commitment, and prayer.

Ocean: I still think sometimes anger is the only thing that can motivate people to act.

Lama: Like a fork of wild lightning or a wildfire, anger can swiftly ignite dry kindling, but, once the fuel is gone, so is the fire. If people are inspired to act out of anger but then encounter difficulties along the way or don't get the results they want, they can despair and find themselves feeling more stuck and less inclined to act or follow through in the future. The anger consumes the merit needed to sustain long-term, positive change and a depth of capacity to benefit others.

Especially when trying to address huge individual or social problems, we need staying power, not something that burns out. The most reliable source of that steady fuel is the power of bodhicitta, because it creates the merit that's an enduring source of strength.

Anthony: I tend to justify my anger, especially if I don't trust the other person. If the other person is speaking or acting in a way that convinces me I shouldn't trust them, I respond with anger.

Lama: Believing the anger is justified is a kind of self-righteousness. That's why it's often helpful to spend time with the Just Like Me meditation as a way to address the self-righteous aspect of anger. That might help support the purification of the habit to anger. Revisit some scenes that have triggered your self-righteous anger where you felt justified and then, in the middle of that, do the Just Like Me meditation.

Ida: You've talked about the pitfalls of righteous anger, but what if we act forcefully to try to protect someone from the consequences of hurting another?

Lama: If we aren't kidding ourselves and truly act out of compassion, creating a boundary to protect someone from the consequences of their own actions isn't anger; it's wrath. The difference between anger and wrath is in the motivation. Wrath is imbued with pure motivation and wisdom, and anger arises from self-centered motivation when we react negatively to what's happening.

You could say the difference between anger and wrath is like the difference between abuse and discipline in raising a child. If we punish a child out of anger, and our negative emotions are in control, then, of course, the child experiences it as abuse. If, out of genuine love and compassion, we create a firm boundary for *their* sake, that's discipline. It might be wrathful discipline, but it's not abuse. The difference is in the motivation.

Anthony: I still respond with anger to things I don't want to happen to me. I can't honestly say I think anger does nothing but cause harm, or I wouldn't do it.

Lama: Anger and aversion are often related to fear. We don't want certain things to happen to us, and that makes us afraid that they will. You're being honest about your motivation and trying to take responsibility through your practice. Although it still arises, does the anger come up less frequently, last less long, and do you see through it and antidote and transform it more quickly? If so, that habit is purifying. Be sure to observe not only its presence but whether it's diminishing.

Even though anger is one of your strong habits, that doesn't necessarily mean you're convinced it isn't harmful. Do you truly believe anger is helpful and that it's benefited you or others? How do you feel when you drop the anger and apologize? I don't think you'd apologize if you thought the anger was justified and helpful.

Anthony: I know a lot of people who get angry repeatedly, apologize for it, but get just as angry the next time.

Lama: For some people, anger is the way they've responded habitually to trauma—to the fear instilled in them by that trauma—or it could just be a force of habit. When it arises, it clouds the mind and makes it hard for us to access our rational thought processes. What we know and believe about something is obscured by the power of the habit, our automatic reactions. I appreciate that you're trying to be so honest here, but I'm not so sure you truly believe anger is beneficial.

Hillary: I'm a parent of two young kids and, although my kids are amazing and fun to be with, they're also extraordinarily stubborn. Every night at bedtime, it's a surprise to my eight-year-old daughter that she has to brush her teeth and get ready for bed, and she rebels. I find myself sometimes seething with anger. Like, "Are you kidding me? We did the same thing last night and a thousand nights before that." I don't know how to bring bodhicitta to that situation. I don't know how to remain open-hearted in the face of her defiance.

Lama: How have others been with you in the face of *your* defiance? What's worked to bring you out of that stubbornness?

Hillary: I don't know the answer to that question. My kids are exactly like me. I need to save them from themselves.

Lama: Try doing the Just Like Me meditation, both formally when you're not with your kids, and once it's become familiar, when you're with them. Then try to find the humor in it. Make fun of yourself in the middle of their resistance. If you can do that, it might help take the charge out of it and allow you to open up more. You're attached to her brushing her teeth, so try to find a humorous way to think of and respond to that.

Investigating Anger

Another method for working with our anger is to examine and disempower it through the power of investigation. What is this thing that's so possessed our mind and heart that it seems we have no agency separate from it? We're completely consumed by anger, and all we want is the expression of it. It's like we're looking through a lens that's so colored by our anger that our entire experience of reality is influenced by it. It's how we experience everything, as if it's truly that way, and no one could make us believe otherwise. When that happens, one thing we can do is explore and examine this thing that's gripped us and that we're so sure is real. We can investigate why we believe it's real and why we're giving it so much power.

Because we believe in this illusory appearance of anger, we act in a myriad of ways that are harmful to ourselves and others, compromise our ability to benefit, and burn up our merit. This tragic cycle is repeated by ourself and others again and again, over and over, perpetuating instead of uprooting suffering.

Just as when working with fear, in the moment when something is pushing our buttons and we feel anger flaring, we can try to find it. To have such a power over us, it must truly exist. So where is it? Is it in our brain, in our head, in our heart? Does it have a shape, a color, a size? Does it move around, or is it always in one place? If we're unable to find it, we stop looking and relax the mind in the not finding. Again, sometimes the not finding is the finding.

When the mind becomes no longer restful, we again examine anger or a different poison—whatever comes up next in our mind. There will usually be plenty of material to work with! Of course, the difficult part is remembering to do this meditation when we're triggered. The swiftest way to cut through is to discover there's no *thing* there to trigger us. We need to have the presence of mind to remember to do the practice and have enough time in with this meditation that it's accessible.

The process is one of trying to find the anger, letting go of the effort, and resting. We alternate between those two—effortful and effortless. We start with bodhicitta and end with dedication.

25 Exploring the Nature of Anger

It's good to do this as a formal practice, because, at first, it's hard to do informally. Always start with bodhicitta. Then, when you're alone, think of something that makes you furious or made you furious in the past. Think about this to the point where your blood is boiling, your face is red, and your heart's pounding. Then try to find the anger. Really explore. If and when you have the experience of not finding it, stop trying, and rest the mind there.

As soon as your mind starts up again, think of another thing that makes your blood boil, and try to find that anger. If you can't find it, let go of trying and let the mind rest. Go back and forth between trying to find the anger and relaxing.

There's ultimately no *thing* there called anger, even though there's the appearance of anger. When you find no *thing* in the midst of the appearance—a glimpse of the illusory nature of your anger—that's wisdom. Rest the mind there and then dedicate the merit.

Tej: How do we have discernment without aversion? How do we have preferences without attachment?

Lama: It depends on the motivation. If our motivation is bodhicitta, there's discernment concerning what's of greatest benefit. The motivation, the mental experience, and the karma we're creating aren't those of attachment and aversion but of love and compassion.

Inez: I have so much anger about the 1% and income inequality. How do I transform that anger?

Lama: Start with the Just Like Me meditation, and begin with bodhicitta, which might be a little abstract in relation to your feelings about the 1%. Then think of a person who represents the 1% and who, "just like me," wants to be happy, doesn't want to suffer, and so forth. Remind yourself that just like you, their true nature is a state of limitless purity and, not recognizing that, they're grasping after all these outer phenomena to find happiness. In the course of doing that, the actions they take are causing inconceivable suffering for the 99%, and that karma will lead to inconceivable suffering in some future experience. Ask yourself how many times, in your pursuit of happiness, you didn't want the ants in your sink and washed them down the drain, or you didn't want the mosquitoes biting so you killed them, or whatever it is for you.

It's easy for us to be righteous when looking at other people, but we need to take responsibility for our own choices and find their actions in us. Remind yourself of when you did whatever you did for your own happiness without thinking of the consequences to others, whether it was other humans or animal beings. If we don't generate pure motivation toward the 1% as we try to address the underlying inequalities, whatever change we're able to create won't be stable. If the heart doesn't change, there can't be such a thing as real equality. We'll simply recreate cycles of history where who's wealthy and powerful keeps trading back and forth, but genuine equality doesn't happen. If we don't create genuine equality in our own minds, how can we expect to see genuine equality outwardly? How can we be creative enough to think of social change and causes and conditions that can produce something truly beneficial if we haven't resolved our own resentment, anger, and hatred?

With this understanding, we work on generating an equal regard for everybody—the rich, the poor, everybody—and an equal compassion for those who are currently suffering as well as those planting the seeds of future suffering. It's not like we've got it all together, and everyone else is planting the seeds of suffering. How many times have we acted without regard for the consequences, without regard or awareness of the impact of our actions on others?

Whether it's the wealthy we feel righteous anger toward or those in power making choices that harm ourselves and others in myriad ways, we need to recognize ourselves in them. If we don't, we'll never change our mind. We'll always have a basis for blaming, for thinking all inequality and suffering is everybody else's fault. We can't be active participants in change that truly uproots the causes of suffering if we're perpetuating the causes in our own mind. The transformation in our minds will occur incrementally, but it will be unfailing if we keep going.

26 Transforming Judgment and Aversion through Alternating Meditation

Start by contemplating the actions of someone who's harming others, and remind yourself why you'd want to do meditations to transform your judgment and aversion. If you find yourself thinking badly of this person and feeling you don't want to benefit them, work through your aversion by contemplating karma, cause and effect, and the fact that they're only creating the causes of their own future suffering.

Alternate each stage of contemplation, compassion, commitment, and prayer with resting the mind. Try to cultivate genuine concern for this person, wanting them to receive as much or more benefit as those you have a more accessible love and compassion for.

Keep stretching the meditation, increasing the scope of people and situations you're contemplating.

Alternate those sequences of contemplation and compassion with resting the mind within a limitless love without objects, without effort or contrivance. If you become distracted, go to the next step of the sequence and continue on from there, finally embracing all beings for all time.

Carolyn: If I keep thinking of everybody else and all their suffering, won't I be even more overwhelmed and depressed?

Lama: As terrible as we think things are for us, we have so much going for us that so many others don't have. Thinking about their suffering helps us realize we have many resources that can be shared with others and used to respond to their suffering. As we recognize the presence of these resources in our mind and lives, we realize we aren't powerless. There's always something we can do to help those around us.

In the past, we've relied on methods that are composite, impermanent, and unfree to try to gain power over whatever we thought was the cause of suffering for ourselves and others. This power we were seeking might have been power over suffering, power over others, power over change. Ultimately, because these methods aren't reliable, sooner or later they hit their limitations, and we felt disempowered, hopeless, despairing. That's another of the old habits that can arise in the mind when we're practicing. Again, we deconstruct these methods and realize that none of them are reliable.

What *is* reliable is the presence of our positive qualities, insofar as we cultivate them. We learn to rely on our practice to recognize, access, and empower them. Our positive qualities, by their nature, aren't finite or limited, but the "we" that's cultivating them is. It's the personality's obscurations that cloud our vision, so we're sometimes not even able to see or recognize the presence of our love or compassion.

Breanna: In the moments when I feel bodhicitta, it isn't a blissful, full-of-joy experience. It's a profound well of sorrow mixed with gratitude and also joy. It's not like I start sobbing in the car or the grocery store. I just want to make sure I'm not missing what bodhicitta is.

Lama: It sounds like you're practicing deeply, and all this stuff is unwinding for you. Within the heart of bodhicitta, we embrace the hearts of every living being. We embrace all that yearning, all the need, all the sorrow, all the joy, all the everything. It's the everythingness being joined with the aspiration that the sorrow be resolved and the joy be fulfilled.

As your heart opens to all of that, sometimes you'll cry, sometimes you'll laugh, and sometimes you'll do something in between. You want to be aware of when the expression of your emotions may not be beneficial or may even be harmful to those around you. It doesn't sound as if the grocery store or driving in the car is one of those situations—as long as you keep your eyes on the road!

Sunlight on Shadows

Carolyn: If I keep thinking of everybody else and all their suffering, won't I be even more overwhelmed and depressed?

Lama: As terrible as we think things are for us, we have so much going for us that so many others don't have. Thinking about their suffering helps us realize we have many resources that can be shared with others and used to respond to their suffering. As we recognize the presence of these resources in our mind and lives, we realize we aren't powerless. There's always something we can do to help those around us.

In the past, we've relied on methods that are composite, impermanent, and unfree to try to gain power over whatever we thought was the cause of suffering for ourselves and others. This power we were seeking might have been power over suffering, power over others, power over change. Ultimately, because these methods aren't reliable, sooner or later they hit their limitations, and we felt disempowered, hopeless, despairing. That's another of the old habits that can arise in the mind when we're practicing. Again, we deconstruct these methods and realize that none of them are reliable.

What *is* reliable is the presence of our positive qualities, insofar as we cultivate them. We learn to rely on our practice to recognize, access, and empower them. Our positive qualities, by their nature, aren't finite or limited, but the "we" that's cultivating them is. It's the personality's obscurations that cloud our vision, so we're sometimes not even able to see or recognize the presence of our love or compassion.

Tonya: Part of my identity for a long time has been that I'm an alcoholic—a recovering alcoholic, but an alcoholic. This is the most important thing in my life—when I was using and now that I'm not using. Because this is part of my identity, I still feel the stigma and degradation of it. That identity carries something with it that keeps me stuck on the bottom, identifying myself and others by our shared woundedness. I'm realizing now that I can change my language in terms of how I identify with this part of my life. Instead of thinking of myself as a recovering alcoholic, I think, "I'm a sober woman." When I do that, I stop identifying with my woundedness and start identifying with my strength.

Lama: This parallels what we've been saying. It all comes down to what we identify with in each moment—the poisons of the mind or our true nature and positive qualities.

Tonya: When we stay so identified with that woundedness— even in our rejoicing of recovery from it—it's like we have a gut connection to it. It's part of our identity as survivors—of substance abuse, PTSD, or any other kind of trauma. It would be so nice not to feel so connected to that part of myself anymore.

Lama: Yes! In every moment, remind yourself of the positive qualities in your mind and heart.

Breanna: I think I'm understanding more deeply that cultivating our positive qualities allows us to automatically overcome our negative habits. I'm seeing that just focusing on the negative habits—which is what I did previously—made them seem bigger.

Lama: Sometimes, the presence of our anger, fear, or triggering is so vivid and overwhelming that we feel we need equally strong antidotes to transform them. When we do so, the power of the negative emotion subsides, and the awareness of the presence of our positive qualities is reaffirmed and can stabilize again.

When we're disconnected from our positive qualities, we're disconnected from our true nature. When the ultimate fulfillment of relaxing into our true nature is inaccessible to us, we usually try to fill that void by looking for causes of fulfillment outwardly. There's a grasping at or pushing away of everything outside of us as we try to get and hold on to what we want or push away what we don't want. In that push-pull, all we know is to react instead of acting from confidence in the radiance of our positive qualities, which are reliable, sustainable, and of benefit to ourselves and others, no matter what's going on.

Our positive qualities aren't composite. We usually only check in with them periodically, so they may seem impermanent, but their presence in our mind isn't impermanent. To the extent that we give rise to and sustain awareness of them, we become free of fear, insecurity, and other old habits. The power of our positive qualities is greater than that of the habits we've developed to try to make it in the world. However, we won't know this unless we spend time with them and experience their strength in the face of inner and outer opposition and hardship.

The more we bring the mind back to bodhicitta, what's obscuring our love and compassion fades and is purified, like the light of the sun dissipating shadows. To the extent that we practice, we become more confident that our positive qualities are limitless, and all we have to do is empower them rather than what's obscuring them.

The process, itself, is completely dependable, because the positive qualities of mind are unerring sources of benefit. Relying on these qualities is the ultimate empowerment, because they're the deepest expression of our true nature. That's why they're more reliable and powerful than the unfree aspects of our personality, more powerful than our obstacles, more powerful than our difficulties. It doesn't matter how great the hardship if we remember it's composite, impermanent, and unfree. But we aren't going to know that, believe in it, trust or rely on it unless we spend enough time in practice to find out it's true.

As we give rise to our positive qualities, abide in them, and develop confidence in them, our practice becomes more stable. Their presence impacts and purifies our own mind but also impacts the minds and hearts of those around us. Less and less, we experience an "us" separate from our positive qualities. There are only those qualities, so there's freedom in the face of objects of fear or adversity, inner or outer.

Our confidence grows—not confidence in aspects of our personality that have been built up over the years but confidence in the presence of positive qualities as the expression of our true nature and that of all beings. That confidence comes through repetition. As we practice and awaken our positive qualities, over time, there's less sense of effort in joining our ordinary mind with our positive qualities. It's just what is. Like the sun dispelling shadows.

The more we practice, the more we develop confidence in the process, the presence of positive qualities in our own mind, and the presence of positive qualities in the minds of others. Everywhere we go and everyone we see is the reflection of the crystalline purity of that true nature.

CHAPTER 9. GATEWAYS TO WISDOM

Most of the methods for personal change that we've been exposed to in our lives in general—whether in formal education or therapy or self-help books—address our "story." They're about our projections, how to accept or survive them, how to better cope with them, or how to be more at peace with them. Those methods all fall within the domain of believing our projections are real. And our true nature—our greatest source of personal empowerment and the greatest source of benefit for ourselves and others—isn't even recognized.

Believing in the presence of positive qualities in ourselves and others, valuing virtue, and wanting our presence in the world to make a positive difference can support our journey but don't necessarily help us to move from the conceptual to the experiential. No matter how strong our belief in inherent goodness, nothing in our background—our education, our political or psychological exposure and training—has offered a methodology to lead us, step by step, to the realization of our true nature. The impulse to work on ourself isn't enough, and spiritual ideas aren't enough, if they're superimposed on the same projections, the same storyline, and the same film.

As we stop identifying with what's obscuring our luminous essence, we have the opportunity to glimpse our true nature. When we act from that awareness, our projections change. They're no longer simply a different turn of the story but a qualitatively different experience of reality, informed by our positive qualities rather than by what's concealing them. Those qualities are like the radiance of the full spectrum of color that makes up the light emanating from the projector—the appearance of our innate wisdom, compassion, loving kindness, and capacity to benefit others—manifesting unfiltered.

Our experience until now has been informed by a lack of awareness of the breadth of our positive qualities. Until we experience the unfolding recognition of our true nature through training in bodhicitta, it's just a concept.

The Four Immeasurable Qualities

We can create this awakening on the path of the bodhisattva by beginning with pure motivation and cultivating the Four Immeasurable or Four Boundless Qualities of equanimity, loving kindness, compassion, and rejoicing. These are considered the cornerstones or the foundation of our bodhicitta. Cultivating any one or more of these qualities can lead us to that purity of motivation.

They're called immeasurable because they abide naturally and limitlessly as expressions of our true nature. Due to our obscurations, the immeasurable, limitless presence of these qualities isn't obvious, so our current experience of them is that they're definitely measurable! As we awaken and expand our awareness of them through our practice, they purify mind's obscuring poisons and the self-centeredness that are the basis of those poisons.

For example, our inherent compassion isn't measurable. It doesn't start over here and end over there. It's not limited to concern for a few but embraces everyone. It includes not only innocent victims but their perpetrators. What limits our compassion is our bias, the habits of the ordinary mind, and the judgments we've developed over time.

Our habits, karma, and poisons of the mind partially conceal these pure qualities, even though they abide in our hearts and minds in a vast, limitless, beginningless, and endless way. They're obscured like the radiance of the crystal is obscured by the ore. Each of these meditations both purifies and removes what's obscuring and allows us to recognize, strengthen, and reveal what's naturally there.

We talk about the Four Immeasurable Qualities as if they're separate and distinct. We can analyze each of the colors of the prismatic radiance of light from the crystal, but, ultimately, they're all the display of the enlightened mind. In our actual experience, when we feel great love, we don't want there to be suffering. In the same way, when we see suffering, in addition to the wish that it be dispelled, there's the wish that beings be happy—that they have what's necessary to create the absence of suffering. Love and compassion are one in our mind and heart, arising as unique manifestations of responsiveness to the needs of beings. As we awaken to the limitless wisdom that's our true nature, there's no separation in the spontaneous love and compassion that arise as its expression. But, until we've awakened and realized that wisdom, we cultivate these aspects of awareness through these four different doorways.

Any time we give rise to pure motivation, any time we make the welfare of others equally or more important to us as our own, we're antidoting self-centeredness through selflessness, which naturally helps to uproot whatever poison is arising, because each of mind's poisons arises from experiencing our needs as more important than those of others.

Similarly, we talk about attachment and aversion like they're two different things. In actuality, they work interdependently. Attachment and aversion are like two sides of the same coin. We're scared of not getting or losing what we want. We're attached to preventing what we don't want. In the same way, love and compassion are two facets of the experience of the wish for others to have what they need and to not have what's harmful.

Gateways to Wisdom

For us to even consider that these qualities are of value and shared by all of us equally represents an enormous sea change in terms of our experience. As we begin, our awareness of them is mostly conceptual. But every practice we do to cultivate bodhicitta purifies and transforms our projections. Just like sunlight on a crystal creates a rainbow-colored radiance reflective of the different facets of the crystal, the light of our awareness gives rise to a radiance of positive qualities that are the reflection of our true nature.

Giving rise to equanimity—equal regard and respect for all— antidotes judgment, bias, and pride. Love antidotes aversion and fear. Compassion antidotes and purifies self-centeredness, desire, and greed. Rejoicing antidotes envy, jealousy, and competitiveness. Through our practice of the Four Immeasurable Qualities, we antidote each of these poisons and approach the limitless wisdom of our true nature, the ultimate antidote to the ignorance of that nature. Thus, mind's five primary poisons—attachment, aversion, pride, jealousy, and ignorance—are antidoted and transformed by our practice of the Four Immeasurable Qualities.

The word for bodhicitta in Tibetan, *Jang Chub Sem*, captures the essence of the path of the bodhisattva as well as the result— realization of mind's intrinsic purity. *Jang* refers to removing what's obscuring our inherent pure qualities. *Chub* means to actualize, realize, or make clear what has always been true— mind's true nature. *Sem* is the Tibetan word for mind. So, Jang Chub Sem refers to both the process we're engaging on the bodhisattva path as well as the final fruition. Our practice of relative bodhicitta purifies everything in our mind and heart that isn't bodhicitta until all that's left is effortlessly arising ultimate bodhicitta, mind's true nature.

The more we practice any or all of the Four Immeasurable Qualities, the swifter the dissolution of mind's duality. As we start out on the path, we're bound by our belief in the solidity of the appearances of self and other as separate from the all-pervasive, completely pure perfection of everything. This is where we start out on the path, so we need to use methods that start from where we are.

Through practice, what starts out as dualistic experience dissolves that sense of separation along with the effort itself until there's simply the effortless expression and recognition of how these qualities naturally abide in our mind. We use effort at first, because it's required to remove the ore from the crystal. Once the ore is no longer coating the crystal, we rest and let it shine like the radiance of the sun on the crystal that casts brilliance in all directions.

Practicing any one of the Four Immeasurable Qualities will lead to that wisdom, but it's helpful to become familiar with and cultivate all four so that the powerful tools to antidote and transform mind's poisons are familiar and accessible. At the same time, if we find we're drawn to one of these qualities in particular, following that inclination can be a swift and effective path.

Say we a have a strong habit to loving kindness, for example, to create happiness and the causes of happiness for others as much as we can. Usually at first, our love is limited—we love a particular person, and we want their happiness and welfare. The more we practice loving kindness, the more we dissolve that limitation through the mere act of loving well, and the rigid experience of separation between self and others starts to dissipate.

We begin by *trying* to practice love, because we're starting with a sense of separation from the ultimate love of our true nature. Then we rest the mind in the spacious sense of uncontrived love—a love that abides in our being without effort. That brings the ordinary mind—which is habituated to the ore—closer to an experience of the crystal—in this case, love without bias or limitation.

However, because the mind is habituated to the ore, we might ask ourselves, "Is this really it? Am I doing it right?" We get conceptual and become effortful, so then we move to the next meditation—for example, giving rise to compassion. We might think of a particular person that it's easy to generate compassion for and then expand our visualization from there to include increasing numbers of beings until we're imagining all beings, alternating each step with letting the mind rest.

We can practice the Four Immeasurable Qualities by transforming each of the poisons as they arise, and we can also practice cultivating each of these qualities in sequence. Practically speaking, it's often helpful to start with equanimity, because it can be difficult to access and practice genuine love, compassion, and rejoicing if we're full of judgment about the people we're trying to be loving toward. We must work with our biases and pride first until we reach the point where we can see ourselves in other people and them in us. Out of that recognition of our common wish for happiness and not to suffer—and the common tragedy of not knowing how to make this happen—love and compassion arise naturally.

27 Cultivating the Four Immeasurable Qualities

Having established pure motivation, generate equanimity as you consider the choices of someone in extreme misery that you consider to be responsible for their circumstances. Instead of judging and blaming them, remind yourself how many times you've behaved in similar ways, unconscious of the repercussions of your actions. Then let your mind rest.

When your mind begins to stir again, give rise to compassion by imagining the circumstances of that person's suffering and what it would be like.

Imagine their fear and need until you feel your heart could break. Then let go of the effort, and rest your mind.

When your mind starts to fill again with thought, meditate on loving kindness. Think of what it would be like for that person to be helped, how it would feel if someone was loving and kind to you in such a situation, and wish that for them. Then let go of trying, and rest the mind.

Next, think of those throughout the world trying to help those who are suffering, rejoice in their virtue, and then rest the mind.

Continue to rotate through the Four Immeasurable Qualities as you imagine different people in various scenarios. Alternate each of these effortful practices with resting in the effortless reflection of each quality, without contrivance.

Carolyn: When I did this meditation, I couldn't open my heart, even though I had the sincere wish to access that open heart, so I could be of benefit to more beings.

Lama: The essence of each meditation is that, with whatever we're experiencing, we at least include the intention that our practice be of benefit to others. If we're suffering, we pray that no one else has to suffer. If we're happy, we pray that all beings have such happiness. In that way, it becomes not just about us. We open it up and include everyone within it.

Hillary: Sometimes I'm open, and sometimes I'm not. Having more methods that work when I'm more closed off seems really valuable.

Lama: Whichever practice we feel the most affinity for is often the most accessible doorway to walk through. At the same time, part of the reason for being exposed to a variety of methods is that each of us will find ones that work for us in different circumstances. Some will be effective when we're challenged by great pain or sorrow, and we'll find others that work for us when we're happy and forget to practice.

If we become familiar with a variety of methods, we'll discover which ones are effective in different situations. Also, as we practice more, it's possible that the methods that work for us in any given moment will change. As we continue to practice, we change, and different methods will be helpful. If we've become versed in each of them, we'll have more tools in our toolbox that are accessible to us.

These are all methods that the Buddha taught to point toward suchness, toward mind's nature. Depending what's going on with us, what our current fixation is, what our current poison is, what our current experience is, there's a way to work with it that leads toward wisdom.

Opening the Shutters

The practice of the Four Immeasurable Qualities is like opening the doors and shutters in a dark cabin to let the sun in. Our true nature is like the sun, which radiates in all directions without effort or bias. It's the nature of the sun to shine, and it's our nature to wish for the benefit of all beings.

However, this radiance is obstructed by the artificial, superficial, impermanent walls that we've erected—ironically, in an effort to try to find happiness. We experience pain, so we put up a wall against pain or against the person or situation we think will cause us pain in the future. Or we erect a wall of anger, because that's the habit we've developed to respond to our own or others' pain. These habitual patterns are like walls that demarcate what we call the ordinary mind. It can be so dark inside that we actually believe there can't possibly be anything sacred in here. If we can imagine the presence of light at all, it seems to only exist outside. That's our experience of reality.

When we first hear teachings that suggest something else is possible, it's like turning on a light bulb. Everything is still shuttered, the doors and windows are still closed, but we can start to see more and begin to believe in the possibility of even more clarity and greater insight. But, even with the light turned on, there are still shadows, and we become equally aware of the light and the shadows. Our shadows can scare or discourage us, but now we can see the shuttered window and realize we can open it, and let in more light.

As we practice, we're able to open more windows and let it in more light. The more windows we open, the more the quality of that light dissipates the appearance of the shadows—the experience of darkness within our mind that has caused us to despair of ever being able to get away from our shadows. Every time we practice—which isn't just the *idea* of turning on the light and opening windows and doors, but actually doing it—we have the *experience* of accessing the light of our mind. In the course of doing that, the shadows dissipate until we realize the walls, the door, and the roof were all a fiction.

When we finally tear down the walls, realizing they were our own construction, it can feel like the line in the Pharrell Williams song "Happy"—"Like a room without a roof!" The practice of bodhicitta helps us to deconstruct those walls and remove the roof so we can have the *experience*—not just the *idea*—that something else is possible. Our awareness is pervaded by the radiance of our positive qualities, and we see there's no self-existing, permanent shadows within our mind. The experience of loving kindness, for example, by its nature, dissipates fear, aversion, resentment, and other negative emotions that have accumulated as part of our biased experience. We're living within wisdom, compassion, and loving kindness.

Even though our efforts, at first, may seem forced, like turning on a light bulb, they offer the direct knowledge that light is possible. To the extent we turn on the lights throughout the room, we dissipate the shadows and get closer to the genuine, spontaneous recognition of things as they are. We're awakening to the realization of how things have always been. Finally, if we open all the windows and doors and the walls themselves dissolve, there's no basis for shadows to arise. The environment of negativity we've been mired in no longer exists, and there's no basis for its continuation. Until that happens, we use effort to turn on the lights and open the windows, so we have an increasing sense of illumination. As we rest in the experience of that luminosity of mind, shadows no longer arise.

We aren't trying to construct something new. In fact, we're deconstructing what isn't ultimately true—the layers of the ego, survival mechanisms, armoring, all the ways we've defended ourselves so we can keep going in the face of our karma, our projections, and our movie. Previously, we didn't know how to see through our experience, and we continued to imprint more frames on the film that only perpetuated our confusion. Now we're deconstructing that mechanism and creating new responses. Each time we practice, we open another window or another door to reveal what's already there.

28 Practicing the Four Immeasurable Qualities in Daily Life

Start your day by choosing to practice any or all of the Four Immeasurable Qualities as you establish pure motivation for the day. Then, in every situation when you find someone creating virtue, you'll be reminded that this is a cause for rejoicing. Each time you see somebody suffering is a cause for compassion and, when you see somebody you want to help, that's a cause for loving kindness. If you encounter somebody who's lashing out because they feel isolated and no one understands them, remind yourself how often you've felt and behaved the same way, and give rise to equanimity. In every situation, there's always an opportunity to practice one or more of the Four Immeasurable Qualities. In this way, your daily life is no longer separate from your practice.

Be aware, in each moment, of the choice between following psychology and identity and all the old patterns of the ordinary mind as opposed to following mind's positive qualities. You can use any of the Four Immeasurable Qualities to antidote the negativity, the old patterns, and whatever poisons of the mind are arising in the moment. Always be aware, and ask yourself, "Am I going to choose ordinary mind, ordinary psychology, my habitual orientation to reality, or am I going to choose one or more of mind's positive qualities?" Be aware, always, of that choice we carry with us in each moment.

Then, at the end of the day, see where you fell short and walk yourself through the situations again, reminding yourself how you could have brought practice to them. When you see where there was virtue, when your motivation was pure, and you did everything you could to try to help, dedicate the merit to those beings you were helping, and all beings, so you aren't just helping them in the short run but in the long run as well.

CHAPTER 10. LOVING KINDNESS

Love is the wish that others be happy—a genuine concern about their short- and long-term welfare. Ultimately, the goal of the bodhisattva is to bring love to every corner of the world in every way we can. We develop a relationship with bodhicitta in order to generate equal love for and bring about the ultimate happiness of every living being throughout time and space.

In cultivating our expression of that love through loving kindness, we make the needs of others equally or more important to us than our own. Every time we do that, attachment and aversion—which arise from self-centered and self-important thoughts—are purified.

Loving kindness transforms the whole spectrum of anger, aversion, fear, and ill will—from mild irritation to hatred, rage, and everything in between—so we can be more available and responsive to others. Instead of pushing away what we don't want, we give to other beings what they want. Our attachment and aversion are purified by making everything—our motivation, our life's purpose, who we are, and what we're doing in the world—about others *at least* as much as about ourselves.

Over time, as the limitations to our capacity to love dissipate, we awaken to our innate, boundless love. Immeasurable love isn't limited to those we're close to or those who share our cultural, political, or other values. "Boundless" means the love we feel is not contrived, effortful, or intellectual. Our genuine experience of reality is one of loving every living being equally, whether close or far, liked or disliked.

Equally, we want everyone to be happy. Equally, we experience our function in this collective movie as bringing about benefit and happiness for all living beings. Boundless also means our wish to be of benefit doesn't only arise when we feel good and things are going well and subside when we feel bad and are having challenges. It's completely pervasive.

The more we practice loving kindness, the more our confidence and faith in love as a cornerstone of bodhicitta deepens so that, no matter how much adversity we face, we always have that connection to our positive qualities. As we practice love, it becomes unshakable. As it becomes unshakable, we develop courage, because nothing can diminish it. When love becomes our guidepost, our moral compass, then, even though we still have the aspiration that things will go well for ourselves and others and concern that things not go badly and that beings not be harmed, we can't be shaken. Our faith and confidence in the power of bodhicitta becomes immovable.

Over time, the ore that's obscuring the crystal thins. Our obscurations diminish, because we're undermining the basis of what's obscuring the crystal to begin with—our belief that we're more important than others and, ultimately, that our existence itself is permanent and solid. Every moment that we make our own needs most important adds ore to the crystal. Every moment we put others' needs first removes ore from the crystal and adds oil to the lamp. As the coating of ore on the crystal thins, we may occasionally catch a glimmer of the gem inside: "Wow, I just had a moment of loving kindness that was completely spontaneous and uncontrived!" The more we practice, the more this happens. Slowly, slowly, it happens more and more, and, slowly, slowly, the crystal is revealed.

The Mess in the Sandbox

When we start out trying to practice love, we often find it difficult to make the welfare of others as important to us as our own. We want what we want, and we don't want what we don't want—which is the same with everyone we encounter. The practice of love means we wish everyone could have what would deeply bring them enduring contentment and fulfillment. Of course, this isn't easy. If it were, we'd be all doing it! People want things that are different than what we want, and they don't want what we want for them. We might try to help them and express our love or our wish for their welfare, but they do the very opposite of what we feel is beneficial for them. No matter how much we try to help, we can't make them change. We encounter our resistance to their resistance. We believe in our resistance, and we become righteous about it. We think, "Why do they have to be like that? Why don't they change?"

We have attachment to them doing things the way we think they should, because we're certain that will lead to better outcomes. We're full of bias and judgment about how they're doing things, and all that push-pull in our own mind gets in the way of loving them well. It gets complex when people are making choices to find joy or pleasure that we believe, in the long run, will only harm them. The classic example is someone using a substance—alcohol or pain pills—to get blissed out or find relief from physical or emotional pain. A simplistic understanding of loving would be to just give them more of the substance, enabling their addiction. Loving well means that, in each moment, we need to balance concern for their short-term enjoyment with their long-term welfare.

We need to bring to each relationship a purity of intention, so we aren't lost in our attachment to what we think they should do to be happy or avoid suffering. That's *our* agenda, and our attachment to our agenda prevents us from listening well so we can become aware of what, from their perspective, would most benefit them in that moment while at the same time not creating causes for more future misery. We need to take responsibility for whatever in our mind gets in the way of that and transform it.

Because our intention is to benefit others, we forget to look at our own mind. We assume everything we're doing is beneficial, so we become righteous when they don't let us benefit them or benefit them in the ways we think they should be benefited. They seem to make it so hard to love them, and it starts to seem as if it's their fault that we can't!

We need to remember this is the script of *our* film. It's our attachment and aversion that are getting in the way of expressing the love that's underneath. We can use our conceptual mind to think this through by asking ourself, "Why do I think they should make it easier for me to love them? Why do I think it's their problem? Why do I think they should be, believe, and act as I think they should?" In this way, we realize we've made it all about us, and not them. If it's truly about them, it can't be about our ideas of how they should be or that they should accept and stop resisting our help or how they should behave differently and make other kinds of choices.

When we find ourselves thinking this way, we remind ourselves that our efforts to be more loving aren't about them being the way we think they should be to make it easier for us to love them. It's about us accepting and loving them just as they are. Loving them doesn't mean we have to share every value and agree with everything they do. If we keep bringing the mind back to this thought of making their welfare equally as important to us as our own, this helps us to let go of all our ideas, attachments, aversions, and negative emotions—and that makes it simple again. We want them to find the depth of contentment and peace that's ultimately fulfilling.

Initially, we may have a sort of bargaining perspective on this— for example, if they feel deeply loved and respected, maybe they'll stop destroying the environment, and it will be easier to love them. There's still attachment at the beginning, because that's just where we are at. The moment we become aware of this attachment, we bring our mind back to our wish for their welfare—unconditionally. We keep it simple—without concept, without ideologies, without debates, without righteousness. We have the thought of, "Here's another sentient being who, "just like me," wants to be happy and doesn't want to suffer. May they have joy—not superficial, fleeting gratification, but a depth of contentment and fulfillment."

For us, this doesn't mean straying to a naïve or simplistic understanding of love. For example, we might ask ourselves what could be the benefit of loving somebody who's destroying the environment when we want to do everything we can to stop them.

It's a misunderstanding to think that, in generating a depth of love for someone, we'll become passive and sit back while they harm others. If we really love someone, we want their long-term as well as their short-term welfare. Harming anything or anyone for one's own selfish purpose creates karma that won't benefit them in the long term, and it doesn't create harmonious relationships in the short term. Understanding this, and out of concern for their welfare as well as the welfare of those they're harming, we want to intervene to protect them from themselves.

It's as if we had several children, and one of them was consistently acting out. Would we love that child less and not discipline them, not think about their long-term welfare? Or would we do everything we could to help them, to protect them from the consequences of their actions and from reinforcing habits that are harmful to themselves and others and will make their lives miserable?

Similarly, this person who's destroying the environment needs help to protect them from themselves. We intervene, not with aversion toward them, attachment to correcting them, or righteousness in creating the discipline, but, instead, from kindness. It's as if they're making a big mess in the sandbox of their lives, and they're not going to benefit in the long run from what they're doing. We think these things through and contemplate deeply the teachings we've been exposed to while balancing the short- and long-term benefit of all beings equally.

Hillary: If we see someone we love creating bad karma again and again, are we supposed to just keep loving them? Shouldn't we say, "I'm not going to participate in this, because I can't watch you do that"?

Lama: The "not watching them do it" is our aversion, not love. We must take care of our own stuff first—because for some people in some situations, it's best to take a step back. Sometimes, it's not. We must be honest with ourselves about when we're hitting the limit of our patience, endurance, and capacity to transform our aversion. That's our stuff, not theirs. If we say, "I'm not going to deal with this anymore," that's us.

If we generate genuinely pure motivation and concern for someone's welfare, and transform our attachment and aversion into loving kindness, the quality of what we say and do comes across differently. If our response isn't influenced by the hope it will produce immediate change, the quality of it will be different. The person will know we love them, even if we set a boundary by walking away. If, instead, our reaction is charged because we're triggered or exhausted and impatient, the impact on them will be different. The karma will be different. If part of us wants what's best for them, without an agenda, but part of us has a huge agenda, we have mixed motivation, mixed karma, and the results will be mixed. We won't be creating the pure virtue and inexhaustible merit that arises from bodhicitta. Then, when we dedicate the merit, it won't have the same power as if we'd practiced with it.

That's why we need to be honest about what's going on in our mind and how much we need to purify to give rise to good heart in an authentic way. That means letting ourselves be honest about all those layers of stuff we've tried to ignore. Perhaps we've stayed busy with the appearance of helping, when actually we're totally freaked out and don't know what to do.

When we sit in formal practice, alone with our mind, those layers of stuff become more obvious. If we're aware of what's there, we can apply the respective antidotes, always bringing the mind back to bodhicitta in every moment.

It's sobering. It was so much easier to think everyone else was the problem.

A Heart Space

To take responsibility for our habits that cause us to want others to be the way we want them to be, we must remind ourself that how we perceive and experience them is our projection. We perceive so-and-so as obstinate, stubborn, or grumpy, and yet, ultimately, the nature of each of these beings is pure. Our beliefs about them are entirely our projection. We're unable to see the luminous expanse within the images on the screen of our mind. Only when we start to own our projections and take responsibility for what's happening in our mind can we change. If we don't do this, we continue to expect everybody else to be responsible for the change we want to see in the world.

As we watch our mind, we may find we have the habit of being considerate of others, but we're motivated by hope and fear regarding the consequences in our own life. There may be the appearance that we're benefiting others, but our motivation is for our own happiness. We behave in a certain way because we want people to like, acknowledge, or praise us, or we hope to get something in return. When we recognize such self-centeredness, we might realize we're behaving this way as a survival mechanism—for example, we're attached to someone liking us because we're afraid of what might happen if they don't. Again, this is all about us. At this point, we redirect our mind and ask ourselves what we can do for that person right now.

We also don't want to act out of fear of being self-centered. When we see ourself having that impulse to act out of hope or fear, and we watch the contrast between the outer behavior and the inner motivation, we bring the inner motivation back to our wish to benefit the other person. This doesn't mean we have to do something outwardly. We can just think about their welfare, remembering they want to be happy as much as we do. Maybe they want to be thought well of for all the same reasons we do. Maybe they're as afraid as we are of not being thought well of. We don't get into the story of their lives or our opinions about the choices they may be making. We just focus on making them as important to us as ourself. Our orientation to reality becomes inclusive of everyone.

Again, this isn't just a conceptual process. It's a heart space.

Through meditation, we begin to cultivate loving kindness in an effortful way when it isn't arising spontaneously, and then we let whatever understanding we've come to in that process sink in without effort. We think of someone, generate love for them, and build out to others from there. More deeply, we're using effort to give rise to what's ultimately effortless, to open up what we're currently experiencing. Through our effortless practice, when we then rest the mind, we cultivate a relationship to the limitlessness of the love in our mind and heart as it abides as a quality of our true nature.

Another way to cultivate loving-kindness is to generate compassion for everyone who's finding it difficult to love as they encounter adversity, who find such a contemplation too daunting or don't have access to the teachings or support for practice. Then rest in the effortless experience of uncontrived compassion.

When the mind becomes active once again, commit to the welfare of a particular person or group. No matter how hard this is, remind yourself that everyone wants to be happy as much as you do, and commit to making their welfare and happiness as important to you as your own, to strengthening your love and compassion, to growing and stabilizing your capacity so that, no matter what you encounter, you'll be able to continue to be a force for benefit. You could commit to increase your practice or a certain kind of beneficial activity. Whatever arises from your compassion, commit to that, let it sink in, and then let go of the effort and let your compassion be experienced with less contrivance.

Then turn the mind to prayer, and rest the mind in the wisdom blessings.

Alternating between each of these effortful practices— contemplation, compassion, commitment, and prayer—and rest, is part of how we change our script. The outcome of our movie shifts each time, and, in the state of rest, we have the possibility to recognize the deeper nature of the film, of our life's experiences.

29 Alternating
Meditation on Loving Kindness

To cultivate loving kindness, begin with pure motivation, reminding yourself that others want contentment and joy as much as you do. Open the scope of your awareness by reminding yourself that everything they're doing is a part of their effort to find stable happiness. Make the wish that their fulfillment be at least equally as important to you as your wish for your own.

Think of someone it's easy to love, and you genuinely wish for their welfare—not just in the short run but in the long run. Think about how you wish them everything good, everything fulfilling, and how you're so committed to their welfare that you'd do whatever you could to help them. Give rise to the wish and then the commitment to develop a greater capacity to fulfill them, to meet their needs, to ensure beneficial outcomes for them in the short and long run, and then rest in the essence of that commitment.

Then, let go of the effort to awaken your love and let it just be—not only the love you've given rise to in relation to that person but your love itself, abiding within your heart and independent of them. Simply allow the love you've cultivated to sink in. Let yourself experience it without concept, being with the experience of love instead of the idea of love and the effort to be loving.

Then pray that, by the blessings of limitless wisdom, loving kindness, compassion, and capacity to benefit, this commitment may come to fruition, your capacity may truly increase, and this person and all beings may know only temporary and ultimate benefit and happiness. Then, rest the mind, one with the experience of those blessings.

When the mind starts to get busy again, go back to cultivating love, this time for a different person or type of person, and then, once again, let the mind rest. Next, think of someone you feel more neutral about, and repeat the contemplation alternated with resting the mind.

Expand the visualization to include others that you find easy to love. Walk yourself through wishing the best for them, wishing you had the capacity to bring that about, committing to developing that inner and outer capacity, and praying, alternating with rest.

Continue to expand at your own pace to those you feel more neutral toward, including those it's more challenging to generate love for.

Then think of someone you feel aversion toward—someone that it's tough for you to wish them happiness. Although it's a lot harder to wish for this person's welfare, ask yourself, if you don't do it, who will? Remind yourself you can't expect everyone else to go around loving people who are hard to love so you don't have to. Ask yourself why wouldn't you want this person's welfare? Why would you want them to suffer? Why would you think their suffering will benefit you, them, or the world?

Really think this through, considering individuals you know as well as groups of people, and alternate these contemplations with resting the mind. Keep expanding the scope of your loving kindness to include more and more kinds of people until it encompasses all beings. Keep expanding at your own pace, alternating until the scope of your intention embraces a vast, limitless love for all beings. Then dedicate the merit.

Inez: I've had a couple of moments while working with these meditations in which I've had the feeling I might actually explode. It gets uncomfortable after a minute, and I don't know how to rest in that.

Lama: If you're trying really hard to concentrate, it's possible that's stirring your subtle energies, which can make you feel as if you're about to burst as the tornado-like energy surges through your subtle channels. This can happen sometimes, especially if our subtle energies are already stirred up due to stressful circumstances in our life or past trauma. You might try some of the things we talked about that are recommended in Tibetan medicine for calming down the subtle energies, such as eating more oil and protein in smaller portions and more frequently.

If, during effortful meditation, you feel you're going to explode, try not to identify with that sensation. You may be grasping at a positive experience. If so, when you rest the mind, try to let go of whatever attachment and grasping may be occurring, and, in a less dualistic sense, let there be joy that isn't differentiated. It's the duality of it, the self-concept, and the subtle and not-so-subtle attachment that causes that experience of discomfort. So, just let it all go.

Breanna: I can experience that kind of more expansive love during meditation when I'm in a good place. However, I find it's also very lonely when you're stuck in the middle of everyone else around you who has a more cynical point of view.

Lama: The ultimate loneliness is our separation from ourselves. The more we meditate, the more we come home to ourselves. This illusory movie-like appearance of a self comes home to the recognition that everything is a vast phantasmagoria of light through film. The actual experience of that is like coming home to something we always knew but couldn't put our finger on— something we've always yearned for but didn't know what it was. As we come home to it, we come home to reality itself. The split of identifying with what's obscuring the crystal instead of the crystal itself is no longer there, so everything is known, non-dually, for the inherent beauty, joy, and purity that it is. In that experience, there's resolution of the loneliness of being identified with what's obscuring instead of what's actually the case.

This isn't the same as companionship or as having our path or our process recognized and supported by others. But it's much more deeply fulfilling, because it's not temporary, not based on outer conditions that we have no control over—such as people who get what we're doing or who happen to agree with it or happen to be doing it in the same way. It's something we can evoke in our own mind through our own choice to practice. In this way, it can resolve the existential loneliness.

We might still have periods where we're alone in relationship to those around us, but I think you'll find that the more you practice, the more you live the meditations, and the more you exemplify those qualities, others will be drawn to you. They'll be inspired by your example rather than judgmental or put off by it. Everyone wants to be happy and no one wants to suffer, so, over time, you'll find more and more people you resonate deeply with. You'll find a community.

At the beginning, when it requires the most effort, you have to be patient. When the boulder is tumbling down the hill, it has its own momentum. In that moment, what will sustain you is what we talked about earlier—the conviction that this is the only way to go for the sake of yourself and others.

Doug: How do those of us working in social justice and environmental activism know that we're ready to do the active work? With the practice of loving-kindness, for example, it seems people take that to mean we get to wait our whole life until we're practically enlightened before we can be sure about our motivation and capacity to really make a difference.

Lama: You said, "Get to wait." If we have the idea that we get to wait, that means our motivation isn't pure. It's more like an aversion to suffering and attachment to some kind of temporary comfort where we get to placate and pacify ourselves.

If you're thinking of people who don't understand the consequences of ignoring suffering, choosing comfort over engagement to address suffering, or are so overwhelmed by their own pain they can't see their way forward, you may feel anger or irritation when you assume they're just going to sit in a peaceful meadow, meditate, and forget everyone else. But we're not omniscient. We don't know their motivation. They could be sitting there with a burning compassion, completely aware—from trying so hard to help and continually running into their limitations—that they can't bear it anymore. Their motivation may be to purify the tendencies in the mind that have caused them to be so ineffective.

Instead of judging them and being self-righteous, take your pride and bias into your own practice, creating merit and dedicating it to them for whatever's best. You might start with the Just Like Me meditation to antidote pride, and then generate loving kindness for this person and ever-increasing numbers and kinds of people.

As you continue, you might include those who are averse to working with their minds, because they think spiritual practice is the opiate of the people, and they don't want to hear anything about love and compassion. Maybe they believe that righteousness and anger is the only way to make change, and they're sure their way is the only way.

We then expand the meditation to include the people we perceive as the perpetrators of harm to others and the planet—for example, those who are responsible for corporate decisions to extract minerals from the earth in such a way that they cause tremendous harm to the earth, the climate, and countless numbers of beings, seen and unseen, who are dying from the processes of extraction. They don't understand the karmic consequences of what they're doing and how much worse it will become. We remind ourselves of how many times we've not been aware or not wanted to look at something.

We keep expanding the scope of our meditation until we're able to give rise to an irrepressible love for all beings. From that point of view, we might feel our calling is to act. Sometimes, we feel a great urgency to act right now and, sometimes, we feel we've been trying so hard to act for so long, but we can't bear our limitations anymore.

Maybe that leads us to take some time away to work on our limitations—perhaps an extra hour a day of practice. Maybe, in the evening after a day of trying so hard, we review our day and assess how we did. Did we create more virtue than non-virtue? Where was our mind at, really? What did we do with our body, speech, and mind? Were we nasty, judgmental, self-righteous, or angry?

We then take responsibility for where we fell short, purify through the Four Powers, refresh our bodhicitta, and dedicate whatever merit we created that day to all those we may have harmed consciously or unconsciously out of self-righteousness or ignorance. Then, we go to sleep with the commitment, prayer, and aspiration that tomorrow we'll do better.

Sometimes, we may feel the need to pull away for longer—a day, a week, a month, or even longer. But, until our practice is more mature, it's very hard to pull away and keep our motivation pure. Unconsciously, we can become self-referencing, thinking about our food, laundry, medicine, temperature of the room, or whatever, and it becomes all about us again instead of about others.

In that case, we might start to feel we're getting too disconnected from our purpose and that we need to go back into activity for a little while. In doing this, we always remind ourselves that the reason we're doing this practice and activity is to be able to give rise to and act upon a completely spontaneous, non-referential love and compassion for every being.

We all have different constitutions, tendencies, and aspirations. Some of us have the impulse to be out there on the front lines, and some of us have a tendency to support those on the front lines. Some of us are inclined to help maintain the practice, so it can be shared with other people who have the inspiration to be on the front lines. This doesn't mean that any person, any choice, or any time of our life is better or worse. What matters for each of us is that, whatever we're doing, it's with pure motivation, it's honest, it's true, and it's for the sake of all living beings and not just temporarily but ultimately.

The more integrated our practice becomes, the more deeply it penetrates our understanding of the needs of beings and of our capacity to help. For example, the more we practice the meditations of Just Like Me and Loving Kindness, we naturally and spontaneously become more aware of others and can put ourselves in their place. We become increasingly aware of interdependence, of the impact of our choices on the lives of others—two legged, four-legged, no-legged and ultimately all beings. Less and less do we experience ourselves and our aspirations as separate from those of others.

As our awareness and commitment to others grows, it's as if we emerge from a bubble of self-centeredness. Increasingly, we experience freedom in the context of liberation from the poisons of our mind and freedom of choice in how we respond to the needs of others—as opposed to the "freedom" to be unaware of the experience of others and do what we want regardless of its impact on others. Our experience becomes increasingly one of having the privilege to be able to truly benefit others instead of the "privilege" of distancing ourselves or being clueless about the experience and needs of others.

As our poisons diminish and our loving kindness and wisdom increase, we gain greater insight and equanimity. For example, if a multi-generational family goes to the beach, the children might have the most attachment, aversion, pride, and competitiveness as they create a sandcastle. As they fight over how and where to build it, they have very little insight, as if the castle is real and not made of sand. When the big wave or dog comes along and destroys it, they're bereft at the loss.

Their parents love and want the children to be happy and not to suffer, so they try to reassure them: "Don't worry, we'll make another one." They know it's a castle made of sand, but they want the kids to be happy, so they help them make another one.

The grandparents sit back and watch the whole scene unfold. They have no less love and compassion for their kids or grandkids. They're equally committed to the joy of the whole family, but they aren't as engaged with attachment or aversion, because they have the perspective that comes with age and years and wisdom. They've been there, they've done that, they know what works, and they know what doesn't work. They chuckle and watch it all happen. They know the grandchildren won't listen to what their parents say, they know their own children won't listen to what they say, but it doesn't bother them so much, because they know, in the long run, it will be okay. It's easier for the grandparents to love without bias, attachment or aversion.

The more we practice, we accumulate not just the momentum of merit but also of wisdom. The time we've put in gives us another support as our practice matures. Everything becomes easier to bear. It's not that the outer conditions change miraculously or the body stops falling apart and there's no more illness. But we gain a greater capacity to deal with what's happening and help others to do so as well. As we further experience the blessings of practice, our commitment to it deepens as well as our insight concerning when time away or time engaged with benefitting others can be the most effective.

Relationship as a Spiritual Path

If we begin to bring this quality of loving kindness to all our interactions, all our relationships become a part of our spiritual path. The extent to which we integrate spiritual practice into our relationships has everything to do with our motivation, with what we want for our lives as well as from our relationships. Whether our orientation to relationships is spiritual or worldly, learning how to love well—wanting, more than anything, the welfare of others—expressing that love in actions of body and speech, and continuing to cultivate that love in our practice, is the basis for enduring relationships.

Rinpoche used to say that if we truly learn to love well, it would be hard for others to stay away from us, because we're devoted to their happiness. If our purpose in relationships is to make others happy, few people would run away from that unless we're doing it in a codependent, hypocritical, or superficial way. If we genuinely love them, we know that expressing that love with contrivance or as codependence won't benefit them, whereas the expression of unconditional love and support will.

Intimacy Is a Powerful Mirror

Romantic relationships can provide powerful opportunities to practice loving kindness. Whether or not we're in relationship with someone who's also practicing bodhicitta, it's important that there be enough trust to practice loving kindness sincerely and act virtuously.

In loving well, we can feel raw as we're taking down our defenses or no longer leaving open all our exit doors. We're just there for the other person, and that can expose where our practice needs work. Whether we're entering into a new relationship or evaluating an existing one, we need to consider how interdependence manifests as we try to bring about the happiness of our partner. Does the relationship support the other person's positive qualities, or does it make them distrustful or more negative? With enough mutual trust, when we love well, the other person will be responsive and inspired to also love well, and both our positive qualities will increase.

If there isn't that basis of trust, if our partner thinks they want love, but they want the Hollywood version or some kind of codependent dynamic that fills their superficial needs but doesn't address the causes of long-term benefit, it will be more difficult for us to practice loving kindness in a genuinely pure way. If we keep giving and the other person keeps taking, we may become resentful or angry and destroy our virtue.

This is why it can be so supportive to be in relationship with another practitioner, because they won't support the old habits of the ordinary mind. They support transformation. Even if our partner is a practitioner in a different tradition or simply a genuinely kind and compassionate person, we can examine the interdependence between us and see if we feel supported and inspired enough to constantly practice. We can gauge whether, in every interaction, we deepen our capacity to love, to give rise to compassion, and to rejoice in the welfare and the happiness of another instead of being jealous or competitive or proud that we're the better practitioner or the better person. Intimacy is a powerful mirror, and we get to look in the mirror all the time in an intimate relationship.

As we become closer to someone, we see if and how frequently we're invited into our old habits to be opinionated, cynical, judgmental, or unkind, for example. If those habits are evoked in the relationship, that dynamic can be counterproductive for our practice. If we find we become a better person when we're with them—our positive qualities are reinforced, affirmed, and appreciated—it's possible that this relationship can support our practice.

We need to make sure the interdependence between us allows us to practice well. If we feel that's the case, and we become more committed to the relationship, no matter what arises in the relationship, we take it as practice. We'll love that person through everything. We close those exit doors and deal with whatever challenges come up—even when we feel we want to run away—because we've made a commitment.

A committed, intimate relationship can be very transformative, because it forces change in our habits much more quickly than relationships in which we have the choice to hang up the phone or walk out the door. Those other circumstances allow the ordinary mind to keep avoiding what's difficult or painful. If we're in a committed relationship and taking it as practice, there's no avoiding anything. It's constant.

For some people, this is a fast path and very effective. For others, even in a harmonious setting, it brings up old habits faster than their ability to practice with them. In that case, it can be better not to be in a relationship at all or to take vows, such as vows of celibacy. If one makes this choice out of bodhicitta rather than avoidance, it can be a powerful means for supporting virtue and avoiding non-virtue. Because it's so easy to slip into non-virtuous patterns in relationships, some peoples' practice thrives within a container of celibacy that protects their practice. We need to ask ourselves, at any given time, what choices are the most supportive for our spiritual path.

When we spend time with someone, we need to check: are our positive qualities increasing, or are our old, negative habits increasing? Are our pride and competitiveness increasing, or are our love and compassion growing? What happens in our mind when we interact? Even if the dynamics start out on a not-so-spiritual level, can we transform our responses? Does the other person support and respond well to the change? All of that is part of seeing if the relationship will work for us as a means of loving well and supporting our practice.

Informal Practice of Loving Kindness

Whenever you interact with others in your day-to-day life, practice making their welfare equally important as—if not more important than—your own. In every situation, ask yourself how you can be of benefit. How can you bring benefit and happiness to this person or these people?

Gently and repeatedly bring your mind back to loving kindness. Allow someone to step ahead of you in line at the grocery store, or don't respond negatively when someone is reactive with you, recognizing there may be all kinds of reasons they're having a bad day. This exceedingly simple practice can serve to calm and focus the mind's tumult while creating benefit for others.

When you start noticing your resistance, concepts, and judgment stirring, pay attention to how they're interfering with your ability to express your wish for the other person's welfare. Whatever comes up outwardly, and whatever your mental or emotional response inwardly, keep asking yourself what this person needs, how you can help them, or how you'd think or act differently if you made their welfare equally important to you as your own. In this way, you can respond to their needs with sincerity and genuine care.

Carolyn: If all we're doing is thinking of the needs of others, how do we get our needs met?

Lama: The key is to understand what the true causes of happiness are. If we keep putting our needs before those of others, we're actually pushing away happiness in the long run. Only our intention and efforts to benefit others plant seeds of happiness.

Ida: How do I make sure I'm not being taken advantage of or becoming some kind of a doormat if I'm being generous like this when no one else around me is? Sometimes, when I've tried to be kind or generous, I regret it later because of other peoples' responses.

Lama: The most important thing (surprise!) is to always generate pure motivation at the beginning of any virtuous action and dedicate the merit at the end. If we truly do something for the purpose of benefiting another, without any expectation of receiving something in return—such as praise or gratitude—we won't have regret, no matter what their response.

Over time, if we're honest with ourselves as we look into the mirror of our mind, we'll see when we've extended beyond our current capacity and our selfish gesture boomerangs back to us in the form of regret. At the same time, this is a mind training—a mental exercise in growing and extending our capacity to love—so we may need to learn to live with some discomfort during the stretch. As long as we've dedicated the merit of any virtuous act, the virtue won't be spoiled by regret at a later time. And our capacity for loving kindness will grow.

Breanna: I find that when I'm in a good mood, thinking about the welfare of others is more difficult. It's harder to settle my mind down, and the practice doesn't feel as deep. It feels so good to feel good, so I just want to have a break and enjoy feeling good. What am I supposed to do with that? I don't want to feel guilty for feeling good.

Lama: Of course, but remember that everyone else wants to feel good, too. You don't have to deny the good feeling, just wish it could be so for everyone. Think of it as not just your own good feeling, but ask what you can do to make such joy possible for others as well.

We often aren't inclined to investigate happiness, because we like it. We want to believe it's permanent, solid, real, and will last forever. But that's a trap, because it *will* change. In proportion to how attached we've been to the happiness, to that degree we'll suffer when we lose it. That's why we need to work with it in meditation as well.

Breanna: How do I sit with that for extended periods of time?

Lama: Include everyone in your motivation, and then rest the mind. Contemplate impermanence—specifically, the impermanence of your happy state. Yesterday you weren't happy, today you are, and tomorrow you might not be. Then, rest the mind. If your contemplation starts to become stagnant and you can't find the depth in it, remind yourself that the impermanence of happiness is true not just for you but for every living being as well.

Whenever any of us finds happiness, no matter how much attachment we have to making it last, there's nothing we can do to assure it will. If we rely on what's composite, impermanent, and unfree in an effort to make it last, we must remind ourself that it won't. Not long ago, we were suffering acutely, and now we have a moment of happiness and contentment. This cycle happens for every living being. Without perspective on our experience, we have attachment to the good times and don't want to acknowledge that it will all change, and we'll suffer when it does. When you practice this way for an extended period of time, contemplate impermanence for others as well as yourself, and then rest the mind. Keep alternating like that.

Ocean: The element of physicality, of desire, is so compelling, and all wrapped up in that feeling of love, especially in the beginning of a relationship. How do we navigate what's real and what isn't, what's love or simply desire?

Lama: This is a good reason to take it slow, because that gives us time to see if this is only desire. If we want this person in our life for all our own reasons, that's desire. We have to ask ourselves, what do we want for them? Do we want them to be happy? Can we make that wish at least as strong as our wish for our own? Does the interdependence in the relationship support making their happiness at least equally important as our own?

Doug: Desire is something I'm continually struggling with— the habit toward self-flagellation for feeling it that's associated with other religious traditions and sorting out my motivation when I want something.

Lama: The chemistry of desire is yet another reason to take the progression of our intimacy slowly. As those sensations arise, examine them. Does this sensation of desire really exist? Does it have a beginning and an end, a color, a shape, a size? What's this thing that's causing me to jump into bed with someone when I could have so much regret a week down the road? Try to find it. If you can't find it, relax the mind. Or, even if you think you've found it, relax the mind.

This is a powerful practice that can purify desire over time. The sensation of desire is so strong and compelling that, to see through it—to be able, even as it's arising, to have the direct experience of there being no *thing* there called desire— transforms our experience of the sensation. It's no longer characterized by the "I" that wants something from "you" and engages in activity to get something "I" want. Desire can be transformed into the experience of its empty nature inseparable from love and compassion. This is extremely profound and transformative.

This is another reason to take it slow—if we rush in, we reinforce the habit to being lost in the desire. We want to know we have a partner we can practice with. These are pros and cons to think about. There's no "should" here, but, on the emotional level of intimacy, jumping in has its consequences. There's karma there. If we become intimate with someone, they're opening their heart, and may have expectations. If we haven't arrived at a mutual understanding of the nature of our relationship, or we haven't had enough time to see if the relationship works for practice or even on a worldly level, and then we realize the person or situation isn't what we'd thought and we want to leave, there's karma—especially if the other person still wants the relationship. We're hurting them. These are things to consider as we decide about the rate at which we energize the relationship. Be careful. You might think about it and talk about it with the other person. Or you might decide together to take it to the next level and sort it out later, with both of you taking responsibility for your part in what happens. If you then decide to go for it, it isn't the same kind of karma if you later decide it isn't a good fit.

Anthony: If we can be in a relationship sincerely for the purpose of cultivating relative and ultimate bodhicitta, it seems every other aspect of the relationship, including its length, would become a secondary concern. Determining the success of the relationship would be based on whether it helps us increase our bodhicitta. Is this correct thinking?

Lama: For each of us, it depends on our goals in life, in general, not just in relationship—how we conceive our life and the purpose of our life. No matter what our goal is, if we practice loving kindness and compassion, it will diminish our negativity and increase our positive qualities. Our ability to be of benefit to others will only increase, and the positive circumstances reflected in our own movie will be infallible. Whether our goal is to completely remove all the ore and reveal all the positive qualities of the crystal in this very lifetime or whether our goal is to find as much happiness as we can along the way or anything in between, if we practice, that will infallibly lead us in that direction. The extent to which we practice is the extent to which the ore will be removed from the crystal, and the nature of the crystal will be revealed.

It's up to each of us, and we must be honest. If our motivation in a relationship is to be able to cultivate loving kindness, bring happiness to another person, and practice with our partner because intimacy is such a fast path, other issues do become secondary to the practice. If this is the case, it's only fair that the partner be someone who shares that goal. Otherwise, our partner may be attached to establishing conditions for happiness that look different from ours and conform more with the way our culture views relationships and happiness. If we aren't looking at it that way, this can cause them pain at a certain point.

To be honest with a partner, we must be honest with ourself about what our real purpose is in life. Within that context, everything falls into place—the purpose of our work, the purpose of our practice, the purpose of our relationships—and it's all consistent with our overall life purpose. However, if we kid ourselves and convince ourselves that our purpose is to cultivate bodhicitta in everything we do, but that's not where we're really at—even though we wish we were—we'll run into trouble. Where our heart and mind actually are at will come into conflict with the practice we're trying to do. If that happens, we might blame the practice and reject the path.

Slowly, as we practice more, it informs our sense of life purpose. What we truly think, who we truly are, and what we truly want will change. Just because, intellectually, we want a particular thing, if we're not there emotionally, this will create disturbance in our mind. We need to do practice aligned with where we are now, what our emotions are now.

If we're considering a partnership or talking with our partner about our relationship, both of us need to be honest about where we are right now but also what our aspirations are for our lives—where we'd like to be, where we're headed—so that, within that honesty, there can be enough trust to determine whether the relationship can be virtuous and a cause of benefit or whether it might potentially be a cause of harm for one or both people. As always, it comes back to looking in the mirror of the mind and being fully honest about what we see.

30 Transforming Fear with Love

Having established pure motivation, bring to mind someone that you find it easy to access your love for. Make the aspiration that, whenever you're with this person, you're nothing other than a force of love for them.

If you have a practice of prayer, pray that this love be stabilized, strengthened, and grow until there are no more limitations. If you have any fear that comes up regarding that person, bring your love to that fear. Does it have the capacity to dispel that fear? If what you're afraid of were to happen—be it death, illness, separation—does that change the love? Does it change your commitment to or expression of love? Is the love reliable in the face of whatever that thing is? Alternate each of these contemplations with resting the mind.

Then think of others you love—members of your family, friends, or community. Think of each of them and how much you wish for their happiness and that you'd do whatever you could to bring that about. Think about their needs and wishes, and make the aspiration to grow your capacity to love, to bring them happiness, to be able to cultivate whatever's of greatest benefit to them. Make the commitment to make that quality of love and caring more accessible and more stable. Then rest the mind.

Pray that your capacity to grow your love might increase so it's equal to or greater than their need. Bring to mind your fears in relation to these people, your fear of their suffering. Practice maintaining your love in the face of that fear. Is that love stronger than the fear and the object of the fear? Is it reliable? If it feels less powerful than the fear or the object of fear, make a commitment to grow that love so it will be reliable in the face of whatever circumstances arise.

Then let the mind rest.

Think of others you don't know as well but that you deeply want nothing other than their welfare. Make the aspiration that their needs and wishes be fulfilled and that your own love become equal to or greater than their need. Commit to cultivate that quality of love, and pray for this to happen, alternating with resting the mind.

Think of others that your feelings are more neutral for. You may not feel an easily accessible love for them, but they also want to be happy and don't want to suffer. Wish that you could be the cause of their happiness. Make the commitment to practice so your love can deepen and grow to encompass their needs and their aspirations—not just short-term but long-term—and pray that this be accomplished. Then rest the mind.

Include those you feel fear or aversion toward, who it's harder to generate love for. There's bias, judgment, and maybe righteousness. However, every one of those beings also wants to be happy, and not a single one wants to suffer. When we think of our love for others, this includes everybody, no matter their temporary choices. We want for them the causes and conditions of happiness and a deep fulfillment, and we pray we can offer that for them. Make the commitment to cultivate and grow your practice to make this possible, pray that it be so, and then rest the mind.

Keep expanding your visualization at your own pace to include more and more beings. When you bump up against any kind of resistance or hesitation about wanting their happiness, ask yourself if your hesitation is about them or about you. Are you hesitating to love them or to want their happiness, or is that hesitation about you wanting what you want and not wanting what you don't want?

Is it true you don't want them to be happy or, deep underneath all those layers of stuff, is there a wish for their fulfillment? Access that wish, and grow it. Make the aspiration that it only grow bigger and stronger, stabilize and deepen. Make a commitment to do the practice to make that possible. Pray that it be so, and then rest the mind. Keep expanding to include more and more beings until there's a sense of your love encompassing the scope of all beings, which is limitless, just like your love is limitless. Then, let the mind settle in the effortless experience of immeasurable love.

When you're aware of the fear you have in relation to all beings or particular categories of beings, look at what's stronger in your mind—the love or the fear. If your fear is stronger, ask yourself what would happen in your life, over time, if you keep giving in to the fear and if that's what you want to underlie your choices. Do you want your life to be informed by love or by fear? Then rest the mind.

When you allow yourself to deepen your love, does that diminish the fear? If you're able to sustain the love, does it allow you to keep going in the face of fear or fearful circumstances? Are you able to continue to love despite the fear? If not, make a commitment to continue to practice, to grow your capacity so that, over time, everything you do comes from love rather than fear, has the capacity to dispel the fear, allows you to be courageous and consistently responsive to the needs of beings. Then, let the mind rest.

Dedicate the merit of your practice with the aspiration that the virtue created be the cause of the happiness and welfare of all beings and of the capacity within yourself and all beings to actualize our limitless, immeasurable love.

CHAPTER 11. COMPASSION

Compassion abides naturally in our mind and heart. It arises interdependently when we encounter suffering. If we allow ourselves to remain open and aware without erecting walls to defend ourselves from it, our compassion will naturally arise as a spontaneous response to the suffering we witness. If we don't close ourselves down through habits such as self-protection, compassion can't help but arise and even overflow.

Once accessed, the power of that compassion is like an open spigot. When we first turn on a spigot that has sat unused, only a trickle of water may emerge because of the mineralization in the pipe. If we turn it on all the way and let it run, the water soon washes away the mineralization and begins to flow freely. Compassion is kind of like that. All we need to do is practice and, the more we practice, the more easily it flows.

There are a number of words we can use to describe the process of accessing our innate compassion—cultivating, arousing, giving rise to, generating—and yet, all we're doing is creating the conditions that allow what's already there to be made evident. Allowing ourselves to evoke it tears down, dissipates, and purifies whatever may be impeding it. This is why, when we're doing practice, we can feel so naked, vulnerable, and raw.

We may find that, between the time when our walls are dismantled and when we develop confidence in the presence of our innate compassion, we'll feel uncomfortable. It takes time to feel at home and identify with our positive qualities. Often, our first initial experience as the walls come down is, "Oh no! There are no walls!"

We can feel naked and exposed—which is the reason we put up those walls in the first place. It can be unpleasant, even terrifying. Throughout our life, we've been trying to protect ourselves using the defenses we developed to survive, to cope, and to keep ourselves going through the projected phenomena of our own film. Now that we're practicing, those defenses are starting to come down. But, as we let ourself be with what remains in the absence of the walls, we find a wealth of compassion and love.

Earlier in our life, we might have experienced situations in which we were overwhelmed with our own or others' suffering, or where letting ourselves feel and exhibit our positive qualities caused unfavorable responses from those around us. Doing practice, we realize we don't need to be frightened by our positive qualities or feel the need to obstruct and hide them. We now have tools to nourish and sustain them, and we're learning, through our practice, that compassion and love are more powerful than all the artifice we've constructed. The radiance of a compassionate heart—like the radiance of the sun—warms and nurtures everything it touches.

Our inherent compassion is boundless—the potential to give rise to equal compassion for victim and perpetrator, for example. We don't just respond compassionately to the victim. We respond equally to both victim and perpetrator to uproot the whole cycle of victim and aggressor. We understand we've all placed our needs before those of others or left others behind or pushed them aside, not knowing how else to find happiness.

Our compassionate responsiveness to the plight of beings is based on the depth of our sorrow. We realize that, in the very course of trying to find happiness, we all create the opposite and so perpetuate the cycle endlessly. Our sorrow gives rise to a deep commitment to interrupt that endless sequence of self-perpetuated suffering for ourselves and all beings. We understand that if we can't interrupt it for ourselves, it's almost impossible to help others interrupt it, so we must start with our own practice.

A story is told of a Tibetan monk who spoke of his terror when he was imprisoned and tortured—not of being killed but of losing his compassion.

Such unbiased compassion is valued in every authentic spiritual tradition. Those who are genuine practitioners within those traditions are recognized by their qualities of love and

compassion, which they share with and express toward everyone equally. Because these traits have been actualized through their spiritual practice, they're apparent to anyone who makes connection with them. Each tradition has its own methodology for achieving those qualities, but the outcome benefits all those around them.

Practicing Compassion

In the practice of compassion, we're allowing ourselves to be aware of the depth of suffering within and surrounding us rather than pulling away or turning a blind eye to its presence. Through our practice, we remember, evoke, or awaken what's already there. The effort of "cultivating compassion" purifies what's in the way. In this process, instead of defending ourselves against suffering—for example, being overwhelmed with feelings of discouragement or despair, being unable to deal with it, or not having the capacity to respond—we sit with it until we're able to respond from the strength of our innate qualities.

We start by bringing to mind a person or situation in which our compassion is more accessible. This process could begin with someone we've never met and likely will never meet in this lifetime but are aware of through the media. It might be a mother in a part of the world rife with famine who has a baby she can't breastfeed anymore, because she's so malnourished. There's no food and, even if there's a rumor of food some miles away in a refugee camp, she doesn't have the strength to get there. Perhaps she had other children that have already died, and now she's dying. She's losing the strength to keep her last remaining child alive. She may have no energy to comfort or talk to her child. This scenario may feel abstract to us if our stomachs are completely or partially full, but we need to remind ourselves that this is the life experience of hundreds of thousands of people in this very moment.

We put ourselves in her place. We might imagine what it would be like for us if all the complex networks in our civilization for producing and distributing food were no longer available, and the stores of food we had were gone—the situation of so many in our world right now. If we don't have kids, perhaps we imagine our parents, our siblings, or our friends. We want to help and give them everything they need, and we can't bear to know they're suffering so deeply. But we can't do anything, because what strength we have is dissipating. No matter how strong our will, it can't break through the weight of our body as our life-force wanes. We have no strength to accomplish our wish to help. There's no food, no water, and, wherever we look, everyone is experiencing the same thing. We imagine how completely desperate we'd feel for any kind of help—if not for ourselves then for our loved ones. All we'd hope for is just a little bit of food to get us or our loved one through another day.

31 Alternating Meditation on Compassion

We imagine ourselves in these circumstances until we have a vivid sense of that experience—what it would look, feel, and sound like. Then, we rest the mind and stop trying to generate these images and feelings and simply let our mind be with that experience. When the mind starts to ramble again, we return to thinking about how many beings are in that situation right this minute—how much suffering there is and how much we want to help.

This way, we become aware of the depth of our compassion—how, beneath all our layers of defenses, what we really want is for that suffering to end. Beneath the discouragement, the conceptualization, the habit to blame others for our problems; and beneath all the strategies, the despair, the sense of powerlessness and hopelessness lies the desire to end the suffering of beings. We let ourselves open to that depth of misery and become aware of the power of our compassion and our wish to do everything we can to uproot that suffering. Then we let go of the effort and rest in that pervasive experience of compassion.

When the thoughts and emotions begin to stir again—"There's no way I can help," or "The problem is so much bigger than me" or whatever they may be—we let the energy of compassion—which, by its nature, is expressive and dynamic—lead to a commitment. The nature of that commitment is different for each of us and may be different each time we do this meditation. It might be the inspiration to volunteer for or send a monthly donation to a humanitarian-aid or social-change organization, or it may be the inner commitment to continue to cultivate compassion so it overpowers any despair or sense of powerlessness. Whatever it is for each of us, it's the dynamic expression of compassion that has the power to purify, cut through, and express itself for the benefit of others.

We let ourselves be aware of our commitment and again rest the mind, letting that commitment sink in and settle.

Then we may begin to wonder how we can uphold our commitment and find the strength and diligence to follow through. At this point, we pray to whosoever/whatsoever embodies limitless wisdom, loving kindness, and capacity to benefit that the compassionate, enlightened intention of their heart may awaken in us our own limitless, enlightened intention for the sake of all beings. We pray from the depth of our heart to have the capacity to uphold that commitment and, again, rest the mind.

32 Expanding Alternating Meditation on Compassion

For some of us, our compassion may be more easily awakened by something closer to home, so we start there—with our family members, friends, neighbors, or coworkers who are dealing with unemployment or food scarcity or other challenges. Or with somebody we know and care about who's seriously ill, perhaps without health insurance. Maybe they're in the hospital and connected to machines. Maybe they're at home, bedridden, and their body is wracked with unstoppable pain. We imagine what that would feel like. They had a life. They had work they did in the world to support and nurture themselves and their family. They felt active and engaged. They believed they could contribute, make a difference, and express what was important to them through their body and speech. Now they're no longer able to do any of this. They're no longer able to follow their intentions with action, because illness has overcome them. They may be unable to express what's in their hearts. They can't support themselves or take care of their family. Everything they associated with a meaningful life they're unable to do anymore.

Imagine no longer being able to live the life we know, because the connection between body and mind has changed. There's the loss of identity, the loss of hope, and the loss of the sense of belonging to a community. There's the despair and hopelessness of not knowing what to do with the mind without the body being available.

Imagine how it feels to be so powerless, to feel so isolated, disconnected, desperate, and to not know who we are anymore. Maybe we have a terminal diagnosis, and there's no basis for optimism—only more powerlessness and more pain. We imagine what that would feel like if we didn't have a spiritual path that offered tools to deal with it.

And then we rest the mind.

Next, generate compassion for others in similar situations— in hospitals, in hospice, or who are alone on the street—homeless, jobless, no family, without dignity, promise, or dreams. Then, we let go of trying, and rest in our heart of compassion.

Again, we let the dynamic energy of that compassion express itself as a commitment. It may be a commitment we make to ourself never to forget the suffering of beings and/or to be responsive in whatever way we can, inwardly and outwardly— whatever it is that arises as an expression of our compassion.

Then, again, we rest the mind and let the power of that intention settle deeply into our mind and heart.

Finally, we pray that our capacity to be responsive, to uphold and express that commitment, be sustained and increase until the causes and conditions of the suffering of every being have been completely uprooted. Then, we rest the mind.

33 Generating Compassion for Those We Feel Aversion Toward

Now we think of somebody we feel aversion toward—to the person themselves, to their choices, or to the role they're playing in our life or the lives of others. We try to put ourself in their place and imagine their experience. Maybe they're not suffering in the moment but are causing harm to others and planting seeds of future suffering. We imagine what it's like to be that person and try to conceive of the world as they do. We imagine that what they choose to do is the only choice they believe they have to get what they want for themselves and those they love. We imagine what life is like from their perspective. Due to the causes and conditions that created their personal karma, they can't conceive of different choices or behavior. It could be that, even if they have exposure to the idea there could be a different way, they don't believe it's possible. They couldn't imagine getting support for doing things differently, or they don't know how else to behave. Maybe it's the power of habit, maybe it's the power of the environment, but all they know to do is to continue to plant seeds of suffering for themselves and others.

We ask ourselves, what would it be like to experience the world as offering no choices other than to hate or kill or destroy or overpower? What would it be like to have no sense there are windows that can be opened and that all our choices are informed by illusion? And what would it be like to have no sense of refuge or safety, inwardly or outwardly, other than in causes of future misery, and no recognition of how profoundly our choices are perpetuating that misery?

We imagine this is our experience—with no possibility of positivity, no possibility of receiving or expressing kindness or even believing that was possible. All we can see is more and more negativity. What would that level of despair or overwhelm feel like?

And then, we rest the mind.

We think of everybody we can imagine who has this experience of reality. The only options they're aware of are options that involve hurting others. Whether this is due to their culture, their habit, their beliefs, their psychology, or their brain chemistry, it's all they know. In their effort to find relief from pain, all they know to do is create more of it. Think of how many beings this is true for.

Once more, rest the mind.

Then the compassionate insight we've awakened wants to express itself. This expression may emerge as a determination to no longer judge, reject, demonize, or ignore that person but rather to try to help them, to do what we can to protect them from themselves and their own harmful actions, or whatever commitment we're inspired to make.

Again, we rest the mind.

We then pray that we can help them, help those they're harming, and help uproot not only the immediate experience of suffering but the deeper causes and perpetuation of that suffering. We pray we might find our way through so we can help them find their way through in a different way than they have been. Then we rest the mind.

Keep expanding the meditation, adding different objects of compassion to include more and more beings. We start with those we feel a more accessible compassion for, so we can develop confidence, and then we keep extending the practice outward to include even those we feel the most negative connection with until, ultimately, it includes all beings. Then we dedicate the merit.

Rely on compassion to dissolve whatever old habits arise in the mind—resistance, overwhelm, powerlessness. Sometimes we may find it easier to recognize our own mental obstacles in someone else. We may see how someone has a huge capacity for compassion and yet they feel devastated, discouraged, or depressed. We generate compassion for them, extend that to all others, and, in doing so, we, ourselves, are included.

Whenever the storyline, old psychology, or old familiar mental habits come up, we can also try the alternating meditation—contemplation, compassion, commitment, and prayer alternated with resting the mind. In the course of practicing these various meditations, we can become more familiar with recognizing our projections as not inherently true and taking responsibility for them, so we can reclaim our power as the screenwriter and change the script. We're writing a new screenplay here, creating new images on the film, and all the scenes are arising as the display of compassion.

Take the time to do formal meditation according to the steps of the Alternating Meditation just described or in a different order, whatever is most effective for you at any given time. If remembering and practicing all these steps seems too contrived, just do the two steps of eliciting compassion through effort and then resting the mind. All these approaches bring us closer to realizing our inherent compassion.

Let the energy of your compassion fuel your practice. It *will* make a difference. This doesn't mean you don't do anything outwardly. But, ideally, everything we do is imbued with this depth of compassion as the basis.

Don't dampen your heart. Don't give in to even the tiniest smidgen of discouragement or despair. Those are our demons of self-centeredness rising up to obstruct our practice and activity for the benefit of others. Don't give them any power. Generate compassion for them, and keep going.

Ignite your compassion. It can purify and carry you through any outer or inner obstacles. But only that depth of compassion can cut through. It's painful, but if we allow that compassion to serve as the basis of everything we do with body, speech, and mind, our world will look very different. Over time, our capacity to benefit others will only expand. If we pull away from the suffering of beings, we compromise our ability to help—whether we're alone in a cave, in the middle of the Bronx, or any place in between. Every moment we pull back from the needs of beings creates an interdependence to not be fully present, to not be available to help.

We balance the short-term responsiveness of our compassion with the wisdom to know we need to tame and train our minds. We need to cultivate patience and diligence, so we can keep going in the face of our own and other's hardships.

Compassion antidotes and transforms self-centered desire, which includes attachment and the whole tendency of the mind to want things for ourselves. This is an extremely strong habit. We're drawn to something, so we grasp after and try to possess it, to uphold the illusion that its presence in our life can remain stable. As we give rise to compassion, the power of that compassion purifies the self-centered wanting of something for ourselves. We transform that wanting of something for ourselves through our wish to take away from others the causes and conditions of their suffering.

This is the formal practice.

Inez: The meditation on compassion is profound and disturbing. Every time I do this meditation, I feel committed to making a change and doing something, but then I think the problems are too immense. I saw a picture in the newspaper the other day of a neighborhood in Syria that had been bombed out. Thousands of people were waiting for promised food and aid that didn't arrive. That made me think, "What can I possibly do that would make a difference?"

Lama: Here's what's so ironic. When we become so overwhelmed by witnessing, hearing, and encountering suffering that we give in to our old patterns—the habits of the ordinary mind to suppress, ignore, give up—we're not letting compassion fully arise in our hearts. If we let ourselves be fully and unceasingly present with our compassion—to the extent that our heart is breaking wide open—the strength of that compassion would be enough to fuel our complete awakening in this very lifetime! If we take that energy—without diminishing it in any way—as the basis for everything we do with body, speech, and mind, our ability to benefit others will increase inconceivably.

Informal Practice of Compassion

Watching or reading the news can be an extremely powerful method for cultivating compassion through exposure to events that we might otherwise try to avoid. By being aware of that suffering and not shutting down to it, we allow our own innate compassion to emerge. The more contact we have with the experiences of others, the more avenues there are for transformation through compassion.

When you see something happening to someone that upsets you, instead of turning away—our usual impulse when something causes us emotional distress—put yourself in that person's shoes. Imagine what it would feel like, look like, and sound like to be undergoing so much suffering. Spend as much time as you need to put yourself in their place until your sense of their experience isn't separate from your own, and then rest the mind. Step back and call to mind how many beings are being devastated by these kinds of circumstances right in this very moment. Generate compassion, and then, again, rest. Generate commitment, and then rest. Finally, pray, and then rest the mind.

Anthony: When I consider my difficulty in being compassionate, I realize I need to deepen my confidence in cause and effect.

Lama: It sounds as if you're saying if someone makes choices that are difficult for you to accept, you're asking yourself how you can have compassion for them if you can't see all the cause and effect at play.

There's one effect that's clear—you don't like that person. This could be because of the choices they've made, the actions they've taken, or the role they're in. One of the consequences is that you have an aversion to them. In the context of the meditation we just did, think of what it's like for them to have not only you but others dislike them.

Anthony: It's not aversion to one particular person, necessarily. When people are in a position of authority, they tend to cut you down—to say you're an idiot or something like that—and, many times, I believed they were right. However, there was something in the back of my mind that said it wasn't true, and that would make me angry at them.

Lama: Right, and that anger is a consequence of what they did. If they're doing that with everybody, they're surrounded by angry people. Think about what it must be like to be them—with no idea of their responsibility in the creation of an environment of people they must work with who are bitter and resentful. You don't have to go very far to see the consequences—just look at how it's affected you. Think about how it's impacted others as well and what it's like for them to live in the middle of that. Alternate that contemplation with compassion, commitment, prayer, and resting the mind.

Limitless Opportunities for Compassion

Through these meditations, we're developing a new habit of responding to our everyday stimuli with compassion instead of trying to prevent our discomfort by erecting defenses or creating coping mechanisms. If we allow ourselves to truly be aware of others, it's obvious there are limitless opportunities for compassion. There are those who are ill or in pain, others who are experiencing great hardship, hunger, or other deprivation. If we let ourselves be aware, every moment of every day is an opportunity for informal compassion practice.

If we react in a knee-jerk way to suffering without balancing that with formal practice, we won't have the necessary staying power in our personal practice or in our efforts to help others. On the other hand, if most of our practice time is spent in solitary meditation, a very subtle self-contentment and self-clinging can arise. We can start to become fascinated with our personal process and think less and less of others. It's subtle and alluring. That demon of self-clinging can easily insinuate itself into our practice if we don't have the benefit of exposure to the magnitude of suffering in the world.

As we're developing and stabilizing our practice of bodhicitta, we need to do both: immerse ourselves in the methods that refine away self-clinging and then emerge to try to help others.

Otherwise, it's very hard to keep compassion foremost in our mind and heart. Whether in the context of solitary meditation or in the context of organized activity, it's so easy to get overwhelmed by burnout, hope, and fear.

We all need to wake up, and, if we're fortunate enough to have access to methods and practices that help us do this, we need to devote ourselves wholeheartedly to them in the short time we have. We can never assume we have another day, no matter our age or health. We can only be certain of having this moment. If we understand the need for benefiting beings and generating compassion, we know we need to use every moment we have to work with our minds. If there's something we can do outwardly to benefit others, we bring the full power of our bodhicitta to every situation in order to make the greatest possible impact. But there's always something we can do inwardly in every moment through our practice to increase our capacity for benefit.

We don't want to feel regret at the moment of death—to look back and think we had the opportunity to be of benefit but didn't take it. Instead, we want to remind ourselves, always, in each moment, that we have an inkling of an understanding of how to practice and increase our positive qualities, so this is our opportunity to do what we can.

Never forgetting what Rinpoche said—that one millisecond of true compassion can purify eons of karma—imagine if we had that compassion in our heart all the time. That's a really fast path!

CHAPTER 12. TONGLEN: TAKING AND SENDING MEDITATION

What we want for anyone—and for all living beings—is the end of suffering and to bring about their stable happiness and fulfillment. It's simply love and compassion. We create as much merit as we can, join that with the power of dedication, and make the aspiration that, by this virtue, all suffering be uprooted and that the health, prosperity, and welfare of all beings come to pass. Our "aspiration" is the expression of pure love and compassion that has nothing to do with our own agenda based on attachment and aversion.

We can generally refer to aversion as mental states that fall along a spectrum from mild irritation to fear to terror to rage. They all have to do with not wanting what's happening or being afraid of something that might happen. At the core of aversion is not wanting—the impulse in the mind to push something away. When we have fear about love, for example—such as about how loving someone might hurt us—we create a push-pull in our intimate relationships and in our relationship to love itself.

We can generally refer to attachment as mental states that range from mild curiosity to fixation to outright obsession, all of which have to do with wanting something—the impulse in the mind to fixate on, grasp at, and hold on to what we want, to the exclusion of the needs and wants of others. It's our grasping and pushing away that fuels endless suffering for ourselves and others. The ordinary, untrained mind's habit is to take for ourselves what's good and to reject what's bad, not realizing that we're creating long-term outcomes that will be the opposite of what we want.

To transform this habit, it doesn't work to pretend we don't have attachment and aversion. Rather, we can use those very poisons to purify themselves by making our wishes about others instead of about ourselves. Changing the object changes the outcome. We replace the wish for our own happiness and the end of our suffering by wishing these for others. The very practice of being attached to the happiness of others and averse to their suffering gives rise to increasingly profound and vast love and compassion which, by their nature, purify those mental poisons. Over time, our love and compassion become more pure, and our attachment and aversion diminish, until all that's left is love and compassion.

It's a process.

There's a powerfully effective meditation that does just that. It's called *tonglen* in Tibetan, which means, "taking and sending." With tonglen meditation, we're reversing our habit of pulling toward ourself what we think will give us happiness—attachment—and pushing away what we don't want—aversion. We do this through compassion—pulling towards us what others don't want—loving kindness—and sending them what they do want. The compassionate wish that the suffering of others would end purifies wanting happiness for ourselves. The loving wish for the happiness of others purifies fear and aversion. It's hard to have pure-hearted compassion and still have aversion.

Our compassion—wanting to take away others' suffering—helps us to transform the habit to take what we want for ourselves. Instead of trying to send away what we don't want—that which is causing us suffering—we send to others the causes and conditions of happiness. Through the loving impulse to send what's good instead of pushing away what's bad, our love transforms our aversion.

In tonglen practice, we're doing both—taking in the suffering of others and sending them happiness—at the same time. We imagine we're taking not only the current conditions of their misery but all the karmic causes of this and all possible future suffering. And we're sending not only temporary conditions of joy but all the causes of unending happiness—limitless positive qualities, virtue, and merit.

It's a tremendously powerful mind training—like developing new muscles of the mind and heart. We're purifying attachment and aversion and the habit to self-centeredness all at once. We're increasing love and compassion and creating virtue. We're developing the habit of regarding others as equally important as—and, eventually, more important than—ourselves. We do this out of love, compassion, and bodhicitta.

34 Tonglen Meditation

As we begin, we refresh our motivation to do this meditation not just for the sake of one or a few people but for all beings—that they, too, may have happiness and the end of suffering.

We start the practice with one particular person in mind, but we do it on behalf of all beings. We think of someone we love deeply. Maybe this is a child, a parent, a partner. It can be anyone who we love purely with an open heart, so much so that we would do whatever is needed to take away their suffering and give them happiness.

We start out by thinking of how much we want them to be happy and not suffer. We might choose someone who's suffering right now. The suffering could be due to a physical illness, their life situation, or their feelings and thoughts related to those situations. We don't think about the details of their suffering or specific ways of addressing it, but simply the fact of it. We imagine we're taking away their suffering and breathing it straight into our heart. We picture all the causes and conditions of their suffering taking the form of sticky tar, swampy water, or a smoky haze rather than as images of the circumstances of their life.

Then we imagine that, from the center of our heart, a pure light—like that of a full moon in a cloudless sky, a radiant pure light that symbolizes all possible causes and conditions of happiness without ideas of what they might look like—radiates out and infuses their body, speech, mind, environment, and entire experience. We imagine that we send them benefit and happiness by joining that wish with our breath. We breathe their suffering straight into our heart, and we send them happiness directly from our heart.

Then we imagine others who we have a similar relationship with—we love them, and we don't want them to suffer. We breathe in their suffering as well and send them short- and long-term benefit and happiness. We breathe all their suffering into our heart, and we send them great joy joined with our breath.

Next, we expand the visualization to include those we may have a more neutral relationship with and can easily access the wish for their happiness and end of suffering. We breathe all their suffering right into the center of our heart. We breathe out benefit and happiness with the wish that these transform their experience.

We continue to expand the visualization to include people that we find it more difficult to wish for their happiness or to take away their suffering. We remember that they, just like us, want to be happy and don't want to suffer. We breathe in their suffering so that they and all beings may have happiness.

We expand the visualization to include an ever-increasing circle of beings that we find it hard to feel love and compassion for. These may be people we know or people we've just heard about. We remember that, just like us, they want to be happy and don't want to suffer. We imagine that, through our intention, visualization, and breath, we completely absorb all of their suffering and send them endless benefit and happiness.

Having started with a pure motivation that's truly selfless, we maintain that motivation as we expand the scope of our visualization until it embraces all beings throughout space and time. We imagine ourself as the vehicle by which their suffering is completely uprooted and the causes of their happiness are fully established. We can't picture everyone, but we have a sense of the enormity of beings and the endlessness of suffering. We're cultivating a vastness of intention in wanting to take away all suffering and give each what they need. Our heart space includes all of them.

When we complete the practice, we dedicate the merit we've created to the end of suffering and the ultimate awakening of all beings.

If we do tonglen regularly and repeatedly, we'll experience a change of heart toward people we have difficulties with and get to the point where we genuinely want their happiness. Whatever else is going on in our lives, we imagine breathing in the suffering of others and sending them happiness.

Over time, we find that the power of our practice overcomes our fear and establishes a loving and compassionate basis for our relationships. Of course, this process takes time, because we've practiced our habits of self-centered attachment and aversion for so long. The more we do tonglen, the more we purify old habits and create a new responsiveness to the needs of others that arises more spontaneously and naturally.

When we take that suffering into our heart and truly generate compassion, it transforms our fear, suffering, judgments, attachments, and aversions. It's as if the fire of our compassion incinerates everything that isn't compassion. This is why it's so deeply purifying. Through our tonglen practice, our increasing love, compassion, and bodhicitta naturally consume suffering and manifest even greater loving kindness and compassion. It's like a fire fueled by suffering. The more suffering we breath in, the more compassion arises, and the more compassion that arises, the more love there is. The more love there is, the more the radiance of bodhicitta arises.

Ocean: Is the aim of this practice to experience suffering? We already know what suffering feels like.

Lama: The purpose of this practice is to purify self-clinging and increase our capacity to be of benefit to others. The desire to take away suffering fuels our compassion, and the desire to give them happiness fuels our love.

Hillary: For my whole life, I've been taught to put others' needs before my own, to always put myself last. This hasn't worked for me. It's why I'm so burned out.

Lama: Many of us put others before ourselves because we're expected to, because it's the social or family norm. If we look more deeply at our motivation, we usually find we have attachment to being accepted, supported, praised, or even protected, and we have aversion to being ostracized, criticized, or considered unworthy. This means that our motivation to help others isn't truly selfless. It's mixed with hope for good outcomes and fear of bad outcomes for ourselves.

Tonglen practice does the opposite. It uproots and purifies our hope and fear and helps us to develop a truly pure motivation—bodhicitta. Through this practice, we're transforming the habit to help others based on our old survival strategies by choosing to give rise to a genuine love and compassion so the pure qualities of our heart can become more available for the benefit of all beings.

Carolyn: Can I imagine that the suffering passes through my heart, so it doesn't get stuck, which is a fear I have? I don't want to breathe in negativity that makes me sick.

Lama: The idea of breathing in someone's suffering can sound really scary and seem like the opposite of everything we've ever believed about how to find happiness and end suffering. However, if we're trying to protect ourself and avoid being harmed by the suffering we breathe in, we're missing the point of the meditation. The purpose is to dissolve self-clinging and our self-centered attachment and aversion. This fear is directly confronted by this meditation, because we're breathing in even more of what we don't want and sending out even more of what we do want. We do this without any sense of protecting ourself, wanting to be happy, or not wanting to be harmed.

This is why we need to take the time to establish pure motivation before we begin the main body of the tonglen practice, and then start by visualizing someone we feel deep love and compassion for. We love this person so much that we'd do anything to take away their suffering. The quality of that compassion is so purifying that what's in our heart at that point is completely selfless, so there's nothing for the suffering we visualize to stick to. There's no uncertainty about or fear of taking on that energy or thought that it can hurt us. It's as if their suffering is incinerated by the pure love and compassion in our heart—as is our aversion to suffering. It's a profound transformation. Over time, tonglen meditation overcomes our fear and gives rise to the courage and joy of a bodhisattva.

Ida: I understand the purpose of doing tonglen to take on suffering, but I don't understand how it can transform our anger toward someone. Are we making the assumption that the person we're angry with is suffering, and that's why they're acting in a way we don't like, which is making us angry?

Lama: Anger arises from self-clinging. If we weren't attached to what we want, we wouldn't be angry when we don't get it, or when we lose it. Through tonglen, we're generating a wish for another's happiness that, over time, becomes so strong that it overcomes and purifies our wish for our own personal happiness. As a result, there's no basis for anger to arise if and when we don't get what we want.

We remind ourselves that whatever they're doing is their way of trying to relieve their suffering and find happiness. They don't know another way. We breathe in their confusion, their wish to avoid suffering, and their behavior that will produce the opposite of what they want as sticky tar or swampy water.

Ida: That seems to contain a lot of judgment.

Lama: When doing tonglen, if you find you can't get past your judgments of the person you're picturing, practice an equanimity meditation such as the Just Like Me meditation as a first step. What you're experiencing is the self-righteous aspect of anger. This is often in the mind when we're angry, because we're sure we're right and the other person is wrong. If that's what's strongest in our mind, we need to transform the self-righteousness, the judgment, and the pride first. We need to remind ourselves that this person is trying to find happiness and avoid suffering the only way they know how—just as we've done and continue to do again and again. They're stuck in this tragic, repetitive cycle of suffering, just as we and all beings have been. Bringing the mind back to our deepest compassion for the suffering of all beings, we want to take away the causes and conditions of that suffering and send out everything good for the short and long term. Within that heart space, anger is purified from its root.

Tej: For how long should we do a single tonglen session?

Lama: Ideally, we do any meditation until we experience a shift—the anger is transformed to love, for example, or intense self-importance is softened into genuine concern for others and an authentic wish for the benefit of people we're practicing for—and then we bring this open heart to the greatest extent possible to our daily lives. Our present habit is to want everything good for ourselves and push away everything bad. We've had that habit all our life. We do tonglen until that habit of wanting what's good for the sake of others and being willing to take on their suffering is as natural as our breath. The more we do it, the more it becomes that. We naturally do what we can to take away the suffering of others and bring them happiness and benefit. This becomes our new habit.

Breanna: In talking about what we're sending and receiving when we do tonglen, this isn't coming and going from our ordinary mind, correct? It's coming and going from bodhicitta. Also, it's sometimes hard to know what to send out, depending on the situation.

Lama: It's not up to us to figure out the ultimate cause of benefit for a particular person or the temporary conditions that lead to the ultimate benefit. We're sending love without trying to problem solve or find the right solution for that person. That's why we learn this meditation as a visualization that's symbolic rather than part of a storyline. If a person believes a bright-red Mercedes Benz is what will make them happy, we don't imagine sending them a bright-red Mercedes Benz. We don't become part of their story or get involved in it in any way. We're not trying to analyze or manage the situation. Instead, we just imagine taking away their suffering—no matter the cause— and sending whatever will bring pure benefit, in the short and long term. Our mind is an open space, and from it we send our wish for and commitment to this person's welfare.

This is why we don't try to insert a story into the tonglen visualizations. We're opening to our bodhicitta—our commitment to their welfare and that of all beings—and our responsiveness to their needs.

Breanna: I can sense the suffering of others intensely and, therefore, I believe in it more deeply than I do my own ability to solve or fix the situation to help people. It's easy for me to see if a person is in pain, but I can't believe that my sending the reflective light of the moon will make a difference. It feels like the scale isn't balanced.

Lama: It's not all up to you—the you that conceives of yourself in the context of your identity and story separate from infinite wisdom, compassion, and capacity to benefit. The bodhicitta you're accessing isn't finite. Immeasurable love and compassion are aspects of your true nature and the true nature of all beings. Awakening to that will purify your old habits, including that of thinking of yourself as powerless to create benefit.

35 A Concise Tonglen Practice

Before beginning the tonglen practice, we remind ourselves that we want to be a cause of happiness and the end of suffering for all beings so they may know the stable joy and fulfillment of awakening to their true nature. Then we visualize someone in front of us that it's easy to feel love and have compassion for. We give rise to the wish to do whatever we can to take away any causes or conditions of suffering and give them happiness.

We start with that intention and our love and compassion for this person. We imagine breathing into the center of our heart all the karmic causes and current conditions of their suffering. As we exhale, we imagine the radiance of all our pure qualities, merit, love for them, and our wish for their short-term and long-term happiness beaming from the center of our heart and completely saturating their body, speech, and mind. Then, as we again inhale, we breathe in their suffering. As we exhale, we breathe out happiness. We join that visualization with our breath repeatedly until the habit to take away suffering and give happiness becomes as natural as our breath.

We expand this visualization step by step to include more and more people, starting with those we already love deeply, expanding to those we feel more neutral toward, extending to those harder to love, those we've had anger or hatred toward, and, eventually, to all beings. We ideally do this meditation until we feel our heart softening and opening, our fear relaxing, and our compassion and love growing.

See what happens in your mind when you do tonglen with different people and situations. Is your fear subsiding and your love increasing, or the opposite?

Does your judgment about and alienation from others decrease or increase? Is your equanimity, respectfulness, and sense of inclusiveness increasing or not?

Ideally, do each step of the meditation with pure motivation repeatedly until your experience changes. Then dedicate the merit.

Ocean: Sometimes, doing tonglen makes me sad. I got really bummed out by thinking about the ways the people I love—or even don't love—suffer. I carried that with me after the meditation to the point of depression. Is that normal?

Lama: As we breathe in the suffering of others, a process of transformation takes place in which we become empowered as an agent of change. Try to imagine their suffering being consumed by the blaze of your bodhicitta so you don't feel as if you're taking on more and more to the point where your heart gets heavy and you get depressed.

The more we breathe in suffering, the more our confidence in the presence of love and compassion in our mind and heart awakens. This strengthens our commitment to help others. We become increasingly inspired, confident, and empowered as someone who can benefit the people we love and all beings. We strengthen our confidence in the appearance of our own positive qualities and our ability to stabilize them and bring them into the world.

Breanna: I had the same thing happen to me. After I finished the meditation, the suffering I visualized—my mom had just had surgery and was in pain—was running through my head for the rest of the day.

Lama: We're not picturing the details or the images of the suffering. There's no content to it—and this is an exceptionally skillful aspect of the practice. Without that content—working only with the visualization of light in and out—there's just the essence of the suffering, and that's what gives rise to our love and compassion. We aren't focusing on the story. We're developing a universal, unbiased love and compassion beyond personalities and circumstances. As we experience the depth and strength of our positive qualities, there's a sense of the power of transformation. We have the confidence that we can become of greater benefit to others.

A great opportunity for developing our tonglen practice can be found in watching the news. Watch it, don't just read it. You'll see a lot of constantly shifting images and can practice maintaining tonglen with your breath as you go.

Tej: You said we should think of people who are suffering without getting caught in the storyline, and then you said to think about people who are suffering in more and more types of ways. How do we do that without storylines?

Lama: Say you begin your meditation by thinking of someone in an extremely frightening situation. As you expand the meditation, you might imagine others who are fearful for other reasons such as unemployment, illness, violence, poverty, hunger, or homelessness, for example. You'd imagine breathing in their suffering as sticky tar or swampy water without trying to visualize the details of their circumstances or what could be done to solve the problem. If you're including someone in your meditation who's sick, you'd imagine breathing in and taking away the causes and conditions of their illness—appearing as smoky haze or sticky tar—as opposed to specifically visualizing them receiving a particular medicine.

Inez: When I do tonglen, I don't just feel the suffering of whoever I'm doing it for. It brings up my own stuff, too. It feels like almost a physical sense of overwhelm, the kind of love that's painful in my whole body. It's hard for me to do the visualization, because what I experience is more of a feeling—

I'll feel the idea of suffering in general but not necessarily the specific situation of suffering.

Lama: The purpose of tonglen isn't to become a great visualizer, although our capacity to visualize improves over time. The purpose is to awaken our love and compassion, which helps to purify the habit of pushing away what we don't want. The act of taking on the suffering of others helps to purify our attachment to our own happiness.

In your case, I'm wondering if, when you take in the suffering, you're holding on to it as something solid instead of letting the radiance of your compassion consume it. It's an active process. It's not like you're breathing in suffering, and it becomes a dead weight that takes over your body. It's transformative and dynamic, and the energy of that transformation expresses itself in the wish for the welfare of others. Also make sure you're not focusing on breathing in suffering more than sending out benefit and happiness. You want to do both, equally.

How to Prepare and Carry Tonglen into our Workplace

To support our capacity to carry tonglen with us throughout our day, before we go to work, as a formal practice, we can do tonglen, imagining ourselves in a super stressful workplace or other situation that we regularly encounter in our lives. Here we'll use the example of a nurse working in the ICU (intensive care unit) of a hospital, where the most critically ill patients are cared for.

Our motivation is that we're doing this practice for the sake of everyone in the ICU, their loved ones in the waiting room, everyone else in the hospital, and everybody coming in and out of the hospital—the paramedics, patients, doctors, nurses, visitors, everybody. As we expand the meditation, it includes not just everyone in and around the hospital but everyone in the community, the state, the country—and, ultimately, all beings throughout space and time.

For most of us, it's easier to start with just one patient who we find it easy to feel compassion for, somebody we see as an innocent victim and hard to blame for their suffering—for example, somebody who was driving along at the speed limit, was hit from the side by a drunk driver, and now is in the ICU in critical condition.

We begin by putting ourselves in their place and recognizing this person is just like us—they want to be happy and don't want to suffer. They were perhaps on their way to work, got hit by a drunk driver, and now their life is on the line. In just a matter of minutes, their life went from being normal—they were thinking about work, their kids, or what they were going to do after work—and now, suddenly, they're in the ICU. Maybe they're in a coma, maybe they're in and out of consciousness. If they're conscious, all they can think about is whether they're going to survive and whether their family even knows they're in the hospital. Perhaps the nature of their injury prevents them from talking. They're fighting for their life, but all they can think about is their fear for their loved ones, of not showing up at work, of possibly being fired—if they survive. All these fearful thoughts may be going through their minds. We put ourselves in their place and imagine what it would be like. Then rest the mind.

Imagine if you suddenly had a heart attack or a stroke and couldn't think or talk or breathe. Just that quickly, our life can go from being completely normal to having no control over our body. Think about what it must to be like for this person in the ICU, and imagine their terror and sense of powerlessness. Then rest the mind.

Then reflect on how fortunate you are. You still have the use of your body. You can formulate an intention and act on it, because your mind can direct your body about what to do, and your body can do it. Then think about the person in the ICU, their terror and desperation, and your wish to be able to do something to help. Then rest the mind.

If we're a nurse or a doctor, we may or may not have the capacity to help in this moment, but what can the rest of us do? Instead of feeling powerless, any of us, at any time, can give rise to a depth of compassion and do this meditation in which we imagine ourselves taking away their suffering. We take on that suffering—because we're alive, conscious, and can do so—and imagine sending them whatever they may need and whatever's best for them, without detail and ideas of what that may be—be it health, strength, merit, or resources—as a radiance of the pure light of bodhicitta. Our awareness of the magnitude of their suffering inspires gratitude for our relative good fortune, a joy and appreciation of what we have to give that energizes us to want to give more.

We do this with a visualization, imagining their suffering is like a sticky tar or smoky haze that we breathe in. All our merit and everything they might need is visualized as radiant moonlight. We join this visualization with our breath and imagine that we're actively breathing in all the causes and conditions of their suffering. We imagine ourselves taking that suffering from them and sending them everything they might need for their short- and long-term benefit. When we send them the causes and conditions of benefit and happiness, that's love. When we take away the causes and conditions of their suffering, that's compassion.

Whatever our job, we do the tonglen meditation before we go to work so that when we enter the workplace, love and compassion are in our mind instead of everything else. This love and compassion are equally available for everybody we interact with.

Imagine, if we worked in the ICU, how our day would go differently if we'd been doing tonglen at home based on our experience with yesterday's patients. Today, we walk into the ICU, and our heart is open rather than closed. We're breathing in suffering and sending out benefit and happiness. We don't know what brought these patients to the hospital, we don't know or have ideas about who's at fault, and we're not blaming. There are just a lot of patients in pain and nurses and doctors trying to help. There are paramedics, EMTs, and other healthcare workers, and everyone is stressed. We breathe all that in, and we send everybody whatever they need. As we inhale, we take away suffering and, as we exhale, we send benefit to everybody equally. There's no judgment and no limitations, just a heart of love and compassion.

During our shift, we do everything we can to help—whether with medicine or medical care or listening or talking—all from this nonjudgmental, unconditional heart of love and compassion. We do everything we can to help and everything we can to take away their suffering.

To the extent that we're able to do this meditation, our day at work isn't just an ordinary day. We're not experiencing "compassion fatigue." There's no limit to our compassion, and the more we practice it, the more we have of it. In the course of those 12 hours, we've been awakening our love and compassion; creating virtue; purifying our attachment, aversion, and judgment; and helping others as much as we can. In doing this, we transformed our workplace into a spiritual practice. It's the same job and the same people, but we have a different motivation that ultimately leads to a different outcome.

Do this meditation imagining your own workplace—the people you work with and situations you encounter—whether they're suffering in the moment or not. Imagine breathing in whatever seeds of suffering may abide in their minds and sending all causes and conditions of benefit and happiness. Starting with pure motivation, walk yourself through this meditation at your own workplace or with your own family and, at the end, dedicate the merit you've created. Try to do this at home before or after work as well as during the workday, and notice any changes that may occur inwardly or outwardly in your work and in your life in general.

Inez: I experience a tremendous spiritual and emotional exhaustion in the work I do at the shelter. I'm trying to find a way to carry on. I know the answer isn't just more sleep. What I need is spiritual nourishment. If I practice tonglen in the morning, will the work I do that day benefit all beings, not just the women I serve? Might this practice reduce the exhaustion I feel from my work?

Lama: If you're able to generate bodhicitta through your tonglen practice in the morning and bring it into your work throughout the day, yes, it will. When we give rise to bodhicitta, it's as if we jump into this great river of blessing of all the great beings who've generated bodhicitta in the past, who are generating it now, and who will generate it in the future. In that sense, we aren't alone, and we're nourished by it. We're being carried by the current of bodhicitta, by this vast accumulation of merit and practice of all great practitioners, and by the positive qualities within our own mind.

However, if we generate bodhicitta in the morning, commute to work, are immediately hit with all this stuff, and we lose it, there might be a little nourishment but probably not a lot. The actual sustenance happens within bodhicitta. The bodhicitta in our heart is what feeds and sustains us. If we have bodhicitta, it transforms our attachment and aversion, because the only thing in our heart is the wish for temporary and ultimate benefit for all beings.

Then we can make a pure offering at our workplace, knowing full well that it may not immediately produce the results we'd like to see. It's entirely possible that we do our best and work hard, and people fight with us or even hate us for what we're doing. But if our motivation is bodhicitta, when we meet people who fight with us, we show them love and compassion in response. Love and compassion are what nourishes us. Bodhicitta nourishes us. What exhausts us is attachment and aversion.

Because we're still creating the habit to bodhicitta, it might be hard to sustain it throughout the day. That's why tonglen practice is so beneficial. If we can develop the habit to tonglen and make it as immediate and natural as our breath, we'll be doing tonglen whenever we meet resistance from others. We automatically breathe in their suffering and wish them happiness. We have no resistance to their resistance, no attachment to them behaving the way we want and fulfilling our need to feel appreciated. We're not yanked back and forth by our hope and fear.

It's like the example of how a big wind can snap the trunk of an oak tree but not the reed that bends. If bodhicitta is our motivation, we're like that reed. We breathe in any and all opposition and difficulty, hatred or anger we meet, and breathe out love and compassion. Trying to push away what we don't want is exhausting.

Inez: Whenever I have to call the police on behalf of one of the women at the shelter, I practice tonglen.

Lama: Whether an abusive husband is trying to break into the shelter, or a woman is being violent to another woman or her children, or the police themselves are being violent, you do tonglen for everyone caught in the drama. Outwardly, there may or may not be anything you can do to resolve the situation in the moment, but the effect of your presence will be different when you're practicing tonglen. It's the effect of the reed that bends, which has a greater power than the brittle demeanor of resistance and attachment. People feel that and are more trusting. If people trust us, we're better able to help.

We know this from our own experience. We can feel it in someone else. Even though a person's whole life might supposedly be about benefiting others, if they're attached to being recognized for how hard they work or for the results, it feels as if it's all about them. That's how people feel about us if our personal agenda is more important to us than our practice.

That can include the agenda of dealing with our exhaustion. However, if the exhaustion is such that, no matter how much we try to practice tonglen, the demands placed on us are stronger than our health and our practice, it might be time to take a break from what we're doing, if we can, to nourish our mind, body, and spirit. Whether we take a break for three hours, three days, three months, or three years, our motivation is to gather all our ability to be fully present and to help every living being to the greatest of our capacity. If that isn't our motivation, if there's a subtle aversion to our exhaustion or an attachment to our health, our motivation is compromised and our efforts to help aren't going to have the same impact.

I know I sound like a broken record, but it all comes down to bodhicitta—everything, again and again. If we have bodhicitta in our heart and recognize that our health is giving out and we can't be present for others the way we want to be, we might have to make some kind of an adjustment in our life circumstances. As long as our motivation is bodhicitta, we aren't abandoning beings when we do that. If our motivation isn't bodhicitta, if we're attached to our own happiness and averse to any impediment to it, and if we're making our needs more important than those of others, we're abandoning beings.

Ida: I deal with a lot of pain as a result of being injured by a roadside bomb—physical pain as well as a lot of guilt that I survived and others didn't. I'm no longer in the service, but, at the same time, I feel like I never left and will never be able to. I've tried to bring tonglen to both my physical and emotional pain, but I haven't had a lot of success so far.

Lama: This is why, to the extent we're able, we cultivate tonglen through formal practice. The more we develop that habit, the more accessible it becomes in our daily lives when pain erupts. The power of bringing compassion and love—not to mention bodhicitta—to that degree of suffering is extraordinary. It has so much power of purification.

Your ability to do that will increase as you stabilize your practice of tonglen, no matter how great the pain. Even in the midst of terrible pain, tonglen is so accessible because it's so tangible. When we're experiencing pain, we wish that everyone else's pain be embraced and purified within our own. Instead of trying to shut out the pain, we bring it in. Instead of trying to hold on to any ease we might feel, we send that to others. In the course of doing that, the aversion that's our natural habit when we feel pain is purified. Normally, when we have pain, we have strong aversion to it, and that increases the experience of suffering. It makes it worse, because we're so focused on it. We don't want it, and we get rigid about it.

When we do tonglen with the pain, instead of bringing aversion to it, we cultivate love and compassion. The component of suffering isn't added to the experience of pain, so we can explore the nature of the pain itself.

For example, if we have pain in our knee, we ask ourselves if that pain is a *thing*. Could a knee surgeon find it? We realize there's no thing we call pain, even though it's such a vivid experience. We examine, we try to find it, we can't find it, and then we let it go. Through that process, it's possible to have a hint of the illusory nature of that pain. It's as if we've wiped clean the film of the ordinary mind and its experience of aversion. When the mind is open, we realize the pain is just sensation, without any attachment or aversion to it.

Through our practice of tonglen, alternated with mind at rest, we can cultivate this ability to transform experience—whether we perceive it as bad or good—to free and purify, at its root, all the attachment and aversion that come with the ordinary mind wanting, not wanting, hoping, and fearing.

36 Tonglen Meditation in the ICU

Again, we start with pure motivation—we're doing this meditation for the short- and long-term welfare of all beings equally.

We imagine there's a patient who's been hit by a drunk driver, who's in and out of consciousness, and who's absolutely terrified. In this moment, there's nothing to be done outwardly but to wait. The medicine has been administered, the family has been called, and this semi-conscious person may be struggling just to breathe. We imagine what it would be like if we were in their situation, what it would mean to us if somebody showed us kindness, displayed a genuine concern, and tried to help in any way they could. We consider that, at least, we can do this meditation for them.

As we exhale, we imagine sending them the radiance of whatever they need. As we inhale, we take away all the causes of their suffering, and the conditions of their suffering. We inhale that directly into our heart. With our exhalation, we send them benefit, the radiance of our love and compassion. With our next breath, we take in their suffering and, as we exhale, we send them benefit.

Do this meditation for a few minutes, imagining this person who's struggling to stay alive.

Next, we think of the other patients in the ICU and do the same meditation with them. Imagine the suffering of each of them, breathe in their suffering, and send them benefit. Do this for several people simultaneously.

Then expand the meditation to include the nurses and doctors who are struggling to help these people. Imagine these stressed, determined, and capable professionals who are trying so hard to help.

Then imagine paramedics in an ambulance bringing in another patient—who, it turns out, is the drunk driver who hit the patient we were just practicing for. We think about that driver and how that person, just like us, wants to be happy and doesn't want to suffer. Maybe that person was having all kinds of conscious or unconscious pain and was drinking to numb the pain —just as we've done so many times when our pain was so bad that we didn't think about the people around us. This person, just like us, made some bad decisions, but theirs caused an accident, and the person they hit may or may not live.

For this driver, we breathe in the causes and conditions of their suffering. We're not trying to analyze or develop stories about this person's life. We're simply imagining all their suffering and fear as sticky tar that we're taking into our heart. Maybe they, too, have a body that was mangled in the accident. We breathe in their suffering, the causes and conditions of their suffering. Our compassion isn't based on liking them or not liking them or agreeing with them or not. Here's a being who's really suffering, and we want to take that suffering away. We want to send them the causes and conditions of benefit and happiness.

We breathe in their suffering as well as the suffering of the paramedics, the police, and whoever came in with them. Maybe there was a big accident involving many people, and everyone is upset. We breathe in all that upset-ness of everybody and send everybody the essence of what's beneficial—compassion, clarity, steadiness, the ability to problem-solve in the middle of an emergency, and anything else they need to help themselves and each other—as radiant moonlight. With each in-breath, we continue to breathe in suffering, and, with each exhalation, we send benefit and happiness to everyone involved.

At the end of our meditation, we dedicate the merit we've created to all those who are suffering in the ICU, all those who are trying to help them—the paramedics who were the first to assist them, the ambulance drivers, and all the medical personnel in the emergency and surgery rooms. We pray they may all know the causes and conditions of happiness and never again have to experience suffering. We wish this not only for them but for all beings.

Questions: Using Tonglen to Remove What's Obstructing Our Bodhicitta

Anthony: Can we do tonglen with our own experience of fear?

Lama: Yes. If your fear is so overwhelming that you can't do tonglen for others, start the tonglen practice with your own fear to dissipate and purify it enough that you're able to breathe in the fears of others. Whatever your own fear looks like, imagine that in the space in front of you and breathe that in—for the sake of all living beings, for the sake of their ultimate welfare. Then breathe out the empty radiance of your pure heart. Do this until you feel enough dissipation of your own fear that you can expand to breathing in the fear of others, and keep expanding until you include all beings. Then dedicate the merit. This will take awhile, so be sure to take some time for your personal practice.

Carolyn: What about our own suffering? Can we do tonglen for ourselves?

Lama: We always do tonglen for others. However, if our stuff is up so strongly that it feels impossible to access the love and compassion we need to do it for others, we begin the tonglen with our own stuff first, whatever that looks like to us. We visualize whatever that is in the space in front of us first, and we start with the same motivation—that we're doing this meditation for the sake of every living being.

Let's use the drunk driver as an example. We want to develop love and compassion for that person, but we may have anger or fear about it. Maybe we know people this person injured, or maybe we ourselves were injured. We might have a response to someone who drinks and drives that's so strong in us that we can't get past it to do the meditation.

We remind ourselves that we're doing the meditation for the sake of the drunk driver, everyone involved in the accident, everyone in the ICU, everyone in the hospital, and for all beings. But, we take responsibility for whatever is in our heart and mind that's in the way of our being able to access pure love and compassion, and we work with that first, to purify and transform it.

If we have a traumatic response, we might visualize it as a tornado, for example. We start the tonglen practice with the motivation that we're doing it for the benefit of all beings. We breathe in the causes and conditions of our suffering, our trauma, our stuckness, our inability to access compassion, or whatever it is, as sticky tar. Then, joined with our breath, we send out the capacity for limitless benefit and love as radiant moonlight to the symbolic form of our trauma until we feel a shift in our mind and heart. When the power of that image in our mind and heart loosens a little bit, we extend the meditation to the person or situation we're doing the tonglen for and continue to expand it until it encompasses all beings.

We start with what's obstructing our practice. This might be something that triggers a memory that makes it harder for us to be present for somebody, or it might be a habit to feel powerless or afraid of our own limitations and our inability to help. We may be on our own trying to help in a situation in which it seems impossible for us to help, so we feel hopeless or powerless. Imagine in front of you whatever you encounter in your own mind and heart that gets in the way of the meditation or of believing in the possibility of change or of being of greater benefit for yourself and others. With the motivation to transform it for the sake of others, breathe that in, and breathe out the transformative capacity for change and benefit. Do that with each breath until you experience a lessening, a shift in which you no longer feel stuck. At that point, extend the meditation to whoever or whatever else you're working with in the meditation until it includes all beings, and then dedicate the merit.

Instead of engaging our ordinary mind—with its mingled feelings of judgment, self-hatred, despair, pride, attachment, aversion, and so forth—we're able to access and cultivate our positive qualities. This helps us to maintain the momentum of positive transformation instead of giving in to our old psychology and stories. We're shifting our focus from the ordinary view of the ore and cultivating the qualities of the crystal.

There are many ways to remove the ore from the crystal. Over millennia, the water from a gently flowing stream will erode the ore off the crystal. Or, we can put the ore-covered crystal in a rock tumbler or a vat of acid, and that will remove the ore much more quickly. There are methods that are quicker but not necessarily gentle. This one—tonglen—is swift and reliable. It will increase our positive qualities and purify our mind. The more we do it—in each situation in our daily life as well as in our formal practice—the more we'll see change.

Tej: You said to picture the thing that's obstructing our bodhicitta, but what do we do when we don't really have a firm grasp on what's obstructing us? PhD students are often anxious about the work they're doing, but there isn't a well-characterized obstacle. It's a mix of feelings and causes, so how do we visualize that?

Lama: Again, we aren't working with the content—the storyline—so much as with our emotional habits. We're taking responsibility for whatever is obstructing our bodhicitta and whatever that looks like for each of us. It could be a memory of a person or event that symbolizes our trauma or an image based on the imbalances in the natural world that represents our emotions—like a tornado, flood, or landslide—and merges with the imagery of the sticky tar that we're breathing in. It's whatever it feels or looks like to you.

Carolyn: I've meditated for many years and tried to walk a path of love. My sister attacked me a few months ago about something that happened 23 years ago. At first, I was able to draw on my practice, and I was totally in control and peaceful. However, after two and a half hours of this behavior, I had to leave my body to handle that abuse, because I'd been physically attacked by her as a child. When your attacker is still attacking you, what do you do? I thought I had tools to handle this.

Lama: You may have had a strong traumatic response triggered by traumatic childhood experiences. With trauma, there are changes that happen both in the body and in our brain chemistry. When we experience the initial trauma, those emotions are stored in a certain part of the brain. When we aren't experiencing trauma, we develop skills and tools that are stored in other parts of the brain that we can draw on in dealing with difficult situations. But when the traumatic memory is triggered, we're suddenly back in that part of the brain where the trauma is stored, and we feel as if we're four years old again. We can't remember that we've learned anything different nor can we access the tools we have, because we're not present—we're in our past, experiencing that trauma.

To heal the trauma, we need to join those two parts of the brain. This is what trauma therapy does. It creates a pathway, like a bridge, between these parts of the brain. In my experience, for some people, working with the tonglen meditation can have a similar impact.

If we find that our personal karma and habits prevent us from being able to practice tonglen effectively, we can start our tonglen practice by working directly with and purifying what's getting in the way. Then, we continue the tonglen by expanding the visualization to include others, as we've been doing. In the case of trauma, we can imagine our trauma in the space in front of us and breathe it in, absorbing it into the center of our heart as sticky tar or smoky haze. Then we breathe out love and compassion, imagining the limitless purity of our true nature radiating from our heart. We have to do this as formal practice before we encounter potentially traumatic situations. Otherwise, we can't expect this new habit to be accessible when we're in the middle of being triggered.

So, do the tonglen meditation when you're home alone and feel safe. Turn off your devices so you won't be interrupted. Bring to mind a traumatic situation involving your sister. Imagine that circumstance in the space in front of you, and breathe it into the center of your heart blended into sticky tar or swampy water, for example. Then, breathe out the causes and conditions of benefit and happiness. Keep doing this until the charge of the trauma lessens.

After you do that meditation with your own trauma, extend it to others. You might start with someone you know who also has a strong history of trauma, extend it to other trauma survivors, and, eventually, include your sister and others with abusive pasts. Extend it to other traumatic circumstances in your childhood, and keep expanding it outward until it encompasses all beings. Do this regularly as a formal practice.

The next time you're with your sister, it's possible that your habit will be to breathe in the abuse and send out love and benefit—or, at least, you might find yourself less likely to be triggered and freeze or disassociate. Instead, you'll be able to make different choices about how to respond. If you do this enough, it becomes a new habit. It takes time. There's no replacement for time in with practice.

Tonya: I was abused by my father, and he was abused. I've been trying to breathe out a happy childhood for him, but I can't imagine what that would look like. I don't know what would have made him happy, and I know I'm not supposed to have a storyline. How to I approach this?

Lama: Keep it really simple. Just imagine radiant moonlight flooding your image of him, pacifying his experience of suffering but without pictures in your mind of what that happiness would look like. He's just happy.

Ida: I understand that if you're in a situation with a person who has difficult emotions, the response would be to practice tonglen, but how do you do that when you're face to face with them? Do you say, "Excuse me, I'm going to practice tonglen on you, and I'll be back in a minute?" What's the practical way to respond to other people's strong emotions?

Lama: You do tonglen, but you do it informally. They don't know you're doing it.

Ida: What if that isn't satisfying to the other person, because you aren't giving them the habitual response—the attention, commiseration, or drama—they're looking for?

Lama: Just make sure you don't depart from the heart of tonglen. Without commiserating with or stroking their poisons of the mind, from your heart, let them know how sorry you are that it's so hard for them. Has your habitual response been to get into their story and try to fix and process everything?

Ida: Mostly I just listen silently.

Lama: Then your partner won't notice any difference.

Ida: But I'd like not to have to listen silently for so long!

Lama: Tonglen helps to disperse the charge of emotions, even though they're not your emotions. Your subtle energies are calming down, so the room is more calm, which can help to cool down the situation. This isn't your motivation for doing tonglen, but pay attention to see if, over time, as you continue to take these kinds of interactions as practice, the episodes don't last as long and if they subside more quickly. Also, while you're listening and present, you're cultivating love and compassion, giving rise to bodhicitta, and purifying attachment and aversion. You're doing so much practice during these times.

Ida: And I won't feel resentment?

Lama: It depends on your motivation. To the extent that you're able to give rise to bodhicitta, you'll be purifying karmic imprints from past resentment and deepening your love and compassion. The more your partner processes, the more chance you have to do really great practice! It can be deeply transformative. Then dedicate the merit to your partner, to all beings that suffer from strong emotions, and, ultimately, to all beings equally, that they may awaken to the true nature of those emotions, to the true nature of the drama.

Hillary: I'm new to tonglen, and I'm wondering how I get through the process without reverting to old ways of dealing with difficult emotions. Thinking of others' suffering reminds me of my own as well as bringing up anger and all kinds of other emotions.

Lama: If you're doing tonglen for someone, and that's triggering and bringing up difficult emotions, work with that first. Visualize whatever is coming up for you and obstructing your bodhicitta in whatever form it takes in your mind's eye. Breathe in all of the causes and conditions of suffering in that situation, and breathe out the causes and conditions of benefit until you feel less triggered. At that point, you can extend it to others.

As you noticed, it's really hard to help others who are triggered and scared when you are, too. If you're triggered, you can't offer them the stability of your love and compassion, so they have an experience of safety when they're around you. Work with your own triggering first, and then you'll be able to access a deeper love and compassion for them.

Inez: With my work, I feel like I've become kind of a sponge for trauma. I've absorbed so much of it just because it's free-floating in the air with so much human tragedy. Then there are specific things that happen—a suicide attempt or a death. How do I deal with that without it taking such a heavy toll on my heart and causing me to just close off and respond in this very matter-of-fact way of, "Yep, somebody tried to commit suicide today. That's what happens when people have trauma."

Lama: To the extent you can stabilize your tonglen practice, you come to understand that everything you do is for their benefit, and you're not resisting the trauma in your environment: Would that you could take it all on for the sake of all beings. If you're generating that aspiration out of bodhicitta, it incinerates your trauma and creates this blaze of love and compassion.

Try to stabilize bodhicitta before you go to work, throughout the workday, and in your dedication at the end of the day. Within bodhicitta is everything you need—the torching of all the causes and conditions of suffering and the generation of solutions for all beings. Your experience will be one of being in the presence of this perfect incubator for bodhicitta, and your strength will increase.

I'm not saying that, physically, you won't be impacted and tired. You're the program director at the shelter, so I assume you have some choice about how everything is structured. Think about that not just for yourself but for anybody who works there, who volunteers there, who might work there in the future, and for the sake of all the women who are there now and will be there. What's the most sustainable, virtuous, supportive, beneficial structure?

Trauma stirs the subtle energies, and the remedy—a stress-free environment—isn't something you have control over. It's important to get enough sleep when you can and, as much as you're able, to let go of effort and striving. Turn off all your devices at least an hour or two before you go to bed. In the Tibetan tradition, people drink warm milk to help them calm down before bed. Do whatever you need to do to get a good night's sleep, because our bodies restore themselves during the night. This will help you wake up feeling nourished with your energies replenished, and you take this into your work environment.

When we have aversion to being the sponge for trauma or suffering, it's the aversion itself that acts as the magnet. That's what's sticky, and it hooks that energetic contamination that wears us down. We can purify our motivation with the aspiration that we really could absorb all their trauma so no one else would ever have to experience trauma again. The power of that compassionate wish will, over time, transform the aversion so you're not weighed down.

As your practice deepens, there's a sense of the dream-like nature of all that's arising. What's arising is so impermanent. It's this constant flow of women and tragedy and sorrow and loss and trauma and grief and rage and violence—wave after wave. Of course, we focus on every single wave, each single woman, and everything that's going on with her. At the same time, we keep in mind the larger picture of all women, all sentient beings, so much tragedy, and, in the face of all of this, we're generating compassion and being as present as we can.

Seeing the larger picture of the play of impermanence, the constant, unceasing expression of the suffering of beings helps us to cultivate a wisdom perspective, recognizing that all appearances arise like a dream, a mirage, a movie, a hallucination. This is not to deny the experience from the point of view of everyone who's in it. However, from the point of view of our mind, we have more breadth of perspective we can draw on to help others in the long run as well as the short run.

Your life is all about helping those very beings—helping them to survive and find a way through. You're present with their pain in a context of compassion and love that's completely nonjudgmental and unconditional. You receive them and their pain, and offer what you can, providing a safe harbor. How extraordinary is that, to have a life dedicated to others in that way?

Always bring this exalted motivation to your work, the aspiration that, through your efforts, no one will ever want to take their life ever again, that every being can find their way through. Through the combination of wisdom, which holds this larger perspective, and your unrelenting compassion, you'll develop more and more confidence in the power of bodhicitta, which will increasingly sustain you.

It's not magic. It doesn't happen overnight, but it *will* happen. Always dedicate to all those who don't have a safe harbor, which is most beings. For these beings, these women, in this time, in this place, there's a safe place, thanks to what you're doing. So, rejoice that you have this opportunity to offer a refuge in the midst of this ocean of suffering, and constantly dedicate the merit that all beings may have safety, comfort, shelter, nourishment, and rest when they're weary.

37 A Concise Alternating Tonglen Practice

Start by doing the tonglen meditation for one person. When your heart starts to open, and you feel you genuinely care about this person—you aren't *trying* to care but actually do care about them—let go of trying and let the mind rest for as long as it's restful. It's okay if you hardly recognize that millisecond of rest because it went by so fast.

At that point, return to tonglen, and do it for another person, and then again rest. Keep alternating like that and, each time, expand the scope of beings you're doing practice for.

If it's hard to even do the meditation, you could start by practicing with the challenges in your meditation.

Visualize and do tonglen first with however the obstruction appears to you, rest with that, expand the practice to others, rest with that, and then continue to expand the visualization, alternated with resting the mind, until it embraces all beings.

Breanna: We've spent time reflecting on and contemplating past experiences and the results of those experiences, but it seems that evaluating situations can be exhausting. How do I learn to let the mind be more restful when I'm working in the ICU and dealing with three patients at a time that are really sick? Even when I have downtime, it's hard to practice.

Lama: We need to learn methods that can be applied in the ICU with a dozen patients who are all critical and having emergencies, which is not to diminish the importance of time dedicated to resting the mind. We must start with methods we can engage at the moment our stuff is coming up, right as everything is coming at us, because that's where most of us spend most of our time.

If we haven't worked skillfully with what's coming up in the ICU, for example, when we come home, even if we have the opportunity to rest, it's not going to be restful. We're going to be processing. Our mind will be churning and full of emotions. Or we'll simply suppress or bypass all the emotional material from the day as we find a moment's peace, without transforming mind's underlying patterns. Then the same thing will happen, day after day, like Rinpoche's example of pushing the pause button on a music device.

However, if we've been able to transform the emotions and slow the rate at which they arise in the ICU, when we come home, if we have a moment to rest, rest is actually possible. To do so, we start with what we can do right in the moment, and then we alternate that with the state of rest.

Carolyn: What can we do to try to rest our mind, and where does resting meditation fit in?

Lama: "Trying to rest" is an oxymoron. The more we try to rest, the less likely it becomes. Instead, when we do an effortful meditation like tonglen and start to experience a shift to a deeper sense of responsiveness and commitment to the welfare of others, we then let go of the effort and let the mind rest. This is so the radiance of the love and compassion that we awakened through our tonglen practice can permeate our mind in an effortless way. It's like stirring ink into water, which blends with and transforms the water itself. We let the love and the compassion we've given rise to saturate our mind, which allows the possibility of love and compassion to arise effortlessly. We can begin to recognize that these qualities were always there, though we didn't know how to awaken them. Alternating tonglen practice with resting the mind is an extremely powerful and swift means to do just that.

When we first start to meditate, as soon as we let the mind rest, we usually get involved with thoughts like, "Is this it? Am I resting in the right place? Is this what rest looks like? Should I be doing something else?" The mind is habituated to trying to get to a place that's different from where we are. Or, if we have a concept that it's not someplace else but "here," we wonder what "here" looks like. There's a habituation to a certain mental state or a certain object or certain things to be done, all of which require effort. If we want change, we all have a strong habit to use effort to get there.

Instead, when we let the mind rest and it starts stirring again, rather than trying to make it stop, we direct the agitation to the next stage of the meditation. We might think about others who are suffering in similar ways or others who are suffering in other ways. We then let go of the effort, and let the mind rest. We alternate in that way—effortful meditation and then rest.

Rinpoche used to say that, at first, we're usually only able to genuinely rest the mind less than 1% of the time. That's why, instead, it's more effective to spend the remainder of our meditation time using effort to transform and purify what's impeding our ability to rest. We purify whatever's obstructing our awareness of and ability to access and empower our positive qualities. We then rest in the warmth of those qualities—when our mind is genuinely restful. Then we go back to the effort and, slowly, over time, the ratio of effort to rest will change. At some point, we'll be doing tonglen 98% of the time, and 2% of the time we'll be resting.

Through that process of alternating, we're practicing both. We're creating transformation in the effortful process, and we aren't using the motion of the mind, which is habituated to effort, in a direction that's only going to cause frustration and impatience. Instead, we take that motion and use it to create transformation by directing it toward something transformative like tonglen. When we do tonglen, the motion itself and the habit to be effortful start to relax a little. When there's genuine relaxation, we rest there. When our mind is no longer restful, we direct it toward the next effort that will produce change. By doing this, every minute is truly transformative. There's not a moment in our meditation that's wasted in frustration and trying to do something we can't do.

Every moment of the meditation is designed to produce benefit for all beings, more virtue, less non-virtue, more positive qualities, less obstruction of our positive qualities, greater capacity to benefit, less obstruction of our capacity to benefit, and more confidence in the process, the methods, and the presence of our positive qualities. Change is happening all the time, and it's change that's always going to be beneficial to others.

Bringing Tonglen to Mind's Poisons

When one of mind's poisons—attachment, aversion, pride, jealousy—grips us, even if we're aware of its presence, we can often feel powerless to do anything about it. Each poison has its own energy and can seem to overpower our mind. We identify with the poison and give into it instead of reinforcing our positive qualities. When we're captured by that poison, we're so identified with it that it's hard to see clearly what would be of greatest benefit and cause the least harm. In the course of trying to find a way through to clarity and happiness, we often end up producing the very opposite. One way to find that clarity is to practice tonglen to purify the poison that's arising and give rise to mind's positive qualities.

38 Transforming Mind's Poisons through Tonglen

Having generated bodhicitta, we let ourselves be aware of whatever poison is uppermost in our mind. We think of everyone else who's struggling with that particular poison—those we know, those we don't know, those near and far who may not have the means to transform that poison into benefit.

Thinking of the suffering that's being perpetuated, and the happiness they yearn for, our natural response is to want to do something to help. We wish we could help even one being cut through, purify, and awaken to their true nature. We give rise to this vast aspiration to have the capacity to help.

From that aspiration to help—which is love—we practice tonglen. We want for these beings the causes and conditions of happiness, which we imagine sending to them as a radiance of pure luminosity that pervades their lives and experience.

We then inhale the causes and conditions of their suffering with the aspiration that they no longer experience it. Through our practice, we imagine we breathe it right into the center of our heart. Then, also from the center of our heart, we radiate limitless love and compassion, and then rest the mind.

As we continue the tonglen practice, we extend the light to more and more beings that are suffering in more and more different ways as the display of other toxic emotions, alternating each with resting the mind. We keep extending and extending until there's a sense of the pervasiveness of love and benefit for all beings and the pervasiveness of compassion that's dissolving and incinerating the causes and conditions of suffering until all beings have been established in a state of complete awakening.

Then, we make a dedication that, through the merit of this meditation, all beings truly awaken to the ceaseless benefit and happiness of knowing their true nature.

Hillary: If we're doing tonglen by visualizing one of the poisons of the mind, how do we imagine that?

Lama: It's your poison, so you visualize whatever it looks like to you. It's your friend, your intimate partner.

Through our practice, we're taking responsibility for whatever is in our mind, the poison of the moment. We can do any combination of meditations on bodhicitta, compassion, loving kindness, and tonglen. You can do this in any order or any sequence. They all have power. You don't have to do tonglen exactly as we just did it. The more you do any one or more of these, the more you'll experience the diminishing of the intensity of the poisons. They'll have a little less hold on your mind. You'll feel a little less powerless in relation to them and more confident in your positive qualities to purify them.

Hillary: In the course of the meditation, I often get distracted, and a strong emotion such as fear might arise. If that happens, should I just keep taking in all beings' fear and suffering along with whatever disturbance is in my mind?

Lama: That's it. That's an example of how we bring our practice to whatever is arising in our mind.

CHAPTER 13. REJOICING

As we continue to develop love and compassion, we see there are different branches of the same tree emerging from one trunk. The roots of self-concept, self-clinging, and self-important thoughts give rise to this well-established trunk, which, in turn, gives rise to these boughs of attachment and aversion. We've been exploring how generating the wish that others be happy and not suffer transforms that experience.

We've talked about the three poisons of the mind—our basic ignorance of our true nature and the attachment and aversion that develop from that ignorance. Our emphasis has been on recognizing the play of attachment and aversion in the mind, the self-clinging within them, and starting to sever that self-clinging by opening our intention to include others within the scope of our motivation, dedications, and aspirations. We've practiced loosening our attachment to wanting things to go our way as well as expanding the breadth of our intention to wish for the end of suffering to include others and not just ourself.

There are smaller offshoots and twigs growing from those two main branches of attachment and aversion, including fifty-two components of aversion that range from raging hatred to the mildest irritation. Fear, for example, falls within that spectrum. As well, there are dozens of aspects of desire. But all those branches and twigs grow from the trunk and roots of self-clinging.

We've been emphasizing effortful methods to uproot self-important thoughts in relationship to others. Practices of love and compassion, alternated with the state of rest, start to create the space within which we can begin to have a genuine experience of selflessness in a more ultimate sense. Wisdom is the direct experience of our true nature. When we rest the mind, we create the space for that wisdom to emerge.

Everything that informs our daily experience arises from lack of recognition of our true nature, like the film passing over the light of the projector. From that ignorance come self-important thoughts that create suffering when we continue to indulge in them as if they're true, non-composite, permanent, and free. We act on that assumption rather than investigating their nature and applying methods to create change.

From the three poisons of the mind—ignorance, attachment, and aversion—arise jealousy and pride, which are like offshoots of our attachment and aversion and opposite sides of the same coin. When things are going well for us, self-contentment, pride, even entitlement can arise—an assumption that we're more worthy of our fortunate circumstances than others. Identifying with what we think is good and can be traced to this self we believe is ultimately true, we find others less deserving than ourselves. We identify with the results of the display of our merit because we think—perhaps on a subconscious level—we did something right and, therefore, we're a little bit better and more entitled than those who are suffering.

However, we mustn't forget that each of us is sitting on a mountain of karma. Right now, for some of us, our positive karma happens to be ripening. For others, negative karma happens to be ripening. With the next turn of impermanence, it will be the opposite. If things are going well for us, instead of lolling about in self-contentment, we need to be grateful, and use our fortunate circumstances to do everything we can to help those whose negative karma is ripening.

On the flip side, preoccupation with our own wish for happiness makes us jealous and envious when others find it and we don't, and this makes it difficult to rejoice in their welfare. When that sense of "Why not me?" seeps into our mind, we can address and transform the attachment to our own happiness and aversion to our own suffering by re-establishing pure motivation and cultivating love and compassion.

Based in that pure motivation, we can also work directly with jealousy by learning how to cultivate the quality of rejoicing. If we find jealousy in our mind, instead of thinking, "Why not me?" we can delight in their happiness and wish for them that it continue and grow until their enlightenment. Rejoicing antidotes jealousy, competitiveness, and envy—the tendency of the mind to compare and place our needs and wishes above those of others.

Finding joy in the experience of another is a way to work skillfully and directly with our tendency to make it about us whenever we see another's joy instead of making it about that person and all beings. We can remind ourselves that we're working on creating the causes of benefit and happiness for all living beings. In the depths of our heart, this is what we truly want: Here's someone who's having a moment of joy, so what's the problem? Why wouldn't we be happy for them? We realize the problem is our preoccupation with our self to the exclusion of others, and we expand our motivation to make our focus about *them*.

Once we commit to benefiting all beings equally, jealousy doesn't make sense anymore. Instead of wondering why they get something that we don't, we can remind ourselves we're trying to benefit all beings. At least one person is experiencing temporary benefit right now, which makes our job a little bit easier! Wherever there's true gratification and its causes in the world, we can be joyful.

If we see somebody having a moment of pleasure, of love, or fulfillment, we rejoice. For example, if we see people coming out of a movie theater and laughing, because we know there's so much suffering in the world, we can rejoice that at least these beings are having a good time. This isn't charged with emotions based on our own agenda. We're just happy these people are happy.

There's also a deeper quality of joy in being aware of the inherent purity of our true nature and that of all beings. If that purity wasn't who we are, there would be no basis for hope or joy, because how can change happen if the potential isn't there and if the reality isn't different from what we've known? But, as we slowly awaken to the fact that the reality *is* different, we have the confidence that this inherent purity is true of ourselves and of all living beings. We then have the joy of doing whatever we can to help bring that recognition to others.

We start by finding joy in the happiness of another, and we wish for them that they never be separate from happiness and that it only increase for themselves and others. For example, we find joy that, in the endlessness of samsara—the ceaseless cycle of suffering—someone may be enjoying a little bit of ease. There's someone who's happy in this moment. We can wish for them that it remain, increase, and become the cause of ultimate happiness. We wish for this to continue until they completely awaken from all causes and conditions of suffering into the stable state of peace through realization of their true nature.

Joy in the Causes of Happiness

We rejoice not only when someone is happy in the moment but also if they're planting the seeds of future happiness by practicing virtue, whether it be in a spiritual context or an everyday, worldly context. When somebody is being kind to another, when somebody wants to uplift another and makes the effort with body, speech, and mind to bring that about, we rejoice. We wish for them that the ability and desire to continue to plant seeds of happiness only increase until they and all beings experience its ultimate fruition.

We delight if we see anyone putting themselves out there and working hard to help another at their own personal expense, making the needs of others at least equally or more important to them as their own. We wish for them that the virtue they're creating serve as the cause of benefit for them—not just in the short run but in the long run—and that it increase until it becomes the cause of ultimate benefit for themselves and all beings.

Of course, we can't know the mind of another or what their motivation really is. It might be mixed. Therefore, we practice rejoicing in all pure virtue, delighting in any aspect of someone's action that's motivated by the genuinely altruistic wish to bring happiness to others, whether we can see it or not. Without doubt, when their motivation is pure, they're planting seeds of benefit for themselves and others. We rejoice in all pure virtue, wherever and whenever that may occur, with the genuine wish that they and all beings may experience the results in their mind and in their lives.

We want to be especially careful not to do anything to interrupt anyone's virtue. Perhaps this is someone who's trying to make the world a better place. Or maybe someone is doing formal practice, trying to create merit, purify obscurations, and cultivate bodhicitta. We want to do everything we can to support and not in any way diminish the power of their virtue, so they may accomplish ultimate happiness—not only for themselves but for all living beings.

Breanna: Do we rejoice if someone has something good happen to them that probably isn't helping others but makes that person happy? Is merit created by simply rejoicing in the fact they're happy?

Lama: Yes, because they wouldn't be happy if they hadn't created virtue previously. Whatever's making them happy is the ripening of a previous act. We rejoice in the roots of their virtue, whatever it was that they did, and that they're experiencing its fruits. Our wish for them is that it be sustained and increase, and that this would be so for all living beings. We rejoice in whatever it is, wish it were so for all beings, and dedicate the merit.

So Much Virtue!

One of the swiftest ways to accumulate merit in everyday life is to rejoice in pure virtue. There are many ways we can remind ourselves of all the virtue going on in the world at any given time. No matter how much someone is suffering in a particular moment, if they're practicing virtue, if they're being kind, if they're being selfless, if they're doing what they can to respond to the suffering of others, they're planting medicinal seeds. It doesn't matter what the context is. It may be in a different religious tradition or no religious tradition at all. It could be in the helping professions or the arts. Whatever the context, if someone is truly motivated to try to help another in a selfless way, they're planting purely medicinal seeds, and all these medicinal seeds will produce purely medicinal fruit.

Even though someone may not be happy in the moment, we rejoice if they're planting the seeds for future happiness. They may be benefiting others and be deeply connected and aligned with that purpose, because this is what brings meaning to their life. In the moment, the firefighter may be in terrifying circumstances but feels aligned and on track with the intention and direction of their life. There's a deep sense of fulfillment when we recognize how many people are creating the way forward to bring benefit into the world. We rejoice in the depth of that, in the seed planting, and then the fruition of that.

We think of the many beings that are being kind right in this moment—millions of beings, or maybe more. We rejoice in all the moments of kindness we'll never hear about or see, but we know they're happening. And then we dedicate all the merit we've accumulated to the short- and long-term benefit of those we're trying to help, and, ultimately, to all beings.

We bring to mind all the virtue we can think of as the basis for giving rise to inspiration. We think of the people helping in homeless shelters and food banks, who, out of a depth of compassion, want beings to have what they need and be protected from what harms them. We can think of all those who are saving lives all the time—medical personnel in hospitals, EMTs, paramedics, firefighters, and the people who go out into the wilderness to try to save the lives of firefighters in the field. We think of all the people who put their lives on the line every day for the sake of others. We consider what that experience is like—when your whole existence is about making the welfare and survival of others more important than your own.

We think of how many people are doing that all over the world right at this moment. There are people who go to places around the world where huge environmental imbalances are causing major disturbances and tragedies. People are losing everything in those disasters and have no shelter, no food, and don't know where their family is or if they're even alive. Many of these people are sick and have no medicine and no doctors. We think of all the people who are working in the refugee camps—at great personal risk—to help bring medicine and food to those who've lost everything. We don't need to catalog each instance and make a long list that we bring to mind every time we rejoice. Rather, in the course of our daily life, as we're exposed to the news or we meet or hear about people who are doing this kind of work, it's an opportunity to rejoice. We remember these people and their efforts when we need to generate inspiration.

We remind ourselves of how many people are doing as much as they can to uproot suffering. Then think of all the practitioners in the different religious traditions who, in the context of their own practice, are generating faith and devotion, making offerings, and practicing generosity, and we rejoice in their merit. Then we can bring to mind all the enlightened beings and bodhisattvas appearing in our world solely to uproot the suffering of beings. We think of all the ways they benefit others. We rejoice in their existence and enlightened activities—everything they're doing for the sake of others with bodhicitta as their motivation—to help change the balance of virtue to non-virtue in the world so there's less non-virtue and more virtue.

Ida: You mentioned people putting their lives on the line. Does that also include people in the military?

Lama: It depends on their motivation. If, instead of putting their lives on the line out of anger or revenge, for example, they do so out of a great love for and commitment to the welfare of others, that's a cause for rejoicing.

Ocean: Is rejoicing always in reference to somebody else's happiness? Can we rejoice in being able to see and appreciate, for instance, an amazing environment we find ourselves in? Is there a way we can take that and share it for the benefit of all beings?

Lama: One way to do that is in the context of offering whatever we're grasping at. If it's a beautiful day, and we're in a beautiful place, the mind could start to grasp onto those appearances. If we think about wanting to spend more time there and coming back often, that makes it all about us. Instead, we can offer to our objects of faith, with the sense of the whole universe being filled with beauty. We pray that all beings may have such beauty, and then we dedicate the merit of that offering that all beings may enjoy beauty, however it appears to them. For some, it may be brightly colored lights and 50-story skyscrapers. For others, beauty is the simplest thing in the natural world. And there's everything in between—a beautiful partner, a beautiful meal—endless options. So, we pray, may all beings enjoy outer and inner beauty that will fulfill them in every way, temporarily and ultimately. In so doing, we're offering whatever it is we're attached to as well as our attachment itself.

This practice can help increase our joy and gratitude for all that we have—a roof over our heads, food when we're hungry, water when we're thirsty, and the health to enjoy it. Our merit increases as we bring to mind and rejoice in all the virtue taking place in the world, all those helping others, all the good heart manifesting around us, and all the ways we've been able to support others as well as in our opportunity to learn and use spiritual tools to be of even greater benefit. As our merit increases, our positive qualities become more available, for the benefit of ourselves and others. We become less depressed, less despairing when obstacles and challenging conditions arise, and our capacity for creative vision, problem-solving, and courage increases. We're increasingly joyful for all we have, and we feel increasingly aligned with a deeper sense of purpose to our lives—to do all we can to benefit those around us and to make the world better for having come through it.

39 Rejoicing Meditation

We start, as always, by establishing pure motivation for doing this meditation—not just to purify our own jealousy and envy but with the aspiration that, through the merit of our practice, all beings may awaken to the true nature of mind devoid of self-centeredness and negativity.

Then we train the mind by rejoicing step by step. We start with someone who it's easy to rejoice for, someone we really love that, when they find happiness, we're delighted. Or maybe it's someone who we've tried so hard to bring happiness to and, when they finally find it, it's effortless for us to rejoice.

Next, we do it with someone that we feel neutral toward, and then with someone who it's hard to feel like rejoicing for. Maybe it's someone who seems to have everything we ever wanted and never got, even after working so hard for it. Maybe we have strong judgment and aversion about the way they appear to be gathering the conditions that produce that happiness. No matter our reasoning, we remind ourselves that here's someone who's happy and, for their happiness to stabilize and increase, they must create rather than destroy merit. We rejoice in their happiness without judgment and without reservation, and pray and dedicate merit that it may increase.

We practice this meditation first with those we love and then with those we feel neutral about and finally with those we judge negatively—and everybody in between. We delight in their happiness, wish it would never diminish and only increase, and wish that they never be separate from the causes and conditions of future happiness. We keep expanding our practice of rejoicing until it includes all living beings. We first rejoice when the seeds that were previously planted ripen. Then we do the same sequence when someone is planting virtuous seeds and behaving in a virtuous way. In between each sequence, we let go of effort and let the mind rest. At the end of our meditation session, we dedicate the merit to the complete awakening of all those we've considered in our practice and, ultimately, all beings.

Hillary: Is there a difference in how we'd respond when someone is actively creating virtue and when they just have happy, positive circumstances?

Lama: In both cases, we rejoice, because they're either planting the seeds of happiness or experiencing the fruition of having planted those seeds previously. Either way, we wish for them that their happiness—and that of all beings—be maintained, never diminish, and only increase. The heart space is the same. We want for them the stability and the increase of that until it's all they know—not just for them but for all living beings.

Carolyn: Rejoicing in the virtue being created by firefighters is easy for me, but when someone right in front of me has something I've always wanted and don't have, there's a little bit of grief in it that's about me not having what they have. The rejoicing isn't pure. How do I work with that?

Lama: Try doing what we do in the compassion meditation when we think of those who are suffering. We put ourselves in their place and imagine what their whole experience is like. In the same way, try doing that with those who are happy. Put yourself in their place and imagine how wonderful it would feel. See if that makes it easier for you to rejoice purely, because it's no longer about you.

Doug: I'm still having trouble rejoicing in someone's pure virtue. If I can rejoice in something somebody else has—for example, skills or the resources to do certain things—that's okay, right?

Lama: Totally. Of course, we can't see into their mind and know it's totally pure, but when you're rejoicing in wherever there's pure virtue, you don't have to get into their story or know what's really going on. It's just a simple, open-hearted rejoicing in wherever the virtue is pure.

Hillary: I can do the general practice about virtue, but, when I start thinking about individuals, it's hard for me to tell if somebody's happy or not. When you think about certain people, you don't really know if they're okay.

Lama: It's true that we don't know what's happening on the inside but instead of trying to analyze their experience, this practice is really just about our own mind. It's a simple, open-hearted attitude without pride, judgment, or the kind of mean-spirited thoughts that can arise when we're only thinking about ourselves.

Say it's a beautiful day, and we see someone sitting in the sun with a contented smile, their face turned upward, and they appear to be happy. Though we can't be sure, we can just make the aspiration that whatever happiness they're experiencing—a moment of rest, of ease—may that always be the case for them, may their happiness only increase, and may it never subside.

What we're cultivating is the clear, quiet openness of rejoicing in happiness and the causes of happiness. We're not trying to cultivate analysis and stories and attempting to probe into everybody else's hearts and minds to see what's really there. It's the spirit of rejoicing in the welfare of others and only wanting that welfare to increase, stabilize, and never decrease.

When we first begin to practice rejoicing, it can seem contrived and effortful. But, the more we do this and all our practices, our heart opens, our judgment and conceptualization purify, our positive qualities become more apparent, and love, compassion, and rejoicing increasingly arise naturally and spontaneously.

Carolyn: When we do this practice, is it appropriate to include beings from other realms, such as animals, some of which are suffering more than others?

Lama: They're sentient beings who, just like us, want to be happy and don't want to suffer, so, if they're having a moment of ease or happiness or creating the causes of happiness, why not? We can't know what's in the mind of a dolphin at SeaWorld, but they sure are creating happiness in the minds of the children watching their shows. Of all the animal rebirths, that looks like a pretty good one, because all day long they're creating joy.

Tej: Can you say more about rejoicing, as one of the Four Immeasurable Qualities, as a basis for bodhicitta?

Rejoicing is an extremely powerful tool for creating and increasing merit. Rejoicing in happiness, the causes of happiness, and every virtuous act is a means for sharing in the accumulation of merit created through each virtuous act itself. Imagine rejoicing in all the pure virtue happening throughout time and space. How much virtue is that? Immeasurable. This is a powerful way to support our path and keep sustaining the positive qualities of mind that are required to uphold bodhicitta. Both formally and informally, practicing rejoicing is delightful, because it creates so much merit.

Remember, always, that the purpose of our spiritual path is to benefit others, temporarily and ultimately. When anyone is suffering, the balance of positivity to negativity in the ripening of the karmic seeds tilts in favor of the negativity. What beings need in the midst of suffering is more merit. We've talked about how the essence of generating merit lies in our motivation—by sincerely wishing for the short- and long-term benefit and ultimate awakening of all living beings. With that motivation as the basis, rejoicing is an extremely powerful and effective way to accumulate merit we can dedicate. By purifying jealousy and envy, we erode our self-clinging and give rise to the pure-hearted wish for the short- and long-term benefit of others.

During the time of the Buddha, there was a king who was so busy he didn't have much time to practice. In order to uphold his bodhisattva vow, the Buddha told him to rejoice three times a day in all pure virtue created throughout time and space, offer the merit of that rejoicing to all enlightened beings, and then dedicate the merit of that rejoicing to the enlightenment of all beings. If we do that at least three times a day, all our positive qualities will increase.

Think of all the virtue of all beings. It's inconceivable! When we rejoice in that, we multiply that merit exponentially because of the limitless number of beings.

The second step is to offer all that merit to all bodhisattvas and enlightened beings on behalf of beings—which, further increases the merit exponentially. The third step is to dedicate the merit of that offering to the enlightenment of all beings, and this, again, results in a limitless increase in the amount of virtue.

In this practice, we use the skillful means of offering the merit created by rejoicing to antidote any attachment to it. We offer it to all those who embody the limitless qualities of enlightened mind, and dedicate the merit of that offering to the awakening of all beings. The merit created is inconceivable in its effect on not only the temporary but the ultimate happiness of all living beings.

Offering to enlightened beings is said to be one of the greatest accumulations of merit we can make, because they appear only for the welfare of others. In the act of offering to them, we recognize and pay homage to their qualities and express our gratitude. We make offerings on behalf of all beings with the aspiration that such blessings pervade the minds and lives of all beings throughout time and space. We follow this by dedicating that merit to the complete awakening of all beings from the endless realms of suffering.

We don't have to limit this practice to three times a day. Because of the depths of suffering, what beings need is merit. So, all day, every day, we could keep rejoicing, offering, and dedicating to the complete awakening of all beings. If there are particular beings you have connection to, dedicate to the enlightenment of those and all beings. Insofar as you feel inspired, act based on that huge, limitless bounty of bodhicitta you're giving rise to. Express it with body, speech, and mind in whatever ways you're able to.

Carolyn: When we're making joyous offerings at least three times a day and reminding ourselves of all the virtue taking place in the world, is this a general offering for the happiness of all beings, no matter where they are?

Lama: Yes, we're rejoicing for wherever there's happiness and the causes of happiness throughout time and space. We can also rejoice, relax the mind, and spend time with the relaxation. It can be spontaneously and effortlessly joyful. Do that without attachment, and then offer and dedicate the merit created.

Being Aware of What We're Rejoicing In

We need to pay attention to what we're doing with our minds when we rejoice as well as who and what we're rejoicing in, because we often have unconscious habits to rejoice in the unhappiness or non-virtue of others. Glancing through the day's news headlines, we become aware of how subtle those habits can be. It may seem like a particular headline can make our mind go this or that way. It seems like it's the headline causing this, but it's really our habits. The headline on the screen appears one way, and our mind creates virtue, and then the next headline appears, and we create non-virtue. Are we recognizing that what we're reacting to is just a scene from a movie? Are we recognizing that everyone wants to be happy and doesn't want to suffer and that we're witnessing the myriad ways in which people try to create happiness and avoid suffering and yet create the opposite?

If someone tells us their news, and we see it makes them happy, we rejoice for and with them. But we can't know all the causes and conditions that went into whatever occurred that made them happy, and that same event could actually end up being the cause of tremendous misery.

For example, we may believe the election of a certain politician would result in less misery and more benefit for more beings. Therefore, we have some attachment to that politician getting elected. When inauspicious things happen to their opponent—their popularity decreases as some scandal erupts, causing them to lose favor with the public—it's easy to slip into rejoicing. We're happy the opponent is failing, because we're so sure our hero politician will create the greatest benefit for beings.

But how can we really know the consequences of all the actions our favorite politician might take if they win? And, when the opponent is losing, we're rejoicing in someone's unhappiness. We must understand that whatever we rejoice in, we're participating in the creation of merit or of non-virtue, and this affects our own accumulation of merit or non-virtue.

One way to understand this is to think about karma, cause and effect. For a karmic act to produce a certain result, four components are required—the identification of an object, the motivation in relation to that object, taking action based on that motivation, and the result of that action. Inherent in this process is the rejoicing that happens at the fruition of an action that we supported.

Say we have cockroaches in our house, and we don't want them there. We identify the object, and our motivation is to harm or kill, which is definitely a form of aversion. Then there's the action to kill the cockroach and the death of the cockroach. If we rejoice when the cockroach dies—"Aha! I got 'em!"—our rejoicing amplifies the power of non-virtue. All four components are there.

If we're vacuuming and don't see a bug, we don't have the intention to kill it. However, if the vacuum sweeps it up, the bug still dies. That accounts for half of the non-virtue, even though we didn't intend to do it. If we realize we killed a bug, feel tremendous remorse, do purification practice, and dedicate the merit to an auspicious rebirth for the bug, this totally changes the karmic thread or outcome.

If we really don't like spiders, and it was a spider we vacuumed up, we might think, "Yay! One less spider in the world!" This means we're rejoicing in its death. Even worse, if we rejoice when we or others intentionally kill spiders, that's huge non-virtue. We're creating the karma of rejoicing in death.

So, if we rejoice when the opposing politician is losing, we're rejoicing in the causes, conditions, and results of their suffering. We're creating the karma of being happy that a sentient being is suffering as well as the karma of pride and righteousness, because we're so sure our politician is better. It's easy to slip into this habit when our emotions are all stirred up and the public discourse is all stirred up.

If our military kills a terrorist responsible for a lot of death and destruction, many people might rejoice. But, in doing so, there's rejoicing in death. Depending on everyone's motivations, this may create more non-virtue than virtue and diminish our collective merit.

On the other hand, when a first responder arrives at the scene of an accident, sees an injured person, does everything possible to get them to the hospital on time, and saves that person's life, they've gathered all four components of a fully ripened karmic act and created the inconceivable virtue of saving a life. They and others rejoice in a life being saved and in the heroism and efforts of the first responder. They all participate in that virtue of a life having been saved, which increases their collective merit.

Anthony: I want to ask you about rejoicing in the planting of the seeds of virtue by other beings. As you said, we don't have the ability to see another being's motivation. Is there a danger that, if we rejoice because we believe a being is planting seeds of virtue when they may actually be planting seeds of non-virtue, we then accumulate the same non-virtue as they do?

Lama: That's why it's often articulated as rejoicing in all pure virtue, wherever it's created, without the concept of knowing what it is. We see something we think is virtuous, and we're delighted. But, as you pointed out, it may be or may not be. That person may be enacting something that looks virtuous on the outside but is, in fact, all about a wish for recognition or praise. This experience of perceiving an action as virtuous can remind us to rejoice wherever the virtue is truly pure, knowing that we may not be able to recognize if it is.

You're right that when we rejoice in something, we join our intention with whatever's going on, which may be mixed with pride, jealousy, attachment, aversion, or other poisons of the mind. So instead, we rejoice in wherever there's benefit that isn't only short-lived but enduring. We always make our intention to rejoice wherever the virtue is pure and truly beneficial.

Anthony: So, we make it an overall generalization, because, otherwise, we'd need discriminating wisdom. How do we apply that without judgment?

Lama: To apply these tools well requires a profound depth of humility—to admit we don't know what's truly best. That's why we rejoice in wherever there *is* pure virtue, because we can't be certain where that is. Until complete awakening, we can't know another's mind.

Now, it's true that, as we dispel the mist of obscuration, we'll experience increasing wisdom and discernment. In the meantime, we want our dedications and rejoicing to be based on pure virtue without concept of where it's occurring.

Doug: If you're aware of a group of people doing non-virtuous things, but, on the outside, most people would regard what they're doing as virtuous, you wouldn't want to necessarily rejoice in what they're doing, correct?

Lama: When you see a group of people who appear to be doing virtuous things, but you're suspicious that the motivation isn't completely pure, just think to yourself that wherever there *is* pure virtue—here, and throughout time and space—you rejoice, offer, and dedicate the merit. Do it like that, without trying to analyze it or figure out, because we can't know the mind of another. Always and with humility, we can rejoice in the possibility and the existence of pure virtue, wherever it is.

Anthony: If we take the example of corporate raiders who are happy as a result of their actions, are you saying there's room for rejoicing if it's in whatever it was that gave them the ease to enjoy this moment?

Lama: Let's take the example of a super-effective corporate raider. Because they're so successful in their work, they have all this money, and many people admire them and follow their lead. It may look as if those are the conditions that are producing their happiness but, in fact, it was some previous act of pure virtue. When we rejoice, we aren't rejoicing in the corporate raiding. That's just the temporary, superficial appearance of what's producing their happiness. We aren't getting into their story—whether what they're doing is contributing to climate change and using up resources. We're keeping it really simple. We're not judging or analyzing what it was that produced this happiness or how much suffering of other beings is being generated as a result. Instead, we rejoice in the seeds of virtue—the virtuous cause that has produced the ease that they then choose to use to raid.

Of course, compassion arises simultaneously if what they're doing to get that ease and abundance hurts others, and they're using the resources they have to harm. They're destroying their virtue through acts of harmfulness, which means their happiness won't last. So, in this case, our predominant practice might be compassion. We recognize they wouldn't be in the position to have the resources they do if they hadn't created merit at some point in the past. We also have compassion for what they're doing with it—destroying the very roots of virtue they planted in the past that are now ripening. They have these resources and are using them to harm others and destroy all their merit instead of creating benefit.

Rejoicing in the happiness of others can be challenging when observing someone who seems to find joy in mistreating others. For example, if we see someone who appears to be delighting in using their power or authority to bully or ridicule another, it looks like they're happy because they sense themselves winning. But we need to remember that whatever looks like the cause of their happiness on a material level isn't the real cause. If they hadn't created virtue, the causes of happiness in the past, they wouldn't be happy winning an argument through intimidation. They'd be miserable.

This is a good example of what we mean when we say, "Don't get into the storyline." The temporary appearance is of a happy bully. But, when they're having a moment of ease, a moment in which they're not drowning in their own suffering, we wish that they may only have the causes and conditions for that ease to continue. It won't continue if they keep destroying the roots of happiness by using their power to harm others. For their happiness to be maintained and grow, they must create its causes through benefiting others. If, instead, they're only creating misery, our primary practice in relation to them might be compassion.

Rejoicing benefits us. We change. We're antidoting our aversion to the bully's behavior and our conscious or subconscious wish that the bully suffer as a consequence of their choices. That allows us to purify our judgment and self-righteousness at the same time as we increase our compassion. It's not like we've never engaged in similar conduct or tendencies when we had the opportunity. We avoid creating non-virtue and, instead, we create merit by transforming our own mind through the purification of jealousy and establishing a more sincere depth of motivation.

We rejoice as a formal practice, with pure motivation as the basis, and then dedicate the merit with the understanding that we're joining our mind and our intention with all those who are creating virtue. This creates a huge accumulation of merit and is a way we can help others who are struggling. We may not know how to help them outwardly in the moment, but, when we practice and accumulate merit, we can dedicate to them that this virtue be the cause for this person and all beings to awaken to the inherent purity of their true nature.

40 Rejoicing Meditation in Daily Life

As an informal practice, every time you notice yourself enjoying something, make the wish that all beings could have such happiness and its causes, and rejoice whenever you see anybody creating the causes of happiness or experiencing its results.

In particular, notice when you're jealous, competitive, or envious because you want what others have. Remind yourself this is the habit of the ordinary mind. Then do the opposite: Wish for others' happiness and the causes of happiness. This purifies your jealousy, competitiveness, and all those tendencies of the mind that want something for yourself without thinking of others.

As a formal practice, you might think of a person or situation you have some jealousy toward or a wish that you had their happiness or their opportunities to create virtue. Do the meditation, and ask yourself why you're thinking, "How come her and not me?" This means all you really care about is your own happiness and not hers. Instead, create the aspiration that all beings enjoy the happiness she's experiencing. May her happiness endure. May it grow and increase. Do this, and see what happens to the grasping for what she has. See how this works on the mind in relation to jealousy, envy, and that whole spectrum of emotions.

CHAPTER 14. EQUANIMITY

On this path, we aspire to the model of the bodhisattva, whose entire purpose is to uproot the suffering of and benefit all beings. A bodhisattva does this ceaselessly—for everyone equally and without bias. We may, theoretically, believe in equality, but we often find ourselves unable to actualize those values in practice. The practice of equanimity—of equal regard, respect, and care for all living beings—is the means by which we can close that gap.

Equanimity lives naturally in us as the ultimate equality of our true nature as a state of limitless purity. Our nature is pure, and yet it's obscured. That's true of all of us, and we're all trying our very best to do what we can with what we have. Yet, if our actions and understanding aren't informed by the wish for the benefit of all beings equally, we'll produce the opposite of what we want. No matter how much we want it, we'll be pushing it away. This is a habit we all share.

Although our true nature is permeated with the positive qualities of natural openness to every living being equally, our present experience is biased. We love those close to us and those who share our values or lifestyle, but we don't love or even tolerate people who we disagree with politically or people we've never met. We want ourselves and those close to us—our family, our community, and maybe even our fellow citizens—to be happy, but it's rare for us to think about—much less wish for—the happiness of every living being equally.

We compromise our commitment to all beings for all time if we condemn someone because they're using their power in what we consider to be a harmful way, if we stop responding to somebody else because the situation feels hopeless, or if we're simply overwhelmed by the suffering in the world. This means we're falling short on our path. Our purpose is to uproot all suffering everywhere, for everyone, equally. To accomplish that, we work outwardly to do everything we can to help others and inwardly to increase our capacity, so there will *only* be less suffering and more benefit in the world. We want everyone to be able to find their way through in a manner that isn't just surviving or causing harm to themselves and others but will bring benefit, joy, and transformation that's positive not just for themselves but for others.

The practice of equanimity is ultimately a practice in humility and recognizing our common capacity for feeling and awareness—not just with human beings but with all living beings. Our shared wish is to be happy and not suffer, but, in the very course of trying to find happiness, we produce the opposite. That's our collective tragedy. We all participate in it, so it's not like we're on a hilltop looking at others who are ignorant while we're completely wise and all-seeing. If we can cultivate that humility, we can find ourselves in others and them in us.

That's why equanimity antidotes and purifies pride, judgment, bias, and the whole tendency of the mind to separate ourselves from others and think we're better than they are or our way or perspective is more "right." Cultivating a heart of humility allows us to access a truly receptive and kind heart toward everyone equally. Then we won't approach our efforts to respond to suffering with an idea that we know better or we've awakened more positive qualities than those we're trying to help.

If our habit is to judge others and see the negativity in them, we recognize that whatever positivity we see in ourselves is also in others. If our habit is to focus on our own negativity and use that lens against ourselves, we come to realize that when we find positive qualities in others, they must be in us, too.

As we develop confidence in our positive qualities, that confidence will be reflected in our interactions with others.

We'll know, from our own experience, the truth of our inherent purity. If we know it about ourselves, we'll know it about others. Truly knowing that about others and having confidence in their ability to awaken and act from their positive qualities will inspire them. As we all know, judgment rarely inspires someone else's transformation. If we truly wish for others' benefit, people can feel it and will trust us. When there's more trust, there's more receptivity. When there's more receptivity, the heart is more open and able to receive what's being given.

We're cultivating equanimity based on our understanding that, although their story may be different from ours, their choices may be different, and whatever karmic wave they're riding right now may be different, deeply, they're just like us. We all play different roles in each other's dramas. Even though our nature is pure—and the potential is limitless for thinking and behaving differently—we're all caught in our own drama, our own projection, our own screenplay, our own movie. We're trapped—all of us, equally.

The truth is, everybody is trying the best they can with what they know and what they have available to them—just like we are. To expect that everybody else should be constantly exhibiting their positive qualities while being totally tolerant of our own negativity—because it feels so justified—doesn't make sense, and it doesn't help us to help others. If our conduct evokes and supports negativity instead of positivity in ourselves and others, we aren't helping to shift the balance and change the direction we're all going in.

Equanimity allows us to remember our connectivity, our shared positive qualities, our shared confusion, and the shared karma we've accumulated based on that confusion. We're all in this together, whether we happen to be riding a wave of merit or a wave of non-virtue. Whatever our current life experience, we can be sure that, with the next turn of karma, we'll have a different one. Today, we may have enough to eat; tomorrow, maybe not. There's no basis for judging anybody—ourself or anybody else—and it's for the sake of all of us together that we practice, we tame and train our minds, and focus on the positivity within ourselves and others. We awaken positive qualities within ourselves with the aspiration to awaken them in others, because we're all the same in both our inherent purity and our lack of awareness of it.

Finding Solid Ground

Until our mind is loosened up and becomes more flexible through practice, it's hard to even recognize the depth and extent of our judgments, because they're so intimately tied to our view of reality. The more we practice, the easier it is to see our pride and biases. Initially, they're a firm part of our identity, and we perceive and interact with others through this lens of what we think is best and how we think things should be. It's easy for us to become righteous, because we so firmly believe in the values we hold, and it's hard to make a distinction between the values themselves and our righteousness about them.

We've often constructed our view of ourselves, of others, and of reality itself in relation to our values and principles. We're oriented to our experience through the lens of that construction of what's good and bad, and, of course, we believe we're more righteous and more right than others, no matter what the subject. After we make a value judgment about something we perceive as virtuous, positive, and beneficial, there's a next step where we think we're right or good because we hold that value, and we regard those who we think don't hold this value as less good.

However, we feel our righteousness is justified, because we think our perspective will result in less suffering and more benefit, so we don't notice the lens of our own righteousness. We then hold on to these views, principles, and values, and they define our sense of life purpose, our sense of who we are, our path, and how we walk through the world.

We hold strongly to our beliefs because they've helped us make our way through a world filled with circumstances that aren't necessarily going the way we think they should. It's understandable that we'd take refuge in how we think things *should* be, because that's been our life raft in this tumultuous ocean of suffering and all these painful things that are happening to ourselves and others. What else is there for us to hold on to except our values and principles and the life goals we've developed based on them?

But, the very act of holding on so tightly contradicts the deeper benefit we want to bring through our practice or our activities in the world. Everyone else is holding on equally strongly to their beliefs and values in an equally righteous way, so, of course, we have conflict. Rinpoche always said that no matter how right we think we are, to try to impose our "rightness" on someone else is always wrong. Although our sense of righteousness is understandable—because we believe our way of thinking brings benefit and diminishes suffering—if we don't see how our attachment to that very belief obstructs our capacity to bring benefit, we won't be motivated to take responsibility for and transform it.

We can usually recognize pride and righteousness in those we disagree with. It's harder to see when it's our own, especially when it's more subtle or we're surrounded by people whose values we share. Whether we judge others harshly or gently, we still hold the belief that the way we see the world is the way it should be.

Through our practice, we begin to see something else is possible besides judging. If we really examine our experience, we find it's more inspirational and uplifting if, instead of acting from our judgments, we act from a sense of common humanity and purpose. Once we abandon our life raft of judgments, it's like we're learning to swim. We discover what will keep us afloat, and we share this with others to help them stay afloat. We're also learning certain principles that become the solid ground we can stand on no matter how strong the storm. These principles, this solid ground, has to do with our positive qualities, which are stable sources of our support for ourselves and others. We no longer need to rely on the old tools we've been using.

We're in a transition, so, as in any transition, there will be a tendency, when things become difficult, to revert to what once supported us. That happens for all of us, but whether we're judging others or judging ourselves according to our righteous standards, this won't support us in finding that solid ground.

We must ask ourselves why we think things should go the way we want them to. Why do we think we're entitled to have what we want, even if we have to harm, neglect, or disregard others to try to get it? Why would we think that someone *should* be and behave the way the way we think they should? Every single time we want others to be something other than what they are, we'll be disappointed, and this will give rise to aversion, reactivity, and powerlessness.

Meditations on equanimity allow us to begin to develop a humility that recognizes we don't know everything, we can't know the mind of another, and we aren't in a position to judge. With humility, we feel grateful to be alive, grateful for whatever good has happened, grateful for those small moments of rest if we ever have them. This feeling of gratitude extends to the life raft we've used all these years to survive. Now that we're learning to swim, we have more tools, but, if we hadn't had that life raft, we wouldn't be here. We're developing more survival tools, and they're not just for our own survival but for the welfare of all living beings.

We each have our own karma, and those beings that behaved in ways that were harmful to us were the agents of our karma. If we didn't have or had purified that karma, they wouldn't have created the non-virtue of harming us. For their sake, we need to purify our karma so that no living being ever acts as the agent of the ripening of our non-virtue and creates karma that will cause future harm to themselves and others.

Doug: You mentioned Rinpoche said that no matter how right we think we are, trying to impose our will on others is always wrong. How do we avoid that when we're so sure we're right?

Lama: Righteousness is particularly difficult to deal with, because often our sense of righteousness is based on legitimate concerns. For example, we may believe that, if we, as a people, don't take care of the environment, the environment will degrade to a point where it won't support life anymore. We have an understandable and strong emotional attachment to protecting the earth, and that attachment is difficult to see through. Our sense of outrage feels true and righteous, so we feel motivated to act on that belief.

So, how do we balance that sense of righteousness with recognizing that a person who expresses an opposite point of view feels as strongly as we do? They may be afraid of losing their job or believe if they don't do certain things, their third quarter won't produce a profit or whatever it is. They're equally as scared and worried about something as we are about the fate of the planet. So, what do we do?

We start by bringing our mind back to bodhicitta, so we can give rise to the wisdom and compassion necessary to create more positive outcomes. To do so, we have to bring practice to and transform what's uppermost in our mind. For example, is our fear that the actions of others will deny the possibility of life on earth so vivid that we're behaving in ways contrary to our values? If fear is our overriding emotion in response to a particular situation, we could, for example, imagine ourselves in the place of that CEO so concerned about third quarter profits. We could remind ourselves that this person, just like us, wants to be happy, doesn't want to suffer, and thinks that disregarding the impact of their actions on the environment in order to make the greatest possible profit is the way to achieve that happiness. We might imagine the board members of that corporation, the employees and stockholders, their families, friends and communities, in ever-expanding visualizations of beings who share our wish for happiness—and our ignorance concerning how to find it—until we're imagining all beings. By generating equanimity, we can begin to purify the righteous pride in our assumption that our way is the only right way forward.

The point of gaining mastery over our emotions isn't to passively accept whatever circumstances we find ourselves in. The point is for bodhicitta to be in charge instead of our emotions, so we can see, think, and act with clarity to create the most beneficial outcome for all involved. This gives us a choice in how we respond instead of simply being reactive and out of control, which we know won't produce the virtue necessary to create enduring, positive outcomes. We gain the clarity to be proactive instead of reactive, which is so necessary given the depth and range of problems in today's world.

Righteous pride can lead to the idea that we're justified trying to impose on others what we think is right and best, which is in itself a form of violence—the violence of forcing our will through speech, thoughts, and even physical actions in our efforts to convince others of our belief in what's right. Trying to impose our will on others isn't effective in the long run, because it only creates pushback and further reactivity. If we don't have control over our own mind and emotions, we'll react to the pushback, perpetuating endless cycles of back and forth with no actual resolution. To truly resolve conflict, we have to abandon our righteousness and set an example for others of equanimity and compassion. Only through the display of our own positive qualities can we inspire others, to allow the possibility of genuine, open dialogue, which is the basis for positive, enduring conflict resolution.

Generating Equanimity—All Beings Are Just Like Me

The first meditation we can do when we see these obstacles in our mind is the Just Like Me meditation. We need to remind ourselves that this person is doing whatever they're doing because they really believe it will bring them more happiness, more money, recognition, or more whatever it is they think they want that will fulfill them. Maybe they're not even conscious of what they're doing. Maybe it's like the example we used earlier of the drunk driver who's just doing whatever they can to numb the pain they're in.

We don't want to judge the choices they're making with a kind of patronizing point of view—"this pitiful person doesn't know any better"—which simply allows the very pride we're trying to antidote to impede the meditation. Instead, we need to remind ourselves that this person is behaving just as we have so many times. When we were careless of the needs of others, when we disregarded the needs of others, when we put our own needs and desires first, we behaved like a racehorse wearing blinders. We weren't conscious of who we were trampling on or what was going on around us.

In the course of trying to avoid our own suffering or establish our own happiness, if we're honest with ourselves, we see the times when we were, at best, careless of the needs of others. We were so self-absorbed that we couldn't even notice how our behavior was impacting those around us. The more acutely we suffer, the more desperately we want to rid ourselves of the suffering, and the more desperately we act without consciousness of the needs of others. We feel justified to do whatever it takes to escape our suffering.

We need to have the humility to recognize that the choices someone is making aren't different from the choices we may have made, even though it might be different objects toward who they're exercising their choices, and a different context with differing degrees of non-virtue and impact. Maybe they're a politician who has a tremendous amount of power to enact their wishes. We didn't have that kind of power, but we might have been in the same mental space. We need to own that and relate to this person as someone who, just like me, wants to be happy, doesn't want to suffer and is working at cross-purposes to their own wish for happiness. They're planting toxic seeds that are going to produce toxic fruit, which will produce suffering for themselves and others in the short and long run—just like we've done so many times before.

We might think of how awful it must be to be the dictator of a country who has the same poisons of the mind we have but doesn't have methods to transform them—and, even worse, has the power to act on them. How many more beings are harmed when this dictator makes the same kinds of choices we make every day?

We've all felt justified in harming others, thinking of them as less important or less deserving than ourselves—maybe not with human beings but perhaps with ants in our kitchen sink. There's a difference of degree between the actions of the dictator and our actions, but, if we have aversion to the ants in the kitchen sink or the cockroaches on the floor, and we act on our aversion by killing them, it's the same poison of the mind at play. We have the power to annihilate an ant or termite colony in our home, and the dictator has the power to annihilate an entire human village or community.

We practice with equanimity formally and informally and bring whatever arises in our mind into that practice. If we have confusion, aversion, a disagreement with someone, or whatever it is, we take that into the Just Like Me practice. Just like me, others experience disagreements. Just like me, each of us wants to be happy, doesn't want to suffer, has the potential to make different choices, and yet is bound to the consequences of our actions. Just like me, their nature is a state of limitless purity, but, not knowing that, they work at cross-purposes to their own wish for happiness.

Ideally, when we practice equanimity, we go through a series of three meditations with different objects—people we love, people we feel neutral about, and people we have aversion toward—and then we expand that outward.

Doug: I've been having difficulty with this meditation ever since you introduced it. It's been my experience that what some people are doing right now will lead to increased famine and much more suffering, so I don't see how I can't judge these people. Also, to have the level of humility you're talking about, it seems we pretty much have to let go of everything, and that will be very difficult for me to do.

Lama: Inwardly, we're letting go of everything except our positive qualities, everything except bodhicitta. We're not letting go of our compassion or our commitment to uproot suffering and its causes. We're letting go of all those artificial, temporary, composite, unfree habits that have limited our ability to help in the past, before we recognized in ourselves and others the positive qualities that are our way through.

Outwardly, we're learning how to practice with and integrate those positive qualities into our actions of body, speech, and mind so we're increasingly able to respond to suffering from bodhicitta instead of attachment, aversion, judgment, and other poisons of the mind.

You've presented a great example to practice with. Try following the meditation instructions with whoever in your mind personifies the causes of others' suffering. Do the meditation again and again, and see if that helps give you another perspective—not from the point of view of the conceptual mind and a political analysis of the causes and conditions of suffering but from the point of view of your heart and your practice. From that perspective, we're empowered to see solutions that are outside the box, creative, proactive, and aren't defined by the limitations of our conceptual mind, which only knows what we've perceived through the filter of our judgments.

In this way, we cultivate the positive qualities to break through all that and see other possible responses. We realize that each one of those people is making those choices based on what they believe will make them happy or relieve their suffering—just like we do. Their nature is pure, just like ours is. Within the context of what they're exposed to and the options available to them, they're doing what they think will produce benefit—just as we've done over and over in our lives. If we can recognize, with humility, our commonality, that will help to antidote and purify the tendency to pride and righteousness. Our mind can start to open and be creative. The more windows and doors that are opened, the more light there is and the better we're able to see how many options there are for intervening and creating more positive outcomes.

Doug: My experience isn't based on some kind of political analysis. What I'm saying is, when people are violent, it's very difficult to be non-violent.

Lama: That's exactly why we need to train the mind to develop a greater capacity when responding to suffering and the causes of suffering. Now, when you think about these things, you get triggered, because they remind you of the pain and powerlessness you've felt. The political analysis grows out of that as a way to protect yourself from that pain. But there's another way to protect yourself, which is to give rise to your love, compassion, and equanimity. These are more powerful. You didn't have training in these methods before so, of course, you used analysis and judgment. That's what we've all done, and that's what's clouded our hearts. But there's another way to go through it.

If you can cultivate love and compassion, they're ultimately stronger than the trigger. You have to repeat them again and again to start to habituate to a different way of responding. But, if you continue to do so, instead of feeling powerless in the face of the collective karma, you'll feel empowered, because you'll know from your own direct experience that something else is possible.

Tej: I see, conceptually, how this meditation can be helpful for combating things like pride. In my own life, I've been fortunate to have loving parents and a nurturing environment. I've been fortunate throughout most of my life in being able to avoid suffering and experience the kindness of others. For that reason, it's relatively easy for me to feel gratitude and to see good in other people. However, I'm not sure that, in practicing this meditation, I'll be able to see how it directly applies to the problem of the self-referencing pride that looks at things in terms of personal success or accomplishment and can see beyond the self to the bigger picture. Is this meditation intended to focus on that kind of dilemma?

Lama: Our current experience is informed by the karmic seeds we've planted in the past. If we're riding a temporary wave of merit, there's nothing about that wave that's non-composite, permanent, and free. It's been created by causes and conditions, and we can be certain that when those causes and conditions change, the experience of riding that wave of merit will also change. To the extent we identify with and take for granted our current circumstances and assume they'll never change, that's the extent to which we'll suffer when they do. It's in this sense that all of us share a commonality.

If we're feeling pride, we remind ourselves we're just riding a temporary wave of merit. It's not because there's something about us that's intrinsically better than anyone else. We're all in this morass of self-perpetuated suffering together. We cultivate equanimity in our responsiveness to others by reminding ourselves of the various ways in which we're equal—the equality of our true nature and the equality of wanting happiness but not understanding its causes.

How our current experience appears doesn't define who we are. You feel you've had a fortunate life, but, if you really look, I'm sure you've had some suffering and pain. You know that the nature of things is impermanence, so, to assume things will keep going as well as they are now contradicts the evidence.

When we do the Just Like Me meditation, it helps us to see that we can't identify with and be proud of the fruition of past actions, because they will only produce temporary results. It's wonderful to have gratitude for it, but don't take it for granted, because the evidence has shown us it won't last.

One of the things that's challenging about such fortunate karma is that the mind is so flooded with self-contentment and pride that when the merit of those around us is exhausted and they lose some or all of their good fortune, there's the tendency to judge them harshly. We might think that they took their good fortune for granted and just used up their merit, or that they got what was coming to them. Whether it's in Hollywood, in great palaces around the world, or wherever beings have that kind of self-contentment, there's a tendency for the pride to blind us and cause us to think that what's happening to everybody else is somehow not going to happen to us.

Instead, we need to examine why we feel proud about something. Why would we think something is fundamentally true about ourselves and not about others? When we do that, the tendency to identify as fixed that which isn't fixed will be purified and help antidote the pride.

We can think of someone we know who's had similar fortune to ours. What's happened to them over the course of their lives? When we examine their experience, we can find no basis for assuming our own good fortune will last, and this awareness antidotes pride. We can remind ourselves that what happened to them could happen to us this very day. How do we know *we* won't be the one to slip and fall or be involved in a car accident or be on a plane that falls from the sky? Why would we think that couldn't happen to us?

The Just Like Me meditation begins to deconstruct the barrier between "other" and "self" in which everybody else is "other" and we have a subtle judgment about them. We start to tear down that wall when we see others in us and ourselves in them. The more we tear down that wall and our pride purifies, the more we'll understand that every single one of us is in this together in every moment. There's no such thing as an individual way out, because, in trying to find that way out, we create the causes and conditions to become even more deeply mired. The *only* way out is for all of us to do this together. This is the hope we have on behalf of everybody, because we all, equally, have a nature that's pure and, equally, out of a lack of recognition of that, we create causes and conditions of suffering. Recognizing this can't help but purify pride and give rise to this sense of the vastness of our common experience and, therefore, the vastness of the solution to our common dilemma.

Breanna: What if you don't have anybody you dislike to focus on in the Just Like Me meditation? Is it okay to focus on people you love and feel gratitude for but don't always like their behavior? Is that the same thing?

Lama: Start with that, do the meditation, and, over time, you'll feel a lessening of the judgment, more acceptance, more equanimity, and more humility. As you do that, you may become more aware of your judgments in general and realize how pervasive they can be. Slowly, you can expand the meditation to include people you realize you do have aversion toward and feel judgmental about.

Ocean: When I think about people who I have a lot of aversion toward—like certain corporate tycoons—I feel I'm still in the intellectual-understanding phase. I intellectually understand how I should have compassion for them, but it's more like going through the motions. I get the concept, but, since they're not close to me, I don't feel my heart changing toward them. It's an intellectual understanding when I try to think of them suffering in their big mansions.

Lama: There are different ways to suffer. People can be sick, or they can be lonely. When you think of these corporate leaders, what arises in your mind?

Ocean: I feel they're evil people. They're corporate moguls who do a lot of bad things, but I'm sure they think what they're doing is the right thing to do.

Lama: Evil people. I'd call that judgmental! When you visualize them, and think, "These are evil people," that's a big judgment, and it gives rise to an emotional response. When you visualize them, you see them hurting people. So, think of them until those emotions arise and then do the meditation. Don't just go into your head when you think of them. You have a lot of judgment toward them, and that's juicy material for meditation.

Political/social activists can have a habit of going to conceptuality as a way to cope with the profundity of their emotions about the suffering they're trying to work with. It's a lot easier to get intellectual. These meditations are teaching us how to stay in our heart and not censor what's there. We bring meditation to it and transform it from something that will produce difficulties for ourselves and others into something that opens us up. Then we can respond creatively and proactively instead of reactively to be of greater benefit to ourselves and others.

You have strong feelings about those corporate moguls, and that's why you dissociate from those emotions and go into your head. The first step is the judgment, which is that what they're doing is evil. Start with that, and bring to mind the basic commonality between yourself and them. They want to be happy and don't know another way other than putting their wish for happiness before that of others. You've done the same thing, in different contexts and to different degrees. Maybe they feel you're evil, and that everything you stand for is evil, so you have a lot in common!

Work directly with your emotions, where your mind and heart are really at. The meditations are meant to be brought directly to those emotions. When you do that, your aversion and judgment *will* change to equanimity, compassion, and loving kindness. Ideally, do each meditation until your experience changes. Over time, that change stabilizes, the poisons of the mind decrease, and your positive qualities will become more apparent and accessible.

We're increasing our capacity, and we have to start with where we're at. We may find that when we start doing the practice with someone we not only have a lot of judgment about but also a lot of aversion toward, our heart doesn't budge. We do the meditation again and again, and it still doesn't budge, so we might need to work *up* to that person. We don't want to abandon them in our hearts, and we don't want to abandon our commitment to transform our relationship to them in our minds.

If we pick an object of meditation that's beyond our capacity, we still need to be committed to the process, so that's why we need to start where we are. However, we don't want to have the idea of, "Well, I'll just *stay* here." The idea is that we're starting where we're at so we can learn the meditation and see what the experience of equanimity is like. Based on that, we can keep increasing our capacity.

The point of meditation is to produce change, so we're trying to repeat something different that will produce a different outcome. If we're not seeing change, either we don't understand how to do the meditation properly or we're biting off too much and need to take smaller bites.

Tej: I have a background in science, and I don't think I could let somebody else believe they're right about something scientific that I know is incorrect, especially if it's something I'm involved with. This is part of my concern about "my needs" and if I'm going to receive what I need.

Lama: When we talk about making the needs of others equally important to our own, this means we're including them in the scope of our intentions. We remind ourselves that this person wants to be right, because they think that will lead them to happiness and allow them to avoid suffering. It's not about the content or about a particular discussion point. It's about you caring about them in the course of that discussion. If you care about them equally to yourself, you'll give them time to express their point of view. You give them the respect that *you* want. You give them everything *you* want out of the conversation. This doesn't mean you'll end up agreeing with each other, but it does mean there will be less non-virtue and more virtue in the conversation, because you're making them equally important to you as yourself. It means they matter to you equally, as much as *you* matter to you.

Tej: Related to that, my usual response is to be competitive by wanting to know more than this other person. How can I antidote that?

Lama: Try making them as important to you as yourself, because then you'll have less of a need to prove you're right and they're wrong. Because they matter to you, the content of the conversation and the argument isn't as important as the respect that's present in the conversation, so then there's less non-virtue and more virtue. There's a basis for resolution of the conflict if there's virtue. If there's only non-virtue, there's little basis for resolution.

Generating Equanimity from Our Collective Amnesia: Have All Beings Been Our Mother?

In the Buddhist tradition, we also give rise to equanimity by contemplating the Buddha's teaching that all beings have been our mothers in previous lifetimes. When the Buddha awakened to enlightenment, he was completely omniscient. He could see all the realms of beings throughout all time and was aware of all the causes and conditions of suffering for all beings.

He could see we'd all lived countless lifetimes—not just a few but more than we could imagine—and, in these countless lifetimes, we've all known each other. We've encountered each other again and again, and we haven't just known each other as strangers but as beings who've been kind to us. In fact, every living being has not only been as kind to us as our own beloved parents but has *been* our parent, and not just once but countless times. Every single one of us has been the parent or the child of every living being. We've all been the parents of every politician, every boss, every person we have judgment about, every person who's harming other beings.

We may never have contemplated—much less believed—in the possibility of multiple lifetimes. To help us understand, Rinpoche sometimes used the example of going to a wedding and drinking too much. Although the next day we can't remember what happened, it doesn't mean it didn't happen. For the purpose of this meditation, we can ask ourselves: What *if* there were infinite lives beyond this one and the one before and beyond that and beyond that—beyond concept. In every one of those lives, our consciousness produced a birth, usually through a mother—a womb birth. What if every being we encounter had given us life and protected and nurtured that life?

In some cultures, most people consider their mother to be the kindest person they've ever known. Some of us feel that way about our mothers, and some of us don't. Either way, we might first reflect on the kindness our parents have shown us in this life. The only reason any of us is here right now is because of our mother. Our parents did enough right that we're here today. They gave us life, and they protected that life when we were young. If they hadn't, we wouldn't have survived a week. At great personal expense, they protected and nurtured that life sufficiently for us to survive. It may not have been what we wanted, it may not have been the kind of food or the kind of discipline we wanted, but they gave us enough that we survived. They gave us enough education in the ways of the world that we were able to make our way, even if we took a different path than they did.

Our tendency is sometimes to feel unhappy about what they didn't give us, but why would we expect our parents, who are human beings, to be perfect and give us exactly what we wanted in the way we wanted it? How could we expect that from beings who aren't enlightened? We only identify with what we didn't get or with getting the things we didn't want when our frame of reference is all about I, me, and mine. From that perspective, we might have developed a view of our parents that's ungrateful, unkind, and, possibly, even unresponsive when they're in need, especially as they age. Focusing on what one or both of our parents—and others in our lives—did wrong instead of what they did right is a perverse kind of mind training that can only lead to disappointment and aversion. If, instead, we can start to look at the positive qualities of our parents and what they did give us, we begin to cultivate gratitude.

This mind training chips away at the self-centered perspective that everything should be how we think it should be and that our feelings are justified in wanting those things. If all we focus on is the negative, we don't cultivate a heart of gratitude and receptivity. We're so busy criticizing and judging everybody and everything we don't like that, when something good comes our way, we can't fully receive it. All we know how to do is reject, distrust, and judge.

Even if they beat or abused us, even if they were psychotic or schizophrenic, if we're here today thinking about these things, it's because of them or because they found the right people to help take care of us. Even if our parent or parents were institutionalized because they couldn't take care of us, if they hadn't given us life and cared for us in our early years, there wouldn't be a "me" to be put into foster care. They did enough right, or we wouldn't be here learning the teachings on how to purify that karma, accumulate merit, create benefit for beings, and help uproot the causes of abuse, violence, and neglect. We couldn't do that if we didn't have this body. Despite all *their* suffering, *we're* still alive.

Alternatively, we can begin this meditation by choosing to contemplate the person who's been the most kind to us, even if it's not one of our parents, and consider, what if they had Alzheimer's and couldn't remember us or were scared of us? What if they tried to attack us or called the police when we reached out to help them? The fact that they have Alzheimer's and don't remember us doesn't mean we abandon them. We still try to be there for them and help them, remembering the kindness they showed us.

If we don't believe in reincarnation, we can still do this as a "what-if" meditation: What if this person, in some long-forgotten time, *had* been that kind to me, what if they *had* saved my life, what if they *had* given me life, what if they *had* protected and nourished that life? Would we abandon them now? How would we respond to them differently? What if this were true not just for this or that person but for every living being? How would we orient ourselves differently toward the needs of all living beings? How would we respond differently to the multitude of beings and their hopes, wishes, aspirations, fears, and suffering? How would we repay that kindness now? We now have the opportunity to repay their kindness, no matter how they appear to us in this moment.

41 Recognizing All Beings as Our Mother

Having established pure motivation, imagine in front of you someone you find it difficult to develop equal regard for, someone you judge harshly. It could be a member of the 1% or a politician who's enabling the 1%. It could be somebody who's been violent toward someone we love, someone we consider an innocent victim. Reflect on the fact that everything they're doing is either motivated by a wish for happiness or trying to avoid something they don't want. It could be a conscious avoidance, trying to push away whatever they don't want, or it could be unconscious. They could be running away from hard feelings. They could be lashing out, acting out some unprocessed anger or trauma. No matter how conscious or unconscious it is, no matter whether they're running away from pain or running toward happiness, they're doing it because they think it will make things better—usually for themselves but sometimes for others.

How many times have we done the exact same thing—grasping at everything we want and running away from everything we don't want and are scared of? We could be running away from our fears, from objects of our fears, from our emotions, from a reality we don't want to face, or from events in our life that we haven't processed. This person is doing exactly the same thing. They may have different objects of desire or aversion, but the action in their mind is the same as the action in our mind—wanting what they want, not wanting what they don't want.

They could be powerless over their hopes and fears. Their attachments and aversions may be undermining their relationships, their job, or values they hold dear. Perhaps they're so consumed by the power of negative emotions that they destroy everything they value, just like we've done so many times. Under the influence of anger and in the name of peace or equality, for example, maybe we've produced more judgment and righteousness—the very opposite of what we value and are working toward.

We think, what if this person had been kind to us in some long-forgotten time? Neither we nor they can remember their kindness or any kindness we ever showed them. They're spinning in their own orbit—following attachment and running away from aversion, just like we are. If we could remember that they'd been so kind, how would we view them differently? How would we feel toward them, how would we think about them, how would we respond to them, how would our commitment to them change, and how could we repay their kindness if they'd given us life, saved our life, or made a fundamental difference in the quality of our life?

Think of others that you judge in similar ways. Each one of those beings just wants to be happy and doesn't want to suffer. Everything they do is motivated by trying to run toward something they want or away from something they don't want, just as we've done. Their actions might seem inexplicable, because we perceive them to be running toward the edge of a cliff, but they don't see it. We, too, have been running so fast that we didn't think ahead or see what was ahead. We've been captured by our feelings in the present moment—both those we want to get away from and those we want to go toward—just like all other beings who are chasing after hopes and dreams or are terrified by their nightmares.

What if each of these beings had been inconceivably kind—given us life, put our needs before their own every minute of every day, stayed up night after night when we were sick, worked hard to put a roof over our head, nourished us, and empowered us with the skills, values, education, or training we needed? How would we respond to them differently if we knew all that about them? How would we conceive our lives in relationship to them to repay their kindness?

Next, think of those you judge harshly because of their behaviors, their habits, and the consequences of these on those around them. They may or may not be trying to hurt those around them. They could just be lashing out, running away, trying to get or find what they think will make them happy. They may be completely overpowered by attachment and aversion, just like we've been so often in our lives. At times, we've been so possessed by or have identified to such a degree with our negative emotions that we couldn't even remember to be guided by our values. What if each of these beings had been so kind that they made a profound difference in our lives—in the length or quality of our life?

Keep expanding the meditation with different kinds of people that you judge more or less harshly. Keep expanding your meditation until it embraces all living beings—each of which wants to be happy and not suffer, and all of which are working at cross-purposes to their own wishes, just like we've done.

If you try to begin with a particular person and find it's too painful and the habit to aversion toward them is too deep, start with whoever *has* been kind to you in this life. Then expand that to include people you feel neutral about, and then people you have harsh judgment about. Expand out from there, eventually including all living beings. When you finish, dedicate to all beings that the virtue of your practice serve as the certain cause of their temporary and ultimate happiness.

Hillary: I feel like my sense of gratitude is being obstructed by this deep-down assumption that my parents should *be kind to me. What do I do with that?*

Lama: One thing you could do is take it to your purification practice, because it's a habit, and it can be purified.

Another thing you could try is to give to everyone you meet what you think others should be giving you. Then take any feelings of entitlement or resentment to your purification practice. That way, instead of reinforcing low self-image—like believing you're a bad person because you're so ungrateful—you purify this view of yourself.

Hillary: When I try to walk myself through a situation that could have gone differently, I draw a blank. I know I didn't have pure motivation in that moment, and often I can see clearly what was going on in my mind instead, but, when I try to imagine what I specifically could have done differently, I either can't think of anything or it's abstract.

Lama: You have to walk yourself through the situation in such a way that the old habits are brought up strongly, so you truly feel those emotions. We're learning which meditations are most effective for changing which kind of negative emotions. For example, tonglen is always effective, because it simultaneously generates love and compassion while antidoting, purifying, and transforming attachment and aversion.

When you look back, watch what arises in your mind in relationship to that person or situation. If it's attachment or aversion, try doing tonglen long enough to experience some kind of change in your experience of the person or situation. If you find that the reason you felt stumped was because you were full of judgment and righteousness or whatever toward that person or circumstance, do one or all of the equanimity meditations. We need to do these meditations not in a rote kind of way but bring them directly to our heart. Of course, we start each meditation with pure motivation and end with dedicating the merit.

If you're truly transforming your feelings through meditation, you won't draw a blank, because, at that point, your mind won't be ordinary. It won't be stuck in the old places in which you didn't know what to do. It will be filled with and empowered by your positive qualities. When we see through the lens of our positive qualities as opposed to the ordinary mind, there are more options. When we see that everyone has been our mother, we love them all so much, we see how much they're suffering, and we find ways we could do this differently, because our mind is naturally opened up.

Anthony: I still have this idea that if some wrongdoer pays the penalty for their wrongdoing, they cleanse their karma. In a perfect world, there would be a penalty for the wrong that was committed rather than us just meditating on how much compassion we have for them because they're idiots like we are. Once we've done that, it might be an even greater kindness to bring them to justice.

Lama: It's all about our motivation. When we bring them to justice, are we bringing them to justice out of righteousness, anger, and a desire for revenge? Or are we bringing them to justice out of love and compassion to protect others from them, them from themselves, and, if possible, to support the possibility for change?

As a way of expressing benefit and a commitment to the equal welfare of perpetrators and victims, you might choose to interact with the justice system to encourage accountability and consequences. However, to be effective, you must have pure motivation. Everything you do has to come from love and compassion, so you're accumulating enough merit for your work to be effective. Not everyone is called to respond to the same things, but, ideally, if we all operate from pure motivation, we'll be more effective when we respond to suffering in whatever way, in whatever situation we can.

Generating Equanimity—
Recognizing the Pure Nature of Every Being

We can give rise to equanimity by doing the Just Like Me meditation or meditating on all beings having been our mother. A third way to do so is to give rise to great equanimity through any number of meditations introduced in the next chapter. In the meantime, we can remind ourselves that the true nature of every living being is sacred, pure, and pervaded with limitless positive qualities. Maybe, in this moment, we don't believe that. Maybe we feel totally cynical about that possibility, but what if our true nature *is* pure?

Anyone we're struggling with, just like us, wants to be happy and doesn't want to suffer. Their true nature is pure but, not knowing that, not being able to believe in or access their positive qualities, they act out of their negative habits, just like we've done so many times. And if this person—and all beings— have been inconceivably kind to us in long forgotten lifetimes, we would orient to them—to all beings and to life itself—as an opportunity to express our gratitude, to repay that kindness.

Combining these three reflections—all beings are just like us in wanting to be happy and avoid suffering; their true nature is a state of limitless purity; and they've shown us great kindness in the past—is a powerful means to antidote and transform our pride and judgment and give rise to a stable and reliable quality of equanimity that will sustain all our efforts to bring benefit to the world.

42 Combining Three Equanimity Meditations

We start by establishing pure motivation, and then we imagine someone we have a lot of judgment, pride, and righteousness toward. We imagine this person in front of us and walk ourselves through a reasoning process, reminding ourself: This person, just like me, wants to be happy. Every single thing they're doing is because they think it will bring benefit. They aren't doing it because they want to suffer. Just as I've done so many misguided things in the course of my life when I thought something would benefit me or those close to me, maybe this person is doing what they're doing because they're trying to avoid some kind of pain or suffering. Maybe they're trying to blame and punish everybody and everything around them for their suffering. How many times have I blamed others for my own misfortune, for my own suffering, for my own difficulties, just like this person is doing?

Their concern for their own welfare is so overwhelming that it wouldn't even occur to them to think about those around them much less take them into consideration, listen, or respond with empathy or compassion. There's just too much suffering, too much desire for their own welfare—just as has been the case with us.

We remind ourselves that this person, who's behaving in these ways just as we've done, has a true nature of limitless purity, like the crystal. Everything they're doing is adding more ore to that crystal, further obscuring their positive qualities and ensuring more suffering for themselves and others now and in the long run—just like we've done so many times. Go through the process of considering how all our natures are inherently pure, and yet, out of not knowing that, we grasp at all of these outer labels and identities. How could we possibly repay any kindness they might have shown us in long-forgotten times?

Next, we imagine others who are behaving in similar ways as this person. Maybe they're in the same organization or the same neighborhood and are making similar choices, behaving in similar ways, and are motivated by similar kinds of poisons of the mind. All these people are behaving in this way out of a misunderstanding of the causes of benefit and the causes of harm, just as we've done so many times, lost in the blindness of our desire for happiness and our aversion toward suffering, disregarding the suffering of those around us.

The tragedy is, everyone we're imagining just wants to be happy. They want things to get better. They're not trying to make things worse, and yet, in the very course of trying to make things better, they make things worse for themselves and for others—just as we've done so many times. We're aware of the deep-rooted tragedy here. Even though their minds are filled with limitless positive qualities—such as generosity, faith, trust, patience, kindness, and wisdom—they instead act out of superficial negative emotions—just like we've done so many times.

What if all these people had been kind to us—the kindness of the kindest mother—and are now lost in their confusion, flinging around the causes of suffering for themselves and others, flailing around in the course of trying to find happiness, and creating the opposite for themselves and others? How would we repay that kindness now? How would we think about and respond differently to them?

We next imagine people who behave differently from those in the previous scenarios and who we also judge harshly. They make choices we find disgusting or terrifying. We think about how many times we've made choices that others—like our parents or people close to us—found terrifying or disgusting. People in our neighborhood or our organization might have been horrified by some of our choices. Did we care about them when we made those choices? Did we care about the impact of our actions on others any more than these people care about the impact of their actions on us?

The people we're imagining behave in these ways in the very course of trying to find benefit—just as we've done limitless times—even though their mind and heart are endowed with limitless positive qualities. And their lives could be going in such a different way. They could be creating limitless merit, but, instead, they're creating so much harm. We think about how these individuals are just like us, may have been kind to us, and consider how we might interact with them differently.

Keep expanding this meditation to include people behaving in different kinds of ways. For example, imagine someone who has shown you great kindness but who you've come into conflict with. Remind yourself: This person, just like me, thinks their way is the best and only way to find happiness. Just like me, in the very course of trying to bring about happiness, they're producing the opposite and creating conflict. How could I respond differently?

Walk yourself through that process with more and more types of people—people you love, people you feel neutral about, and people you have aversion toward—and continue to expand the visualization to include *all* living beings—two-legged, four-legged, no-legged, many-legged. Just like us, the true nature of each one is a state of limitless purity, but, out of not knowing that nature, each one produces the opposite of what they want, again and again. How can we orient ourselves differently to repay their kindness, in our lives, in our work, and in our communities?

At the end of your practice, dedicate the merit of your meditation to them with the aspiration that whatever virtue you've created may be the cause of short- and long-term happiness for them and all others, throughout time and space.

Ocean: When I did this equanimity meditation, a lot of self-righteousness and anger came up. When I know someone is hurting other people with their actions, I don't want to become complacent. I feel I can recognize my judgments, but that doesn't make me less angry.

Lama: It's great that you're seeing your habit to react to injustice with anger rather than equanimity and compassion. If you've been feeling a lot of anger about all the injustice in the world, that's been eating up your merit.

The purpose of all these meditations—and the purpose of the bodhisattva path—is to increase our capacity to be of benefit and decrease the limitations to our benefit. If we're only trying to help innocent victims and not the perpetrators, the perpetrators will keep perpetrating, and there will be more innocent victims forever. We must address the perpetrators as well as the victims.

To be of greater benefit, we need to accumulate the virtuous causes of that benefit, which means planting medicinal seeds. To do that, we must transform whatever is going on in our mind that isn't virtuous. We're not giving a free pass to the perpetuators. We're working with our mind to become more effective. To the extent that we add ore to the crystal through our negative thoughts and emotions, we obscure our capacity to be of benefit. To the extent we remove ore from the crystal, we reveal the qualities of our true nature. This means, when we act, we draw on those positive qualities—which aren't composite, aren't impermanent, and aren't subject to causes and conditions. They're a reliable source of strength, empowerment, and benefit for ourselves and others. If we understand these principles and want to practice according to this understanding, we need to remove what's obscuring our positive qualities and recognize, enhance, and express them.

You might find the stories of the lives of great masters who've created extensive benefit for others to be extremely compelling in showing you why we need to tame and train our mind. For example, for Mahatma Gandhi to be able to have the equanimity he had toward the British and to be able to say to the British governor that the Indian people were going to liberate India with the governor's help, he had to see the British governor not as an enemy but as a person equally worthy of respect. Gandhi had to go through a lot of mind training to be able to respond to the degree of suffering going on in India at that time in a way that was truly transformative. He and his followers did a lot of practice. He started *ashrams* where people undertook spiritual practice so they could look the British soldiers in the eyes with love and compassion instead of hatred as they were being attacked. He understood they needed to prepare spiritually.

I'm using that example because Gandhi produced a level of transformation we can't even conceive of as long as we're involved in or buying into the victim psychology that says perpetrators need to be punished and victims are powerless against them. What empowers us to respond differently, to think creatively, is our positive qualities, because then we're plugged into a source of power that isn't finite and impermanent. We're not looking through the same lens of confusion and self-referencing and hope and fear. Through our practice, we're able to purify those so we can see things more clearly. The courage of the bodhisattva comes from these positive qualities. It may sound like a platitude, but the truth is that, ultimately, the only thing stronger than our fear is loving kindness, compassion, and wisdom—our positive qualities.

Otherwise, we remain in our ordinary mind and feel perpetually powerless.

We're not letting anyone off the hook. We're empowering ourselves to be more effective and proactive in order to protect those perpetrators from the effects of their own actions as well as the victims in the moment. We don't only have compassion for those we perceive as innocent victims and feel judgment and anger toward those we see as the perpetrators. We have a deep conviction that the only difference between the two is time—the current perpetrator will be the future victim when the karmic fruition of their actions ripens. We're helping to uproot and intercept causes of suffering, now and in the future, and planting seeds that will produce a momentum of benefit and virtue.

If we want to see positive change, but we react to injustice with anger, we're incinerating the very causes of the positive change we seek, burning up merit. If we want to see positive change, we must create positive causes. We must gather the causes and conditions of positivity if we want a positive outcome, so we must be well informed about what produces that positivity, how to gather it, how to increase it, how to protect it, how not to destroy it, and how to give it to others. When we do that, we begin to develop a momentum that can create, support, and sustain change that's positive.

Ocean: In a practical sense, Gandhi didn't just sit at home and pray.

Lama: On the foundation of spiritual principles and practice, he organized people so that suffering was made more visible, using what he called Truth Force. He brought the suffering to the surface. He made the truth evident through the media. He also took the truth to the governor and the powers that be and engaged them in the process. And, consistently, again and again, he refused to fall into a mindset of praise and blame, victim and aggressor.

Ocean: It's still hard for me to not think of pulling away to do spiritual practice as complacency, even though I understand we ultimately need a more skillful method.

Lama: It's the opposite of complacency. If we only have compassion for the victims, it's easier to become complacent, because we aren't as aware of the degree of suffering in the world and how it's being perpetuated. If we have enough merit, we can carve out our little comfortable niche and just hang out where we're happy—until, of course, impermanence happens. However, if we have equal compassion for the perpetrators *and* the victims, the urgency increases vastly, and it's much, much harder to become complacent. Those who have power and wealth have those things due to past causes and, if they're using their power and wealth to harm others, they're incinerating the basis of everything they have and want. They're destroying it for themselves, and they're destroying it for others.

We can't become self-contented and sit back. The way of the bodhisattva is inconceivably active. Sometimes, that action involves taking time for formal meditation to prepare our minds. We need to put the time into formal practice, but the whole purpose is to benefit others. Depending on circumstances, we're called to act in different ways. How can we be complacent if our hearts are opening and we're more and more aware of the degree and depth and vastness of suffering? There's no such thing as a safe space that can fully protect us, because, everywhere we look, beings are suffering, and our purpose is to end that suffering.

CHAPTER 15. GREAT EQUANIMITY

Our practice of equanimity supports all those around us through unbiased love and compassion, like nurturing every plant equally in a drought-stricken landscape. Even more so, great equanimity—the direct knowing of the true nature of all beings—is like the blessing of a summer rain that nourishes and transforms our entire environment without effort, showering limitless love and compassion on all beings equally, near and far.

One way we can develop that capacity is to rely on the Four Immeasurable Qualities, each of which serve as gateways to recognition of our true nature. Just as what appears as undifferentiated ("white") light contains the full spectrum of colors, the pure essence of being is saturated with a vast array of positive qualities, any one of which, in itself, can serve as an unerring path to awakening and to believing in each other's infinite capacity as well. Ultimately, every method we use to cultivate bodhicitta leads us to wisdom by purifying what's obstructing it.

Through our practice, we come to know, from direct experience—beyond concept and duality—that love and compassion are true and reliable, and that our essence is fundamentally pure. Although we must cultivate this knowledge through effort at first, we start to make space in our mind for the genuine experience of our true nature to emerge effortlessly.

For example, we use effort to cultivate love, and then we rest the mind. In this way, we come to recognize—without analysis, investigation, or artifice—that love isn't a *thing*, yet it's completely pervasive and we can develop confidence in its flawless presence. We're unable to find substantial things called our true nature, positive qualities, or love, even though our experience of them is undeniable.

Every time we're introduced to the idea of our natural purity—however conceptual our understanding may be—it shatters our view of reality. The process of investigation alternated with rest starts to break down the conceptual extremes of the ordinary mind. We're developing a quality of knowing that arises through experience rather than simply through the intellect. It's not abstract. It's not like knowing the answer to something in school. We know what's true, and we know this from our own experience.

We've used the metaphor of buying food, storing it in our pantry, combining ingredients, and cooking a meal. If we don't take the food out of the pantry and cook it, it can't nourish us. But what does it *mean* to take the food out of the pantry, cook, chew, and ingest it? It's our lived experience that gives strength to our spiritual practice, the confidence that comes through *knowing* what's really true. It didn't come from the outside. We weren't forced to learn it. We came to that recognition from our own experience. In this way, we come to *know* our true nature is pure; we *know* our natural qualities of love, kindness, and compassion; and we *know* that nothing is fundamentally self-existent—because this is our experience of reality. Everything we do with body, speech, and mind is the expression of that knowing.

We've created a different movie.

Our True Nature is One of Wisdom and Compassion

The true nature of mind is a state of limitless purity endowed with limitless positive qualities and capacity for the manifestation of those qualities. Within that limitless potential is everything from the most negative and obscure to the most positive and awakened—and everything in between.

We experience the appearances on the screen of our life as fundamentally true, separate, and distinct from us. That confusion is a misunderstanding of reality arising from ignorance of our true nature. We identify so deeply with the images on the big screen of our life that we become completely absorbed in and fascinated by them. Within the commotion and drama of our grasping after the appearances we like and rejecting those we don't, we have no awareness of the true nature of that experience. Our attachment to the story of our lives obscures the essential radiance of mind itself—mind that's absent of solidity yet luminous.

We can't capture the lucidity radiating from the movie projector to put in a box as a gift for anyone. Although it can't be captured, it's something that can be known. The more we awaken to the wisdom of knowing the essence of movies, the essence of being, the essence of everything, we begin to experience genuine freedom—the freedom to make choices that uplift and benefit rather than reacting reflexively and habitually to our projections.

Our wish to make the greatest beneficial impact in the world is supported when we realize our entire experience is like a movie. Otherwise, we continue to be lost in a universe of endless filmmaking. As long as we think the movie is real, those appearances have power over us.

Wisdom awareness is like being aware of the light passing through the frames of film. Even as appearances arise, we know they're not ultimately true. That knowing loosens our fixation on the appearances themselves. Wisdom is the recognition of things as they are, which seeps into our experience of reality, opens it, loosens it up, and relaxes it so that, even as we experience the imagery on the screen, we know it's none other than light through film. Our relationship to the imagery is freed up and purified, and the imagery itself, over time, frees up and purifies. As long as we relate to the imagery as ultimately true, we reinforce our present relationship to appearances and are unable to experience a deeper recognition of things as they are.

Every practice we're working with here leads us toward that more profound knowing, our essential wisdom. As we relax into this awareness, everything that isn't this, falls away. It dissipates without effort. The qualities that benefit others—such as love, compassion, generosity, and patience—are naturally expressed. No matter how hateful or angry someone is, we respond with love and compassion. As we're able to realize that those emotions themselves are none other than the play of light on film, we're less captured by them, less reactive to them, and our toxic emotions begin to dissolve. Whatever's unfolding on the movie screen won't entrap and imprison us. We begin to gain more freedom of choice in how we respond as the power of our awareness becomes greater than the power of appearances. That's wisdom.

From this wisdom arises not only compassion for beings overwhelmed by great suffering but also compassion for the predicament of beings. All of us are held captive by the scenes in our movie and believe they're real, not understanding how we perpetually produce the opposite of what we want. We're trapped by our own ignorance.

Once we begin to awaken, our compassion becomes increasingly vast until it evolves into the profound equanimity of knowing so deeply the true nature of reality that we experience nothing but an equal concern for all beings along with the wish to benefit them equally and help them to realize their true nature. If we're still bound by the appearances of our film and reacting with yoyo-like emotions, we can't help others, who are equally trapped, to cease perpetuating the causes of suffering for themselves and others.

For most of us, as we embark on this path, methods that introduce us directly to our true nature aren't as effective as starting slowly and simply. As long as our understanding of reality is based in confusion, no matter how many teachings we receive, we'll only experience them through the filter of the film itself and develop only a conceptual understanding of the practice rather than living it. That conceptual understanding obstructs rather than supports a genuine experience of mind's true nature, because we're defining truth through our interpretation of the images on film. Instead, it's through the practice of the heart of bodhicitta that we're able to swiftly remove enough of the confused imprints that we can develop genuine insight into our true nature.

To do so, we need to stabilize our experience of the positive qualities that are an expression of our true nature. We must know, from our lived experience, that they don't ultimately exist—no heart surgeon or brain surgeon could find them—and yet they appear, arising as the radiance of our heart.

Inez: How can I develop confidence in my ability and that of others to be of greatest benefit?

Lama: When we know the inherent purity of our own mind, we then know the inherent purity of mind itself, the mind of all beings. When we know so deeply that the potential of every being is infinite, we can convey this to others. This usually happens not through words but in the way we love and respond compassionately to others. It comes not from our own personal agenda but from a quality of love and compassion, of knowing that every living being has infinite potential. If we really know that about someone, we empower them to know it about themselves. When we're certain about that in ourselves, we can help others to be certain about it as well.

Through our own process of discovering the power of our positive qualities, we come to know the same is true of others. It's not inaccessible, conceptual, or hidden. It's infinite responsiveness to infinite causes and conditions that can arise. We're not separate from that. As we gather more of those moments of insight, we express those positive qualities for the sake of others. That's the path. These are the causes and conditions that produce awakening.

We engage in the effortful practice of the Four Immeasurable Qualities again and again to lead us to the effortless awakening to things as they are. From that knowing, that great equanimity or ultimate bodhicitta, arises the limitless positive qualities that allow us to become ceaselessly responsive—sometimes outwardly, sometimes not; sometimes physically, sometimes not—with a mind that's always present.

Breanna: How can I be certain that my meditation is leading to that awakening?

Lama: Ultimate bodhicitta—wisdom—is inseparable from relative bodhicitta—all that we've been learning. So, there's no possibility of expression other than endless bodhicitta. If that's not happening, we need to return to one or another methodology that brings the mind back. With that as a basis, we again let go of effort and rest the mind. We go back and forth. Maybe we alternate with compassion, or maybe we alternate with prayer. We keep pulling together the causes and conditions that will produce the effortless, ceaseless expression of bodhicitta, of spontaneous love for all beings equally, of a heart of compassion that's beginningless, endless, drama-less, and without victim or aggressor—simply unceasing compassion for the plight of beings. We know our collective confusion is superficial, temporary, and tragically recurring, but knowing this doesn't mean it all stops. It means we're empowered with the certainty of the natural perfection of things to take actions that are virtuous and, in and of themselves, the causes of future awakening and benefit. We know there are always more options than the ordinary mind sees.

Beyond Somethingness and Nothingness

To explore, practice, and realize the meaning of great equanimity, we have to break down the assumptions that cause our fixation—the uninvestigated belief that things are solid and non-composite, because that's how they appear. For example, if we see someone causing harm, we might see and label them as a "bad person." Based on that label, we project all kinds of judgment and hostility, and we may even act based on that view. We aren't seeing this person as an accumulation of many causes and conditions that have come together to produce this moment in time—a gathering together of molecules and subatomic particles or as a bag of bones and blood and flesh. We aren't seeing their mind as the result of previous imprints, from their family of origin, their community, the culture they grew up in. If we were aware of the constellation of beliefs, behaviors, and habits created by these imprints, we'd see how change is possible. But, instead, we see this person as fixed in time just the way they appear to us now.

When we look at our own minds, we can feel overwhelmed and discouraged by the power of habit, psychology, and mind's poisons. This is an aspect of eternalism—the materially oriented belief in the permanent, non-composite existence of things. We see ourselves as fixed, our psychology as fixed, our personality as fixed. We believe we can't change any of this because it's fixed. It's true that if everything in the moment isn't in a process of endless change due to endlessly shifting causes and conditions, there would be no way to create change.

However, if we realize nothing is fixed or ultimately true, we might think there's nothing there. We could go to the other extreme of nihilism and feel as if nothing matters and everything is hopeless. We can develop that view about ourselves, others, and everything in our lives.

Our culture—and humankind in general—is largely permeated by eternalism. It's hard not to think of the lack of permanence as something other than nothingness. So how do we explore the meaning of our true nature as a state of natural perfection that's beyond both something and nothing? We start by investigating our beliefs about our true nature alternated with resting the mind. This examination starts as a conceptual process, but this is how we need to begin to break down our assumptions, or we'll be bound by them forever.

Great equanimity arises through recognition of the true nature of everything as limitless purity beyond the extremes of existence and non-existence. If we try to find that limitless purity, what some call the sacred, we may ultimately decide there's nothing there. However, this perspective denies appearance.

Different cultures and traditions relate to the idea of the "sacred" as what's inherently pure, transcendent, positive, beyond the material world. In the Buddhist tradition we use the term "Buddha nature" or the pure nature of all beings and all phenomena, "the true nature of mind," "the true nature of reality." But every one of those terms involves a noun. The sacred is a thing, our true nature is a thing, Buddha nature is a thing. All the metaphors we've used—the crystal, the movie, a rainbow—refer to a thing. So, let's explore and see if we can find and identify that thing.

On the surface, of course, we can't find our true nature, but we still have assumptions, or we wouldn't conduct ourselves based on the belief we're self-existing—and, not only that, but the most important self-existing something in the whole universe! If we truly knew that, ultimately, there's no thing called the self, there would be no basis for self-clinging and all our other habits. The methods we're using to purify and counteract our habits wouldn't be necessary if we knew, through our own experience, there's no thing called the self, no thing called our true nature. But, if we go to the opposite extreme and think there's no self, who's thinking about these things and asking these questions?

Then we walk through our assumptions about "other." We can think about a person or any outer thing—a mountain, a city, or any object with a name—and use the same line of reasoning. Then we explore the existence of objects of hope, objects of fear, the self, other, the sacred, and the absence of the sacred.

What we're doing here is beginning to explore the meaning of great equanimity—what's beyond fixation and nihilism, beyond somethingness and nothingness. Within the view that recognizes all appearances arise due to causes and conditions, there's the understanding that everything is in a constant state of flux. This means there's infinite potential for transformation.

43 Trying to Find Our True Nature

Explore and contemplate to see if you can find a *thing* called essential purity, the sacred, and, if so, where is it? Does it have a beginning and an end, a color, a size and a shape? Then rest the mind.

Does it live in our body, and if so, where? If our true nature is a sacred state of purity, is there a place inside our body we can call "the sacred" and, if so, where does it live? When the body dies, does the sacred die with it? Explore, then rest the mind.

If our true nature isn't a thing, how could it come to be? Why are we exploring bodhicitta if there's no such thing as our true nature to wake up to? We must believe there's some thing to be achieved, and we're trying to learn methods to discover that thing. So, what is it? What does it look like? What are its characteristics? How could the sacred be in everybody and not be the same in all of us? Is it like the oxygen that everyone breathes? Is it like the space in which endless appearances arise? Contemplate, then rest the mind.

If you can't find the sacred, if it's not a thing that's identifiable, with characteristics, does that mean it doesn't exist? If it doesn't, what accounts for the boundless positive qualities in our minds and hearts and those of others? What accounts for spiritual, meditative, and religious experience? Contemplate and rest the mind.

If our true nature isn't in the body but in the mind, where, within the endless stream of thoughts, emotions, memories, and mental events, can it be found? Is it in the beginning, the end, or the middle of any particular thought or emotion? Before each thought arose, was there no sacred, and, after the thought dissolves, is there no sacred? If that were so, the existence of the sacred would be dependent on causes and conditions, unstable and impermanent, so how can we say everything is sacred?

Examine these lines of reasoning, alternated with rest, compassion, commitment, and prayer.

Doug: I feel I may have missed a step here. You've asked us to try to find the sacred essence of everything, but we won't be able to find it, so we rest the mind. For me, the idea is still shaky that there's sacredness in everything, that our true nature is pure. It seems we must begin with that belief, and that's the step I think I may have missed.

Lama: In exploring the meaning of great equanimity, we're examining our beliefs about the spiritual path, about the sacred, about the nature of mind. All beings are equal in wanting to be happy, not wanting to suffer, and in the consequences of not knowing the causes of happiness and suffering. This whole phantasmagoria of endless suffering arises from our lack of awareness of our true nature. To antidote that ignorance, we try to find, explore, and realize the sacred.

This involves investigating the nature and source of our positive and negative emotions to discover if they're affected by causes and conditions. For example, when we're angry, we can't remember our compassion or our love or equanimity. On the one hand, there's our relationship to the positive qualities, which strengthens and stabilizes through repetition and practice. But, when we try to discover if our positive qualities are self-existing, we find there's ultimately no "us" trying to give rise to positive qualities. There's only love or compassion within that experience, without duality or separation. As a result, there's no basis for negative habits and obscurations to occur. These only stem from a lack of recognition of the true nature of our experience.

When we let go of the effort to cultivate love and rest the mind, for example, the radiance of love arises without effort, but the experience of it isn't fundamentally true, any more than a love scene in a movie is true. Ultimately, there's no subject witnessing, no thing to witness, no process of witnessing or examination going on. There's just a knowing without a subject knowing an object. You could say it's love knowing itself, compassion knowing itself. That's wisdom—when our awareness realizes itself, knowing its own nature without duality. There's just the knowingness of it.

As we practice giving rise to our positive qualities alternated with rest, we develop a different relationship with ourselves, with others, and with what's happening between self and others. It all relaxes within wisdom awareness. That wisdom is like a solvent that dissolves our fixation, attachment, and aversion. Everything relaxes and opens. The more we practice, that wisdom becomes more stable. Our relationship to self, others, and what's happening between self and others opens. As wisdom infuses our lives, increasingly we recognize the pure nature of everything. That knowing of our true nature is what purifies previous imprints in the ordinary mind. From that awareness, positive qualities arise as a natural response to the needs of beings.

Is the Flame Empty?

This isn't a conceptual process nor is it always the same, because the nature of mind itself is empty, meaning there's no substantial thing we can call "mind." If we look for mind, we can't find it—it's not there to be discovered.

The word "empty" in this context is often misunderstood. It doesn't mean nothingness or a void but the illusory essence of mirage-like movie or dream sequences. The nature of mind is, in fact, inconceivably dynamic and expressive. The reason mind has limitless potential is because it's not substantial. If it were solid or permanent, the boundless manifestations of mind couldn't possibly occur.

Although there's no thing called mind, ceaseless, dynamic expressions of mind arise in limitless ways as the brilliance of that empty nature. The union of the two—the empty aspect of mind and the radiance of its dynamic qualities—is one way to understand mind that can help us not get lost in a nihilistic idea of nothingness.

In the projections of light through film, there's *no thing* to ultimately be found. If that "no thing" pervades all of our experience, we might then think that everything is ultimately "no thing" The ordinary mind is habituated to appearance and its consequences, cause and effect, and it can go to the opposite extreme by believing that emptiness means denying cause and effect. It's a huge trap to think nothing ultimately is there, and, therefore, consequences don't exist. In thinking this, we deny karma and the importance of paying attention to our conduct. We can fall into a kind of depression from this profound misunderstanding and wonder what the purpose of life is if nothing really exists.

All we have to do to wake ourselves out of that delusion is to hold a flame to our finger and tell ourselves the flame is empty. That, in itself, may purify confusion and point out the contrast between conceptual understanding and direct experience. If we'd truly realized the flame is empty, we wouldn't suffer from the heat of the flame. However, we have an experience of pain, and that's why it's consequential.

We need to investigate and not take anything for granted, because actions lead to consequences. We don't want to fall into the trap of denying the importance of virtue, love, compassion, and beneficial action for the sake of others.

This line of reasoning may sound silly, but our experience can be extremely subtle. We can be examining like crazy but still think emptiness is a thing. We may think emptiness is the nature of reality, but then we project our habit to *thingness*—solidity—onto our idea of emptiness. So, we need to examine this thing called emptiness.

Outer appearances—no matter how we try to understand or grasp them or wish they'd slow down—keep arising and subsiding unceasingly. We have the appearance of our body being born, developing, aging, and dying—and we sure wish we could slow *that* down. We have the appearances of mind—the process of thinking, feeling, fixating, and rejecting, and the unceasing self-referencing arising from our fictitious experience of self. As we start to purify self-centeredness, we more fully experience the pure qualities of mind—an unceasing display of love, compassion, rejoicing, and equanimity.

In what we call mind-in-motion, there's no thing we can find that isn't constantly changing. The equalness of great equanimity abides in both its empty and unceasing aspects. We need to explore both to determine if they're equally true for ourselves and for all beings. We explore, investigate, and try to discover our true nature, and then we relax the conceptual investigation and let the mind rest.

Breanna: You said that when we're resting in the recognition of the true nature of reality, we have spontaneous love and compassion for all beings. I'm curious about what that feels like or what that means, because sometimes when I meditate on impermanence, I feel way more spacious, and love is easier.

Lama: If you think spaciousness exists, you might cling to that as a thing. Now you're starting to notice the difference between that belief and the spacious experience of mind—which is less stressed, traumatized, and invested and has a greater ability to give rise to love and compassion.

Without contrivance or effort, there's just the union of appearance and emptiness—not like a union of two things that are put together but a timeless unity. The very nature of appearance is empty, and the very nature of emptiness is to express itself. Within that view, love and compassion are naturally occurring, inseparably and spontaneously.

In Rinpoche's metaphor of the grandparent watching their grandchildren on the beach, the grandparent has more wisdom than a parent—less attachment and less aversion. The grandparent loves the kids, regardless of what the kids are playing or the drama of the sandcastle.

We could also think of love like the rays of the sun. It's the nature of the sun to shine, everywhere, equally. It doesn't have to think about it or try to shine. Love and generosity are natural expressions of great equanimity.

Breanna: In the example of the grandparent, there's this experience of spaciousness, but I'm hearing you say that's different from what I was experiencing. The spaciousness is actually filled with love and compassion.

Lama: Yes. That's why "emptiness" is a hard word for us to get our minds around, because it's an absence of solidity and yet imbued with the vast potentiality of "everythingness." What arises occurs according to interdependence. You're beginning to break though some old ideas you had about both extremes and to see through the tunnel vision of the self-centered perspective. Self-centeredness with space is very different from the spaciousness of bodhicitta.

Anthony: Is the next extension of equanimity—regarding other people as equal to us—to not judge a person or a situation?

Lama: The meditation on equanimity is a basis for that, because ultimately, in any situation, we can't find a *thing,* and yet, there are unceasing appearances arising. The true nature of what's going on is the inseparability of the two. We're dealing with both extremes—finding there's no thing, resting, thinking there's no thing, and finding there are unceasing appearances, resting, recognizing the inseparability of the two as direct experience, and then resting. That's the best way to cultivate the ability to see through these appearances and experiences.

Incidentally, this empowers us to make choices that are more beneficial to others, because, when we bring that view to everything that's happening, our vision isn't as clouded by attachment and aversion, pride, jealousy, and so forth. What arises is just love and compassion for everyone who believes in things as they appear. We're motivated by our love and compassion, and we have more wisdom and discernment about how we respond or the ways we can find creative alternatives to what's going on.

"I'm Pretty Sure I'm Sick"

If the ordinary mind rebels and tries to convince us there's nothing illusory about the pain in our knee, we can use the mind that's rebelling to antidote its beliefs by breaking them down: Our experience is that there's nothing illusory about this pain in my knee. Okay, so, if the pain isn't illusory, that means it's solid and true. So what color is the pain? What's its shape and size? Is the knee itself solid or a composite of bone, cartilage, blood, muscles, and so forth? If we examine each of *those* things and break them down, we find they're composed of tissue that's composed of cells that are composed of molecules that are composed of atoms that are composed of subatomic particles—and, ultimately, we discover there's nothing there. Quantum physics tells us there's nothing there. The Buddha taught us 2500 years ago there's nothing there. We *know* this conceptually, but we haven't realized it, or we wouldn't have the same experience of the pain in our knee. The causes and conditions producing the appearance of the pain are still there, but, if we had full realization, we'd know, deeply, it's an illusory pain, an illusory experience.

There was a great master in our tradition, Nyoshul Khen Rinpoche, who lived in Bhutan and passed away a number of years ago. He'd been poisoned earlier in his life and had terrible headaches as a result. One of his students sponsored him to come to the United States to get medical treatment for the pain. The specialist they consulted asked him, "How have you treated the pain until now?" Nyoshul Khen Rinpoche replied, "I meditate." The doctor looked at him skeptically and asked, "Does that make the pain go away?" Rinpoche replied, "No, the pain is still there, but my mind is more comfortable."

This is the difference between pain and suffering. Suffering is the mental experience of pain. Nyoshul Khen Rinpoche was free of suffering, because he knew the pain was illusory. As he was able to rest in that recognition, he wasn't overcome by the experience of pain.

As we realize the illusory nature of our experience—as opposed to just having the *idea* that it's empty yet appearing—we're not bound by it. The power of that awareness is greater than the power of the appearance.

Tej: I find the phenomena of the body to be so compelling. I've been sick for about four days, and the idea of using this process of examination as an antidote for my illness seems to take a much more advanced practice than I have. It requires deconstructing the illness, but, to do that, it's necessary to deconstruct the self that has this body.

Lama: We must bring practice to our experience in a way that corresponds with where our mind actually is. If the intensity of your experience of illness makes it difficult to use this analysis to see through it, use a method that *will* help you to purify it.

Tej: You said to use whichever methodology works for us. My body doesn't seem to be light through film. It seems very real. I'm pretty sure I'm sick.

Lama: You're learning that even as you try to pierce your experience with analysis and resting the mind, the habit to identify with the body is stronger. We need to use whatever practice corresponds with our assumptions. Otherwise, we'll be doing a practice of appearance emptiness that doesn't penetrate that experience. As a result, we're reinforcing the idea that the body is solid. We need to employ a more dualistic method to help purify, as quickly as possible, that duality. We want to do whatever practice will permeate and purify our experience as swiftly as possible.

If we're cultivating wisdom and haven't been able to give rise to or stabilize great equanimity—this is when we rely on relative bodhicitta. When we have that kind of physical experience—

pain or illness for example—to the extent that we have a habit to invest this body with a substantiality it doesn't ultimately have, to that degree, we struggle with our hope and fear in relationship to it. Unless we've cultivated the power of wisdom, it can't penetrate and overpower the delusion that gives rise to the hope, fear, attachment, and aversion.

That's when we think of others who are having the same experience. In your case, you could start by thinking of others who are also ill and can't do what they want to, can't follow with their body the intention of their mind, because the physical karma is so overwhelming. Perhaps the next step is to pray, By my illness, may no one else be ill. May the illness of all beings be purified by my own. With that aspiration as a basis, the next step is breathing in the illness of all beings and sending out absolute purity and healing, which is ultimately the expression of great equanimity. Through the practice of tonglen, we breathe in the illness and send out natural purity.

If we always give rise to relative and/or ultimate bodhicitta, that will transform our mental, physical, and verbal experience. The power of that is ultimately greater than the power of any of the temporary, superficial, composite phenomena that appear to be coloring our experience. Whether we're directly resting in the recognition of great equanimity or are cultivating the qualities that lead to it, both are extremely powerful, because everything else is due to causes and conditions that aren't ultimately true.

As you think of everyone else who's ill, pray that all their wishes and aspirations be fulfilled by your virtue: May your cultivation of bodhicitta create the merit that's necessary for all those beings to find health. This is the basis of the tonglen practice for all beings who are ill—to breathe in the causes and conditions that produce illness and send out the causes and conditions that bring health. Then dedicate the merit to all beings.

Over time, the cumulative effect of your practice will erode the power of self-clinging and, more deeply, of self-concept, so that, increasingly, you'll be able to see through and transform old habits even as they're arising. Until then, continue to rely on whichever relative method is most effective in any given moment to produce change.

Metaphors for Great Equanimity

Metaphor is another way to explore the meaning of our true nature beyond the extremes of existence and non-existence. We started out with the metaphor of the projector, the film, and an exploration of how we project and label appearances. Within the habit of labeling, there's a more subtle habit—a belief that appearances are inherently true. Based on that, we label the appearance and, based on that labeling, we fixate. Then we give rise to an assessment or judgment of whether that appearance is good or bad. Based on those judgments, toxic emotions arise followed by a sequence of habits.

At the same time, we know that when we're watching movies, all the characters and everything that's unfolding isn't ultimately there. If the drama is really gripping and, especially, if we're the hero, it's very hard to remind ourselves that these appearances are just light through film. Within the context of that metaphor, the unfolding of the drama on the screen is what we call the "relative aspect of truth" or the "relative truth" within which actions all have their inevitable consequences. There are experiences of happiness and sadness and good and bad that are consequential, even more so when we identify as the hero. Our hearts race as we watch the film, whether it's the film of life, a film in a theater, or a film on our phone. Our hearts race because of the habit to invest legitimacy in something where it doesn't exist. It's so compelling that we think it's true. That aspect of truth—where non-virtue leads to harm and virtue leads to benefit, where fire leads to heat and water leads to wet—is completely consequential within that sphere of reality. And yet, ultimately, that whole drama isn't really happening. All we have to do is turn off the projector or our phone, and the drama stops.

This means that, ultimately, there's no drama there, even though it's arising in a fashion that's so compelling. The aspect of truth in which we realize there's no drama there is called the absolute or the ultimate truth. What's ultimately true about it is that there's no drama unfolding, even though, relatively speaking, there's obviously a drama unfolding that's completely consequential to everybody within it. The tendency of the ordinary mind to go to the extremes of existence and non-existence is just the means by which it tries to capture, contain, and make sense of our experience, especially when we're introduced to the deeper nature of that experience.

There are skillful ways for working with metaphor to loosen the habits of the ordinary mind to try to understand and make sense of, organize, negotiate, and survive our experience. We use metaphor to lead the mind toward an understanding that's a less conceptual way of seeing that, even as the drama unfolds on the big screen we call reality, there's nothing ultimately there. Then we let go of the effort to understand through metaphor, and rest the mind. Then, even though there's nothing ultimately there, appearances arise unceasingly. This is one way to practice recognizing their illusory nature, a way to begin to understand our experience more deeply when we talk about the true nature of reality as a state of pristine purity. These contemplations and meditations lead us toward a recognition of the inseparability of these two aspects of experience.

Great equanimity arises when we recognize, experientially, that our projections are just light through film. The Buddha used a number of metaphors to illustrate that even as appearances arise, they are, by their nature, illusory, not inherently self-existent. He used the metaphors of the dream, a reflection of the moon on water, a rainbow, an echo, a hallucination, and a mirage to point to the illusory nature of reality.

44 Meditation on the Movie of Our Life

When you awaken in the morning, remind yourself that every moment of your day is like a scene from the movie of your life: the getting out of bed scene, the brushing your teeth scene, the making breakfast scene, and so forth. Continue reminding yourself, throughout the day, that everything that's happening is like light through film, and maintain that awareness as your go to sleep.

As the events of the day unfold, remind yourself that you wrote the script of this movie. Everything that's happening is like an imprint on the frame of a film that you created. All the appearances are light passing through film. If you don't like the appearances, how could you change your relationship to them? Which meditations that you've learned could change the quality of your experience of the events unfolding in your life? If you like the appearances, how could you share them with others?

Maintain awareness throughout the day of yourself as the main actor in your film. Watch yourself act, then let go of watching, as if you're one with the action itself. Remind yourself that each action is nothing other than light on film, then rest in the play of the light of mind itself. Watch yourself speak, then let go of watching your speech, as if your mind is becoming one with your breath on vocal chords. Watch yourself think, remember, or feel, then rest the mind in the knowingness of your thoughts, memories, and emotions.

The Dreamlike Nature of Reality

Using the dream metaphor, we know that, when we're dreaming at night, if we don't recognize we're dreaming, all the events appear real and vividly consequential. The appearance of self, other, and of what's happening between self and other seems true—until the alarm goes off. We wake up and realize it was "just a dream." It was illusory and, by its nature, non-existent. Yet, when we didn't *know* it was a dream, we were captured by everything going on. The good scenes made us happy, and the bad scenes made us sad or scared.

If we're able to realize, as we dream, that it *is* a dream—not just be aware conceptually but *know* it's a dream—the power of that awareness can change our experience of the dream. Instead of those appearances having power over our mind, our mind is able to have power over the appearances. That metaphor can help us to cultivate wisdom, because our whole life is like one long dream.

In one way, we can say the purpose of life is to make better dreams for ourselves and others. However, if we're lost in our own dream, even if it's a pleasant one, we can't help awaken those trapped in nightmares. It's not enough to refrain from the causes of our own nightmare or to try to make better dreams just for ourselves. We need to *wake up* so we can help everyone else wake up.

Through great equanimity, we recognize that everything is illusory—like a movie, a dream, a hallucination, or a rainbow. We can't *deny* appearances, nor can we deny that the nature of those appearances is ultimately illusory. One way to practice great equanimity is to remind ourselves our life is like a dream or light through film.

The Buddha's metaphors of the moon's reflection on water, the rainbow, and the dream can help us start to understand what's beyond understanding. What do we mean when we say appearances are empty and yet appearing at the same time? They're not one or the other, nor do they exist or not exist or both or neither. They aren't two separate things happening at the same time or appearing in union. They aren't the union of a duality but rather dwell in timeless unity, meaning they were never two things that were joined.

Rinpoche said that trying to understand the true nature of reality with the conceptual mind is like trying to use a net to catch water. The net of conceptualization can't capture reality as it is. Instead, we approach our exploration of great equanimity through investigation, contemplation, the practice of the Four Immeasurable Qualities and metaphor alternated with resting the mind.

All the practices we're doing help us to refine away our intense fixation on the apparent existence of self, other, and what's happening between them. We're refining away the ore obscuring the crystal and starting to have glimmers of what may be underneath. Slowly, our obscurations purify so that we can begin to have a direct experience of reality beyond concept.

45 Meditating with Metaphor for Illusion

As you watch a movie, without analyzing or thinking about the appearances in each scene arising through light on film, simply let your mind settle on the images themselves, without story. Then let go of the effort to settle on luminous images, and let the mind rest.

Let your mind settle on a rainbow in the natural world or light refracted through a crystal. Simply let your mind be with the rainbow appearance without looking away or analyzing the conditions producing the appearance or separating your process of inquiry from the appearance itself. Then let the mind rest.

When you awaken from a dream that's still lingering in your mind, let your attention settle on the appearances without making sense of them or following their story. Simply let your awareness blend with the dreamscape, then let the mind rest.

Hillary: When thinking about the inherent purity or essence of being we've talked about, I'm wondering whether the knowing of the not knowing splits the mind into concepts, and we just keep reinforcing our confusion?

Lama: We perpetuate and increase our confusion every moment that we believe our projections are true. It's natural for the ore to think that's all there is, that there is no crystal. The more we purify, the more we realize what else there is.

What we do with our mind can lead us in fundamentally different directions. Spiritual evolution isn't assured. It depends on our choices. Every moment, each of us makes choices about the direction we're going. It's up to us—if we have the tools. This is what's so precious about this opportunity we have. We have access to the tools and enough trust in them to use them. We have some degree of choice about the conditions within which to practice. If we don't have the tools and the faith to use them, we don't have the same power of choice. That's what we call a precious human birth. How precious is that? And how impermanent! This is our chance to wake up, to realize our true nature, so we want to use it well while we have it.

CHAPTER 16. RIDING THE WAVE: DAILY LIFE AS SPIRITUAL PRACTICE

Rinpoche sometimes used the metaphor of surfing to help us understand how, if we can remain present with the turn of events in our lives, our practice will be swift and clear. The surfer has to stay with the crest of the wave in order not to fall, just as, in each moment, we need to try to stay one with our practice consistently, no matter the shift of outer and inner phenomena in our lives. Otherwise, if we get a little ahead of or behind the wave, we can lose our balance and fall.

We can have a certain amount of awareness, trying to bring bodhicitta to everything that's happening, but then the next person, the next need, or the next drama arises, and we aren't able to stay present and, instead, we fall off the wave.

We can see our deepest habits in the midst of sudden change: what's our response? When we fall off the wave—when we lose our mind in the unforeseen twist of events—are we able to realize we've lost our practice? If we recognize that's happened, we can use one of the tools we've been learning to bring ourselves back to bodhicitta.

Each of these tools will help us to be better able to stay with the wave, because we're reinforcing our positive qualities. We're deepening the habit to orient to the turn of phenomena in our lives in the context of bodhicitta. That's the mode we're cultivating to be able to swiftly change our response when the force of appearances overpowers our practice. The trick is to develop both the mindfulness to stay with bodhicitta and also the vigilance to be aware when we fall away, so we can bring the mind back.

One way to know our practice is working is that less and less time transpires between the times when we fall away and when we realize we fell away. When we first receive teachings, it might not be until the next time we review the teachings that we realize we've forgotten to practice, which could be six months later! As we practice more, we may realize we haven't remembered bodhicitta for a month or a week. Over time, we'll be able to remember daily and then hourly. The time we spend having fallen away from our practice or getting lost in detours diminishes.

The important thing is to contemplate the teachings we've received and stay present with the big questions we started with such as karma and the choices we're making in our lives so that, at the time of our death, we won't have regret. For example, we may become sick and, while lying in bed, we could remember to ask ourselves what our priorities have been. It's not the illness itself that takes us away from or brings us back to the path. It's what we do with the illness that can bring us back. If we bring bodhicitta to our circumstances and ask all the right questions about our lives and priorities, we can bring ourselves back to practice.

Once we feel aligned with our purpose and orientation to life, we practice while remaining mindful of that purpose always and in any situation. If we fall off the wave, we bring the mind back. We try, as much as possible, to stay right with the phenomena with our mind as they crest, without falling off. This helps develop stability of practice. We notice, when we fall off, the imprints of thoughts and emotions so they can be purified. Ideally, if we remain present with the wave of our bodhicitta, we won't even make those imprints. This is the fastest way forward. If our practice isn't slipping away, there's less and less to purify, and the path is smoother.

That's the stance of the true practitioner. We've developed a relationship to the practice, a relationship to life, that's allowing us to take appearances as the path, to purify karma as we go, and to not continue to create more unfortunate karma going forward. We can eventually even develop a sense of "Bring it on!" because we're confident about having a precious human birth that's impermanent, and this is our chance.

Anthony: Only rarely is my practice one in which something arises, I remember the tool to practice with it, I move on to the next thing, and that tool pops up, so it's like riding a wave. Sometimes I find myself sitting there for a half hour or more just trying to bring up bodhicitta. It's almost like I'm completely impervious or I'm apathetic. If there's no bodhicitta, should I just get up from the cushion and go create merit? What do I do at that point?

Lama: We could say this is a metaphor for the momentum of our practice, the momentum of bodhicitta, which is what's sustaining us in our actions of body, speech, and mind. Everything we've been learning is about how to create and maintain that momentum. You're right, sometimes we don't feel it as momentum. Past karma can come up, poisons of the mind can come up, we can get triggered by all kinds of things, and we fall off the wave. The wave goes this way, the surfboard goes that way, and it's all we can do to catch a breath.

In general, everything we've been talking about helps us to create that momentum. We start the day by establishing bodhicitta, even if it's conceptual and even if we don't have time to do formal practice. We at least bring to mind the intention that everything we do this day, this life, be of temporary and ultimate benefit for all beings—or, simply put, the cause of the awakening of all beings. Then, we bring our mind back to that motivation with everything we do as we go through the day.

If possible, we try to take time for formal practice at the beginning of the day. If we're not able to do this, in every moment that we act during every day—no matter what's happening outwardly—we bring that intention to what we're doing. Even though we may not be fully engaging bodhicitta, just that motivation transforms what appears to be an ordinary day or an ordinary action into an extraordinary one. That simple act of reestablishing our motivation bathes everything in our day with the blessing of bodhicitta as does the huge accumulation of immeasurable merit when our day is consecrated by dedicating that merit for the sake of all beings. When what appears ordinary—washing the dishes, sweeping the floor—is done for the sake of all beings, it contributes to the momentum of our accumulation of merit, which will support giving rise to the depth and stability of bodhicitta we aspire to.

At the same time, we practice bringing wisdom recognition of the deeper nature of our experience to all that we're doing. Insofar as we're able, we recognize everything is impermanent. Whether we think it through, or just let ourselves be aware there's a deeper truth at play that we haven't fully awakened to, as we bring the mind back to bodhicitta, we create merit. That merit is the basis for the momentum of our practice, so, if we don't create merit, it won't happen. That's the path. That practice, in itself, purifies everything that needs to be purified, keeps us on track, prevents us from making imprints, and purifies previous imprints.

A number of factors could be contributing to your inability to generate bodhicitta at any given time. You could be super stirred up because of events in your life, or something could have triggered you. Whatever's going on for you, think of everyone else going through the same thing who may not have the insight or the tools for dealing with it. Wish that, through your suffering, their negative karma may be exhausted.

Always bring others to mind. This is the simplest and most radical shift you can make and, if you can do that, it will help give birth to love and compassion, create merit and bring you back to bodhicitta. If you experience real love and compassion, you don't want just temporary benefit or temporary relief from suffering for others, and you don't want it for just a few but for everybody.

Anthony: Sometimes, I'll be focused entirely on trying to think of others, but I'm so deeply entrapped in whatever's going on for me that it's impossible to imagine or care about other people.

Lama: When we're riding a wave of negative karma, and there's so much negativity in our mind that we can't see through it, we can use one of the powerful methods for gathering merit, such as rejoicing in others' virtue.

Over time, we learn that when we're running away—such as staying busy out of a habit to avoid—we need to rely on the tools we've learned to bring the mind back to bodhicitta. We won't always be clear every time, but the more we bring the mind back again and again, this becomes our frame of reference. If this becomes the wave we're riding, when we're not riding it, the contrast is obvious and uncomfortable, even painful.

Our accumulations of merit and wisdom—bringing the mind back to pure motivation, antidoting and transforming negative emotions through the Four Immeasurable Qualities and other bodhicitta meditations—contribute to the momentum of our practice. The greater the momentum, the more it will sustain us and the harder it is to fall away from it. No matter what arises, it will be experienced in the context of bodhicitta. At a certain point, bodhicitta itself becomes the momentum—not just trying to give rise to it but its actual presence in our mind will become stable. Everything is purified swiftly within the stability of that space of heart and mind.

Until that happens, we're pulling together the causes and conditions to support it. In each moment, the trick is to do whatever we can to use whatever method is available to us at the time to bring the mind back to bodhicitta. We don't want to waste time letting the mind drift away from it, so we do everything we can to bring the mind back, again and again and again. This is what builds the momentum that will sustain us. It will become not a practice but the realization that it's already a part of us. The point of practice is to help us catch up with our deeper heart.

Doug: To what extent does sharing our practice experience help others?

Lama: Usually, it doesn't, because we each have our own experience that arises and subsides according to what's happening in our own practice and karma. If we compare our practice experience to that of others, they might feel discouraged about their experience or they might feel proud or they might think that nothing is happening in their mind, because they aren't having the same kind of experiences as us. However, it can be helpful to share our practice experience with our teachers, so they know what we're doing with our mind and can offer feedback to make sure we stay on track.

We can think about our dharma practice as a big pot into which we're putting all these ingredients according to the Buddha's recipe. We set this pot on a fire—the warmth of our practice— and something happens when we apply heat to those ingredients. However, if we poke a hole in the pot or release the lid of a pressure cooker at any point, what's happening inside will change. Similarly, when we share our practice with others, it's like taking the lid off the pressure cooker. It will change the process itself.

Doug: Are you saying that the benefits of my practice only come out in how I treat people outwardly, how I express myself, and not in how I try to help others understand how practice can support us?

Lama: It's also in your heart. The more you practice, the more your heart changes. The expression of your positive qualities manifests in all kinds of acts of kindness. Also, you're creating huge amounts of merit that you're dedicating to others. As a result, the world has more virtue and kind-heartedness in it.

Doug: I feel that sharing with other practitioners is a significant part of my practice, specifically with the meditation group I facilitate in prison. It seems to be helpful for all of us to share our experiences of where we've seen our own practice being of benefit or how we've learned to deal with a challenge differently.

Lama: Sharing your flaws and how you work with them is always beneficial, because it helps people feel safer to admit they have flaws as well, accept support for how to work with them, and receive guidance on which meditations can be most helpful. This can help others not to feel like there's something wrong with them because they have stuff.

But to share our meditation experiences or how we experience our positive qualities isn't so helpful. Rinpoche was strict with us about this. There were always new people coming in who got discouraged, because they weren't having the kind of dreams or insights that someone else was having. People were always comparing themselves to each other, and it wasn't a source of virtue or benefit.

Tonya: What happens when I fall off the wave and I don't want to get back on it? I don't want to bring my mind back to bodhicitta. I can see that I've fallen off the wave, so it's not a lack of awareness. It's just a stubborn resistance.

Lama: For many of us who grew up in a culture unfamiliar with bodhicitta, unless we have an extraordinary karma ripening for the path, usually we need to take a bite from the teachings, and then chew and digest it, because the whole framework of bodhicitta is so different from what we've known. We can like the idea of the path conceptually, but it takes time for the teachings to sink in. We may hear the teachings, and they may click for us, but we have to work with them to see if they make sense to us as the basis for our path, our lives, and our choices. It takes time to assimilate and digest them. Some people take a big bite, and it may take 15 years to digest it. Others may only need a few months.

If we don't take time away when we're feeling rebellious, it can start to feel like another authoritarian structure being imposed on us. That just reinforces our own psychology of being a bad this or that, which doesn't benefit anybody. We're simply bolstering our oppositional tendencies toward authority. Maybe we need to go away for some time and try to stay afloat without the surfboard in the midst of big waves to see if we can catch a breath, try to swim, and see how we do. Do we want that surfboard, or do we want to get swept back by the wave? Sometimes, we just have to play it out.

I've seen many people that play it out, hit the limitations of their ordinary mind, and then come back for the next bite. That seems to happen more often than people connecting, diving in, and staying—or getting onto the surfboard and staying upright—so your experience isn't uncommon.

I've noticed that each time you fall away from formal practice, at some point, when you return, your faith in the power of practice becomes more consistent and integrated. So, just accept that's the way you're doing it.

We each must approach practice in our own way. Sometimes, much of the path is finding out what that way is, which is what you've been doing. You've been asking the right questions and going deeper into your practice. Your positive qualities are increasing, and negativity is decreasing. Don't judge or punish yourself or give yourself some label. Just accept that this is the way you're doing it.

Tonya: I have a really hard time accepting the way I've been doing it, because I get more and more miserable the more I persist in doing it my way.

Lama: You just have to play it out.

Tonya: I just have to keep getting more and more miserable?

Lama: Maybe...until you hit some kind of limit and bring your mind back. Spiritual practice only works if it's an active choice. If we don't want to do it and try anyway, usually that isn't so effective.

This is different than learning how to cultivate discipline, concentration, and other factors that support the path that we call upon once we've decided we want to practice. If we're still fighting with our self about the path itself, and we're hitting ourselves over the head about the fact that we're fighting the path, that doesn't help. If we're not sure, sometimes we just have to try the alternatives.

Tonya: It makes me sad, because there have been times when I've been so, so sure of the path. How did I fall away from that certainty?

Lama: Remember, we're all sitting on mountains of karma. We've all planted all sorts of seeds, maybe enough virtuous seeds that we end up on the spiritual path but also seeds of doubt, of misunderstanding, all of which have made imprints. It's not as if we're bad if we've done it, it just happens. When those seeds ripen, we can experience that as doubt overcoming us as we proceed on the path. It's just those previous karmic seeds.

Trying to stay within a large corral, as you've done, is perfect for this karma. You're in this corral of virtue, and you approach and pull back, although you never leave the corral. Slowly, over time, you've developed more clarity. This doesn't mean all previous seeds of doubt and resistance are purified. They still come up sometimes, but a lot less often, and they don't capture you as strongly as they did, and they don't take you away for as long as they used to.

Tonya: The longer I've had a connection with bodhicitta, and the more moments I've had of being able to practice, I have a tangible experience of walking away from my positive qualities when I follow my resistance. I can tell I've given something up.

Lama: You've spent enough time becoming familiar with your positive qualities, and that's increasingly become a frame of reference. When you're away from it, you notice the contrast, and it doesn't feel good. That's exactly why we come back, if we find this path to be beneficial.

Tonya: Another thing I think about is, if I were to die today, I'd have regret. So that plays on my mind when I walk away.

Lama: The problem is, when you follow your resistance, it's like a different lens. It's a different karma ripening. If you say to yourself that whenever you're in that place, you're going to ask yourself whether you'd feel regret if you died today, you'd rebel even more strongly. You'd say to yourself that you'd have no regret, that you went and did this other thing that was beneficial. It won't work. When that lens is clouding the mind, we see everything through it.

When you come back to your practice, you create enough of a momentum of merit and wisdom and mind training that it becomes the more predominant force in your life. Previously, it was the time with your practice that was uncomfortable, and now it's the time away that's uncomfortable. That's a huge shift. We have to work skillfully with our karma. It would be really easy for you to put me in the position of saying to you, "You *must* practice!" Then you get to rebel against me and not take responsibility.

Tonya: I've already tried that countless times, as we know.

Lama: You've done it perfectly, for you, with your karma, and it's working. With this insight, you may choose, during your formal practice, to spend more time in purification practice and work with regret—regretting whatever it was you did that created this doubt or oppositional karma or loss of faith—and then dedicate the merit to everybody who encounters those kinds of difficulties. Really own it, and take it onto the path.

Tonya: Before this moment, I had the experience of a greater faith and a greater devotion than I ever had before.

Lama: It's like the rubber band that stretches and snaps back. Each time, just like the rubber band, you stretch more, and the resistance decreases while the elasticity increases. You can see that, because it's working for you.

Bringing Bodhicitta to Everything We Do

Rinpoche used to tell us to rejoice when we wake up in the morning, because not everyone does. We rejoice that we have another day, because we don't know how many more we'll have, and we have this day—or at least part of this day, this moment to do what we can to increase our capacity to help others.

We then establish bodhicitta as our motivation for everything we do. If we have time, we might do some formal practice before we go to work. We can reflect on the previous day, and think about situations where we fell short, where we could have done better, and practice whichever meditation is the most relevant. This helps us think through the situation differently, so we create a new habit to respond differently if and when similar circumstances arise again.

We give rise to bodhicitta before entering the workplace, and dedicate merit before each break. Then, we generate bodhicitta as our motivation for all our interactions during the breaks and, again, dedicate. All of this helps to keep our mind active with bodhicitta. And we dedicate merit before the possibility of weakening or destroying it in moments of regret or strong negative emotions such as anger.

We go through the day doing everything we can to bring practice to every circumstance. At the end of the day, we look back and see where we fulfilled our intention and were able to practice, responding in ways that we believe were genuinely beneficial.

At the same time, we need to be watchful that we don't get proud or identify with what we did well but rather give it away. We dedicate whatever virtue we've created: may it be the cause of certain benefit for the person who may have been nasty as well as the person who was the recipient of that nastiness. May it benefit everybody equally, and may they all benefit from this virtue not just in the short run but in the long run.

We then look back to see where we fell short and walk ourselves through those scenarios in our mind. As we reimagine what happened, we can feel the anger, the heat rising in our mind and heart, the aversion, the jealousy, or whatever it was. We antidote those emotions with the appropriate meditation to bring our mind back to pure motivation Then we walk through the situation differently by practicing with positive qualities instead of negative responses.

As we do this again and again, we're making new habits. Unless these new habits become as ingrained as the old, we'll respond out of those old patterns. We all do this, and we can't expect it to be otherwise. However, the good news is, because these methods were given to us by great masters and enlightened beings, they're super effective and powerful, which means we don't have to put as much time into changing them as we originally put into creating them.

We do need to practice, and the most effective way is to do this every single day—not just abstractly but in the context of walking ourselves through situations we wish we'd handled differently. At the time, we couldn't think of a different way to handle them, so we walk ourselves through these situations again and again until we're able to respond to life's challenges from our positive qualities instead of our old habits.

When we see where we've fallen short, we can also do the Meditation on the Four Powers of Purification. Wherever we feel merit has been generated, we dedicate that, so the day is sealed in that context.

In every day and every practice, we begin with bodhicitta and dedicate the merit at the end. In the middle, we don't let ourselves get carried away or lost in our thoughts, nor do we suppress them. Instead, we maintain awareness and bring the mind back to relative and ultimate bodhicitta, again and again. This undermines and purifies the habit to becoming caught in webs of self-involved thought, and it steeps our mind, our practice, and our efforts for the benefit of beings with limitless virtue and merit, which we dedicate to all beings. This is called the Three Excellences: the excellent motivation at the beginning; the excellence of our awareness in the middle; and the dedication of merit at the end.

Doug: With all that we're learning, and when we're in the midst of our workday, how do we remember what practice fits with what situation?

Lama: Each practice is a tool, and some tools will be more effective at different times than others. The more you develop a familiarity with each of them, the more they're going to help you, because you know what to use at any given point.

As we go through our day and interact with different people and circumstances, we'll see various things come up in our mind. We identify which of the poisons are uppermost in any given moment, and antidote them with one or all of the Four Immeasurable Qualities to bring the mind back to bodhicitta. We use tonglen and love and compassion meditations to antidote attachment, anger and aversion. We use rejoicing to antidote jealousy and competitiveness. Practices of equanimity antidote pride, judgment, bias.

We remind ourselves that we're all equal in our wish to find happiness and avoid suffering, and in our confusion about the causes of happiness and suffering. We're also equal in that our true nature is a state of limitless purity. We can bring that to mind, even though we may not be having the more profound, non-conceptual insight of great equanimity. Or, we can focus on a practice that has to do with one specific person, who like me, wants to be happy, emphasizing the "just like me" part so it doesn't become patronizing or paternalistic.

If we're so bound by our ignorance and confusion that we're completely lost and have no idea how to proceed, we can practice cultivating wisdom by alternating contemplation of impermanence with prayer and resting the mind.

As a general practice for cultivating a wisdom perspective, we can pay attention to the rate of change. Whatever's arising in this moment wasn't arising a moment before and won't be arising in the next. We want to do this especially when things are hard—objects of attachment are fading away, objects of aversion are arising. We remind ourselves it's all impermanent. None of it will last, so we allow it to arise and subside without clinging to or analyzing it. If that feels accessible, it will lead toward Great Equanimity. Bringing that perspective into our day helps to loosen our grip, our fixation. Even though, in that moment, we may not be able to access limitless wisdom, this way we can open the door, open the window, take down the shutters, and allow that ray of light to illuminate, within and without, a way through that's beneficial to ourselves and others.

When you do your formal practice that evening or the next morning, you can play through your memory of the previous day's events—where you lost your practice and how you could have brought your mind back to bodhicitta more effectively. Obviously, the emotions won't be as strong as they were at the time, but you'll be able to feel some shifting in your orientation. Your heart may soften, and you'll have more perspective. As we spend more time with these tools in formal practice, they become more easily accessible in our daily life. This is the point—not that we use them all every day but that we have some relationship to each of them, so they become resources.

46 Daily Life Practice

Begin by establishing pure motivation for your practice.

Then reflect on a recent interaction with someone where you lost your practice. Walk yourself through what happened so that you're clear about the point at which the interplay became about you and not bodhicitta.

If you became angry at how you were being treated, start by thinking of everyone else who's feeling mistreated but who doesn't know what to do with their anger other than express it and create non-virtue. Do tonglen meditation for them, breathing in their anger and misery and sending all your merit and bodhicitta. Expand your visualization in ever-widening spheres of benefit until it encompasses all beings, including those who were mistreating you.

If you still find residual anger in your mind, try bringing it to the Four Powers of Purification meditation, regretting whatever past actions you took that are ripening in your current circumstances as well as your habit of anger and aversion and all the karma you've created by acting on those emotions instead of transforming them.

If your primary response to that incident was feeling judgmental and righteous, try bringing to mind the three combined Equanimity meditations with the person(s) mistreating you, expanding the scope of your intention to ultimately include all living beings.

If you find you were envious of those who were being praised instead of mistreated, practice rejoicing in the causes and current conditions of their happiness and wishing for them that these never diminish but only increase until their enlightenment.

Then dedicate the merit of your practice to those you felt were mistreating you, and then to all beings, that it may serve as the cause of their complete awakening from the causes and conditions of suffering.

Creating Merit Throughout the Day

We don't need to wait until we're substantially farther down the path to bring benefit to beings. There are many things we can do on a daily basis to increase and dedicate our accumulation of merit. For example, any time we find something we like or enjoy, instead of holding onto that as our own personal experience, we offer it. If we notice a beautiful day, a beautiful place, or a beautiful flower, we offer that experience. Instead of owning it as our own moment of happiness, we offer it. We imagine that flower multiplying until the whole universe and beyond is filled with emanations of this beautiful flower and offer it to wherever limitless wisdom and compassion abides, on behalf of all beings.

The act of letting go of and offering what we've unconsciously held on to as our own moment of pleasure creates a great deal of merit because it's so selfless. Since attachment is the source of so much suffering, when we let go and, instead, practice generosity, we're not only antidoting our attachment but further increasing the merit of our offering by visualizing it multiplying through space and dedicating on behalf of all beings.

If we start thinking this way, we'll notice how many times in the course of the day we tend to own these moments of happiness and don't think to share them—a beautiful sight, a wonderful meal, a moment of intimacy with someone we love, a moment of comfort, the ability to fall asleep when we're exhausted. Although it's far better to notice and feel grateful for all we enjoy rather than taking it for granted, ideally, instead of just reveling in them for our own sake, we offer them with the wish that every living being could have the opportunity to sleep deeply when they're tired, eat well when they're hungry, have beauty surrounding them, and so forth.

If we honestly look at our mind, we'll see how often we experience enjoyment by holding on to it. When we see that, we can, instead, immediately offer it with the wish that all beings could have such joy, beauty, fulfillment. We offer wherever we see the mind's tendency to grasp. This applies to little moments as well as when we're given a gift or praise or whatever brings us joy. Instead of simply accepting the praise with a thank-you, we offer: May all beings have such fulfillment. The more we do this practice, the more we see the many opportunities we have to practice generosity.

Tonya: I feel the change in my heart when I set my motivation—my intention—to be of benefit to all beings. With anything I used to do before—yoga or meditation practice—I felt like I was cheating a little, because there was an element of wanting to be of benefit to others, but a lot of it was just about wanting to feel good, to heal and center myself, or to not be a burden on others. How do we do the things we do and still maintain that motivation? Maybe when you enter this path, your whole life changes.

Lama: The *experience* of your whole life will change. And I don't think you're cheating. You're practicing. It's up to you if you want to make any outer changes or not, and your desire to make outer changes may transform over time. You may find that the deeper your practice goes, the more contented and at home you are with the choices you've made and your ability to bring practice to those choices.

Each of us walks the path differently, in our own way. Our experience of and orientation to everything changes profoundly insofar as we're making everything we do a cause of benefit for all beings—not for just the short term but for the long term and not just for a few but for all beings. This casts a very different perspective on everything and, from that perspective, we may find ourselves reevaluating certain things. However, this doesn't mean you have to stop doing the things that help you keep going, that fulfill and nourish you. Just don't forget everybody else as you're doing them. You can send health and joy to others. You can breathe in their suffering and, as you do that, you can make an offering of everything that's good in your life.

The most important thing is to include the short- and long-term welfare of others in absolutely everything we do. When we do that, we see things differently. It's an inner change. It's a change in our orientation.

Tonya: I feel slightly paralyzed in that I'm setting my intention, but I don't know if what I'm doing is of benefit.

Lama: It's wonderful not to know—if you have the freedom to hang out in the not knowing for a while.

Tonya: I've been a body worker, and I set my own hours. I'm also part of a team in my family that caretakes my nieces. So, I do have some time at the moment.

Lama: You're caretaking children and you're healing people, so it sounds like the main things in your life are beneficial to others. Be aware if your mind starts to close in on "just these people, just these nieces, just these people who are sick." Make sure you're always opening it up by remembering you're serving the needs of everyone who's sick through the person you're working with in this moment—not just their temporary sickness but the ultimate dis-ease of not knowing our true nature. You could pray, Through this healing, may all beings have the ultimate healing of awakening to their true nature. Let the things you're already doing in your life be the expression of bodhicitta.

Start out by stabilizing that when you do your personal yoga or exercise. Bring that motivation: By the virtue I'm creating, may all beings have the freedom, the tools, and access to what they need for their body to be healthy and to find temporary and ultimate health.

Stabilize your pure motivation and bring it into every aspect of your life. Once that's more integrated, you may find you want to ask yourself some questions about other things you could be doing that would be of greater benefit. But these are hard to know until you've stabilized your motivation, and that takes time.

It's wonderful that you have some space in your life to let yourself be with the not knowing. Think of everyone else who doesn't know what's best—even if their motivation isn't bodhicitta—for themselves or those they love. Don't forget everyone else. And pray, May what's truly best—not just for myself, not just for those close to me, but for all living beings and not just temporarily but ultimately—become clear. May I recognize the best use of this precious time I have on earth, the best use of this healthy body, the best use of my wish to benefit others. Keep praying for that to become clear.

The power of your bodhicitta is unfailing, and you're connecting that with dedication, aspiration, and prayer. You're creating all this interdependence for clarity to arise in a way that will be recognizable to you, so you can have confidence that it's beneficial. Bring your motivation to everything you do. Rejoice in how wonderful it is to bring bodhicitta to every aspect of your life. Enjoy that, and dedicate.

Dedicating Merit Throughout the Day

It's important to dedicate frequently all the merit we're gathering, especially as we're starting out in our practice, because it's another act of generosity. As we create merit, instead of holding on to it—like, *we* want the results of that merit to ripen for *our* good experience—we give it away with the wish that everyone may experience the fruits of our merit. This is a supreme act of generosity. Because it's so selfless and we're giving it away, it goes out of the realm of the self and our personal karma and into the realm of the inexhaustible, positive karma of all the beings who've benefitted, continue to benefit, and do everything they can to benefit others.

The more we give it away by dedicating it, the more protected it is—a seeming contradiction. We want to make the habit of generating pure motivation, creating as much merit as we can, dedicating that merit, refreshing our motivation, and creating more merit. We just keep going until it becomes a rhythm throughout the day, a palpable, positive momentum. We might even start to experience ourselves as a kind of merit generator.

No matter what else is happening, we just keep going, creating and dedicating merit to all beings.

Whatever's in our mind when we accumulate merit creates the interdependence for how that merit will ripen. If what's in our mind is for all living beings to be completely free of suffering and to have stable happiness, the merit we create will contribute to the fulfillment of that aspiration in this and future lives. But if we're only thinking of our own personal wishes for short term happiness, we're missing an unparalleled opportunity to create more substantial benefit for ourselves and others.

Rinpoche used to tell the story of a moment during a big ceremony in a shrine room in Tibet when a rabbit ran in and hopped right up onto the highest throne and just sat there. A yogi with great wisdom could see that, in the rabbit's previous life, it had been a monk in this same monastery. That monk had done decades of practice to create virtue, yet sometimes had the wish to sit on a high throne someday. Even though it was unconscious, the merit he created through his practice joined with that wish to sit on a high throne, so that, in his next life, he did—but as a rabbit! As a rabbit, he was relatively limited in his ability to benefit others, although he must have created a lot of merit through the collective hilarity he caused during that ceremony!

We may not be able to relate to a Tibetan story involving the wish of a rabbit in a past life to sit on a high throne, but we need to be aware of any and all ways that our attachment to our short- term personal happiness can unconsciously join with our accumulation of merit. We might wonder what's the problem if we have enough good karma to be able to buy some expensive article of clothing or fancy new digital device.

The problem is the lost opportunity. We've planted the seed for a lovely annual plant that will produce a lovely blossom for one season only when we could have, with the same effort, planted a perennial seed for a medicinal plant that will bring benefit to ourselves and others for countless seasons to come.

Ida: How can we help someone who seems to be so deeply into their suffering that they actually start to enjoy it, so that their suffering has started to define them, and they wear it as something they're proud of? How do we even approach that person?

Lama: It may not be that they enjoy the suffering but rather that they need the comfort of the familiar. If suffering is all they've known, it feels like home, and perpetuating it is part of their identity, the survival strategy they've learned as a way to keep going. We can't *say* anything to that person. Words won't work. We have to *be* different than their experience and model a way of being in which we walk through the world trying to benefit others.

Sometimes, just for them to have the experience of seeing someone doing it differently—and who's joyous in doing it differently—is enough. It depends on that person's karma—how much habit, how many waves of consequences of previous actions are hitting them in that moment, and so on.

When people are drowning in the effects of previous negative actions, they need virtuous influences—and merit—to shift the balance of their experience. We can't see all the causes and conditions affecting someone's current experience. But if we can't benefit someone outwardly because the wave of negative karma is so strong, we can always create and dedicate merit.

Because they're drowning, it can seem impossible for them to create this for themselves, but we can create and dedicate it for them. It could be that the tsunami of suffering is all they've known. It's so pervasive that they don't have any other experience of reality or even the idea that anything else could be true for them.

That's the purpose of the dedication of merit: We're committed to gathering as much merit as we can to dedicate to them. But because we don't want to be attached to the needs of that person over the needs of every other suffering being, we dedicate it to this person and to all beings that they may swiftly know the end of suffering. We create and dedicate, create and dedicate, and, over time, that person's experience will change.

We can have doubt about things that are unseen that seem impossible to prove, but, if we do this again and again, there will be change, though it may not look like the direct result of what we're doing. For example, that person may unexpectedly get a job or a new apartment. Change may come in fits and starts, but, slowly, the conditions in their life will change.

Putting "Time In" on Practice

We need to spend time with both formal and informal meditation and become familiar with how to use these tools so they're available at all times and we can bring whichever methods will help to transform whatever isn't bodhicitta into bodhicitta. For the benefit of ourselves and others, we need to ensure that bodhicitta arises as our abiding, lived experience— not just an effortful response to temporary, impermanent, composite phenomena. Working with these meditations can bring us to that quality of steady practice. There's absolutely no replacement for the time we put in on practice.

If we don't spend time with our practice in this way, our emotions will be swept away by life experiences that arise more quickly and powerfully than our ability to transform them, and they'll destroy our practice instead of enhancing it. If we have tools but not the right motivation, we won't know how to use them properly, and we can make a mess and hurt ourselves and others.

Ideally, we're making time each day for formal practice and giving rise to bodhicitta throughout the day as we do our usual activities. It's a matter of bringing bodhicitta repeatedly to mind and developing confidence in it. The more we do these practices, the more bodhicitta will be our lived experience, the foundation of everything we do, and allow us to awaken to the radiance of our true nature.

Bodhicitta provides the understanding for why, how, and when to use these tools. Without cultivating bodhicitta, we won't feel an urgency to use them. Bodhicitta assures that these tools create vast, swift, and powerful benefit for ourselves and all beings.

Ocean: How do we help others and still spend all this time helping ourself? How do we live in the world an equal amount of time?

Lama: First of all, the time we're putting into formal meditation isn't for ourself; it's for all beings. If we understand and believe in the necessity of spiritual practice as indispensable to be of greater benefit to others, we can do meditation for the sake of others without any sense of contradiction. Otherwise, we might be able to address some of the needs of some beings in the moment, but there are so many more needs and beings than we can currently help, so we need the greater capacity that comes through formal spiritual practice.

If we've put in a lot of time trying to help others, and again and again hit the limitations of our capacity, we can find that our ability doesn't match our aspirations. The frustration that comes from our awareness of this gap makes us absolutely convinced there's no alternative but to bridge that chasm. If we keep hitting our head against the wall—we've tried this and that and every other thing—but we haven't practiced bodhicitta, we're limited in our ability to bring benefit to others. We've tried to change the politics, we've tried to change the law, we've tried to change the team, we've tried to change everyone in our family, we've tried all kinds of things, but we haven't tried to change ourself. Sometimes, this process is necessary for those of us who have a strong habit to activity and action. We have to hit our heads against the wall a certain number of times until it becomes clear there's no other choice but to apply the methods that will change *us, deeply.*

Never compromise your commitment to others. If you're not convinced that putting time into spiritual practice is an important part of that commitment, keep going—for the benefit beings—in all the outer ways you're doing. If, at some point, you come to feel the time and energy you're putting into helping others with the methods, the heart, and the capacity you currently have aren't enough—and the urgency you feel and the scope of your intention is so vast compared to your current ability that you can't bear it anymore—you may want to try to put some time into formal practice.

Ocean: That makes a lot of sense. I try really hard, and I've hit that wall. I keep trying to help beings and, pretty soon, I'm not even sleeping. I meditate, but I hit that wall in my practice, too. I'm not feeling it, because I'm just exhausted.

Lama: That's a good way to destroy your body, which means you won't even have that as a vehicle to be of help. If we have a strong habit to activity and a sense of urgency because so many being are suffering, it may take hitting our head against the wall a lot of times before we get some sense knocked into us. We don't put the time in until we can't bear our limitations anymore, until our sense of ineffectiveness becomes more unbearable than the unbearableness of the suffering we want to respond to.

Hillary: How can I bring bodhicitta to obstacles that come up in my life and practice?

Lama: Bodhicitta always has the power to transform what appear to be obstacles, because they're only obstacles if we give them power. The only thing that gives them power is the ordinary mind, and the ordinary mind is only active when we forget bodhicitta. So, they're not, ultimately, obstacles. They're just temporary expressions of not knowing, not remembering, or not believing in our positive qualities. All we have to do is bring the mind back to the power of bodhicitta, which, like the rising sun, dispels darkness and brings the clarity that lights our way through.

Firmly establishing and stabilizing bodhicitta will give rise to our positive qualities and a greater capacity to cut through whatever challenges come up as we learn additional methods to empower our practice. This is the power of intention and of confidence in those positive qualities which are far more powerful than the upheavals in our temporary experience. We can have confidence that the ore is coming off the crystal and, eventually, the crystal will be completely revealed. It's that simple, although, from the point of view of the rock being tumbled, our experience doesn't necessarily feel simple, easy, or obstacle-free!

Tonya: I'm in a transitional period right now with work, but I find I'm being drawn to the kind of work I used to do. I'm trying to look at it and ask myself if my identity is wrapped up in this idea of finding work that benefits others, or am I coming from a genuine heart space where I recognize that this work is something I have a capacity to do, so I should do it.

Lama: Ask yourself which choice regarding your work is of greater benefit to others, which choice creates more virtue and less non-virtue. Your answer to this question has nothing to do with your identity. It has to do with the benefit of beings. We can all use questions like this as a gauge for every choice in our lives: Where is there more benefit for others? Where is there more harm? What creates more virtue in the world? What creates less non-virtue in the world? What are we contributing to? What's the collective karma that we're a part of? Does that collective karma benefit or harm beings?

We want to keep our frame of reference one of avoiding the causes of harm and suffering for ourself and others, undertaking the causes of benefit and happiness for ourself and others, and taming and training our mind to actualize our limitless capacity to do so. This is what the Buddha said: "Do no non-virtue; practice virtue; and tame your own mind. This is the essence of my teaching." If we use this as a framework for our lives, for decisions we make, it can help guide us as we undergo the pendulum swings of the ordinary mind.

Tonya: I can see that even wondering if I have confidence in an identity built on bodhicitta is making it about me. I just need to have confidence in bodhicitta, keep an expansive view and look for interdependence.

Lama: Keep an expansive view, give rise to the expansive motivation of bodhicitta, and pray for what's best without any attachment or concept of what that is: may interdependence make completely clear what's truly best for yourself and all beings.

Hillary: I'm a judge who mediates domestic violence cases. The last time I had to do this, I tried so hard, using bodhicitta and trying to appease in a highly contentious situation, but it just didn't work. Maybe it's because I'm looking for an outcome. I'm in a situation where who knows what's going to arise. It's like jumping into a waterfall—I have no idea what's going to carry me through. I don't know what to work on to bring what's best into the situation.

Lama: When we're working with people who are feeling strong emotions—such as a wish for revenge or retaliation—and don't have an altruistic point of view, we can't talk to them about virtue and non-virtue or karma. However, we can point out consequences. You can give both parties involved in the mediation a context that can allow for the most favorable outcomes for everyone involved, diminish the unfavorable ones, and help them to see from that perspective. If they're super attached to their own favorable outcomes and super attached to unfavorable outcomes for their opponents, try to talk to them about why they think succeeding in their revenge or punishment will help. Then explain that, in your experience, in the long run, it doesn't feel good and creates unfavorable outcomes.

Remember what the Buddha said to the man who became discouraged with how far he had to go every day to receive teachings. The Buddha advised him to look back every once in a while to see how far he'd come. So, remember how many resources you have—worldly resources, spiritual resources, skills, aptitude, intelligence. Even though you're not feeling confident in the moment, that doesn't mean you have no capacity to help. When your fears, insecurity, and lack of confidence come up, don't energize them. Keep bringing the mind back to bodhicitta and prayer: May every action of my body, speech, and mind be of benefit to all parties involved, may there be more peace and less hostility in the world as a result. Keep bringing your mind back to prayer and bodhicitta. Don't scare yourself with your doubts.

Boundaries with Bodhicitta

Part of developing a greater capacity to benefit others often involves establishing healthy boundaries with bodhicitta as our motivation. The more common understanding of the need to set boundaries—doors to our personal space and time that we can open or close depending on circumstances—is usually explained in the context of protecting ourselves in order to continue to be available to others. But assumptions about our own needs being more important than those of others can seep into such choices.

If that's the case, such actions only reinforce instead of dissipate self-clinging.

Setting boundaries with bodhicitta as our motivation means doing so not out of attachment to our own welfare but thinking about the short- and long-term welfare of everyone equally. Our actions can look the same in both instances, but the outcome, over time, can be as different as night and day. Are we leaving work at the end of a long shift because we have attachment to our time off and aversion to our boss's demands? Or are we genuinely thinking of the needs of all those we serve and concerned about getting the rest and nourishment our body needs to be as available to them as possible the next day? Are we thinking about establishing pure motivation, so our actions are creating immeasurable merit that we can dedicate to those we encounter at work and to all beings' long-term as well as short-term benefit? In both instances, our actions can appear outwardly the same, but the outcome is completely determined by our motivation, not the actions in and of themselves.

Doug: I'm in a new romantic relationship and am already running into questions about boundaries. How can I think about our lives and time together that's healthy and supportive from the point of view of practice?

There's something to be said for going slow, for really checking things out to see if the basis for loving well is there. Does this person have good boundaries? Do they respect your boundaries? Do their boundaries or certain behaviors trigger you? It's difficult to practice at first if we constantly feel provoked, and intimacy can be deeply challenging. We need to have enough trust in the other person to be able to learn how to practice even in the middle of being hugely triggered. If we take our time at the beginning of a new relationship to notice if the right dynamics are there and try to love well, it can be an extremely profound spiritual practice.

However, it often happens that it's difficult to practice in relationship, especially if we're super compatible. It's very tempting to become involved only with people who share what's obscuring our true nature—our attachments, aversions, and values. The comfort provided each other can reinforce rather than challenge our self-centered habits and ego-centric identity.

Establishing boundaries with bodhicitta naturally involves honoring others' boundaries and helps us to love well. If someone needs space, we give it to them, even if it's hard, even if, in the moment, we feel we desperately need their attention or presence. If they need space, we give them that space with the aspiration that all beings may have what they need in this and every moment.

If we're involved with someone who doesn't have good boundaries, doesn't understand the need for good boundaries, doesn't respect our boundaries, and, especially, if they're not inspired by our love to practice loving well, we'll eventually get drained. Trying to respond to their needs and wishes can go beyond our capacity to practice.

Doug: I think I have confusion about boundaries in general. For example, there was a time one evening when I needed gas and pulled into a gas station. This guy immediately came up and started pumping the gas for me. I thought that was strange. Then he said to me, "I noticed when you pulled up that there's something wrong with your brakes. Can I check them out for you?" I said, "Sure." He opened the hood and asked me to pump the brakes so he could see if they were working. Then he suggested we take the car for a drive to make sure the brakes were okay. He got into the driver's seat, I got into the passenger side, and we drove down the street. After a block or two, he pulled over and said, "I need to get out here, but I'd really like $30 for fixing your brakes." I gave him the $30, and he got out and walked off. I knew I'd been scammed.

Lama: Bodhicitta doesn't mean we have no boundaries. By not making boundaries, we allow the other person to make non-virtue. Rinpoche used to call that "idiot compassion," when we respond only to someone's short-term needs without any larger perspective of what's beneficial in the long run. What makes it less idiotic is when we think about the long-term consequences to that person and the karma they're making. If we truly care about them, we don't want to enable them.

The guy who claimed to have fixed your brakes created the full complement of all four components of non-virtue: He identified you as an object, he had a motivation to scam, he undertook the action to scam you, and the result was that he scammed you. That's a complete act of non-virtue for him.

One way we bring bodhicitta to our boundaries is we think about not just the short-term but the long-term consequences for that person, and all beings. It's like the difference between the actions of a parent or an adult friend toward a child's repeated requests for candy. The friend might give the candy to make the child happy in the short term, not thinking of the long-term consequences on the child's health and habits, whereas the role of the parent is to balance both. On the bodhisattva path, we want to protect beings, as much as possible, from making bad karma. But, in this case, you enabled it!

Carolyn: If you're committed to helping certain individuals in a particular way—for example, with school costs—is it all right to draw boundaries in other areas? I'm helping a family with their kids in school, but they're really poor and often lack money for food, medication, transportation, etc., and I find myself getting resentful at the constant barrage of requests.

Lama: The consequences of your actions will depend completely on your motivation, not on how others perceive you. You have to take these principles, integrate them, and determine for yourself what you think will be most beneficial. The fact that you're having resentment means it's gone beyond your capacity.

Out of bodhicitta, you want to act skillfully with the recognition you don't have limitless resources. What you do have is XYZ, and you can offer that freely with a good heart. That way, you're not making the karma of attachment to your own welfare and aversion to theirs. It can be helpful sometimes to practice giving a little bit more than you think you can in each instance, to stretch your capacity for generosity beyond the confines of self-cherishing so it doesn't remain confined in a comfortable bubble that lets your practice stagnate.

You never want to deviate from your wish that they have everything they need always for all time and not just for this family but for all families. You give what you're able to give, with bodhicitta, and dedicate the merit that, over time, they have everything they need—and not only this family but all beings, and not just in the short run but in the long run. Again, as always, it comes down to motivation.

Carolyn: Sometimes I struggle in dealing with people in my life who may have lots of money, yet they're still grasping at resources. I believe that underneath their wanting and grasping for things is a real hunger for a spiritual path. I struggle with where to set the boundary of wanting to be generous and wanting them to have the same generosity of feeling or spirit. Sometimes, they don't want to hear that what they're really grasping after isn't things and money but something else.

Lama: They definitely don't want to hear that! You can't tell anybody anything, usually. You can only set an example. Are you talking about a context in which everyone is putting money into the pot for a certain purpose, this particular person is putting in very little, you're putting in a lot, and you don't know if you can continue to afford it?

Carolyn: That's one example. It's not that I don't think I can afford it, it's that I become impatient with continuing to show by example, and they're not getting it.

Lama: I see a little bit of attachment and aversion there! Our practice isn't to change others. It's to change our own mind so we're more able to help others. We aren't using the teachings as a lens through which to judge other people.

Carolyn: But what if, after a decade, you see no change?

Lama: Then you remind yourself: It's been a whole decade that I've had this attachment to them changing, and I'm still making myself miserable, because they aren't changing. Maybe I need to let go of this attachment and decide that I'm going to make a boundary, because I'm not able to hang in there with a pure heart in every situation. I need to make a boundary for their sake, so that when I do interact with them, I'm not judging them. I'm not trying to change them. I'm not attached to them being different nor averse to them being the way they are. I'm simply being of as much benefit as I can possibly be.

Carolyn: With your family, you can't say, "I'm done with you." They don't understand it. They just keep coming back. I set a boundary, but they don't get it.

Lama: You're not setting the boundary to make *them* get it. You're setting a boundary that *you* need to be able to sustain bodhicitta as much as possible in every interaction. It's not about changing them, because they probably don't want to change. The more you try to change them, the more they really don't want to be changed. It's not going to work. We're present and loving with a vast aspiration for all beings, but we have no expectation or need for these particular beings to change when we need and want them to.

Carolyn: Are you saying the boundary is in our mind?

Lama: Sometimes it's only in the mind, and sometimes it's outward, but it has to be a boundary of bodhicitta. If the motivation is something other than bodhicitta, whatever that motivation is influences the karma we're making, the fruition we'll experience sometime in the future. Really contemplate karma. Do you believe it's unfailing? Do you believe virtue leads to benefit and non-virtue leads to harm? If not, we're left with asking ourselves, "Why am I doing this?"

With a generosity of heart, we pray that they may have what they're looking for, deeply. This isn't uttered outwardly. Whenever we see or experience ourselves holding back, we need to open up and offer whatever it is—unless, out of pure motivation, we feel that doing so will bring more harm to them and others in the long run.

You're very attached to your family being different, and I'm sure they're attached to you being different, because that's the nature of that relationship in general. You have to find the balance in what they think is best for them and what you think is best. Sometimes, we might feel we're enabling and contributing to non-virtue. You might need to make a boundary there. You always have to consider which choice will make more virtue and which choice will make more non-virtue. As much as possible, try to stay away from the non-virtuous choices and engage the virtuous ones.

Inez: When I was a child, I used to get on top of the washing machine when my family was tense and sing and tell jokes. I've been on top of the washing machine my whole life. When it gets scary, there I am! When I see intense suffering going on in somebody that I truly love and care for, it's wearing on me to see the pain being perpetuated. Is there anything we can say or do to help them snap them out of it? What would be appropriate to do without being a "fixer" acting out of idiot compassion?

Lama: Whether we're "fixers" or not depends mostly on our motivation. The outer actions can be the same whether or not our motivation is attachment to short-term benefit. First of all, we never tell anybody what we think they should do or not do unless they ask, and people are more inclined to ask if they're inspired by our example. This is especially true if these are people we have an ongoing connection with. Insofar as you're practicing, you're staying steady, present, available, and helpful. People may start asking you more questions, wanting your opinion. You don't want to give long lectures in response but rather answer the question as concisely as you can. If they want to know more, they'll ask you.

Continue to bring your mind back to bodhicitta and pray for interdependence to make clear if there's anything further you can do to be helpful. Sometimes, interdependence will change when we pray. An opening will happen, or the person will bring up something in the course of the ongoingness—a doorway to offer something that might help them or to give them a different perspective. It's usually most effective to speak from our own experience, not as some kind of expert. If there's an opening, you can share that.

Inez: Is it wrong to say you can't listen anymore? When my daughter was really suffering from her mental illness, she was constantly going over and over things, and it was very difficult to listen to.

Lama: It depends on the person. It's really up to your motivation and bodhicitta and prayer. At any moment, try to see if there's interdependence to be able to intervene. With some people, you have a level of intimacy and trust that allows you to give input. If you don't, be sure to own your response, and be clear why you feel the boundary you're creating will benefit them. There has to be a lot of trust involved. Otherwise, people will experience your response as meaning you don't love them, and you don't care. With each relationship, try to find the boundaries that are most effective and allow the other person to hear in a way that doesn't diminish their trust in the relationship or in you and allows them to experience your feedback as an act of love and not of abandonment.

If these are people who are regularly in your life, you might be able to introduce the subject of "too much talk" in the context of reflecting on your day and mentioning someone they don't know that you couldn't stay present for because of the way they were processing their pain. If you talk in the third person about somebody they don't know, sometimes they can hear it that way. After a few weeks or months of trying that, you might say to the person that you're encountering the same dynamic in your relationship with them as well, that going over the same problem again and again isn't the best way for you to help. If you've laid some groundwork, you have a better chance of it not being seen as a breach of trust.

Inez: That makes sense, because my habit is to take it and take it until it feels like my head will explode. Then my response is either to shut down or complain to someone else. I see it's important to lay that groundwork, because these are long-term, important relationships.

Lama: You're making boundaries with bodhicitta for the sake of these relationships, so you don't blow up or pull away. How you define and express these boundaries will be different with each person. They'll be more or less receptive at different points in their life depending on what's going on with them, so it's a dance of interdependence. From the viewpoint of bodhicitta, how and what we do depends on our motivation. If we're really doing it for their sake and for the sake of the relationship so we can continue to be in their life and offer support in ways they can receive, we have to make boundaries.

We don't abandon the people in our lives. We make boundaries that allow us to keep going with them and with our practice and try to communicate with each person in a way that they'll understand according to their worldview. Saying that you're taking time for healing or to recover may be a framework that some people can relate to. For their sake, you're expressing the boundary in a way that works for them, that they're able to understand to the best of their ability and also letting them know you're not abandoning them. You can make it clear that it's for their sake that you're taking the time away. Be confident in where you want to put your life energy at this point, stay focused, and make boundaries that allow you to continue to create and sustain the outer container for your practice that will support the inner container of bodhicitta.

Inez: There are folks who, no matter what we do or how we do it, feel abandoned and think that we don't love them. How do we stay the course when there's a huge display, and someone thinks we're the worst person ever and we're destroying their life by setting boundaries?

Lama: Chances are they're not just doing this with you. It's a psychological stance they take with others as well. If it's somebody you're intimate with, you could offer to go to counseling with them as a segue to encouraging them to go to counseling on their own. Explain to them, in the context of your mind and your life, why you're doing this—for example, your effort to change your habits to try to fix things for others, when it's really your own need to fix that needs to change.

Again, you're not telling them how to be or what they should do. You're owning your own perspective and being honest, which is a really loving thing to do. They may or may not accept it. Approach them with all the love you have and let them know that what they're asking for is something you're unable to do, but you *can* do XYZ and that you want to do this because you love them. You say no to their request, but you also say yes to something else.

Inez: So even if the person is spinning out, we aren't reactive but stay open-hearted and loving. Is that all we can do?

Lama: If there's any part of their spinning out that triggers you, you need to work on that in your formal practice when you're away from them. Play it in your mind again and again, so the next time they're spinning out, you won't be so triggered and can remain present and loving and clear. When you're doing the formal practice, pray for clarity about what you can do.

When you're in the moment with them, keep bringing the mind back to bodhicitta, and keep praying, under your breath, for insight about what you can do that will be most effective. In doing that, you may find something opens up. In the endlessness of the display of the acting out, there might be a turn, a question, an example, or something that provides a doorway you can walk through to try to meet them where they are. Prayer can be a powerful means to access wisdom and compassion and stay steady.

Tonya: I understand that we have to work with people's capacity and try to meet them where they are and give them what they need. At the same time, we don't want to participate in their creating bad karma for themselves for future lifetimes. I struggle with that. For example, maybe you have a relative who's old and they don't have much time left, so you put up with a lot of their stuff, which is fine, but then you see them creating bad karma for themselves. Where do you draw the line?

Lama: There isn't one way for every situation. It depends on each person and circumstance. We don't have control over what they do or say. The only thing that we can develop certainty about is the power of our practice to gain more control over our own mind and responses. That's how we can learn to take whatever's happening into our practice so we can transform our judgment or our resistance to their resistance. We work with our own mind to transform that into love and compassion and bodhicitta. That can take a while, depending on the person and the situation.

We start by trying to generate pure motivation, and then we pray. If we attempt to pray, but we haven't gotten our stuff out of the way, we'll interpret the interdependence that arises in the context of our stuff. We have to get that out of the way to generate a pure-hearted prayer for this person and all beings and not just for the short term but for the long term. What's best? We don't have a clue. Is there anything we can do here? We must transform our attachment and aversion through our bodhicitta. Without an agenda, we pray for clarity about whatever way is truly best, in the short and long term, for this person and all beings.

Sometimes, there will be a little opening. Sometimes not. If there's an opening, try to walk through that door as gently and respectfully as you can—not pushing, not trying to bring your own agenda through the door, but just meeting them where they are the best you can. Each person has their own karma. There's no general rule other than to always refresh pure motivation. Through your practice, transform whatever's in the way of that, and pray for clarity to know what you can do, if anything.

47 Meditation on Boundaries with Bodhicitta

With every action you take for the benefit of others, ask yourself, is this of benefit not just in the short term but also the long term, and not just for this person but for all beings?

Is your motivation to help protect somebody from themselves, from non-virtue, and from the consequences of their actions, or simply to try to get them to do what you want and need or think is best for them?

In the evening, as you review your day, check every single action you took against those criteria.

Did you have attachment or aversion to certain outcomes? Were you able to purify and transform those habits by re-establishing bodhicitta? If not, practice repeatedly transforming your mind's poisons by bringing the mind back to bodhicitta as you review the day's events.

CHAPTER 17.
THE POWER OF BODHICITTA

In the first chapter of *Way of the Bodhisattva*, the great master, Shantideva, says:

"As when a flash of lighting rends the night
And in its glare shows all the dark black clouds had hid,
Likewise, rarely, through the Buddha's power,
Virtuous thoughts rise, brief and transient in the world."

No matter how dark the night, one virtuous thought, one wish to truly benefit another, is like a flash of lighting illuminating the landscape of possibilities temporarily concealed by layers of confusion atop ignorance of our true nature.

The force of virtue, of bodhicitta, of good heart, can overcome the dark, composite, impermanent conditions of our lives. If we've genuinely practiced bodhicitta, we'll have confidence in its power. We know the capacity of that flash of lightning that we can draw on no matter what's happening inwardly or outwardly. It will always be more powerful. It will always illuminate. One virtuous thought, and another and another, imbued with bodhicitta—that's our way through.

Bodhicitta is an unfailing foundation to our path and to our lives. When in doubt, no matter what other practices we may be learning, no matter how we're engaged in the world, and no matter how compelling the projections of our movie, we always need to remember to check whether what's going on in our mind is of benefit to all limitless beings, in both the short and long term, and how we can change anything that might be impeding that benefit.

Understanding and applying this practice over time, there's less and less negativity and drama obscuring the radiance of our mind's positive qualities. Over time, we have more insight that all our experience is none other than the play of light on film, and we begin to see the brilliance of our mind and heart illuminating all those around us. We develop a greater capacity to transform our mind and our experiences. We realize there's nothing but infinite potential for change, because there are no solid, self-existing, inherently real imprints in the mind. Ultimately, they don't exist. If they did, we'd be in big trouble!

Just as shadows dissipate when the sun rises and illuminates the landscape, our negativity decreases and our positivity increases. As the projection of our imprints changes, our experience changes. We enjoy an increasing capability of mind and heart that enhances our awareness of and ability to actualize our positive qualities. To the extent that we do that, we're enriched with everything necessary to create benefit for ourselves and each other. We become agents of action that's of benefit to beings.

Ocean: I work with an organization that educates teenagers, and I've noticed the teachers and people in charge of educating these kids are so involved in their own suffering they can't benefit the kids they're supposed to be helping. It's part of the school culture that everything is so difficult that there's no way to get anything done. The dissatisfaction comes from thinking you have to do something, so it seems like the best thing you can do is nothing.

Lama: You *are* doing something. You're being *different*. You're modeling a different thing. That's huge. For some, you might be the only person they ever meet who's doing it differently. Continue to live your good heart. Even if there's nothing more you can do outwardly other than demonstrating good heart, you can always create and dedicate merit.

To the extent you can help your kids to recognize that positive qualities exist in themselves and others, that shows something other than what they've known is possible. There are so many words in the world now. More concepts can't penetrate that, but the quality of your heart can.

Rinpoche used to say that these days the real miracle is helping someone's heart to open, helping them give rise to genuine compassion. As we cultivate our own good heart, it can penetrate all that karma and help to open the heart of another—and that's the miracle.

Ocean: It took me a long time to recognize how important pure motivation is and an even longer time to start to generate it. To develop pure motivation, I found I needed to develop a mind of renunciation, but, given the tremendous suffering in the world, it doesn't seem that these small things we do in the moment are having an effect.

Lama: I'm reminded of the story of a little girl tossing starfish back into the sea as she walked down the beach after a storm. A man approached her and, gazing down the beach at hundreds of stranded starfish, asked what difference her efforts could possibly make. Without pausing, the little girl replied, "It makes a difference for that one!"

We don't want to deny the immensity of the task, but we also don't want to deny what a difference it makes to each starfish that's saved. When we despair at how little we're able to help, we need to remember how it made all the difference in the world when someone made the effort for *us*. It might have been the difference between life and death. It might have made the difference between being able to keep going or not. We all know when someone did that for us. So, we shouldn't downplay the difference it makes when we do it for someone else.

Given all the starfish on the beach, it can seem as if we can't do enough, but it's enough for each one we save. Each time we return a starfish to the water, we bring pure motivation to that: By this virtue, may all beings be where they need to be. We establish that motivation, and dedicate: by this merit, may all beings find what they need, and may our capacity to fulfill the needs of all beings be completely and fully accomplished without compromise.

You've probably seen the bumper sticker, "Think globally, act locally." In this case, we're thinking universally. We're thinking about all beings in all realms of experience, throughout all time. But we can only act in relationship to those we have direct connection with in this moment. We keep all beings in mind as we act on behalf of those we *can* help. At the end, we dedicate the merit to all beings and also to our own capacity to close the gap and be of unceasing benefit.

This helps us to keep going. We're not denying the immensity of the suffering nor are we denying what we can do right now. We're creating merit joined with dedication and aspiration prayers to increase our capacity. The more merit we create and the more we dedicate, the more our capacity grows by not denying what we can do in any given moment.

Also, every moment in which we indulge discouragement because we can't be of more help is a moment we could have helped more. We don't have the time—and others don't have the time—for us to be discouraged. They don't have the time for us to feel guilty or ashamed. Beings need us to keep going. We keep going outwardly, doing everything we can with whatever opportunities we have. And we keep going inwardly by practicing with everything that comes up. We keep going, and we keep dedicating.

If we do that, slowly, over time, our capacity will increase. If we're trying to work on one aspect or another of our practice and it seems as if we're not making an impact, we can ask ourselves how we can create more merit. The more merit we create, the more our positive qualities will naturally unfold.

Remember to rejoice in virtue. Short cut! In any given moment when our mind is feeling dark, we're feeling powerless, despairing, or confused, or whenever we encounter *any* kind of obstacle, remember how many people, right in that moment, are putting their lives on the line for others. Remember how many people are filled with faith in virtue. Let yourself be uplifted as you bring to mind all these acts of selflessness because there are so many ways in which people are being virtuous right now.

To create even more merit, offer the merit created through rejoicing to all awakened beings throughout time and space. To increase that merit even more, dedicate the merit of that offering to the awakening of every living being.

Carolyn: How does making money to pay your bills and survive in the world fit with self-confidence without being selfish? I'm a realtor, and I have to present myself in a certain way. How can I project confidence so people trust me? I want to blend my practice with my work in the world.

Lama: It's the same thing. You're a loving person and want to be a force for benefit. You can have confidence in that. Before you go to work, you could do tonglen meditation. When you walk into your workplace and see people, you want to benefit them, and you can have confidence in that. The confidence isn't about you or whether you can convince them of this or that. You can have confidence in your motivation for what you're offering to them. They'll feel the power of your pure heart and pure intention, and know you're working for them and want what's best for them.

If you're showing a house to a particular family, start with bodhicitta, and do your best in the course of showing it to bring bodhicitta into every interaction. Maintain the wish for the welfare of your clients and help to match them with housing that's aligned with their goals. Then, at the end of the showing, when you drive away, dedicate the merit of that interaction. If you have a series of these types of exchanges, you can dedicate as you go.

Carolyn: I'm trying to not be selfish but instead to be confident as I attempt to make people understand what's involved in a contract for buying or selling a home. I have confidence in doing the right thing and making sure they understand. My whole motivation is to make sure we go through the process with clarity and honesty.

Lama: All you can do is make your pure offering. You're offering honesty, accountability, and transparency for their sake. These are all the things a good realtor would offer. Purify your mind and motivation, and be as diligent as you can. The rest is up to them. In this way, you're not acting from attachment. If you make a pure offering, there's more space in your mind. Most of us respond better to salespeople with space in their minds than to salespeople with an agenda. Offer from the point of view of pure motivation, wanting what's truly best for them and all beings.

A Drop of Water in the Ocean of Enlightened Intention

Bodhicitta is based in the Four Immeasurable Qualities, but we don't want to confuse the development of those qualities with bodhicitta itself. The Four Immeasurable Qualities are the foundation of bodhicitta, and bodhicitta is the foundation for the whole path.

What makes the practice of the Four Immeasurable Qualities become a practice of bodhicitta is when we bring a limitless aspiration to the practice of equanimity, loving kindness, compassion, or rejoicing. When we do that, the merit we create and the actions based on that merit are of benefit not just to a particular being but to all living beings and not just in the short run or in this life but for limitless time. Our motivation is as limitless as space, the object of our motivation—all sentient beings—is as limitless as space, and the time frame and the goal are as limitless as space. Our heart space is limitless—unbounded by mental gymnastics, gimmicks, or identification with self or other. So, the virtue that's created is limitless—even when the action itself can seem so limited, like planting one tomato plant or washing one pile of dishes or saving one tiny being as it crosses the sidewalk.

At times, it can seem that, compared to the amount of suffering throughout time and space, one song, one cup of coffee, one moment where we have some capacity to benefit, has no impact. If we identify the mind with the apparent limitation of that moment—of that object or opportunity—the virtue that's created will be confined by the constraints of our ordinary mind. But by giving rise to bodhicitta, limitless virtue is created from the same, seemingly small, action.

Ordinary virtue, like drops of water on hot desert sand, may be of benefit in that brief moment, but, because of the limitations of that drop and the vastness of the outer conditions, it will vanish quickly, even though it may briefly benefit the blade of grass it falls on. If that same intention is imbued with bodhicitta, it's like a drop of water falling into the ocean that will never evaporate. It joins the vast sea of the enlightened intent of all awakened beings whose motivation is for the awakening of all beings. The ocean of enlightened mind can't be depleted, as it is the all-pervasive, timeless presence of the true nature of reality itself, constantly nourishing the actions of body, speech, and mind of all the great beings throughout time and space, whose entire existence is dedicated to the welfare of others.

If bodhicitta is the basis of everything we do, it will inevitably lead to the removal of the ore from the crystal—even if our relationship to the idea of complete awakening as a goal seems completely abstract or artificial. If we truly want the ultimate benefit of all beings equally, it doesn't matter what we call it.

We're going to get there, and everyone we have connection with is going to get there, eventually, because every single one of our actions and dedications is based in bodhicitta. With that motivation, every motion in every millisecond, the mind is purifying what's obscuring and awakening to what's ultimately true, so enlightenment is inevitable.

Ocean: I think about this misconception, especially in the art community, that we have to suffer, on some level, to be able to create or help others. Pain and suffering are glorified, and there's this idea that if we get to a place of love and compassion, we'll lose our ability to create. The belief is, if we're able to make something that's imbued with suffering, people connect to it, and that's what makes it great art. Or that we can only be effective as activists through generating outrage.

Lama: I'm reminded of a friend who's a playwright. When he first encountered the Buddhist teachings, he started writing plays filled with love and compassion. Everybody he showed them to said, "This doesn't work—there's no conflict, no drama." Nobody wanted to produce his plays! So instead, he did research on African-American history and shined a light on times of uplifting individual and community responses to agonizing suffering and tragedy.

Of course, the world is full of conflict, pain, and suffering, so if there's no connection to that, the audience isn't able to relate to it. But the point is, what's the perspective? What's the message? We can shine a light on suffering and, at the end, make the audience feel completely despairing, as if there's no hope. Or we can shine a light on suffering and show that change is possible—outwardly and inwardly.

If we see injustice or great suffering, it's not that we're just trying to change our own mind about it and not be responsive outwardly. Instead, if we're moved to respond, we understand that, to be effective, we need to respond with a purely motivated heart. We understand that if we engage with injustice from the point of view of attachment, aversion, judgment and pride, we won't be nearly as effective as we need and want to be. We'd be burning up whatever merit we've accumulated, especially if we're fueling our anger. And then we wouldn't have the necessary momentum of merit to bring positive change in our lives and in the lives of others.

In proportion to how much we want justice, in proportion to how much we want to be a force for ending suffering and creating benefit, to that extent, we must accumulate merit and purify the poisons of the mind so there's no more obstruction to the expression of our positive qualities. Then we'll be able to interact with others from the point of view of an equal commitment to everybody involved. That gives us clarity and insight that isn't compromised by our toxic emotions, all of which cloud our ability to see clearly what will be most beneficial. Otherwise, all we can do is react, and then we're not free. We're actually extremely un-free, because we're under the power of our negative emotions. If we're in a constant state of reactivity, there's no space or freedom in the mind for creative solutions—which, as we all know, are deeply needed.

As well, if all we're doing is reacting and being angry, we're alienating everyone around us—unless we're inspiring others to be angry and reactive as well, in which case we're a force for the collective burning up of merit, creating a downward spiral because of the collective outrage in every direction.

We have to be a force for virtue if we want to see things turn around and go in an upward direction. We have to do everything we can, in every moment, to give rise to, stabilize, and act from pure motivation and not empower and energize any of our negative habits or emotions. We must do everything we can to empower and express our positive qualities and recognize and inspire them in others. Then we can become a force for the awakening of the positive instead of its destruction.

It's important to be conscious of the positive when we engage with other people because of the interdependence we're creating with the collective karma. If we join or are working with a group of people who are all super angry, we're participating in a collective burning up of merit. If we can be a force for positivity and an inspiration for uplifting, we create the possibility of making a positive impact and helping others as well to turn away from the poisons of the mind, to turn away from non-virtue, and to turn toward what's truly beneficial.

If the collective karma outweighs our individual capacity to help, we need to be more skillful with our time to find or create activities that are wholly virtuous. We do whatever we can, in every moment, to create pure virtue with pure motivation—not just with *these* people, not just for *these* beings, and not just right now but for all beings for all time. When we dedicate the merit of that again and again, we're accumulating and building a momentum that will, without question, produce benefit. That's what the world needs now.

Whether times are good, bad, hopeful, or scary, these principles underlie everything we do. However, we won't have the confidence this is the case or the courage to rely on them unless we've practiced them again and again and seen for ourselves that they work. Is our compassion stable? Is our equanimity stable? If we're in the middle of a big kerfuffle with lots of people, lots of chaos and emotions, can we keep a steady love and compassion? Can we do tonglen? Can we breathe in all that kerfuffle energy and send out a radiance of pure qualities? We want to develop and stabilize our practice to the point where we can generate and sustain bodhicitta no matter where we are and what's going on.

To do that, we must have confidence that these methods work, and we have to be completely sure this is the cause of happiness. Otherwise, we'll get caught up in the tsunamis of our personal and collective karma and be swept up in waves of emotion and reactivity. Maybe a certain wave creates temporary conditions we happen to like, but can we be sure, if we haven't been acting from a place of mutual regard, respect, and concern, that those who don't like this particular wave aren't going to react and swing the other way? We'll be in this perpetual pendulum swinging back and forth. If we want to create stable benefit and happiness in our culture, in our family, in our mind, we have to create those causes. To create those causes, we have to contemplate deeply what they are, diligently practice integrating them into our life and mind, and relying on them as a method for benefit.

Inez: I can see myself having a sense of equanimity while also having a sense of power, as in the phrase, "This, too, shall pass." How does everything you've talked about help if we're powerless and being hurt?

Lama: Our ultimate experience of powerlessness is when we don't have access to our positive qualities, when we're separated from realization of our true nature. Then all we're able to relate to is the negativity in our hearts and all around us. Any time we do meditation to elicit positive qualities and transform the negativity in our minds to positivity, we'll feel empowered. It's not power in relationship to others. It's power in relationship to existence, to life itself. The more we feel genuine loving kindness and compassion for anybody—but especially for all beings—the clearer we are about why we're here. It's not about outer identity. It's about being here to benefit others and having no question about that. This gives us a confidence and a sense of empowerment that serves as a compass to guide us no matter how tumultuous and disorienting the storm.

You mentioned the phrase, "This, too, shall pass." We can think of that in a vindictive sense, that those we see as opponents are old and won't be here so long. Or we can think of it in a way that's wise and profoundly compassionate, reflecting that they're trying so hard to do what they think will bring benefit and happiness. We can't see their motivation, but it appears they're creating a lot of karma that's causing a lot of suffering for beings, and that's something they carry with them whether or not they're conscious of it.

We remind ourselves that we have this opportunity as human beings with an amazing, infinite potentiality of mind that we can use to create the greatest benefit in the world or the greatest harm or anything in between. To use this potentiality of mind for anything other than the greatest possible benefit is tragic. We've all been there, and that's why we know how tragic it is. Now we're trying to get more clarity so we don't feel so lost and can develop compassion for others who are confused and making choices in trying to find happiness that cause suffering to others. It's the tragedy of the endless cycles of suffering.

Tonya: I think of power as my ability to effect a change in something outside of as well as within myself. I can be all peaceful in retreat and feel empowered while the world is burning around me, but that's not what I've chosen to look at. How do I cultivate power that benefits others, not just myself?

Lama: The only way you can have that kind of power to benefit others is when you're fully empowered by your own positive qualities. To be fully empowered that way, your reliance on those qualities has to be unshakable. It's a misunderstanding to think we only feel our positive qualities when we're *away* from suffering. The whole purpose of practicing is to be able to maintain a heart filled with nothing but love and compassion for everybody, equally, no matter what's going on around us. That's the point of bodhicitta meditation, and we have to put enough time in to be able to do that.

Mahatma Gandhi practiced for years, and the ashrams he developed supported a depth of practice. The Satyagraha movement took off not just due to his skill and genius at organizing but also because he and so many others had prepared spiritually by putting in years of training in meditation and prayer. They couldn't go to the front line until they could look at a British soldier pointing a bayonet at them with genuine love.

The purpose isn't to pull away so we can feel peaceful and loving all by ourselves. Say you want to be a healer and have a strong inspiration to try to end as much illness as possible. If you just rushed out and tried to help everyone who was sick, your capacity to heal would be limited. You've got to go to medical school and train. You've got to put the time in. During the time when you're reading textbooks and studying, you're not with sick people, but you're getting ready to be able to be effective in helping them. We have to spiritually prepare as much as possible to be of the greatest possible benefit to others.

Tonya: I've been encountering a lot of disharmony and divisiveness in my activist work, and I feel much of it comes from misperceptions of one another that could be remedied through dialogue. I get very discouraged when I see how the people we're working with can become so hurtful to each other.

Lama: You always have to begin by working with your own mind, so you're not coming from a place of judgment, anger, and reactivity toward people who are saying and doing things you don't like. They won't receive your judgment in a positive way, and it won't produce the kinds of outcomes you want.

Could you create a forum or formal structure for supporting active listening? Otherwise, dialogue isn't really possible. Not everyone will want to do it, because some people are just pissed off, and they're sure it's everyone else's fault. They aren't going to want to engage, and it will be hard for folks like that to listen well until they see it's working. They need to see the evidence.

Perhaps you can start doing it with a small group of people who are equally troubled that what started out as such an inspiring activity has had the effect of producing a lot of bickering and backbiting. In your larger network, I'm sure there are people who are concerned and want to turn things around to make it the uplifting experience it was in the original vision.

Tonya: There's a shocking level of violence and PTSD among all of us, and we all have different levels of awareness of it. It's amazing how quickly things can get tense and go bad. I don't want to give up, but it feels as if what I've been through is like trying to break up a dog fight and getting bitten. It's like my only decision is to choose the hill I'm going to die on when it comes to fighting all these layers of stuff going on. Just in the way we talk about each other, we're undoing all the progress we could have made on issues that actually matter. When I meditate now, I just get angrier, and I run out of patience. How can I maintain my patience? I'm caught by my own limitations.

Lama: We need to remind ourselves that we don't have the room to become impatient, we don't have the room to give in into our old habits, because the need is too great. Knowing you, you won't stop until you've tried everything you can. You don't want to give up, or else you'll have regret later. You need to work with people who want to help you to turn it around and understand that they have to be a part of the solution to not be a part of the problem.

Try to involve more people who share your desire to turn things around and develop guidelines for working together that feel nourishing and supportive to everyone involved. Then, if and when the group expands, you're inviting others into a format that's already developed that protects against that kind of negativity, so you can become a force for benefit together.

Ocean: As you talk about great equanimity, I get a sense of a switching from negativity to positivity, but I'm thinking negativity and positivity are self-existing. Then I had this welling-up sensation of a great wave of the switching of negative habits to positive qualities on a global scale. Is there any truth to that?

Lama: Going back to the metaphor of the film, we're learning how to transform the scenes that are filled with suffering and harm to ones filled with benefit and auspiciousness. Yet, ultimately, whether those appearances are arising as terrible horror shows or wonderful love stories, they're all just light through film. That's why we need to proceed, method by method, to cultivate love and compassion and change the screenplay. Then, when we realize it's all light through film, we aren't acting from attachment to the heroes or aversion to the villains. When the mind is free of all of that, the creative process is extremely different. It's not expressed through the filter of the ordinary mind. It's the radiant expression of naturally pure, endlessly creative potentiality.

Ocean: If more and more people start practicing, wouldn't the merit and the wisdom they create be so vast that it would affect everybody, even if they weren't practicing?

Lama: Within the unfolding of collective karma, our individual karma has more of an impact. What each of us is doing with our mind is a cause. In each moment, every thought, word, and deed plants a seed.

Take, for example, the Buddha's cousin who was around the Buddha for many years. It's hard to have a more positive support system than that. Yet, his cousin continued to have a misperception of the Buddha, because his personal karma overrode the positive collective conditions. He hadn't created the causes to allow that seed to ripen even in the midst of those supportive conditions. You can have perfect weather, perfect soil, perfect moisture, but if the seed isn't in the ground, it's not going to grow. Each of us has to plant those seeds.

Ocean: So, if somebody is stubborn and decides, "I don't want to wake up," or they don't believe it can happen for them, there's nothing we can do for them?

Lama: We can accumulate and dedicate merit to them, and include them in our prayers, and that will have an impact over time. However, if, in every single moment we're accumulating and dedicating merit to them they're burning up merit and creating more and more negative causes, we may not have much immediate impact.

Ocean: I'm feeling hopeless and frustrated right now. It seems that no matter how much I do, there's still self-referencing. I can spend every millisecond of my life dedicating and practicing, resting and alternating, and doing everything I've been given, but it's really only for my *mind, because I can't really have any effect on or control over the karma of another being.*

Lama: It depends on your karma with that person. It also depends on your qualities. The Buddha couldn't immediately affect his cousin, but he affected countless millions of other beings at the time and so many centuries later and so many continents away. The impact is inconceivable to us. As we awaken to our true nature, we're able to impact those around us who have enough karma and merit and, hopefully, inspire them to give rise to love and compassion which, over time, will purify their negative karma and create virtuous causes for beneficial outcomes. It becomes a different kind of cycle. It seems you're asking yourself if it's worth it if you can't do this for every being immediately but, like the little girl on the beach, it was worth it to each starfish she saved.

Ocean: *Is it even possible to get to the goal? Maybe I can affect all these people and they can affect all these others, but can we arrive at the goal of all waking up together while we're so overwhelmed with the appearances in our movie?*

Lama: It depends on what each of us does in response to those appearances. What direction it all goes is up to each of us and all other beings.

The only thing that's stronger than all our habits, our emotional states, and everything that ultimately arises from self-clinging is bodhicitta. If you ignite that and practice diligently, you can completely awaken in this lifetime. In all your future lives, the impact you can have on others is beyond concept. Just imagine if every single one of us aroused immeasurable compassion and brought it to the practice path. Imagine all these enlightened beings working for the sake of everyone throughout time and space. The world would really look different. This is why our spiritual practice must be based in bodhicitta. In every moment of the day, we bring the power of relative and ultimate bodhicitta to whatever's happening.

One version of the bodhisattva vow states, "Samsara is endless. I vow to end it." Ultimately, what other purpose could our lives have? To step over the starfish on the beach? To pretend they're not there? Or to do what we can to help everyone we encounter and to develop the capacity to help as many as possible?

From Fixation to Freedom

We've been emphasizing the effortful aspect of giving rise to bodhicitta, the effort it takes to turn the tide from the causes of suffering to the causes of benefit and happiness. Within that, there's the wish that things be different—for ourselves and for others. Just in that wish there's effort.

Within the habit of wanting to "fix," there's the constant effort to repair what's inherently irreparable as long as we're all bound by the seeming reality of our movie. Within that, we reinforce the ignorance of mind bound by belief in the seeming reality of appearances as they play out on the big screen of life. In that context, there's nothing to do but change old habits and cultivate new ones. This is difficult, and effort is required. The boulder is rolling down the hill, and we're trying to catch it and change its course.

But, in doing so, we can bring the habit of wanting to fix what may not be fixable in this moment. We squeeze our understanding of bodhicitta into endless attempts to fix. This prevents us from accepting that when karmic fruit have ripened and are falling from the tree, there's nothing to be done other than to accept what's happening and bring practice to our emotional responses to create the basis for more fortunate outcomes in the future.

If we're trying to fix something with this narrow understanding, we're trying to make things different from what they are. Integral to that process is a solidification of what's happening. We think that what's happening is ultimately real and consequential and that we're solid and real and consequential. In that act of trying to fix, we reinforce duality—the mind that's bound by belief in appearances as real. In that context, there's nothing to do but to try harder. Trying to change what we perceive as solid requires a lot of effort and can distract us from discerning what kind of change is actually possible and what isn't.

If all we do is approach our practice and the benefit of beings through endless attempts at "fixing," we won't have access to the limitless potential that arises from the ease, the space, and the confidence of ultimate bodhicitta—of knowing the true nature of things as they are, which is that they're *not* static. As long as we try to change things with a belief in their solidity, we'll be making a lot of effort. When we realize that nothing is immovable but rather all appearances arise like a movie, dream, or mirage due to causes and conditions that also aren't static, all we have to do is insert different causes and conditions to produce different results.

When we recognize that everything is actually arising like the reflection of the moon on water. a dream or mirage, we aren't denying the appearance of the moon on the water, the drama in the dream, or the appearance of beings who are suffering endlessly. To the extent that we realize the deeper nature of all that's appearing, we're empowered to respond to it by drawing on the limitlessness of the positive qualities of our own mind and those of others instead of the rigid perceptions of our ordinary mind. There's more space, more freedom, and, therefore, more perspective and more room for creative, unconventional solutions.

Acceptance

To give rise to freedom from fixation within our own mind—so we believe deeply in the freedom of others' minds and can display the compassion and loving kindness that arises from the effortless state of freedom—we practice relative bodhicitta and the development of wisdom, ultimate bodhicitta.

To develop that wisdom, first we examine and break down the web of endless thought that has impeded our awakening so that all the old constructs, beliefs, habits, and orientations of the ordinary mind are disassembled. Then, when we rest the mind, we're allowing the mind to steep in the nature of all of that. Some of it has been disassembled and some of it hasn't, so we have questions. We examine those questions, let them go, and rest the mind.

On the one hand, as part of the process of deconstructing, we're examining what's impeding and obscuring, and, on the other hand, when the mind is at rest, we're starting to develop a relationship with the deeper nature of our storylines, hopes and fears, attachment and aversion. That relationship isn't conceptual or effortful, but experiential.

We accumulate merit alternated with moments of insight through the steeping. As we remove what's obscuring, we're headed toward an effortless resting in the nature of everything as it is without contrivance, without effort, without attachment to fixing or fear of not fixing. It's simply the natural sacredness, perfection of everything as it is.

Carolyn: Often, when I see critters, I have a sense of connection and an immediate love and openness. I don't necessarily have that with people because I have an agenda, so that's probably something I need to practice with for the next several months—if not my whole lifetime!

Lama: It's great that you see how the power of having an agenda changes the experience. An agenda involves effort, duality, and wanting things to be other than they are. And, of course, we believe our agenda is the best agenda, so we justify everything we do to try to accomplish it!

Ocean: You said the effort to always try to fix reinforces duality. Would you explain that?

Lama: Within the effort is a lack of openness to what is and wanting it to be different. That's duality. There's what is, there's an idea of how we want it to be, and there's effort to make that happen. There's a self that conceives of a different outcome and makes an effort to create that. This is what we call the Three Spheres: subject, object, and what happens between subject and object. So, within effort, there's inherently duality.

When we practice the wisdom teachings directly—not the mental breaking down of appearances but resting the mind— that's effortless effort. It's not an effort based in duality to try to get to some place that we're not. It's simply remembering to let go within a state of rest.

Ocean: Is it harmful to create duality when you're trying to ease the pain of beings?

Lama: We're in duality, and all of us experiencing that pain are in duality, so we have to use dualistic methods. However, these dualistic methods—such as giving rise to bodhicitta—will, by their nature and over time, purify our obscurations and, ultimately, duality itself. Dualistic effort is purified through the skillful means the Buddha gave us to practice in the midst of suffering so we can be confident we're doing as much as we can to help in the moment, while, at the same time, everything we're doing is leading beyond duality. Over time, for example, we purify attachment and aversion through love and compassion, and accumulate vast amounts of merit. We can be confident we're on track for a greater capacity to be of benefit to all beings in the short and long run.

Ocean: I was confused by the idea that there's nothing to do but keep trying harder even though that reinforces duality.

Lama: If we try harder with the methods for giving rise to bodhicitta, they will, in and of themselves, over time, dissolve self-clinging, the basis of duality. However, we also need to be skillful in balancing the effort of trying harder with mind at rest, so we can create a basis for recognizing mind at rest within the motion, because the deeper nature of the motion is the empty luminosity playing through the film. If we're only focusing on effort, we'll never be able to gain the insight that can ultimately liberate the suffering of ourselves and others. As the Buddha said, "Things aren't as they seem, nor are they otherwise." That's wisdom.

Tej: Does this mean that when we don't have recourse to effortless methods, we have to just sort of grind away?

Lama: Yes and no. Sometimes, if we have a big habit to trying hard, the best way to exhaust it is to try harder, which can help purify the habit to effort through sheer exhaustion. But, for some people—for example, someone who's experienced a lot of trauma—to try harder only stirs the subtle energies more and makes it even more difficult to recover. That's why it depends on each person's situation.

We're all familiar with mind in motion. Yet, the essential nature of that motion is mind at rest, spacious and free. Rest is the essential nature of all the motion that's empty yet appearing. Through the alternating meditation, we become more familiar with this natural openness and start to train the mind in a different habit. Instead of holding on, we're learning to let go. Then we can have glimpses of the possibility of rest by starting out between the two extremes of motion and rest, which seem to be two entirely different things. But, as we alternate, we refine away the extremes themselves, so that, within motion, we can, over time, experience rest, and, within rest, we can experience the ceaseless play of motion. That's the middle way.

The middle way is the experience of mind, the experience of reality, that knows things just as they are: not inherently self-existent and yet appearing ceaselessly, endlessly, and dynamically expressing. And yet, even in the expression, there's no thing that's expressing. That quality of knowing the inseparability of what we call emptiness and appearance isn't an intellectual knowing. It's not mind that knows something that's separate from mind. It's the nature of mind knowing itself. It's our intrinsic wisdom knowing itself, and that self-knowing awareness or self-knowing wisdom arises spontaneously when we've gotten what's obstructing it out of the way. We've gathered enough merit and wisdom for it to become boundlessly clear without artifice and, in that knowing, everything is resolved, everything is fixed in the ultimate sense.

Within that understanding, we don't have to worry about abandoning the fixing of sentient beings, because the wisdom that knows the natural perfection of everything ceaselessly expresses itself without lenses, without stories, without imprints, karma, habits, and obscurations. The ceaseless expression is nothing but infinite positive qualities, infinite openness, and the infinite compassion and loving kindness that are ceaselessly responsive to the needs of beings. That response doesn't arise from attachment to things being a certain way or aversion to them being another way. It has nothing to do with having agendas and trying to make everything be the way we want it to be. Within the profound acceptance of the natural perfection of appearances lies the potential for infinite responsiveness according to the needs of beings.

48 Finding Rest Within the Three Spheres

Keep examining, self, other, and what happens between self and other. Then alternate your examination with resting the mind.

Examine, probe, and try to find the thing that's motivating everything you do. Let go of the process of trying to find, and let it sink in, let it steep.

When the mind becomes busy again, use that busyness to go back to a practice that's designed to transform the busyness. Go back to contemplating: What's this thing I'm trying to find? Who is the me that's trying to find it? How did I let my mind get so busy? There must be "me," because I have hope and fear. That's why my mind has become busy. So, where's the me? Where's the source of the complications?

Whatever arises, examine that, and then, in the course of examining it, let it go. Alternate back and forth between examining and resting the mind.

Anthony: I'm going through all the mental breaking down of conditions and time and so on, and it seems contrived.

Lama: It is, at first, because the ordinary mind is completely contrived. Even though the ordinary mind is experienced as reality, it's actually nothing but contrivance. We're using contrivance to antidote and purify contrivance, so we can eventually rest in non-contrivance.

Courage

Through practice, we slowly develop the capacity to accept with less resistance the ripening of our previous karmic seeds. Instead of blaming others or ourselves or indulging knee-jerk reactions of attachment, aversion, hope and fear, we develop the capacity to simply accept that sometimes past karmic seeds have already ripened, and there's nothing more we can do at this point to change the immediate outcome.

We also become clearer that we *can* change our *response* to those events so we're more confident going forward that the choices we make now are virtuous and will only produce benefit in the future while purifying as swiftly as possible any toxic karmic seeds that we've planted in the past.

As Saint Francis noted in his Serenity Prayer, we can learn to accept what we can't change and also cultivate the courage to be able to change what we can, whether these be changes in our own minds or outwardly in our lives.

All our hopes and fears arising from self-clinging slowly subside through our practice. Through bodhicitta, we're able to develop the quality of selflessness needed to be courageous in all situations, so, naturally, we experience less fear and more love and compassion. And, because our love and compassion are the expression of our inherent positive qualities, they're a source of strength and courage that's far greater than any hopes or fears we may have.

When we're motivated by a commitment to the temporary and ultimate welfare of all beings, that commitment—over time and through practice—becomes stronger than our attachment to our personal goals, identity, and self-cherishing. As that motivation becomes stronger, it becomes a force for transformation in our own practice as well as in our work and activities in the world. Through the power of bodhicitta, we not only purify karma but also the poisons of the mind. As all our habits—including the most subtle habits of self-clinging and self-concept—are purified, their presence in our mind weakens and has less of a hold on us.

At the same time, the accumulations of merit and wisdom that arise through our practice of bodhicitta gain more power and momentum. As that happens, these can overpower our psychology and our ordinary mind. At first, we learn to equalize concern for others with concern for ourselves. But, the more we practice, the concern for others becomes greater than our concern for ourselves. Because our self-clinging is diminishing and our bodhicitta is increasing, we find that the courage to make necessary changes—both in our own minds and outwardly in our lives—naturally increases. As long as our motivation is bodhicitta, we find we have the courage to do what's needed in our practice and in the world.

As we cultivate wisdom, the idea that the self is substantial and real relaxes. Selflessness—not just in relation to other beings but in relation to the seeming solidity of appearances— increases. The rigidity of mind formed out of hope and fear in relation to fixated ideas of self and other weakens. Our love, compassion, and responsiveness to the needs of others arise naturally and powerfully. The courage we pray for becomes possible through our practice of bodhicitta joined with the blessings of all great bodhisattvas of the past, present, and future.

There are three ways we can give rise to the courage of the bodhisattva. The first is the kingly way, where we have the wish to awaken inspired by the confidence that, once we awaken, we'll have all the necessary qualities to be able to free all beings from suffering.

The middle way is the boatman's way, where the oarsman rows the boat across the river and takes everyone with him.

The most courageous way is that of the shepherd, who tends his flock by sending everyone ahead and then comes in behind, closing the gate after making sure everyone else is okay. This courage arises from the depth of selflessness needed to truly make the needs of others more important than our own. Chagdud Rinpoche said that, ideally, we develop the heart of the shepherd, but, practically, we need to gain the capacity of the king.

We have to be careful, because as soon as we start trying to develop the kingly capacity, self-clinging can seep back in, and it can become all about us again. Our practice might start out with the genuine motivation: "I'm doing this practice for the sake of *others*," but, over time, it can become more like: "*I'm* doing this for the sake of others." The ego is so slippery. It's easy for it to creep into our practice so we can kid ourselves into believing we're doing what we're doing for the sake of others, when, in fact, we've slid back into self-referencing, being attached to being the best king, the most highly praised king, and so forth. We must be careful not to give power to our ego and all the psychological and emotional patterns that have gripped us and prevented us in the past from being able to benefit beings as much as we've wanted to.

Hillary: On the bodhisattva path, do we have a responsibility to respond to all the suffering we witness? Are we responsible for the people who are creating huge negative karma that's bad news for them in the long run and for those that are most immediately impacted?

Lama: When we take the bodhisattva vow, in essence, we commit to uproot the suffering of every living being until all abide in a state of complete awakening. A part of that vow is that we never abandon a single being.

We've talked about practicing for every living being equally, and also about being committed not just to their short-term but to their long-term welfare as well. The classic situation is of the victim and the aggressor. The victim, in the moment, is experiencing suffering at the hands of the aggressor. We want to intervene to protect the victim, but we also need to intervene to protect the aggressor from planting seeds that cause inevitable suffering in the future. The compassion and equanimity of the bodhisattva heightens the sense of urgency to respond to save every being equally—not just those we perceive as innocent victims but also to protect perpetuators from themselves. Each of us will find our own way to respond according to our inclinations and capacity.

Hillary: Do we have that responsibility if we haven't taken the bodhisattva vow?

Lama: That depends on each person. If we think it's true that virtue leads to positive outcomes and non-virtue leads to suffering, we might go through the meditations and ask ourself if that process has led us to a place where we want to commit to the short- and long-term welfare of all beings equally. If people are new to these ideas and practices, that concept might sound appealing but may not be where they're actually at.

You've been to a number of bodhicitta trainings, and you also have your own Quaker practice that you've been doing diligently for years. You've been integrating these principles into your life and mind for a long time, which is what it takes. We start out with an idea and values that we'd like to embrace and integrate, but, in truth, in a situation where there's a victim and an aggressor, we might still find ourselves responding with compassion for the victim and anger, aversion, and judgment toward the aggressor. That's just where we are.

However, if we understand these principles, we want to be more effective, and to create more virtue and less non-virtue, we can do the meditations again and again to change our habits and develop different responses to suffering than we've had in the past. This requires putting time in on the meditations. So, it's up to each of us to look at the question you asked, because, in some ways, it's the essential question.

Hillary: That's helpful, because equanimity is where the rubber meets the road, I think.

Lama: That's right. We say, "All beings for all time." It's right there.

Wisdom

Insofar as we're bound by appearances, we react to them only because things appear to be happening *to* us. We react nicely if we like what's happening, and we react badly if we don't like what's happening. We're in a constant state of reactivity, which is, ultimately, completely powerless.

We're empowered insofar as we practice bodhicitta and understand the deeper nature of our experience. Then we can make different choices in relation to what's happening. Non-virtue and harmful things can be happening around us, and we can choose to not respond in harmful ways. To the degree we understand that, we're empowered.

No matter what's happening around us, we can always choose to give rise to and stabilize bodhicitta. The more we cultivate bodhicitta, the more we can respond in a way that is proactive rather than reactive. Ultimate creativity is possible through recognizing that appearances, by their nature, are empty illusions, like a nighttime dream.

Contemplations and meditations for the cultivation of wisdom, ultimate bodhicitta, lead us toward a recognition of the inseparability of these two aspects of experience. Using our projector metaphor, even as the movie unfolds, there's no thing there, and yet, although there's no thing, the movie is unfolding. The night dream unfolds, even though there's no thing that can be seen when we awaken. Whether it's waking out of the dream or waking within the dream, there's no thing, but there are constant appearances unfolding.

If we're watching a film about others' lives, we have more perspective on the choices the characters are making than we usually do in our own lives. We feel sad when our hero suffers, but, at the same time, we recognize the tragedy of their continuing efforts to find happiness by digging themselves more deeply into the hole of suffering.

Through our wisdom practice, we're able to watch our self as if in a movie as we go about our daily life; we can more easily maintain a greater perspective: that everything unfolding is impermanent, the play of scenes we've written previously, and that our responses to changing events will determine our future experience. Cultivating this wisdom perspective can help us to refrain from causes of future suffering, to undertake causes of future happiness, and to begin to have more control over our mind and choices and future experience.

As we continue to practice bodhicitta and purify obscurations, we gain more wisdom and insight, and our confusion diminishes. As that happens, we develop more certainty about the causes of suffering and the causes of happiness and become more skillful in refraining from harm and in undertaking benefit.

A reflection in a mirror couldn't occur without the reflective capacity of the mirror. Nor would it occur if our image didn't appear in front of it. If we don't like the reflection in the mirror, it doesn't work to try to scrub the surface of the mirror, any more than if we don't like the movie it works to go up to the screen and try to change it. We have to change it at its source.

As we practice the wisdom perspective of knowing everything is arising like the reflection in a mirror or the projections of a movie, slowly our perspective broadens, and we gain greater insight about what change is possible within the context of our individual and collective karma as they ripen. We're less distracted by our personal agendas, and more able to see the larger interplay of all the characters in our film. We become aware of what causes and conditions can be introduced, if any, to produce the change we think will be most beneficial, and more confident that that change could actually help. Until we're able to develop enough wisdom to have confidence and certainty in all circumstances—and eventually the omniscience that comes with our full awakening—we rely on bodhicitta and prayer. Through the power of blessings of limitless wisdom, compassion, and capacity to benefit—unobscured by our personal attachments and aversions—we gain insight and perspective about what can be of greatest benefit, what's possible, and what's not possible for the sake of all beings.

49 Watching Ourselves in Our Own Movie

Practice, both formally and informally, watching yourself as if watching a movie and notice how your perspective on your choices changes.

How does it change your relationship to objects of attachment or aversion, and your attachment and aversion itself, if at all?

How does it change your perspective on possible avenues for change, if at all?

Do you find more perspective on whether karmic fruit has fully ripened and/or if there might be a possibility to change certain conditions that would prevent or further its ripening, and if so, which ones, and how?

How does practicing love, compassion, or tonglen shift your experience of the movie, of yourself and other characters within it, and avenues for benefitting them?

How does prayer expand the scope of your awareness, if at all?

Doug: In situations in which we see people—strangers—who are suffering or in difficulty, we want to fix it or, at least, make it better. Often, in those cases, I don't have clarity about how to act. Especially if someone is negative toward me, like in a restaurant, or on the street.

Lama: In situations with strangers, there's often not a lot we can do outwardly. We can try to make a connection in some way, and the strongest connection is through some kind of physical or material connection. The next strongest way to make a connection is to say something, or, at least, look at the person. For example, if someone sitting near you in a restaurant seems to be upset in some way or having difficulty, you could look them in the eyes as you get up to leave, smile, and say, "Have a really great day." Or you could talk to the server and pay for their meal.

If we've made some kind of a connection with them, our dedications of merit to them will have a stronger impact. Most importantly, we want to always hold them in our hearts, our prayers and dedications, and never abandon them. Maybe when we walk by them in the restaurant, that's the only connection they have with the path of enlightenment. In some lifetime, due to the power of that connection, and our dedications and prayers, they'll connect with an authentic spiritual path and find freedom. We have to be patient. It might not happen in this lifetime or for a number of lifetimes. It's very possible you'll never have any awareness of the consequences of your connection. That's why we need to take a long view.

It's great that you're wanting to purify your tendency to try to fix everything right now. The longer-term fix is our own awakening and, through that, their awakening. The stronger the connection we make, the greater the chances of that happening. We must have practiced enough so that, when we pay their bill, help them into their chair, or wave goodbye, that gesture is full of genuine care and concern. If they can experience just a moment, just a flash of good heart, that may open up something for them in this lifetime. By smiling at them or paying for their meal, you may be defying their assumptions and expectations by being good-hearted and generous. Who knows what that does to their world view? Maybe nothing, maybe something. If you keep accumulating merit and dedicating, there can be benefit for them even in this lifetime.

We have to remind ourselves to be patient and loving. It doesn't matter what the situation or result looks like now. With each interaction, each person, each place, we try to move it along towards virtue as much as we can according to the situation. We feed the pigeons. We save the lives of fish. We smile at people who hate us. We move the needle a little bit each time, as much as we can. What will determine the strength of the impact is the quality of our heart and of our practice.

Carolyn: Instead of beginning with cultivating love and compassion, what if we went in the other direction and just worked directly with the true nature of reality? Could that become our experience? What kind of knowing do we get doing that? Would our knowing evolve out of creating a container that isn't love and compassion?

Lama: We need a strong foundation to support the building we're constructing, which means we have to be able to give rise to a view of reality that's completely authentic without even the slightest, most subtle misunderstanding. Such misunderstanding is easy to fall into, because our experience of mind is so subtle. When we talk about our meditation experience, it's difficult to find the words to describe how we take detours. It can be the difference between full awakening and endless confusion. In other words, it's the difference in where we're heading. Although it's possible for some to spontaneously awaken without step-by-step training, it's extremely rare. That's why the Buddha and the great masters have given us methods for constructing a building that can support that lofty view, authentically. It's a lot faster to build a strong foundation from the ground up, because you can be completely confident that what's happening with your mind is authentic.

It's a disservice to ourselves, our practice, and other beings to think of these practices as only introductory, beginning practices that we dash through so we can get to the deep, high teachings and practices that will liberate ourselves and all beings more quickly. To think there's something more profound than bodhicitta is confusion, because it's bodhicitta that leads to and sustains the wisdom view of the true nature of reality. Giving rise to completely selfless compassion and loving kindness leads infallibly to this view, because there's no longer a concept of self. That's why, in our practice, we imbue the mind with the completely selfless wish to benefit others.

Within the purity of that intention, our experience of reality isn't separate from the needs and aspirations of all beings. There are no longer fictitious walls in the fictitious room of the ordinary mind. It crumbles under the strength of the sun's radiance streaming through the windows and doors we've opened. There's nothing to sustain those walls, because they're ultimately fictitious, composite, superficial, and temporary. That's why bodhicitta empowers us to benefit ourselves and others in the short term and is indispensable for giving rise to the deeper wisdom that's the cause of ultimate freedom for ourselves and all beings.

Bodhicitta serves as the container to hold and sustain our most vast and exalted aspirations. If we don't have this foundation, no matter how high and sublime the teachings, how great the practice, it will all crumble like a tall building constructed on shifting sand. Our ability to go deeper and sustain the highest wisdom view is in proportion to the strength of our foundation. If we have that foundation, the whole path represented by that great building will benefit all beings.

Carolyn: If positive qualities are truly the nature of reality, it seems that, no matter what direction you went, that true nature should reveal itself.

Lama: If the true nature of our mind revealed itself naturally, without methods to support that awakening, we'd all be enlightened. Spiritual evolution would be a principle, and we'd all be evolving no matter what we do with our minds. The reason we need a spiritual path is because it *does* matter what we do with our minds. We're creating habits that either obscure recognition of our true nature, lead us on a detour away from it, or lead us toward it. What we do and the habits we cultivate are immensely important.

We can have a moment like this, where we're sitting and talking about it, and it seems very abstract. But the evolution—or not—happens in every millisecond. What we do with our minds is leading us in one direction or the other in every moment, so it's hugely consequential. We don't know how much time we have to purify the confusion that binds us to endless suffering.

This is our chance.

DEDICATION OF
THE MERIT OF THESE TEACHINGS

As we complete these teachings, we dedicate whatever virtue has been created through our exposure to, contemplation of, and meditation on these teachings and the virtue of our past practice and our practice and activity going forward. We dedicate not only to those who appear as heroes or villains in our personal drama—whether they've helped us, and we've been able to help them, or they've harmed us, and we've harmed them—but to every living being who's been kind to us in the past not just once but throughout time beyond concept. We pray that, by this virtue, their kindness be repaid and they connect with an infallible path of virtue and the full awakening of their positive qualities. We pray they ride that wave of merit to the ultimate benefit and happiness of themselves and all living beings.

As you do so, if you feel drawn to, you can recite the following prayers of dedication and aspiration that Rinpoche composed and compiled. We recited these at the end of every training with him to join our virtue and aspirations with the vast intentions of all enlightened beings. May they be fulfilled!

50 Dedication Prayer*

Throughout my many lives and until this moment,
whatever virtue I have accomplished,
including the merit generated by this practice,
and all that I will ever attain,
this I offer for the welfare of sentient beings.
May sickness, war,
famine and suffering be decreased for every being,
while their wisdom and
compassion increase in this and every future life.
May I clearly perceive all experiences
to be as insubstantial as the dream fabric of the night
and instantly awaken to perceive the
pure wisdom display in the arising of every phenomenon.
May I quickly attain enlightenment in order
to work ceaselessly for the liberation of all sentient beings.

51 Prayer of Aspiration*

Buddhas and bodhisattvas all together:
Whatever kind of motivation you have,
whatever kind of beneficial action,
whatever kind of wishing prayers,
whatever kind of omniscience,
whatever kind of life accomplishment,
whatever kind of benevolent power, and
whatever kind of immense wisdom you have,
then similarly I, who have come in the same way to
benefit beings,
pray to attain these qualities.

52 The Auspicious Wish**

At this very moment,
for the peoples and the nations of the earth,
May not even the names disease,
famine, war, and suffering be heard.
Rather, may their pure conduct,
merit, wealth, and longevity increase,
And may supreme good fortune and
well-being always arise for them.

* The "Dedication Prayer" and "Prayer of Aspiration" are from the concise practice of Red Tara composed and compiled by H.E. Chagdud Tulku Rinpoche.

**"The Auspicious Wish" was composed by Kyabjé Dudjom Rinpoche.

ACKNOWLEDGMENTS

Without the wisdom, kindness, patience, and unbounded compassionate responsiveness of Chagdud Tulku Rinpoche, these teachings and the informal format in which they were offered never would have happened. Nor would I and so many others have had the opportunity to receive further teachings and guidance from other extraordinary masters. Everything he gave us has become my heart and the essence of this book.

These pages were compiled from edited transcripts of a series of trainings that occurred over a number of years and is the result of an extraordinary and dedicated team effort to bring it to fruition. Those who made this offering did so from the compassionate intention to make available to others the power of transformation they experienced through their study and practice of the path of the bodhisattva. Their contributions included extensive, diligent efforts to record, catalogue, transcribe, coordinate, and edit retreat recordings. To you all, thank you beyond words.

As well, my appreciation is enormous for the careful review of many pages of material both by individuals and groups, including those devoted to the study and practice of Chagdud Rinpoche's teachings in *Change of Heart: The Bodhisattva Peace Training of Chagdud Tulku*; the inmates at the Arizona State Prison in Florence, Arizona; and the women in the CREATE program at Sister José Women's Center in Tucson, Arizona. I extend my heartfelt gratitude to all who collaborated to offer invaluable feedback that made the material in this book more accessible to readers unfamiliar with the path of the bodhisattva.

I'm deeply grateful for the tireless efforts of the Iron Knot Ranch staff, who kept everything going outwardly and inwardly while I worked on this project. And, finally, without the sincere, thoughtful, persistent engagement of all those who took part in the Bodhicitta Immersion trainings—and whose voices coalesced into the fictional participants in this book—it could never have happened.

May all our efforts support the awakening of every being to their limitless wisdom and compassion.

Additional resources to support your understanding and practice of the material in Sunlight on Shadows can be found at
www.ironknotinstitute.org/sos/resources

Made in the USA
Las Vegas, NV
19 September 2022

55592726R20272